ALL MUSIC GUIDE REQUIRED LISTENING

OLD SCHOOL RAP AND HIP-HOP

All Music Guide Required Listening Series, No. 2

ALL MUSIC GUIDE REQUIRED LISTENING

OLD SCHOOL RAP AND HIP-HOP

Edited by

Chris Woodstra
John Bush
Stephen Thomas Erlewine

Backbeat
Books

An Imprint of Hal Leonard Corporation
New York

Published in 2008 by Backbeat Books
An Imprint of Hal Leonard Corporation
19 West 21st Street, New York, NY 10010

Printed in the United States of America

Book design by Snow Creative Services

Library of Congress Cataloging-in-Publication Data is available upon request.

All Media Guide has created the world's largest and most comprehensive information databases for music, videos, DVDs, and video games. With coverage of both in-print and out-of-print titles, the massive AMG archive includes reviews, plot synopses, biographies, ratings, images, titles, credits, essays, and thousands of descriptive categories. All content is original, written expressly for AMG by a worldwide network of professional staff and freelance writers specializing in music, movies, and games. The AMG databases—All Music Guide®, All Movie Guide®, and All Game Guide™—are licensed by major retailers, Internet sites, and other entertainment media providers and are available to the public through its websites (www.allmusic.com, www.allmovie.com, www.allgame.com) and through its published works: All Music Guide, All Music Guide to Rock, All Music Guide to Country, All Music Guide to Jazz, All Music Guide to the Blues, All Music Guide to Electronica, All Music Guide to Soul, All Music Guide to Hip-Hop, and All Music Guide to Classical Music.

All Media Guide, LLC, 1168 Oak Valley Drive, Ann Arbor, MI 48108
T: 734/887-5600. F: 734/827-2492
www.allmediaguide.com, www.allmusic.com, www.allgame.com

ISBN: 978-0-87930-916-9

www.backbeatbooks.com

CONTENTS

PART I: THE ROOTS OF RAP

Although frequently defined as cutting edge, hip-hop took to celebrating its roots rather early. Of course, rap was not music that came out of nowhere—it only seemed that way. It bubbled up from funk, jazz, soul, reggae, and disco, taking elements of each, but belonging wholly to none. The commonly acknowledged first hit single, "Rapper's Delight," came in the early '80s, and by the end of the decade, the "old school" had already been enshrined. All the elastic, disco-electro beats and party rapping seemed ancient in the wake of the sample-heavy collages coming from the D.A.I.S.Y. Age, the tough social consciousness of Boogie Down Productions, the incendiary noise from Public Enemy and the Bomb Squad, the loose, lewd P-Funk samples from Digital Underground, and the jazziness of Tribe Called Quest. Although it was only a few short years later, this was music that was several generations removed from the block parties of early hip-hop; it seemed eternally modern and filled with boundless possibilities.

Like many similar moments, it passed faster than seemed possible. Soon, hip-hop fractured as the mainstream turned into a gangsta playground and the riskier stuff proudly went underground, with only a few artists (such as the mavericks in the Wu-Tang Clan) playing to both sides. By this point in the mid-'90s, the arc of the first act (plus pre-history) of hip-hop had been pretty much set, and that arc is even more evident in retrospect. Also in retrospect, that late '80s and early '90s vanguard—dubbed "the golden age" for reasons that are readily apparent—morphed into the "old school," and the two became one in the same. The "golden age" is now used as the name for the early days of hip-hop overall.

What this volume of All Music Guide's Required Listening does is provide a map to that golden age of the old school and the music that helped it come about. It's easy to pinpoint where recorded rap starts—right as the '70s gave way to the '80s, just as labels like Sugarhill and Tommy Boy took off. However, it's hard to say where the old school stops, because like all music, it exists on a continuum, with each phase and era giving way to the next. The golden age ends around the end of 1994, once the aftershocks were beginning to be felt from three landmark albums—Wu-Tang Clan's *Enter the Wu-Tang*, Nas' *Illmatic*, and the Notorious B.I.G.'s *Ready to Die*, all of which honored the past while leading the way forward. It was also around this time that the south became known for more than the Geto Boys and OutKast, while gangsta rap (once considered a passing fad, just like hip-hop itself) re-upped to become a commercially dominant force.

But where does it begin? It begins years and years before those first block-rocking singles, back when James Brown was laying down the heavy funk, when Miles Davis was incorporating Hendrix and Sly into his thick fusion, or even further back, when Jimmy Smith and Jimmy McGriff were creating funky soul jazz grooves on their Hammond B-3s. There are crates and crates of great jazz, soul, and funk LPs that provided the foundation of hip-hop, both spiritually, and quite literally, as these old records were sampled and scratched to create new music.

What we do here in our "Roots of Rap" section is highlight some of the best of these old LPs, including those albums that were sampled heavily during the golden age. (For more details on what was sampled where, turn to our playlists.) Not all of the great old records are here—there are, after all, too many to count—but there are enough to get you going on your own search through the dusty aisles of your local used-record store to find the roots of rap.

Yet the heart of this book is in the heart of hip-hop, the glory years when Run-D.M.C. first taught us a DJ could be a band, when Kool Moe Dee and LL Cool J traded barbs, when N.W.A. came straight out of Compton, and when De La Soul were plug tunin'. Not one of those artists sound the same as another; however, they all share a few things in common: they define their times, they illustrate how rich and vibrant the scene was and continues to be, and they're all part of AMG's Required Listening.

ALBUM DIRECTORY

Above the Law

Livin' Like Hustlers
1990, Ruthless

With albums by Ice-T, N.W.A, the Geto Boys, and Eazy-E having popularized gangsta rap in the late '80s, the stage was set for the success of Above the Law. The members of this South Central L.A. group had close ties to members of N.W.A—Above the Law produced their own debut album, *Livin' Like Hustlers*, with Dr. Dre, and recorded it for Eazy's Ruthless label (which was going through Epic as well as Priority and Atlantic). Though not in a class with Ice-T's or N.W.A's work, *Hustlers* is a sobering depiction of ghetto life in L.A. Violent, profane, and graphic, songs like "Another Execution," "Menace to Society," and "Murder Rap" let listeners know exactly what life in South Central was like. The imaginative Dre's input as a producer is consistently beneficial, and he sees to it that the CD comes alive musically. ATL's lyrics would sound increasingly clichéd as the 1990s progressed, but *Hustlers* shows that at the dawn of the decade, the Angelenos had some freshness.

Alex Henderson

Black Mafia Life
1993, Ruthless

Above the Law's second album had three things working against it. One: over two years had passed since their debut (unless you factor 1991's *Vocally Pimpin'* EP), which certainly left many with the impression that they were no longer. Two: they had to follow up a strong Dr. Dre-produced debut with in-house production. Three: it was nearly half an hour longer than the debut, leaving it wide open for filler issues. Despite these factors, the members of Above the Law proved with *Black Mafia Life* that they were more than a one-album wonder. They returned with a record that was both more laid-back and assured, yet the sound was tougher all the same. The tales spun by Cold 187um, KM.G, Big Hutch, and Go Mack are as unrelentingly grim as ever, yet this is—if anything—a party record, full of grooves and licks swiped from Bootsy Collins, the Fatback Band, and Curtis Mayfield. Cold 187um's slick sampling work—almost as accomplished as Dre's on the debut—combined with live instrumentation more than makes up for the fact that none of the thoroughly convincing MCs are lyrical masters. Lop off a few substandard moments, replace them with one or two big singles (admittedly, nothing here is as hot as the debut's "Untouchable"), and you'd have a West Coast classic.

Andy Kellman

Afros

Kickin' Afrolistics
1990, Ral

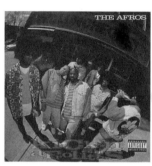

A side project of Run-D.M.C.'s Jam Master Jay, *Kickin' Afrolistics* was a satirical look at '70s blaxploitation films and the ever popular Afro. Filled with Jay's signature production and Beastie Boy DJ Hurricane helping to supply the rhymes and beats, it's a solid album that doesn't fail to deliver musically. However, while the satirical concept was original at the time, it seems a bit dated at present and wears thin after a while—especially when bordering on Digital Underground territory. For serious heads only.

Rob Theakston

AMG

Bitch Betta Have My Money
1992, Select

Men are from Pluto and women are from Jupiter. Fine. But after listening to *Bitch Betta Have My Money*, one wonders if AMG had ever actually experienced up-close and personal contact with any genuine members of the female species prior to recording his second effort. The music is—not to put more of a fine a point on it than it deserves—misogyny raised to the nth power. As sophomoric potty talk, offensive (tongue-in-cheek?) sexism, and blatant female-bashing goes, though, the album is fitfully amusing and more than mildly entertaining. Or rather, to be more precise, if you can bring yourself to swallow or overlook the more insulting vulgarities and self-styled roll-pimping—not, it should be noted, an easy task at times, considering the extent of some of the nastiness—*Bitch Betta Have My Money* is a far sight more diverting than the average 2 Live Crew horn-fest, partly because AMG seems to include himself in the joke more often than not, and because P-Funk-laced tunes like "The Vertical Joyride," "Mai Sista Izza Bitch" (on which Boss delivers a decidedly non-dainty pimp-slap of her own), and the DJ Quik-produced "Nu Exasize" are undeniably fonkay ear-candy. The album, on the other hand, is nowhere near as jocular or sociopolitically hard-hitting as either N.W.A or Ice-T—or even Sir Mix-A-Lot—and it would be difficult to envision the impulse that would lead to selecting an AMG album off the shelf before one of his musical superiors. That being said, the title track, in particular, is a classic bit of disrespectful smack-talk, and so obviously the artistic apex of AMG's career that the rapper tried to bottle the magic once again a decade later with the far less memorable or successful *Bitch Betta Have My Money 2001*. Cautiously recommended, then, if you collect locker-room gangsta rap, and so long as you also have access to a shower nearby.

Stanton Swihart

Arrested Development

3 Years, 5 Months & 2 Days in the Life Of...
March 1992, Chrysalis

Widely adored when it appeared in 1992, Arrested Development's debut album, *3 Years, 5 Months & 2 Days in the Life Of...* seemed to herald a shining new era in alternative rap, when audiences and critics of all colors could agree on the music's importance. Of course, that didn't happen, as Dr. Dre instead took gangsta rap to the top of the charts with *The Chronic*. In retrospect, *3 Years...* isn't quite as revolutionary as it first seemed, though it's still a fine record that often crosses the line into excellence. Its positive messages were the chief selling point for many rock critics, and it's filled with pleas for black unity and brotherly compassion, as well as a devotion to the struggle for equality. All of that is grounded in a simple, upbeat spirituality that also results in tributes to the homeless (the hit "Mr. Wendal"), black women of all shapes and sizes, and the natural world. It's determinedly down to earth, and that aesthetic informs the group's music as well. Their sound is a laid-back, southern-fried groove informed by rural blues, African percussion, funk, and melodic R&B. All of it comes together on the classic single "Tennessee," which takes lead rapper Speech on a spiritual quest to reclaim his heritage in a south still haunted by its history. It helped Arrested Development become the first rap group to win a Grammy for Best New Artist, and to top numerous year-end critical polls. In hindsight, there's a distinct political correctness—even naïveté—in the lyrics, which places the record firmly in the early '90s; it's also a bit self-consciously profound at times, lacking the playfulness of peers like the Native Tongues. Nonetheless, *3 Years...* was a major influence on a new breed of alternative southern hip-hop, including Goodie Mob, Out-Kast, and Nappy Roots, and it still stands as one of the better albums of its kind.

Steve Huey

Audio Two

What More Can I Say?
1988, First Priority

Aided by Stetsasonic's Daddy O on a pair of cuts ("Make It Funky" and "Top Billin'"), Audio Two's full-length debut is a patchy affair, just like the albums that would follow from the Brooklyn duo. Neither Gizmo Dee nor his brother Milk

are proficient rappers with above average lyrical capabilities, but the way they play off each other is occasionally enough to cause some excitement. "Top Billin'" stands easily as the best track here, thanks in no small part to Daddy O's sparse yet infectious work—the beat would later reappear in Mary J. Blige's "Real Love." Other entertaining moments include "Hickeys Around My Neck" and "Make It Funky."

Andy Kellman

Awesome Dre' & Hard Core Committee

You Can't Hold Me Back
1989, Priority

The Midwest is the one region of the U.S. that—unlike the Northeast, South and West Coast—hasn't had a lot of well-known rappers. One hardcore rapper who created a buzz on Detroit's rap scene of the late 1980s was Awesome Dre', who showed some potential on his debut album, *You Can't Hold Me Back*. This CD is a bit uneven, and at times, Dre' sounds like he's being inflammatory just to get a reaction. For example, he rails against fellow rappers L.L. Cool J and Kool Moe Dee without really articulating what he has against them. But the Motor City native does have an appealing flow and a lot of spirit, and he uses his gut-level emotion advantageously on riveting cuts like "Frankly Speaking" (which decries censorship), "Committing Rhymes" and "Sackchasers," a denunciation of materialistic women. "Sackchasers" isn't misogynist, as some claimed, but it does put golddiggers in their place. Dre' comes across as someone who has the guts to be himself—instead of emulating East or West Coast rap styles, Dre' makes it clear that he's quite happy to represent Detroit. Nationally, however, he didn't receive much attention.

Alex Henderson

Awesome 2

The Awesome 2 Present: The History of Rap, Vol. 1
1990, Select

Presented by the Awesome 2, Special K and DJ Teddy Tedd, *The History of Rap, Vol. 1* is a devastating collection of classic old-school tracks, compiling both the familiar ("The Message" by Grandmaster Flash, "The Breaks" by Kurtis Blow, "Planet Rock" by Afrika Bambaataa) and a few of those more familiar to DJs ("That's the Joint" by the Funky 4+1, "Feel the Heartbeat" by the Treacherous Three").

Keith Farley

Afrika Bambaataa

Planet Rock: The Album
1986, Tommy Boy

Afrika Bambaataa, one of hip-hop's progenitors, was known as a talented DJ before his single "Planet Rock" came out in 1982 on Tommy Boy. The song, which sampled (actually re-recorded in the studio) elements of Kraftwerk's "Trans-

Europe Express" and was the first R&B track to use an 808, helped define a new movement in music, electro, which then inspired Miami bass and Detroit techno, and pushed the musician's status toward near iconic. *Planet Rock: The Album*, a collection of singles that came out four years later, captures Bambaataa's energy and innovation. This is his work with Soulsonic Force, which means his collaborations with James Brown ("Unity") and John Lydon ("World Destruction") are missing, but it's a good collection, the equally interesting "Renegades of Funk" (in remix form) and "Searching for the Perfect Beat" also present. There are also three previously unreleased tracks, which although not quite having the impact of the first half of the record, are much more than filler, and include guest appearances from famed Furious Five rapper Melle Mel on "Who You Funkin' With?" and D.C.'s Trouble Funk, appropriately, on "Go Go Pop." The original 12" version of the title track is enough to make *Planet Rock: The Album* a worthwhile purchase, but the inclusion of the other material pushes that to necessary.

Marisa Brown

Looking for the Perfect Beat: 1980–1985
March 2001, Tommy Boy

As a major architect of early hip-hop, Afrika Bambaataa is perhaps more deserving of a respectable compilation treatment than anyone. And while his considerable influence has largely been brushed aside by a rap world that sadly ignores far too many of its innovators, *Looking for the Perfect Beat* may help to change that. Whatever your opinion on the shelf life of his music, Bambaataa was an innovator of the highest order. While many rappers would be content to sample and name check James Brown ad nauseam, Bambaataa collaborated with the Godfather of Soul himself on the sharp "Unity Part 1 (The Third Coming)." The amazing double-punch of "Planet Rock" and "Looking for the Perfect Beat" serve as the centerpiece of this disc, while "Zulu Nation Throwdown" sits as a perfect opening track, in its time initiating a back-to-roots aesthetic that was years ahead of the Afrocentric rap explosion of the late '80s. *Looking for the Perfect Beat* also nicely augments the résumé of producer Arthur Baker, a trailblazing dance remixer of the early '80s. Sadly missing are any significant liner notes or photographs. Also available as a limited edition two-LP set.

John Duffy

Rob Base

It Takes Two
1988, Profile

Without question, Rob Base & DJ E-Z Rock had the party anthem of 1988 in "It Takes Two"—an insanely infectious rap/dance gem using a James Brown/Lynn Collins classic of the same name as a reference point. While the song was a major hit in dance music and club circles, Base won over hip-hop's

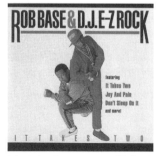

hardcore with his strong technique as a rapper. Though most of this debut album falls short of that mega-hit's excellence, it's a generally decent effort that has both hip-hop and R&B appeal. A reflection on societal breakdown, the sobering "Times Are Gettin' Ill" is atypical of this album—which favors soul-flavored party music over social and political commentary. From Maze's "Joy & Pain" (which the duo used without Frankie Beverly's permission, inspiring him to threaten legal action) to the house-influenced "Get on the Dance Floor," *It Takes Two* thrives on strong hooks and unapologetic escapism.

Alex Henderson

Basehead

Play with Toys
1992, Imago

An alternative rap cult favorite, *Play with Toys* is the mysterious Basehead's shining moment. Originally released by the long-gone migré label—an American 4AD wannabe with a design wing and everything—the album is Basehead rapper/producer/leader Michael Ivey's snoozy vision of "slacker rap," which is organic, lazy, smart, and head over heels in love with beer for some reason. Hops and barley and their negative effects on the body are the topic of "2000 B.C.," a slow shuffling track with loose guitars, real live drums, and Ivey's echoing mumbles pining the loss of 2000 brain cells. "Ode to My Favorite Beer" opens with the sound of a poptop, then slides into a strange soundscape that comes very close to the dream pop of A.R. Kane, making another 4AD connection. When Ivey delivers "Clair and Cliff Huxtable never lived around here" on the great "Better Days," he's depressed, not ghetto proud like the hardcore ballers would sound. Filled with these lackadaisical, down-and-out moments, this debut album with a hangover isn't for everyone. It really didn't have much of an influence once alternative rap and indie rap began to flourish, either, but *Toys* deserves its cult status and sounds like little else in the hip-hop universe.

David Jeffries

Not in Kansas Anymore
1993, Imago

Although it retains many of the same qualities of their critically-acclaimed debut, Basehead's second album, *Not In Kansas Anymore*, is missing a key ingredient—charm. Where *Play With Toys* was a unique record, creating its own world with stoned, hazy funk and psychedelic, lo-fi hip-hop, *Not In Kansas Anymore* sounds lazy. Musically, it is a continuation of the debut—in fact, it's a replica of the debut, offering the same tricks without any new flourishes. That doesn't mean it's a bad record. There are several tracks that rank with the best songs on the debut, but there's nothing that has the same sense of discovery that made *Play With Toys* an interesting record.

Stephen Thomas Erlewine

Beastie Boys

Licensed to Ill
1986, Def Jam

Perhaps *Licensed to Ill* was inevitable—a white group blending rock and rap, giving them the first number one album in hip-hop history. But that reading of the album's history gives a short shrift to the Beastie Boys; producer Rick Rubin and his label, Def Jam; and this remarkable record, since mixing metal and hip-hop isn't necessarily an easy thing to do. Just sampling and scratching Sabbath and Zeppelin to hip-hop beats does not make for an automatically good record, though there is a visceral thrill to hearing those muscular riffs put into overdrive with scratching. But, much of that is due to the producing skills of Rick Rubin, a metalhead who formed Def Jam Records with Russell Simmons and had previously flirted with this sound on Run-D.M.C.'s *Raising Hell*, not to mention a few singles and one-offs with the Beasties prior to this record. He made rap rock, but to give him lone credit for *Licensed to Ill* (as some have) is misleading, since that very same combination would not have been as powerful, nor would it have aged so well—aged into a rock classic—if it weren't for the Beastie Boys, who fuel this record through their passion for subcultures, pop culture, jokes, and the intoxicating power of wordplay. At the time, it wasn't immediately apparent that their obnoxious patter was part of a persona (a fate that would later plague Eminem), but the years have clarified that this was a joke—although, listening to the cajoling rhymes, filled with clear parodies and absurdities, it's hard to imagine the offense that some took at the time. Which, naturally, is the credit of not just the music—they don't call it the devil's music for nothing—but the wild imagination of the Beasties, whose rhymes sear into consciousness through their gonzo humor and gleeful delivery. There hasn't been a funnier, more infectious record in pop music than this, and it's not because the group is mocking rappers (in all honesty, the truly twisted barbs are hurled at frat boys and lager lads), but because they've already created their own universe and points of reference, where it's as funny to spit out absurdist rhymes and pound out "Fight for Your Right (To Party)" as it is to send up street-corner doo wop with "Girls." Then, there is the overpowering *loudness* of the record—operating from the axis of where metal, punk, and rap meet, there never has been a record this heavy and nimble, drunk on its own power yet giddy with what they're getting away with. There is a sense of genuine discovery, of creating new music, that remains years later, after countless plays, countless misinterpretations, countless rip-off acts, even countless apologies from the Beasties, who seemed guilty by how intoxicating the sound of it is, how it makes beer-soaked hedonism sound like the apogee of human experience. And maybe it is, maybe it isn't, but in either case, *Licensed to Ill* reigns tall among the greatest records of its time.

Stephen Thomas Erlewine

Paul's Boutique
July 1989, Capitol

Such was the power of *Licensed to Ill* that everybody, from fans to critics, thought that not only could the Beastie Boys not top the record, but that they were destined to be a one-shot wonder. These feelings were only amplified by their messy, litigious departure from Def Jam and their flight from their beloved New York to Los Angeles, since it appeared that the Beasties had completely lost the plot. Many critics in fact thought that *Paul's Boutique* was a muddled mess upon its summer release in 1989, but that's the nature of the record—it's so dense, it's bewildering at first, revealing its considerable charms with each play. To put it mildly, it's a considerable change from the hard rock of *Licensed to Ill*, shifting to layers of samples and beats so intertwined they move beyond psychedelic; it's a painting with sound. *Paul's Boutique* is a record that only could have been made in a specific time and place. Like the Rolling Stones in 1972, the Beastie Boys were

in exile and pining for their home, so they made a love letter to downtown New York—which they could not have done without the Dust Brothers, a Los Angeles-based production duo who helped redefine what sampling could be with this record. Sadly, after *Paul's Boutique* sampling on the level of what's heard here would disappear; due to a series of lawsuits, most notably Gilbert O'Sullivan's suit against Biz Markie, the entire enterprise too cost-prohibitive and risky to perform on such a grand scale. Which is really a shame, because if ever a record could be used as incontrovertible proof that sampling is its own art form, it's *Paul's Boutique*. Snatches of familiar music are scattered throughout the record—anything from Curtis Mayfield's "Superfly" and Sly Stone's "Loose Booty" to Loggins & Messina's "Your Mama Don't Dance" and the Ramones' "Suzy Is a Headbanger"—but never once are they presented in lazy, predictable ways. The Dust Brothers and Beasties weave a crazy-quilt of samples, beats, loops, and tricks, which creates a hyper-surreal alternate reality—a romanticized, funhouse reflection of New York where all pop music and culture exist on the same strata, feeding off each other, mocking each other, evolving into a wholly unique record, unlike anything that came before or after. It very well could be that its density is what alienated listeners and critics at the time; there is so much information in the music and words that it can seem impenetrable at first, but upon repeated spins it opens up slowly, assuredly, revealing more every listen. Musically, few hip-hop records have ever been so rich; it's not just the recontextulations of familiar music via samples, it's the flow of each song and the album as a whole, culminating in the widescreen suite that closes the record. Lyrically, the Beasties have never been better—not just because their jokes are razor-sharp, but because they construct full-bodied narratives and evocative portraits of characters and places. Few pop records offer this much to savor, and if *Paul's Boutique* only made a modest impact upon its initial release, over time its influence could be heard through pop and rap, yet no matter how its influence was felt, it stands alone as a record of stunning vision, maturity, and accomplishment. Plus, it's a hell of a lot of fun, no matter how many times you've heard it.

Stephen Thomas Erlewine

Check Your Head
April 1992, Grand Royal

Check Your Head brought the Beastie Boys crashing back into the charts and into public consciousness, but that was only partially due to the album itself—much of its initial success was due to the cult audience that *Paul's Boutique* cultivated in the years  since its initial flop release, a group of fans whose minds were so thoroughly blown by that record, they couldn't wait to see what came next, and this helped the record debut in the Top Ten upon its April 1992 release. This audience, perhaps somewhat unsurprisingly, was a collegiate Gen-X audience raised on *Licensed to Ill* and ready for the Beastie Boys to guide them through college. As it happened, the Beasties had repositioned themselves as a lo-fi, alt-rock groove band. They had not abandoned rap, but it was no longer the foundation of their music, it was simply the most prominent in a thick pop-culture gumbo where old school rap sat comfortably with soul-jazz, hardcore punk, white-trash metal, arena rock, Bob Dylan, bossa nova, spacy pop, and hard, dirty funk. What they did abandon was the psychedelic samples of *Paul's Boutique*, turning toward primitive grooves they played themselves, augmented by keyboardist Money Mark and co-producer Mario Caldato, Jr. This all means that music was the message and the rhymes, which had been pushed toward the forefront on both *Licensed to Ill* and *Paul's Boutique*, have been considerably de-emphasized (only four songs—"Jimmy James," "Pass the Mic," "Finger Lickin' Good," and "So What'cha Want"—could hold their own lyrically among their previous work). This is not a detriment, because the focus is not on the words, it's on the music, mood, and even the newfound neo-hippie political consciousness. And *Check Your Head* is certainly a record that's greater than the sum of its parts—individually, nearly all the tracks are good (the instrumentals sound good on their subsequent soul-jazz collection, *The in Sound From Way Out*), but it's the context and variety of styles that give *Check Your Head* its identity. It's how the old school raps give way to fuzz-toned rockers, furious punk, and cheerfully gritty, jazzy jams. As much as *Paul's Boutique*, this is a whirlwind tour through the Beasties' pop-culture obsessions, but instead of spinning into Technicolor fantasies, it's earth-bound D.I.Y. that makes it all seem equally accessible—which is a big reason why it turned out to be an alt-rock touchstone of the '90s, something that both set trends and predicted them.

Stephen Thomas Erlewine

Ill Communication
May 1994, Grand Royal

Ill Communication follows the blueprint of *Check Your Head*, accentuating it at some points, deepening it in others, but never *expanding* it beyond the boundaries of that record. As such, it's the first Beastie Boys album not to delve into new territory, but it's not fair to say that it finds the band coasting, since much of the album finds the group turning in muscular, vigorous music that fills out the black-and-white sketches that comprised *Check Your Head*. Much of the credit has to go to the group's renewed confidence in—or at least renewed emphasis on—their rhyming; there are still instrumentals (arguably, there are too many instrumentals), but the Beasties do push their words to the forefront, even on dense rockers like the album's signature tune, "Sabotage." But even those rhymes illustrate that the group is in the process of a great settling, relying more on old-school-styled rhyme schemes and word battles than the narratives and surreal fantasies that marked the high points on their first two albums. With this record, the Beasties confirm that there is indeed a signature Beastie Boys aesthetic (it's too far-ranging and restless to be pegged as a signature sound), with the group sticking to a blend of old school rap, pop culture, lo-fi funk, soulful jazz instrumentals, Latin rhythms, and punk, often seamlessly integrated into a rolling, pan-cultural, multi-cultural groove. The best moments of *Ill Communication* rank with the best music the Beasties have ever made, as well as the best pop music of the '90s, but unfortunately, it's uneven and rather front-loaded. The first half overflows with brilliant, imaginative variations on their aesthetic: the assured groove of "Sure Shot," the warped rap of "B-Boys Makin' With the Freak Freak," the relentless dirty funk of "Root Down," the monumental "Sabotage," and the sly "Get It Together," highlighted by a cameo from Q-Tip of A Tribe Called Quest. After that, the album seems to lose its sense of direction and momentum, even if individual moments are very good. Any

record that can claim jams as funky and inventive as "Flute Loop" and "Do It," or instrumentals as breezy as "Ricky's Theme," is certainly better than its competition, but there are just enough moments that rank as obvious filler to slow its flow, and to keep it from standing proudly next to *Check Your Head* as a wholly successful record. Even if it is a little uneven, it still boasts more than its fair share of splendid, transcendent music, and it really only pales in comparison to the Beasties' trio of classic records. By any other measure, this is a near-masterpiece, and it is surely a highlight of '90s alternative pop/rock.

Stephen Thomas Erlewine

The Beatnuts

Intoxicated Demons
April 1993, Relativity

Flashy, booty-slapping Latino hip-hop created by horny substance abusers. What's not to like? This mini-LP debut by Colombian/Dominican producers the Beatnuts passes the booze and spliffs in such a high-volume block-party quake of ungainly rhymes that one instantly remembers why careless hip-hop used to be so fun. Imagine a lewd and sentient wife beater and you have "World's Famous." Picture some good luvin' take on Public Enemy and you have "Reign of the Tec." Squint real hard and one can see a winking jab at A Tribe Called Quest's "Butter" strutting around until it gets the attention it wants ("Third of the Trio"). This is an intentionally offensive group just begging to be let out of their underground cages. Don't let anybody tell you otherwise: *Intoxicated Demons* is a fine debut, no matter its raunchy hubris. Because the more hardcore rap fans the Beatnuts annoy, the better they sound.

Dean Carlson

The Beatnuts
June 1994, Relativity

The Beatnuts' first full-length album is as pure a document of raw, hardcore hip-hop circa 1994 as is possible to get. No pop hooks, no slick production, no ballads or lyrics about money and girls. The individual cuts don't really stand out, instead flowing seamlessly into a powerful whole. It's almost a period piece, given the way that hip-hop eventually gave way, as the '90s progressed, to the excessive bling-bling of the Puff Daddy era, but it also sounds strikingly minimalist and stark, which prevents it from sounding too dated. In retrospect, with its emphasis on lean, jazzy beats and lyrical flow, it can clearly be viewed as a harbinger of the underground hip-hop of the late '90s (such as Company Flow and the Def Jux crew), all the more ironic since at the time the Beatnuts were widely considered just a half-step removed from the mainstream, which is not to say that it is dry and arch, since any album with cuts like "Lick the Pussy" and "Psycho Dwarfs" isn't attempting to be overly thoughtful or intellectual. Even if the lack of lyrical depth and reliance on cheap humor (the last sound on the album is a belch) can get a bit wearying, the impressive production and skilled flow are still a welcome sound. Though mainstream hip-hop fans will probably find *Street Level* too spare and monotonous, hardcore hip-hop fans will find it a welcome addition to their collection.

Victor W. Valdivia

Big Daddy Kane

Long Live the Kane
June 1988, Cold Chillin'

Even though he spends a good 90% of the album boasting about his skills and abilities on the microphone, and cutting those of other MCs, Big Daddy Kane consistently proves himself a thrilling artist on his debut album, *Long Live the Kane*, one of the most appealing creations from the original new school of rap. This debut captures the Big Daddy Kane who rocked the house at hip-hop clubs and verbally cut up any and all comers in the late '80s with his articulate precision and locomotive power—the Big Daddy Kane who became an underground legend, the Big Daddy Kane who had the sheer verbal facility and razor-clean dexterity to ambush any MC and exhilarate anyone who witnessed or heard him perform. There are missteps here, to be sure—especially "The Day You're Mine," on which Kane casts himself as a loverman over a stilted drum machine and lackluster, cheesily seductive singing (offering a glimpse of the particular corner into which he would eventually paint himself). But there are also plenty of legitimate early hip-hop classics, none of which have lost an ounce of their power, and all of which serve as reminders of a time and era when hip-hop felt immediate, exciting, fresh, and a little bit dangerous (in the figurative, rather than literal, sense), and when hip-hop spawned commercial tastes of the moment rather than surrendering to them. Although his next album would be nearly the artistic equal of the debut—and, in many ways, even bettered it—Big Daddy Kane would never sound as compelling or as fresh as on this first effort.

Stanton Swihart

It's a Big Daddy Thing
September 1989, Cold Chillin'

If Big Daddy Kane's debut album painted him as an enormously talented battle MC, his follow-up, *It's a Big Daddy Thing*, finds him aggressively expanding into new territory and gunning for a wider audience outside the hip-hop faithful. Unlike later efforts, most of it is rousingly successful, making for an album that's arguably just as strong as his near-classic debut. This is where Kane starts to take his place as one of hip-hop's first sex symbols, thanks to the gliding "Smooth Operator," the somewhat dated ballad "To Be Your Man," and the Teddy Riley-produced new jack swing track "I Get the Job Done." If the latter is a blatant attempt at crossing

over, with a vastly different sound than anything else on the album, it's also a player's statement of purpose. Elsewhere, Kane plays the anti-drug, pro-education social commentator, bringing his Nation of Islam beliefs further into the spotlight on tracks like "Another Victory," "Children R the Future," "Calling Mr. Welfare," and "Rap Summary (Lean on Me)." "Pimpin' Ain't Easy" sits a little uneasily alongside that progressive-minded material, not just for its obvious subject matter but for the line where Kane declares himself "anti-faggot"; nonetheless, it remains something of a favorite among fans who look past that slip. And of course, there are plenty of showcases for Kane's near-peerless technique, including "Mortal Combat," a live version of the rare B-side "Wrath of Kane," and "Warm It Up, Kane." There's some filler in the second half, like the amusing, blaxploitation-styled "Big Daddy's Theme," but overall *It's a Big Daddy Thing* is a strong, varied album that captures every important side of one of rap's major talents.

Steve Huey

Taste of Chocolate
October 1990, Cold Chillin'

Big Daddy Kane gave one of his most consistent efforts with *Taste of Chocolate*, his third album. Kane not only had first-rate technique and rhyming skills working to this CD's advantage, he also had quite a bit of excellent and varied material to choose from. Though he still spends too much time bragging about his microphone skills, such hard-hitting numbers as "Mr. Pitiful" and the sobering "Dance With the Devil" show just how substantial he can be. This time, Kane is joined by a number of distinguished guests, including Barry White (who is typically charismatic on the rap ballad "All of Me"); Malcolm X's daughter Gamilah Shabazz (with whom he duets on "Who Am I") and the raunchy comedian Rudy Ray Moore. When Kane and Moore exchange insults on "Big Daddy Vs. Dolemite" things get outrageously entertaining.

Alex Henderson

Looks Like a Job For...
May 1993, Cold Chillin'

After the stylistic missteps and weak self-productions of *Prince of Darkness*, Big Daddy Kane returned to the rhyme with 1993's excellent *Looks Like a Job For...*, an album that updated his sound for the early '90s but left plenty of room for the greatest to freestyle. And led by a pair of TrakMasterz productions, the title track and the casually, hilariously dismissive "How U Get a Record Deal?," it started off incredibly strong. Nearly all of these were the usual battle raps, but Kane also had much to say with tracks like "Rest in Peace" and "Brother Man, Brother Man," the latter featuring him smoothly trading rhymes with his protégé, Lil' Daddy Shane.

John Bush

Daddy's Home
September 1994, MCA

It looks like the return of the loverman on the cover of Big Daddy Kane's sixth LP, *Daddy's Home*, though hardcore fans who bought it anyway were treated to a tight, tough record that alternated classic Kane with a few surprisingly successful detours and enough space to salute the next generation of East Coast hardcore. He set it off on an excellent opener, breaking up his usually quick flow for a few gems of carefully phrased, lyrically lurching rap that make him sound like the return of the drunken master. "Brooklyn Style...Laid Out" and the hands-in-the-air jam "In the PJ's" are great double features for Big Daddy Kane and Big Scoob. For the irresistible "Show and Prove," Big Daddy Kane invited a pair of young rappers, Jay-Z and Ol' Dirty Bastard, well before they would appear on their own records (both MCs' styles are definitely in place, and Jay-Z gets in a few zany speed raps). One detour that didn't work was "Don't Do It to Yourself," an attempt at duplicating West Coast G-funk that doesn't come across. Despite a few choruses that sounded a little tired, *Daddy's Home* proved that Kane was still in prime form.

John Bush

The Very Best of Big Daddy Kane
March 2001, Rhino

How do you become a hip-hop legend and still remain somewhat underappreciated? If you're Big Daddy Kane, you hit the scene right after one of the greatest MCs ever to pick up a mic (Rakim), record lots of battle rhymes when your peers (KRS-One, Chuck D.) are getting political, and cross over to R&B listeners before hip-hop figured out that it didn't have to compromise to do so. Kane was one of the prime movers behind the quantum leap in lyrical technique that took place during the late '80s, rapping with excellent diction at a more frantic pace than the smooth, effortless-sounding Rakim. Time has been kind to his work, as Rhino's *The Very Best of Big Daddy Kane* demonstrates. Its selections concentrate mostly on Kane's first (and best) two albums, pulling six tracks from *Long Live the Kane* and seven from *It's a Big Daddy Thing*. The opening trio of classics—"Raw," "Set It Off," and "Ain't No Half-Steppin'"—are flawless bids for immortality all by themselves, and haven't lost an ounce of energy, nor has the storming live cut "Wrath of Kane." Despite his reputation as a battle MC, Kane's Nation of Islam beliefs did pop up in the occasional message cut, represented here by "Word to the Mother (Land)" and "Another Victory." And even if they made purists uneasy at the time, Kane's crossover efforts were where his image as hip-hop's leading loverman came together. "Smooth Operator" and "Cause I Can Do It Right" hold up just fine, and while the Teddy Riley-produced "I Get the Job Done" has a jarringly different new jack sound, the spirit behind it is pretty infectious all the same. (The ballad "Very Special," on the other hand...well, it made the charts.) Even so, there's no better place than this to get acquainted with one of the golden age's greatest rappers.

Steve Huey

Big Mike

Somethin' Serious
1994, Rap-A-Lot

Being a member of the now forgotten Convicts didn't make Big Mike a hood household name, but taking Willie D's place in the Geto Boys for an album sure did. Cashing in on his new fame and keeping the momentum rolling, Big Mike's

solo debut, *Somethin' Serious*, is a mother. Hard, swampy tunes with Big Mike stone-cold thugging like UGK dominate, but occasionally Mike comments on society, like when "Piece of Mind" damns the get-rich-quick hood kids who can't "wait till the fruit is ripe." With its funky punch and infectious, hiccupping chorus, "Comin' from the Swamp" is unforgettable and almost matched by the slow, observant, and poignant "World of Mind" that follows. Big Mike isn't fronting with his toughness, but his tales of good vs. evil prove there's a heart in there and leave no doubt about an active brain up top. "Daddy's Gone" (with Scarface) is Mike's best writing showcase, with food stamps, bad examples, and hard choices all swirling around in the world of the song's single-mother protagonist.

David Jeffries

Biz Markie

Goin' Off
February 1988, Cold Chillin'

The Cold Chillin' class clown, Biz Markie debuted with *Goin' Off*, one of the most unrelentingly amusing sets of productions and performances of anyone during hip-hop's golden age. Markie was an oversized teenager with lyrical talents (if not finesse) far beyond his years, and material opposed to most every rapper around—trading in nightclubs for the mall and striking a pose for picking your nose. Yes, the rhymes were often rudimentary or obvious (and many of the best were actually written by Big Daddy Kane), but his infectious optimism and winning flair (plus the masterful production of Marley Marl) carried Biz Markie far beyond the status of a novelty act. His first single, "Make the Music With Your Mouth, Biz," introduced him as a human beatbox, but he went on from there to encompass a straight-ahead but hilarious game of the dozens ("Nobody Beats the Biz"), a tribute to his favorite haunts around Brooklyn ("Albee Square Mall"), and a track with some wry cynicism about the price of fame ("Vapors"). The rangy Marley Marl cued up some classic backing tracks for these songs, with any hint of braggadocio counteracted by his carnival-esque production sense. Since a 1995 reissue on Cold Chillin' substituted new Marley Marl remixes for a few of the originals, it's best to spring for the 2001 two-fer *Goin' Off/The Biz Never Sleeps*.

John Bush

The Biz Never Sleeps
October 1989, Cold Chillin'

On the cover to *The Biz Never Sleeps*, Biz Markie's in the lab with his chemistry set, cooking up a concoction of colorful liquids that's bound to explode sooner or later. Inside, however, the music wasn't quite as dynamic; Markie decided to produce and write this record entirely by himself, instead of relying on help from Cold Chillin' beatmaster Marley Marl (who'd produced his excellent debut). The results veered dangerously close to the standard indulgent sophomore album, though Markie's natural charm and a blockbuster hit ended up carrying the proceedings. It certainly didn't start out very well, the opener being a long-winded "Dedications" that was little more than the title indicated, and "The Dragon," a one-joke track about odd smells. Rap fans with a sense of humor, however, were willing to forgive nearly anything after hearing "Just a Friend," the result of an intriguing story rap interspersed with a bizarre bout of crooning that, once again, ably demonstrated how far Biz's charm could take him (in this case, all the way to the Top Ten). "Spring Again" and "I Hear Music" were yet more loopy productions with a universal theme, while Markie even sounded intoxicating while freestyling about a non-existent dance over a simple loop ("Mudd Foot"). It was obvious the (teenage) lunatics had been released from the asylum; the wonders of visual technology allowed the Biz and T.J. Swan to have their thank-you lists super-imposed, inside the credits, on their bared boxer shorts.

John Bush

I Need a Haircut
August 1991, Cold Chillin'

Biz Markie, rap's clown prince, can usually be counted on to deliver goofy humor, and *I Need a Haircut* is as wildly entertaining as anything he's ever done. Biz isn't one to rap about his sexual prowess, drive-by shootings near the projects, or Louis Farrakhan's ideology. In contrast to the sobering gangster rap of N.W.A. and Ice-T, the angry political protests of Public Enemy and Boogie Down Productions, and the machismo of L.L. Cool J, Biz Markie seeks only to amuse, entertain, and have fun. Indeed, rap doesn't get much sillier than "T.S.R. (Toilet Stool Rap)" and "Kung Fu." The Brooklyn native's third album also contains "Alone Again," the song that incorporated Gilbert O'Sullivan's pop hit "Alone Again Naturally" (allegedly without the pop singer's permission) and inspired a major lawsuit.

Alex Henderson

Make the Music with Your Mouth, Biz
2006, Cold Chillin'

Before the "human orchestra" Biz Markie's debut album, *Goin' Off*, came out, Prism Records (which became Cold Chillin' in 1989) released the rapper's EP, *Make the Music with Your Mouth, Biz*, in 1986. Twenty years later the label remastered and reissued that classic 12", adding to it seven live tracks recorded in 1987 at *Club Uptown* in Worcester, MA, plus "Biz Beat," which shows off both his beat-boxing skills and his sense of humor (throwing in a line from the Meow Mix commercial, for example). As the original EP can be hard to find (though it was repressed in 2002), this album is a convenient way not only to hear the standout title track, but two songs that didn't make it onto *Goin' Off*, "They're Coming to Take Me Away (Ha Haa)" and "A One Two." Most interesting, however, are the live cuts—a rarity in hip-hop—which, though the quality suffers occasionally (generally because someone is too close to the mic), do an excellent job of conveying Biz's energy, showmanship, and goofiness. With help from fellow Juice Crew members T.J.

Swan and Big Daddy Kane, Biz spits his way through the show with enough enthusiasm that you can practically see him leaping around the stage. Is he the best rapper ever? No, but he was never trying to be, and even though songs like "Protection" and "XXX-Mas Freestyle" are rather crude, they're also entertaining and fun. *Make the Music with Your Mouth, Biz* is not only an important introduction to one of rap's most spirited performers, it's an important look at hip-hop's earlier days, too.

Marisa Brown

Black Moon

Enta da Stage
November 1993, Nervous

Released in 1993, Black Moon's debut, *Enta da Stage*, was a real departure from the high-energy extroverted hip-hop of the time. MCs Buckshot and 5Ft Accelerator (though Buckshot dominates) attack their verses with an aggressive nihilism not heard since Kool G Rap's peak. Theirs is a grim reality, filled with guns, weed, and violence. Buckshot displays none of the usual gangsta remorse; he is a willful public menace. The Beatminerz production crew craft subterranean beats to match Buckshot's mayhem. The tracks are dark, layered with muted jazz samples, and seemingly bottomless. *Enta da Stage* is hip-hop made for headphones and basements rather than for the clubs. It set the tone for much of the hip-hop to follow. Biggie Smalls' suicidal thoughts and Noreaga's boisterous thuggery both have their roots here. The album marked a turning point in hip-hop.

Chris Witt

Black Sheep

A Wolf in Sheep's Clothing
October 1991, Mercury

Playfully satirical, witty, and incredibly imaginative, *A Wolf in Sheep's Clothing* introduced one of the freshest talents in early '90s rap, a self-produced duo who caught the tail end of the Native Tongues family. Though Dres and Mista Lawnge didn't match the brilliant wordplay of A Tribe Called Quest or De La Soul, their topics were well-chosen, they were presented in a hilarious context, and every song was backed up by strong productions and great rapping. *A Wolf in Sheep's Clothing* wasn't a comedy record, but it was difficult to tell when the duo were half-serious or half-joking, especially since they were often the objects of their jokes. They poked fun at many aspects of black music and culture of the early '90s, everything from the persuasive gangster mentality ("U Mean I'm Not"), obsessions over the Afrocentric viewpoint ("Are You Mad?"), and lewd sex raps ("La Menage"), as well as an amusingly incorrect response to feminism ("L.A.S.M."). They also dropped a few of the best hip-hop club tracks of the era, the insanely catchy items "The Choice Is Yours (Revisited)," "Try Counting Sheep," and "Flavor of the Month." (Another smooth dance tune, "Strobelite Honey," was dreadfully honest about girls who look better under the lights than upon closer inspection.) Polar opposites to the ranks of somber political rappers, and deftly counteracting the indulgence and self-seriousness of many alternative groups, Black Sheep hit a height with their debut that few hip-hop acts would ever reach.

John Bush

Kurtis Blow

Kurtis Blow
1980, Mercury

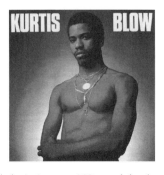

Back in hip-hop's old school era—roughly 1978–1982—albums were the exception and not the rule. Hip-hop became a lot more album-minded with the rise of its second generation (Run-D.M.C., Whodini, the Fat Boys, among others) around 1983–1984, but in the beginning, many MCs recorded nothing but singles. Two exceptions were the Sugarhill Gang and Kurtis Blow, whose self-titled debut album of 1980 was among hip-hop's first LPs and the first rap album to come out on a major label. Thus, *Kurtis Blow* has serious historic value, although it is mildly uneven. Some of the tracks are superb, including "The Breaks" (a Top Five R&B smash in 1980) and "Rappin' Blow, Part Two," which is the second half of Blow's 1979 debut single, "Christmas Rappin'." And "Hard Times" is a forceful gem that finds Blow addressing social issues two years before Grandmaster Flash & the Furious Five popularized sociopolitical rapping with 1982's sobering "The Message." Some of the other tracks, however, are decent but not remarkable. Switching from rapping to singing, Blow detours into Northern soul on the Chi-Lites-influenced ballad "All I Want in This World (Is to Find That Girl)" and arena rock on an unexpected cover of Bachman-Turner Overdrive's "Takin' Care of Business." While those selections are likable and kind of interesting—how many other old school rappers attempted to sing soul, let alone arena rock?—the fact remains that rapping, not singing, is Blow's strong point. And Mercury really screwed up by providing only the second half of "Christmas Rappin'"; that landmark single should have been heard in its entirety. But despite its flaws and shortcomings, *Kurtis Blow* is an important album that hip-hop historians should make a point of hearing.

Alex Henderson

Ego Trip
1984, Mercury

By the time Kurtis Blow recorded 1984's *Ego Trip*, the Harlem MC was no longer considered cutting-edge in hip-hop circles. Blow, who was at the height of his popularity around 1979–1981, had come to be regarded as old school—and in 1984, cutting-edge meant Run-D.M.C., LL Cool J, the Fat Boys, the Beastie Boys, and Whodini. But even if Blow's rapping style was sounding somewhat dated in 1984, he still had impressive technique. Although uneven, *Ego Trip* has a lot going for it. Some of the material is excellent, especially the hit "Basketball" (which salutes the sport's big names), the skeletal "AJ Scratch," and the sociopolitical offerings "I Can't Take It No More" and "8 Million Stories" (which features Run-D.M.C. and puts an 1980s spin on the old TV series *The Naked City*). Other tracks, meanwhile, are decent but not great—like Blow's previous LPs, *Ego Trip* isn't without filler. Hip-hop was becoming increasingly album-minded

in 1984, but Blow had come out of an era in which singles dominated hip-hop and albums were the exception instead of the rule—which may explain why his albums tended to be inconsistent. But *Ego Trip* has more plusses than minuses, and its best tracks are first-rate.

Alex Henderson

Bone Thugs-N-Harmony

Creepin on ah Come Up
June 1994, Ruthless/Epic

Bearing the kinship of West Coast gangsta rap legend Eazy-E, Ruthless Records signees Bone Thugs-N-Harmony scored a left-field anthem in summer 1994 with "Thuggish Ruggish Bone," the lead single from their debut release, the eight-song *Creepin on ah Come Up* EP. The group's harmonious, fast-paced rapping sets them apart from their gangsta rap contemporaries, as does their Midwestern locale. Another highlight here is "For tha Love of Money," which features Eazy shortly before his unexpected passing away. Capturing Bone in their prime, back when they were still a cohesive, functional unit with nothing to lose, *Creepin on ah Come Up* isn't such a worthwhile listen on its own, but "Thuggish Ruggish Bone" is perhaps the group's signature recording and undoubtedly essential listening for fans, either here or elsewhere, as the song would later be compiled on the *Collection, Vol. 1* best-of (1998). [The 1999 re-release of *E 1999 Eternal* appended the *Creepin on ah Come Up* EP as a bonus disc.]

Jason Birchmeier

Boo-Yaa T.R.I.B.E.

New Funky Nation
1990, 4th & Broadway

While most rappers have been very reliant on technology, L.A.'s Boo-Yaa T.R.I.B.E. insisted on using "real instruments" both on stage and in the studio. On stage, they definitely strived for the type of spontaneity that funk bands generated in the 1970s. The Samoan-American gangster rappers and their associates use plenty of actual horns, bass, guitar, drums and percussion on *New Funky Nation*—an enjoyable debut album clearly influenced by WAR, Parliament/Funkadelic, Tower of Power and other '70s bands. Their reflections on gang violence in L.A. aren't all that memorable, but the T.R.I.B.E.'s knack for strong hooks and a blend of rap and old-school soul/funk instrumentation make this CD well worth hearing.

Alex Henderson

Boogie Down Productions

Criminal Minded
1987, M.I.L. Multimedia

Criminal Minded is widely considered the foundation of hardcore rap, announcing its intentions with a cover photo of KRS-One and Scott La Rock (on his only album with Boogie Down Productions) posing with weapons—an unheard-of gesture in 1987. BDP weren't the first to rap about inner-city violence and drugs, and there's no explicit mention of gangs on *Criminal Minded*, but it greatly expanded the range of subject matter that could be put on a rap record, and its grittiest moments are still unsettling today. Actually, that part of its reputation rests on just a handful of songs. Overall, the record made its impact through sheer force—not only KRS-One's unvarnished depictions of his harsh urban environment, but also his booming delivery and La Rock's lean, hard backing tracks (which sound a little skeletal today, but were excellent for the time). It's important to note that KRS-One hadn't yet adopted his role as the Teacher, and while there are a few hints of an emerging social consciousness, *Criminal Minded* doesn't try to deliver messages, make judgments, or offer solutions. That's clear on "South Bronx" and "The Bridge Is Over," two of the most cutting—even threatening—dis records of the '80s, which were products of a beef with Queens-based MC Shan. They set the tone for the album, which reaches its apex on the influential, oft-sampled "9mm Goes Bang." It's startlingly violent, even if KRS-One's gunplay is all in self-defense, and it's made all the more unsettling by his singsong ragga delivery. Another seminal hardcore moment is "P Is Free," which details an encounter with a crack whore for perhaps the first time on record. Elsewhere, there are a few showcases for KRS-One's pure rhyming skill, most notably "Poetry" and the title track. Overall it's very consistent, so even if the meat of *Criminal Minded* is the material that lives up to the title, the raw talent on display is what cements the album's status as an all-time classic.

Steve Huey

By All Means Necessary
1988, Jive

The murder of DJ Scott La Rock had a profound effect on KRS-One, resulting in a drastic rethinking of his on-record persona. He re-emerged the following year with *By All Means Necessary*, calling himself the Teacher and rapping mostly about issues facing the black community. His reality rhymes were no longer morally ambiguous, and this time when he posed on the cover with a gun, he was mimicking a photo of Malcolm X. As a social commentator, this is arguably KRS-One's finest moment. His observations are sharp, lucid, and confident, yet he doesn't fall prey to the preachiness that would mar some of his later work, and he isn't afraid to be playful or personal. The latter is especially true on the subject of La Rock, whose memory hangs over *By All Means Necessary*—not just in the frequent namechecks, but in the minimalist production and hard-hitting 808 drum beats that were his stock-in-trade on *Criminal Minded*. La Rock figures heavily in the album opener, "My Philosophy," which explains BDP's transition and serves as a manifesto for socially conscious hip-hop. The high point is the impassioned "Stop the Violence," a plea for peace on the hip-hop scene that still hasn't been heeded. Even as KRS-One denounces black-on-black crime, he refuses to allow the community to be stereotyped, criticizing the system that scoffs at that violence on the spoken recitation "Necessary." "Illegal Business" is a startlingly perceptive look at how the drug trade corrupts the police and government, appearing not long before the CIA's drug-running activities in the Iran-Contra Affair came to light. There are also some lighter moments in the battle-rhyme tracks, and a witty safe-sex rap in "Jimmy," a close cousin to the Jungle Brothers' "Jimbrowski." Lyrics from this album have been sampled by everyone from Prince Paul to N.W.A, and it ranks not only as KRS-One's most cohesive, fully realized statement, but a landmark of political rap that's unfairly lost in the shadow of Public Enemy's *It Takes a Nation of Millions*.

Steve Huey

Ghetto Music: The Blueprint of Hip Hop
June 1989, Jive

The second Boogie Down Productions album devoted mostly to consciousness raising, *Ghetto Music: The Blueprint of Hip Hop* finds KRS-One evolving into a fierce advocate for both his community and his chosen art form. He's particularly concerned about the direction of the latter: he's wary of hip-hop being co-opted by the pop mainstream, and the album's title comes from his conviction that real hip-hop is built on the vitality and rebelliousness of the streets. Accordingly, *Ghetto Music* contains a few more battle rhymes than usual, plus some showcases for pure MC technique, in keeping with the most basic elements of the music. The production, too, is still resolutely minimalist, and even if it's a little more fleshed-out than in the past, it consciously makes no concessions to pop or R&B accessibility. There are more reggae inflections in KRS-One's delivery than ever before, audible in about half the tracks here, and the production starts to echo dance-hall more explicitly on a few. Meanwhile, as the Teacher, he's actually put together lesson plans for a couple tracks: "Why Is That?" and "You Must Learn" are basically lectures about biblical and African-American history, respectively. This is where KRS-One starts to fall prey to didacticism, but he has relevant points to make, and the rapping is surprisingly nimble given all the information he's trying to pack in. Elsewhere, "Who Protects Us from You?" is a bouncy anti-police-brutality rap, and KRS closes the album with the point that "World Peace" can only be achieved through a pragmatic, aggressive struggle for equality. Although *Ghetto Music* has a few signs that KRS is starting to take himself a little too seriously (he dubs himself a metaphysician in the liner notes), overall it's another excellent effort and the last truly great BDP album.

Steve Huey

Edutainment
July 1990, Jive

KRS-One's artistic winning streak continued with *Edutainment*, Boogie Down Productions' fourth album. True to form, he focuses on black history and speaks out on homelessness, racism, police excesses, and materialism with clarity and insight. KRS was often compared to Public Enemy leader Chuck D because of his consistently sociopolitical focus, but there's no mistaking the fact that his unique mixture of black nationalism, Eastern religion (both Hinduism and Buddhism), and Rastafarian philosophy is very much his own. From a commercial standpoint, he had become a little too intellectual and wasn't selling as many albums as many in rap's gangsta school. But from an artistic perspective, *Edutainment* is as commendable as it is riveting.

Alex Henderson

Sex and Violence
February 1992, Jive

The final album released under the Boogie Down Productions name, *Sex and Violence* is a partial return to form after the overly preachy ego trip of *Edutainment*. Specifically, it's a return to the aggressive beats of KRS-One's earlier work, except with a more contemporary sound—this is the first BDP album to rely on multiple outside producers, which supplies a much-needed sonic update. As a result, some BDP fans feel that *Sex and Violence* is an underrated effort—it packs more of a punch, and KRS-One is refocusing on the art of MCing, not to mention his dancehall reggae influence. That said, it isn't a complete success, since his usual consistency of vision isn't quite there. There are a number of good moments: the single "Duck Down," "Like a Throttle" (which fears that Islamic spirituality has become nothing but a hip-hop fad), and "Poisonous Products." But elsewhere, some of his observations are more provocative than immediately insightful. He urges the "Drug Dealer" to invest his profits in the black community, and on "Build and Destroy" he brands high-ranking black officials like Clarence Thomas and Colin Powell nothing short of devils for their assimilation. Plus, "13 and Good" and "Say Gal" both have a discomforting undercurrent of misogyny unbecoming a teacher. There's enough vitality on *Sex and Violence* to make it worthwhile for fans, but overall it doesn't rank with the best of KRS-One's work.

Steve Huey

Boss

Born Gangstaz
1992, Def Jam

Just as fantastical and less forced than plenty of other gangsta rap records released in 1992, Boss' *Born Gangstaz* is a remarkable album that has gone underappreciated in the hip-hop world. Abetted by a laundry list of reputable producers—Jam Master Jay, T Ray, MC Serch, Def Jef, AMG, Erick Sermon—MC Lichelle Laws and DJ Irene Moore shrug at a cruel world, claim to not care, drink like fishes, smoke like Cypress Hill, live like thieves, and accord the opposite sex no respect whatsoever. In fact, no one and no thing is given any degree of respect, and it's clear that they've got a death wish. All of this would be met with a shrug if Laws had less-than-remarkable vocal and lyrical skills, but she's just as adept at painting vivid scenarios while riding the rhythms as any of her producers. She doesn't simply flip the gender roles of the average gangsta record; "tricks" expecting to get some end up getting some in the form of bullets. Her delivery consistently sounds collected but set to blast, and the productions almost always complement her detached, matter-of-fact viewpoint. Too bad the answering-machine messages left by Laws' parents soften the blunt impact of this cold, cold record.

Andy Kellman

The Brand New Heavies

Heavy Rhyme Experience, Vol. 1
August 1992, Delicious Vinyl

"Brand New Heavies play the sh*t that/People used to listen to in '70s Chevys." With that succinct and flawless couplet from the awesome opening track, "Bonafide Funk," Large Professor helped to explain why there was a certain herd of influential rappers who were enthralled by the Brand New Heavies' sleek (some would say slick) and urbanely stylish Anglo take on classic American funk and soul after the quartet released its eponymous debut in 1991: They were

pulling the very same vintage-groove LPs from their crates for inspiration. When the Heavies made their first trip to American shores, both Q-Tip and 3rd Bass' MC Serch were quick to show their respect by hopping on-stage with the band (likely the event that planted the seed for *Heavy Rhyme Experience*), and the latter rapper even predicted that *The Brand New Heavies* would be the source material for a decade's worth of loops and samples for rap producers. Serch's enthusiastic forecast never quite materialized, but it is hard to argue with his logic after you hear this landmark collaborative experiment. A live hip-hop band wasn't a complete novelty at the time—proto-rapper Gil Scott-Heron utilized jazz backing, Tackhead was the house band for Sugarhill Records all the way back in the late '70s, and the self-proclaimed "world's one and only hip-hop band," Stetsasonic had been fully live for several years by that point—but never before had rap taken such an on-the-fly, jam-like approach. Spontaneous combustion resulted. Never before (and perhaps never since) had the Heavies managed to sound this deliciously in-the-pocket and playful, and the MCs beautifully follow their lead. Guru sounds looser and more whimsical on "It's Gettin Hectic" than on any Gang Starr track. Simon Bartholomew's teasing guitar lines poke holes in Grand Puba's swollen-tongued bluster on "Who Makes the Loot?" Kool G. Rap is given the blaxploitation backing he had always deserved. And Ed. O.G. and Pharcyde do verbal gymnastics that must be heard. But every vocalist here blooms from the pairing. The only regret is that N'Dea Davenport was not included in some capacity, considering how much she added to the Heavies. Too bad, as well, that there was never a volume two. One wonders what sort of magic Posdnuos and Trugoy of De La Soul, the Leaders of the New School trio, Rakim, or Chuck D. could have conjured had they been tapped as collaborators, or from the West Coast Ice Cube and Del tha Funkee Homosapien. Still, *Heavy Rhyme Experience, Vol. 1* is a match made in heaven.

Stanton Swihart

Brand Nubian

One for All
1990, Elektra

Brand Nubian never sold as many albums as the many West Coast rappers burning up the charts in the early '90s, but the New York group commanded great respect in East Coast rap circles. In black neighborhoods of New York and Philadelphia, Nubian's debut album, *One for All*, was actually a bigger seller than many of the platinum gangsta rap releases outselling it on a national level. Influenced by De La Soul and the Jungle Brothers, Nubian favored an abstract rapping style, and Eastern rap fans were drawn to the complexity of jams like "Dance to My Ministry," "Ragtime," and "All for One." Grand Puba, Lord Jamar, and Sadat X had a lot of technique, which was what hip-hoppers favored in the East. On the whole, Nubian's Nation of Islam rhetoric isn't as overbearing as some of the recordings that other Five Percenters were delivering at the time. The CD is a bit uneven, but on the whole is likable and exhilarating.

Alex Henderson

In God We Trust
February 1993, Elektra

When pre-album single "Punks Jump Up to Get Beat Down" was issued—along with its violence-laced video—it was clear that Brand Nubian would not be the same minus Grand Puba. It was a safe bet that *In God We Trust* wouldn't have attempted any new jack swing crossovers or tie-dyed imagery. Though the makeover is drastic, it is convincing, with Lord Jamar and Sadat X stepping up with some of the era's fiercest, most intense rhymes, a higher percentage of which referenced the likes of Louis Farrakhan and the Nation of Islam, Marcus Garvey, and self-defense by any means necessary. Multiple, indefensible homophobic taunts and the silly "Steal Ya 'Ho" aside (did they really think the use of the two words was so necessary?), *In God We Trust* is nearly faultless, packed with rumbling acoustic basslines, Jeep-rattling breakbeats, and rhymes written and delivered with a great deal of hunger and an equal amount of self-assuredness—as if to say, "No, Brand Nubian was never Grand Puba and a couple sidekicks." The Diamond D-produced "Punks" outshines everything else, but the group more than holds its own as a self-contained production team. Had a high-profile beat maker been responsible for "The Godz...," "Pass the Gat," or "Brand Nubian Rock the Set," they'd certainly be present in his or her highlight reel.

Andy Kellman

Candyman

Ain't No Shame in My Game
September 1990, Epic

When a rapper does well in the R&B or pop markets, hip-hop's hardcore tends to view the artist with suspicion, however strong his or her rapping skills might be. That was exactly what happened to Candyman when "Knockin' Boots" (a catchy single that sampled Betty Wright's "Tonight Is the Night") enjoyed considerable crossover action. Some hardcore rappers questioned Candyman's legitimacy, but make no mistake: *Ain't No Shame in My Game* proves that the Angeleno's rapping skills are solid. While this decent debut album has its share of lighthearted R&B-flavored fare (including "Playin' on Me," "Melt in Your Mouth," and of course, "Knockin' Boots"), more aggressive, in-your-face tunes like "Today's Topic," "5 Verses of Def," and "The Mack Is Back" demonstrate that Candyman has no problem handling hardcore b-boy rap. The overall result is a generally likable, if a bit uneven, album.

Alex Henderson

Neneh Cherry

Raw Like Sushi
May 1989, Virgin

Those arguing that the most individualistic R&B and dance music of the late '80s and early-to-mid '90s came out of Britain could point to Neneh Cherry's unconventional *Raw Like Sushi* as a shining example. An unorthodox and brilliantly daring blend of R&B, rap, pop, and dance music, *Sushi*

enjoyed little exposure on America's conservative, urban, contemporary radio formats, but was a definite underground hit. Full of personality, the singer/rapper is as thought-provoking as she is witty and humorous when addressing relationships and taking aim at less-than-kosher behavior of males and females alike. Macho homeboys and Casanovas take a pounding on "So Here I Come" and the hit "Buffalo Stance," while women who are shallow, cold-hearted, or materialistic get lambasted on "Phoney Ladies," "Heart," and "Inna City Mamma." Cherry's idealism comes through loud and clear on "The Next Generation," a plea to take responsibility for one's sexual actions and give children the respect and attention they deserve.

Alex Henderson

Homebrew
October 1992, Virgin

Neneh Cherry doesn't get into the studio nearly often enough. Three years passed before the British singer/rapper came out with a second album. Thankfully, she more than lived up to the tremendous promise of *Raw Like Sushi* on the equally magnificent and risk-taking *Homebrew*. Cherry shows no signs of the dreaded sophomore slump—everything on the CD is a gem. She triumphs with a seamless and unorthodox blend of hip-hop, R&B, dance music, and pop, and on "Money Love" and "Trout," the presence of R.E.M.'s Michael Stipe brings rock to the eclectic mix. As humorous as Cherry can be, her reflections on relationships and social issues are often quite pointed. While "Money Love" decries the evils of materialism, the moving "I Ain't Gone Under Yet" describes an inner-city woman's determination not to be brought down by the poverty and drugs that surround her. And "Twisted" is about keeping yourself sane in a world gone insane. Unfortunately, *Homebrew* wasn't the commercial breakthrough Cherry was more than deserving of.

Alex Henderson

Chill Rob G.

Ride the Rhythm
1990, Wild Pitch

Ride the Rhythm doesn't look like other rap records from the early '90s—in fact it looks sort of like a techno-pop record. The title rides along in a heavily stylized font across the bottom while in the foreground an image of a city-steppin' Chill Rob

G presides as cool as his name, which hangs above riddled with bullet holes; meanwhile, in the background an op-art pattern dominates to the right of Chill, while cops and street-prestige symbols of cars and women compete on the left. The dichotomy is puzzling but understandable. Chill Rob G is a tough East Coast rapper, but the song he's best known for is an international pop hit, "The Power," by Snap! Granted Chill was only sampled by the Europop group but, perhaps in an attempt to grab some of the cash, he covers Snap!'s version of "The Power" on *Ride the Rhythm*. Even though the song would sound perfectly normal on one of Snap!'s albums, here it nearly derails an otherwise solid album. The other songs represent classic early '90s chopped-funk production, courtesy of Flavor Unit producer the 45 King. The pinnacle of their collaboration is the classic "Let the Words Flow," which manages to maintain its bulldog stance and be danceable at the same time. And that is the attempt of the rest of *Ride the Rhythm* as well, only in the hands of Chill it sounds more like a command than an invitation.

Wade Kergan

Cold Crush Brothers

Live in 82
1994, Tuff City

This live album is low quality by most sonic standards, but it is one of the only ways one can hear hip-hop as it was originally performed before DAT machines rendered the DJ a mere ornament who occasionally "scratched" over pre-recorded tapes during live performances. Further, it captures a moment in time when hip-hop was party music, before Grandmaster Flash's "The Message" opened up the possibilities for more reality-based raps. One can feel the energy in the interaction between the MCs and the audience who chanted to the looped beat created by the DJ spinning two of the same records, alternately returning each record to the beginning of the breakbeat in a seamless fashion.

Kembrew McLeod

Cold Crush Brothers vs. Fantastic Romantic 5
July 1998, Slammin

The second (official) live Cold Crush tape to surface, this one earns classic status not because it's the best that's ever been heard, but because it's the best-sounding—and the only one coming straight from one of the sources: DJ Charlie Chase. He offered it as a way to beat the bootleggers (and finally earn some proceeds himself), also explaining in the intro, "I cleaned up the vocals and recut the beats." As dangerous as the word "recut" sounds, this battle tap really *is* a classic (and if parts were redone, they certainly don't reveal any artificial sources). Chase gives plenty of time to the Cold Crush (it's possible he didn't even like the Fantastic Five section on tape), who take up nearly all of the 45-minute disc. Though a few tracks are crammed front to back with line after line of dizzying, single-cadence old school rapping, it's clear that the Cold Crush were masters of keeping the beat going at their frequent club dates.

John Bush

Common

Can I Borrow a Dollar?
1992, Relativity

A former *Source* magazine "Unsigned Hype" winner, Common Sense almost single-handedly put Chicago hip-hop on the map in the early '90s with his excellent debut, *Can I Borrow a Dollar?*, which displayed a truly unique sound that, nevertheless, situated the rapper somewhere between the ground staked out by A Tribe Called Quest and Gang Starr. *Can I Borrow a Dollar?* features the fabulous, oddly muted production of 2 Pc. Drk Productions (Immenslope and Twilite Tone). They opt for a spare, minimalist production that prominently features understated keyboard loops over simple drum tracks, occasionally augmented by saxophone or flute for an overall jazzy, laid-back feel. The production perfectly complements Common Sense's hiccuping/singsongy vocal style and involved rhymes. His lyrics are packed with allusions and references to pop and street culture nearly as eclectic as those of the Beastie Boys. Though sometimes lighthearted to the point of aimlessness and occasionally veering into harder-hitting (vaguely misogynistic) sentiments, *Can I Borrow a Dollar?* acted, for the most part, as an antidote to the exaggeratedly hardcore rhymes of a lot of early '90s hip-hop. Standout tracks such as "Charms Alarm," "Take It EZ," and the only outside production, the Beatnuts' characteristically bell-driven "Heidi Hoe," are calls to arms to all hangers-on and fakers in the hip-hop community. This is one of the most underrated hip-hop debuts of the '90s.

Stanton Swihart

Resurrection
October 1994, Ruthless

Although Chicago is often praised for its blues, jazz, and house music, the city has failed to be successful when it comes to rap. One of the few Chicago MCs who has enjoyed any type of national attention is Common Sense, whose complex style of rapping and jazz-flavored tracks inspire comparisons to De La Soul, Digable Planets, A Tribe Called Quest, and the Pharcyde. On his sophomore effort, *Resurrection*, the South Sider doesn't hesitate to let you know that he has considerable technique, and in fact, he sometimes displays too much of it for his own good. Nonetheless, his intelligence, wit, and originality make this CD impressive. *Resurrection*'s standout track is "I Used to Love H.E.R.," which seems to describe a lover's moral and spiritual decline, but is actually addressing what Common views as hip-hop's decline (in particular, gangsta rap's exploitation of sex and violence). Also quite noteworthy are "Nuthin' to Do" (which speaks out on the deterioration of Chicago's neighborhoods), and the introspective "Book of Life," a commentary on trying to keep it together in a society that has lost all traces of sanity.

Alex Henderson

Compton's Most Wanted

It's a Compton Thang
February 1990, Orpheus

Rudimentary yet undoubtedly cornerstone, *It's a Compton Thang* brings together for the first time a talented group of rap artists highlighted by future and former West Coast legends—MC Eiht and the Unknown DJ, respectively—that would build upon the prototype N.W.A had established two years earlier on *Straight Outta Compton*. Compton's Most Wanted follow that prototype very closely here, even going so far as sampling N.W.A on the album opener, "One Time Gaffled 'Em Up." *It's a Compton Thang* is more than simply a second-rate *Straight Outta Compton*, though. In fact, it expands upon that prototype, specifically with late-album highlight "Late Night Hype," a laid-back G-funk ballad that would set the stage for a million others in the coming years. Beyond historical significance, *It's a Compton Thang* doesn't quite measure up to what CMW would do in subsequent years. The Unknown DJ and DJ Slip piece together some memorable productions from classic samples, among them James Brown's "Payback" on "Final Chapter," and the rappers similarly deliver some uniquely old-school style, yet all of this is more novel than anything, particularly to contemporary listeners—more reminiscent of the much-treasured golden age than the much-criticized gangsta age. And while that golden age sense is precisely what's so much fun about this album, it's not what CMW would embody thereafter, as they hardened both their production and their rapping, which are anything but hard here. All of that aside, the true beauty of *It's a Compton Thang* is the initial synthesis of former electro legend the Unknown DJ with future gangsta icon MC Eiht as well as the pleasant reminder that West Coast gangsta rap was once more about old-fashioned fun than cheap thrills.

Jason Birchmeier

Straight Checkn 'Em
July 1991, Orpheus

Compton's Most Wanted's second CD got more sullen, combative, and sexist in its language and themes than their debut. Where "Duck Sick" and "It's a Compton Thang" at least had some swagger and a taste of humor to offset the posturing, "Can I Kill It?" and "Compton's Lynchin'" were more surly, while "Gangsta Shot Out" and "Growin' Up in the Hood" were fatalistic and "Raised in Compton" despairing rather than informative. Only "Mike T's Funky Scratch" sounded a lighter note, and that was due to its being a declaration of rap prowess rather than street superiority.

Ron Wynn

Music to Driveby
June 1992, Orpheus

The third and commercially most successful album by Los Angeles rappers Compton's Most Wanted contained such terse narratives as "Dead Men Tell No Lies" and "Hit the Floor." If there hadn't been such an abundance of similar material in the early '90s, these tales might have triggered intense scrutiny and analysis. Instead, the most common response is that MC Eiht's raps aren't quite as loose or expressive as those of Spice 1, Ice Cube, Nas, or many others telling identical stories.

Ron Wynn

When We Wuz Bangin' 1989–1999: The Hitz
January 2001, The Right Stuff

The 1989–1999 time span cited in the subtitle of *When We Wuz Bangin'* is a little misleading. Compton's Most Wanted did in fact span a decade, forming in 1989 and debuting a year later, but the group spend most of the ensuing decade inactive, releasing only three albums during a three-year span (1990–1992). Throughout most of the '90s, group leader MC Eiht trudged on with his up-and-down solo career and took producer DJ Slip along for part of the ride. The remaining members of CMW meanwhile remained mostly confined to old-school obscurity. As short-lived as the talented group had been, though, they did release a wealth of blueprint West Coast gangsta rap during their three-album span, each album—*It's a Compton Thang* (1990), *Music to Driveby* (1991), and *Straight Checkn 'Em* (1992)—offering a few standout singles. Many of those singles are compiled here ("One Time Gaffled 'Em Up," "Late Night Hype," "Growin' Up in the Hood") as are several of Eiht's bigger solo hits ("All for the Money," "Streiht Up Menace," "Days of '89") and even some rare recordings (DJ Premier's remix of "Def Wish II"). The inclusion of Eiht's solo work is key, since he did have a few great gangsta ballads, but you could argue that those songs had little to do with Compton's Most Wanted and occupy precious disc space that could have instead featured gang-bangin' songs like "Hood Took Me Under" or "Straight Checkn' Em."

Jason Birchmeier

Coolio

It Takes a Thief
July 1994, Tommy Boy

Coolio's debut, *It Takes a Thief*, brought him immediate success, establishing his reputation as a hard-knock, gunslinging gangster with a biting sense of humor. Maybe it was because of his appearance—heavy eyelids and finger-in-a-light-socket hairstyle—or maybe it was because of his laid-back vocal delivery, but he never seemed quite as menacing as other West Coast rappers spitting verses about the same thuggery. Instead of trying to incite fear in his raps, he complained that he didn't like having to live that way, and noted that he wasn't really a choice in the matter. Practically all the songs on *It Takes a Thief* are about one of two things: gang-banging and robbing in the ghettos while trying to make ends meet, or about hard times as a crack addict on the streets. Not exactly the most uplifting topics, but when the stories of strife are rapped smoothly over melodic funk anthems, people automatically shake their butts and overlook the darker subtext. In actuality, the content of the album is pretty similar to Marvin Gaye's *What's Going On*, if you can believe that, with

Coolio wondering why society is so messed up and trying to find a way to make ends meet. Like Nas (who also came out with his debut in 1994), his lyrics are justifications and apologies for living the thug life in an era when most popular rappers glorified the hardcore lifestyle. Rather than hyping his toughness, he explains ghetto trials and tribulations. It's hard to imagine Snoop or 2Pac rapping about standing in the welfare line ("County Line"), or being impoverished and malnourished and eating out of a garbage can ("Can-O-Corn"), but Coolio tells these tales of woe matter-of-factly while candy-coated beats and playful melodies bounce along like P-Funk. With its infectious "Slide, slide, slippity slide" chorus, it went unnoticed that his breakthrough single, "Fantastic Voyage," was actually a song about escapism, and that "I Remember" was about the angst of getting shot by a gang member for unknowingly wearing the wrong colors, rather than a sentimental ditty about the good ol' days. Regardless of the commonly misinterpreted underlying meanings, the songs are undeniable party jams, and with future albums, the lyrics would focus more and more on the dancefloor aspect. The whole journey is a fantastic and underrated juxtaposition between good times and bad times, and ultimately, even though his second album, *Gangsta's Paradise*, sold more copies, this debut represents Coolio at his finest hour.

Jason Lymangrover

Gangsta's Paradise
November 1995, Tommy Boy

Most of Coolio's hit debut *It Takes a Thief* was fairly upbeat material, but the appearance of the stark single "Gangsta's Paradise" in the summer of 1995 signaled a change in the rapper's music. Driven by an ominously deep bassline and slashing strings, the creeping, threatening funk of "Gangsta's Paradise" was the most chilling thing Coolio had recorded to date, but the menace didn't come at the expense of his considerable talent for immediate, catchy hooks. Consequently, the single shot to the top of the charts and hovered in the Top Ten for many weeks. The album followed shortly afterwards, and it didn't fail to deliver on the promise of the single. Not only did Coolio expand his sound, but his songwriting skills improved, as *Gangsta's Paradise* has very few weak moments. Alternating between slow, funky grooves and elastic, party-ready anthems, *Gangsta's Paradise* is proof that Coolio is one of the most exciting and interesting hip-hop artists of the mid-'90s.

Stephen Thomas Erlewine

Fantastic Voyage: The Greatest Hits
July 2001, Tommy Boy

Over the course of three albums in the 1990s, Coolio took West Coast hip-hop even farther into the mainstream than Dr. Dre. Even though he nearly succumbed to the perils of the streets in his youth, Coolio's take on the '70s funk-obsessed L.A. sound was usually far more good-humored than the menacing Death Row crew. His gangsta roots could play to the hardcore faithful, but he also snagged plenty of younger listeners with his fun-loving party music and genial (if profane) comic persona. (In fact, it's difficult to imagine Puff Daddy becoming an across-the-board pop star without Coolio first sparking that younger audience's interest in hip-hop.) Coolio's broad appeal, combined with a knack for finding (often borrowing) memorable hooks, helped make him one of the best pop-rap artists of the '90s, as demonstrated by *Fantastic Voyage: The Greatest Hits*. It's a straightforward 13-track collection centered around Coolio's signature party anthems—"Fantastic Voyage," "Too Hot," "1, 2, 3, 4

(Sumpin' New)"—plus his moody masterpiece, "Gangsta's Paradise," and one previously unissued track, "Aw Here It Goes" (a theme for the Nickelodeon comedy series *Kenan & Kel*). Yet the lesser-known tracks are often pretty catchy themselves, proving that Coolio's talents extend beyond the handful of irresistible singles for which he's primarily known. Even if nothing else quite matches the heights of those few classics, *Fantastic Voyage: The Greatest Hits* is still an infectious, consistently entertaining listen.

Steve Huey

Cybotron

Clear
1990, Fantasy

The only old-school electro LP with any amount of staying power (thanks in part to its release on Fantasy), this CD release of the Cybotron album—previously known as *Enter*—includes crucial, early singles like "Alleys of Your Mind," "Cosmic Cars," and techno's first defining moment, "Clear." The collision of Atkins' vision for cosmic funk and the arena rock instincts of Rick Davis result in a surprisingly cohesive album, dated for all the right reasons and quite pop-minded. Ecological and political statements even crop up with the final tracks, "Cosmic Raindance" and "El Salvador."

John Bush

Cypress Hill

Cypress Hill
August 1991, Ruffhouse

It's hard enough to transform an entire musical genre—Cypress Hill's eponymous debut album revolutionized hip-hop in several respects. Although they weren't the first Latino rappers, nor the first to mix Spanish and English, they were the first to achieve a substantial following, thanks to their highly distinctive sound. Along with Beastie Boys and Public Enemy, Cypress Hill were also one of the first rap groups to bridge the gap with fans of both hard rock *and* alternative rock. And, most importantly, they created a sonic blueprint that would become one of the most widely copied in hip-hop. In keeping with their promarijuana stance, Cypress Hill intentionally crafted their music to sound stoned—lots of slow, lazy beats, fat bass, weird noises, and creepily distant-sounding samples. The surreal lyrical narratives were almost exclusively spun by B Real in a nasal, singsong, instantly recognizable delivery that only added to the music's hazy, evocative atmosphere; as a frontman, he could be funny, frightening, or just plain bizarre (again, kind of like the experience of being stoned). Whether he's taunting cops or singing nursery rhyme-like choruses about blasting holes in people with shotguns, B Real's blunted-gangsta posture is nearly always underpinned by a cartoonish sense of humor. It's never clear how serious the threats are, but that actually makes them all the more menacing. The sound and style of *Cypress Hill* was hugely influential, particularly on Dr. Dre's boundary-shattering 1992 blockbuster *The Chronic*; yet despite its legions of imitators, *Cypress Hill* still sounds fresh and original today, simply because few hip-hop artists can put its sound across with such force of personality or imagination.

Steve Huey

Black Sunday
July 1993, Ruffhouse

Black Sunday made Cypress Hill's connection to rock & roll more explicit, with its heavy metal-like artwork and noisier, more dissonant samples (including, naturally, stoner icons Black Sabbath). It's a slightly darker affair than its groundbreaking predecessor, with the threats of violence more urgent and the pot obsession played to the hilt (after all, it was a crucial part of their widespread appeal). Apart from those subtle distinctions, the sound of *Black Sunday* is pretty much the same as *Cypress Hill*, refining the group's innovations into an accessible bid for crossover success. In fact, it's a little startling how often *Black Sunday* recycles musical ideas and even lyrical catch phrases from the endlessly inventive debut. And the rock-derived, verse-chorus song structures start to sound a little formulaic by the end of the record (how many choruses feature Sen Dog repeating part of whatever B Real just said?). But in spite of that, *Black Sunday* still sounds vital and lively, since the group has a surer sense of craft. Most of the tracks are fleshed out into structured songs, in contrast to the brief sketches that punctuated *Cypress Hill*. The album benefits immensely from the resulting clutch of excellent singles (and songs that could have been), and while a couple of tracks feel redundant and underdeveloped, *Black Sunday* is overall a consistent, engaging listen, especially the flawless first half or so. Unfortunately, it's also the group's last great album, thanks to the musical recycling operation that began here and would handicap much of their subsequent work.

Steve Huey

D-Nice

Call Me D-Nice
1990, Jive

D-Nice had two albums as a DJ with Boogie Down Productions under his belt when he went solo with *Call Me D-Nice*, and he was still a youngster at the time. Though hardly a masterpiece, his debut album proved that he didn't go out on his own for the sake of ego. Anyone expecting something on the level of BDP's best work was clearly asking for too much; that's a big cloud that many put over D-Nice's head. After all, there are few MCs you can compare to KRS-One, so why compare an MC whose primary talents are as a DJ and beatboxer? The album delivered a bona fide classic with the title track, full of boastful rhymes and instantly memorable swollen organs and buzzing basslines. Only once does he attempt edutainment, and that's on "Glory," a school report in the form of a song that summarizes the Civil War film of the same name. Otherwise, he keeps it to bragging, throwing requisite bones to the R&B lovers ("It's Over") and the fellas who stood poised to label him a softie ("Pimp of the Year"). The production is spare and basic for most of the duration, and it complements the remainder of the BDP-related releases just fine.

Andy Kellman

Da Brat

Funkdafied
1994, So So Def/Chaos

The first album by a female rapper ever to sell one million copies, *Funkdafied* is a promising debut effort that finds da Brat still solidifying her style. She's a very good rapper without a strong identity of her own yet, and despite her own obvious intensity, she seems infatuated with the offhanded drawl of Snoop Doggy Dogg on much of the album. She's not just influenced by him, but cops recognizable inflections, phrasing, and vocal riffs, and producer Jermaine Dupri sometimes supports her with Dr. Dre-style G-funk tracks, most obviously on the single "Fa All Y'All." But even at its most derivative, *Funkdafied* has spirit. Repeatedly announcing, "I ain't no muthaf*ckin' joke," da Brat paints herself as a cussin', weed-smokin' badass bitch who can hang with the boys and beat them at their own game. Cuts like "Da Shit Ya Can't Fuc Wit," "Fire It Up," and "Give It 2 You" effectively establish her tough-talking persona, and the smash title cut is a breezy, laid-back party jam. On quite a few tracks, da Brat augments her Snoop fixation by referencing lines from '80s classics, almost as though she feels compelled to prove she knows her history; she can also rely a little too heavily on her catch phrase, "Brat-tat-tat-tat." But even if she isn't quite there yet, da Brat knows who she wants to be, and she has the talent and production to make the journey entertaining.

Steve Huey

Da Youngsta's

The Aftermath
April 1993, East West

With Mobb Deep and Illegal at one end of the spectrum (the more authentically streetwise one), Kris Kross and Chi-Ali on the (more commercially savvy) other, and Leaders of the New School occupying the eccentric, artistic center, the early '90s did not want for teenaged rap artists. Philadelphia's Da Youngsta's was yet another trio of underage MCs who made a brief but fairly impressive splash on the hip-hop scene. Impressive enough, in fact, to draw the attention of some of the genre's major personalities. *The Aftermath* leans toward the street side of the divide, but has some of the artistic heft of L.O.N.S., mostly as a result of the production work of a quartet of heavyweights: the Beatnuts, Pete Rock, Marley Marl, and DJ Premier. Unlike the clear legitimacy that was immediately bestowed upon by the community on Mobb Deep's Prodigy and Havoc, however, it is not always easy to take the relentlessly hardcore stance of Da Youngsta's seriously. First, though, it is somewhat superficial as a reason, the voice of at least one of the group's members was still stuck in puberty hell at the time the album was recorded. It is cartoonish, in a decidedly sinister way, to hear such a voice making physical threats and lyrical boasts. Secondly, Lawrence "L.G." Goodman, who oversees the proceedings (and comes up with some strong beats of his own), just happens to be father to two-thirds of the crew (the third member was a cousin). The fact that Da Youngsta's, in reality, were not exactly callous street urchins takes some of the wind and conviction out of their more menacing rhetoric. Those failings aside, the album still has a bevy of platinum moments, especially the Beatnuts track "Wild Child," Pete Rock's "Iz U Wit Me" and "Who's the Mic Wrecka," Premier's "Wake Em Up," and Goodman's own "Count It Off."

Stanton Swihart

Dana Dane

Dana Dane with Fame
1987, Profile

Rap was many things in the '80s: sociopolitical, cutting-edge, innovative, in-your-face, insightful, angry, thought-provoking, intellectual, entertaining, funny, crude, and so on. Eighties rap could describe tragic social conditions (Ice-T's "Colors," Grandmaster Flash's "The Message") or it could be unapologetically silly (Biz Markie's "Pickin' Boogers"). Rapping with a fake British accent, Dana Dane represented the goofier side of '80s rap. *Dana Dane With Fame*, the New Yorker's debut album, is a classic of its kind. Occasionally, this 1987 release touches on social issues, but for the most part, *Dana Dane With Fame* (which was produced by Hurby Luv Bug) doesn't take itself too seriously. Dane's greatest asset is his sense of humor, and the East Coast MC is wildly entertaining on goofy, nutty items like "Nightmares," "Love at First Sight," and the hit single "Cinderfella Dana Dane." But while social commentary isn't the CD's main focus, Dane isn't oblivious to the social problems that plague a major city like New York. On "Delancey Street" (another major hit), Dane raps about three women trying to rob him at gunpoint on Manhattan's Lower East Side. The dark-humored tune manages to be funny and disturbing at the same time; even when he's rapping about urban crime, Dane maintains the silliness that made him so endearing. "Delancey Street" was a song that New Yorkers had no problem relating to in the '80s; back then, the area of Delancey Street near the Williamsburg Bridge was infamous for its high crime rate (although much of Manhattan's Lower East Side became a lot safer in the '90s, thanks to Mayor Rudy Giuliani's war on crime). *Dana Dane With Fame* isn't the MC's only worthwhile album, but it is definitely his best and most essential.

Alex Henderson

Das EFX

Dead Serious
April 1992, East West

Das EFX—part of EPMD's Def Squad crew, which also included K-Solo and Redman, among others—made such a wide breakthrough in 1992 with their debut album that their hit "They Want EFX" was even referenced in the lily-white teen serial *Beverly Hills 90210*. That *Dead Serious* could have that sort of broad impact and still retain its credibility within the underground hip-hop community says something about its appeal, which was considerable. But the album wasn't just appealing; it was also enormously influential,

ushering in an entirely unique rhyming flow that influenced any number of rappers, established and novice alike. What exactly the duo is rapping about is anyone's guess. One thing is for sure: their lyrics are about as far removed from hard-core realism as they could possibly be, and although there are certain elements of boasting, it is so cut up and contorted that it never sounds like there's even a hint of the humdrum here. None of the lyrical clichés that can occasionally bog down even the finest hip-hop artist are present. Members Dre and Skoob (tellingly, "books" spelled backward) instead engage in lightning-fast, tongue-twisted word association and stream-of-consciousness rants rich in pop cultural references and allusions. It was a completely original rhyming style in 1992—one of the reasons it had such an impact both in the insular world of hip-hop and on the wider public—but it also had an invigorating looseness that lent itself to commercial radio. "They Want EFX" is clearly the creative highlight of the album; the other songs work the same basic template, and each one is nearly equal in execution and charm, particularly the jaunty "Mic Checka" and "Jussummen."

Stanton Swihart

Straight Up Sewaside
November 1993, East West

By the time *Sewaside* saw the light of day, the public hadn't fully absorbed Das EFX's innovative debut, *Dead Serious*. The hardcore rap game had barely caught up with the brilliance of their rapid-fire vocal delivery and sample-laden beats. But then again, another crew from Staten Island emerged in 1993 and took the rap game by total storm, leaving the genius of *Sewaside* somewhat overshadowed by their dominance. However, this change in climate shouldn't overshadow *Sewaside* as a crucial record in the Das EFX canon. While the duo's methods of madness were slowly emulated by a large plethora of MCs, Das EFX stayed with the same effective blueprint laid down in *Dead Serious*. By maintaining this consistency, *Sewaside* lacks the punch in the gut that *Dead Serious* delivered, but it's still a solid record that completists and newfound fans will equally enjoy.

Rob Theakston

De La Soul

3 Feet High and Rising
1989, Tommy Boy

The most inventive, assured, and playful debut in hip-hop history, *3 Feet High and Rising* not only proved that rappers didn't have to talk about the streets to succeed, but also expanded the palette of sampling material with a kaleidoscope of sounds and references culled from pop, soul, disco, and even country music. Weaving clever wordplay and deft rhymes across two dozen tracks loosely organized around a game-show theme, De La Soul broke down boundaries all over the LP, moving easily from the groovy my-philosophy intro "The Magic

Number" to an intelligent, caring inner-city vignette named "Ghetto Thang" to the freewheeling end-of-innocence tale "Jenifa Taught Me (Derwin's Revenge)." Rappers Posdnuos and Trugoy the Dove talked about anything they wanted (up to and including body odor), playing fast and loose on the mic like Biz Markie. Thinly disguised under a layer of humor, their lyrical themes ranged from true love ("Eye Know") to the destructive power of drugs ("Say No Go") to Daisy Age philosophy ("Tread Water") to sex ("Buddy"). Prince Paul (from Stetsasonic) and DJ Pasemaster Mase led the way on the production end, with dozens of samples from all sorts of left-field artists—including Johnny Cash, the Mad Lads, Steely Dan, Public Enemy, Hall & Oates, and the Turtles. The pair didn't just use those samples as hooks or drumbreaks—like most hip-hop producers had in the past—but as split-second fills and in-jokes that made some tracks sound more like DJ records. Even "Potholes on My Lawn," which samples a mouth harp and yodeling (for the chorus, no less), became a big R&B hit. If it was easy to believe the revolution was here from listening to the rapping and production on Public Enemy's *It Takes a Nation of Millions to Hold Us Back*, with De La Soul the Daisy Age seemed to promise a new era of positivity in hip-hop.

John Bush

De La Soul Is Dead
May 1991, Tommy Boy

On their notorious second album, De La Soul went to great lengths to debunk the daisy-age hippie image they'd been pigeonholed with, titling the record *De La Soul Is Dead* and putting a picture of wilting daisies in a broken flowerpot on the cover. Critics and fans alike were puzzled as to why the group was seemingly rejecting what had been hailed as the future of hip-hop, and neither the reviews nor the charts were kind to the album. It isn't that De La try to remake their sound here—*Dead* keeps the skit-heavy structure of the debut, and the surreal tone and inventive sampling techniques are still very much in evidence. But, despite a few lighthearted moments ("Bitties in the BK Lounge," the disco-flavored "A Roller Skating Jam Named 'Saturdays'"), a distinct note of bitterness has crept into De La's once-sunny outlook. On the one hand, they're willing to take on more serious subject matter; two of the album's most powerful moments are the unsettling incest tale "Millie Pulled a Pistol on Santa" and Posdnuos' drug-addiction chronicle "My Brother's a Basehead," both true-life occurrences. Yet other tracks betray a brittle, insular state of mind; one running skit features a group of street thugs who ultimately throw the album in the trash for not having enough pimps, guns, or curse words. There are vicious parodies of hip-house and hardcore rap, and the single "Ring Ring Ring (Ha Ha Hey)" complains about being harassed into listening to lousy demo tapes. Plus, the negativity of the bizarre, half-sung "Johnny's Dead" and the hostile narrator on "Who Do U Worship?" seemingly comes out of nowhere. *Dead* is clearly the product of a group staggering under the weight of expectations, yet even if it's less cohesive and engaging, it's still often fascinating in spite of its flaws.

Steve Huey

Buhloone Mindstate
September 1993, Tommy Boy

The last album of De La Soul's creative prime, *Buhloone Mindstate* was also their last with producer Prince Paul. After the claustrophobic *De La Soul Is Dead*, *Mindstate* is a partial return to the upbeat positivity of *3 Feet High and Rising*, though not its wildly colorful invention. Instead, *Buhloone Mindstate* takes a calmer, more laid-back approach—the music is often more introspective, and the between-song skits have been jettisoned in favor of a tighter focus. The surrealism of *Buhloone Mindstate*'s predecessors has largely evaporated, and the production, while still imaginative, doesn't quite dazzle the way it used to. Then again, it's admirable that the group is trying to mature and progress musically, and they would never experiment quite this ambitiously again. There's quite a bit more live instrumentation here, with extensive, jazzy guest work by the JB Horns. In fact, the guests threaten to overpower the first half of the album; "Patti Dooke" and "I Be Blowin'" are both extended showcases for the horns, and the latter is a full-fledged instrumental led by Maceo Parker. They're followed by a group of Japanese rappers on "Long Island Wildin'," and it isn't until the terrific single "Ego Trippin', Pt. 2" that De La really takes over. Many of the record's best raps follow: the reflective old-school tribute "Breakadawn," the jazzy "I Am I Be" and "In the Woods," and the Biz Markie collaboration "Stone Age." If *Buhloone Mindstate* is a great deal more straightforward than De La's earlier work, its high points are still excellent and well worth the time of any fan. In fact, many De La diehards feel that this album is hugely underrated.

Steve Huey

Del tha Funkee Homosapien

I Wish My Brother George Was Here
1991, Asylum

Del Tha Funkee Homosapien may be the cousin of gangsta rap icon Ice Cube, who was the executive producer on this debut, but it would be hard to imagine two more dissimilar artists. Yet, just as Ice Cube helped popularize and legitimize West Coast gangsta rap with NWA, Del helped lay the foundation for what would become California's thriving underground scene with his seminal debut, *I Wish My Brother George Was Here*. Predating similarly seminal debuts from like-minded artists like the Alkaholiks, Souls of Mischief, Freestyle Fellowship, and Pharcyde, *Brother George* takes the Parliament-Funkadelic-derived G-funk sound popularized by NWA and spins it into exciting new directions, replacing gangsta rap's nihilism with a healthy sense of the absurd. Released while Del was still a teen, *Brother George* offers a take on city life that's wry and bemused rather than tense and violent, addressing such crucial issues as having to ride the bus ("The Wacky World of Rapid Transit") and shiftless friends ("Sleepin' on My Couch") with a refreshingly assured comic sensibility. Bolstered by a pair of terrific, typically irreverent singles, ("Dr. Bombay" and "Mr. Dobalina"), *Brother George* imbued the otherwise grim West Coast hip-hop scene with a welcome dose of irreverence, proving that you didn't have to conform to any single image to be taken seriously as a rapper. Although for the most part an endearingly lightweight effort, *Brother George* does address serious topics on occasion, with "Dark Skin Girls" attacking media and personal perceptions of African-American beauty with a viciousness that borders on blatant sexism. Del has accomplished much since the release of *Brother George*—the *Deltron 3030* album completed his evolution from smart-ass b-boy prodigy to indie rap superhero—but nothing he's done since has quite matched the charm, fun, and sheer exuberance of his stellar debut.

Nathan Rabin

No Need for Alarm
1994, Elektra

After helping create the West Coast underground scene with his 1991 debut, Del tha Funkee Homosapien made a radical departure with 1993's *No Need for Alarm*, eschewing the familiar G-funk of his debut for a jazzier, more sophisticated sound more akin to East Coast acts like Black Moon and Main Source. The thematic and lyrical content of Del's work underwent a considerable change as well, with *No Need for Alarm* largely avoiding the endearing comic vignettes and blunted utopian vision of his debut for a never-ending string of battle raps. Del's loopy sense of humor remained intact, but without the structure and pop savvy of *I Wish My Brother George Was Here*, *No Need for Alarm* feels a bit aimless, even if it does contain some of Del's best work to date. "Catch a Bad One" showcases Del's new direction to the best effect, driven by Casual's sinister, hypnotic, string-laced production and some of the fiercest and most potent battle raps of Del's career. When *No Need for Alarm* works, it's terrific—funny, skillfully produced, and wonderfully propulsive. Unfortunately, it only works about a third of the time. Critics have taken Del's debut to task for having a fairly generic P-funk-dominated sound more in line with executive producer Ice Cube's work than Del's unique sensibility, but Del has always functioned better when paired with strong collaborators. Sure, it could be argued that *I Wish My Brother George Was Here* and *Deltron 3030* reflect the sensibilities of producers and co-producers Ice Cube and DJ Pooh and Dan the Automator as much as they do Del, but working with strong-willed peers has a tendency to temper the artist's tendency toward self-indulgence and bring out the best in him. Without a strong sense of direction, *No Need for Alarm* is frustratingly uneven, rich and transcendent one moment and aimless and repetitive the next. Still, it's a challenging, unique, and uncompromising follow-up, one well worth picking up for anyone interested in either the evolution of West Coast hip-hop or just the evolution of one of its most talented, eccentric, and gifted artists.

Nathan Rabin

The Best of Del tha Funkee Homosapien: The Elektra Years
February 2004, Rhino

"Alright this is D-E-L, and I'm calling from 3838 [unintelligible] Way, yeah I just wanted to call to say '*F*ck the radio!*'" And so began the unpredictable, uneven, but ultimately fruitful career of Del tha Funkee Homosapien. This unlikely introduction came at the end of "Turn Off the Radio," from his cousin Ice

Cube's first solo album. When Del the lovable ragamuffin's first Ice Cube-produced single was released later on, in early 1992, most expected a junior version of Ice Cube—but what they got was something pitted between that hard-edged funk sound and party-down, proto-backpacker indie rap. From this one song—and the equally silly video that accompanied it—it was plain to see that Del would not be dealing in the kind of vicious material mastered by his cousin and his former crewmates in Da Lench Mob. The friend who would not leave and front-porch golden-shower revenge were his domain, not white devils and spraying AK-47s. As debut album *I Wish My Brother George Was Here* swelled in stature after release, Del's path took a few twists and turns, but this set for Rhino—somewhat mislabeled as a best-of—sticks with the MC's time spent on Elektra. This includes most of the best moments from *George* and 1994 follow-up, *No Need for Alarm*, making it valuable for those who haven't been able to track them down. However, those who have followed Del all along should also take note; this set also contains a small bounty of B-sides, most of which are of some import. A few extraneous remixes make the set drag—and, boy, that *Judgment Night* collaboration with Dinosaur Jr. should never leave its point of origin—but it's still a win-win situation for all of those involved. The package scores bonus points for its informative liner notes, not to mention the shout-out to borderline-genius writer Kodwo Eshun.

Andy Kellman

Diamond and the Psychotic Neurotics

Stunts, Blunts & Hip-Hop
July 1992, Chemistry

Diamond D had quietly provided some exciting production work and made strides within the rap music industry and community throughout the early '90s, but his name didn't become immediately recognizable until his classic guest appearance rapping on A Tribe Called Quest's "Show Business" ("Take it from Diamond/It's like mountain climbing/When it comes to rhyming/You gotta put your time in"), off their masterful second album, *The Low End Theory*. Even amid vintage verses by such lauded hip-hop company as Tribe's Q-Tip and Phife and Brand Nubian's Lord Jamar and Sadat X, something about Diamond D's forthright and rock-solid, but totally laid-back, style stood out. Hip-hop heads waiting to hear more from him were rewarded with a veritable wealth of treasures when *Stunts, Blunts & Hip-Hop*, Diamond D's debut album, was released the following year. The album instantly became—and remains—something of an underground masterpiece. *Stunts* is a hugely sprawling, amorphous thing. Nearly 70 minutes would generally seem far too long for a hip-hop album to sustain any degree of good taste, especially one that is mostly song-based and keeps the *de rigueur* between-song skits to a minimum. There is, in fact, a fair amount of filler here; but even that filler, after several listens, is so ingratiating that the album would seem incomplete without it, and it helps the album to actually be listenable in its entirety, as a single, long, whole statement. Part of the reason even the filler works is because the production—most of it by Diamond D himself—is uniformly excellent. The music he comes up with is just as steady as his rhyming. As for his simile-heavy lyrics, they can occasionally seem stilted or awkward, and aren't exactly complex, but Diamond spins a long yarn—sometimes autobiographical, sometimes fantastical, sometimes a projected scenario—with the best of them, although he can also delve too often into blanket boasting, and sometimes his words lack any particular direction. It's the everyone-in-the-studio ambience, though, rather than any particular standout aspect, that propels the album. Certain songs do stand out from the overall tapestry of the album: the woeful girl-gone-wrong tale "Sally Got a One Track Mind"; "*!*! What U Heard," with its bouncy bassline; the insistent "Red Light, Green Light"; the Jazzy Jay-produced "I Went for Mine"; the loping "Check One, Two"; the groovy "Freestyle," co-produced by Large Professor; "K.I.S.S.," co-produced by Q-Tip; and the jazz-tinged "Feel the Vibe." But they make far more sense as part of the album's cycle. The most enjoyable way to listen to the album's individual parts is to also listen to the stuff that surrounds it.

Stanton Swihart

Digable Planets

Reachin' (A New Refutation of Time and Space)
September 1993, Pendulum

Landing in 1993, Digable Planets' *Reachin' (A New Refutation of Time and Space)*, settled in on the consciousness of a large cross section of listeners ranging from alt-rockers, metal freaks, and headz worldwide. A surprise hit with the press and the general populace alike, *Reachin'* was released at the most opportune time of the '90s. The so-called alternative scene had just blown up in '91 and '92, so commercial radio was actually playing something close to variety and major labels were signing acts and developing them at an unprecedented level. Played on rock and urban stations, Digable Planets' debut represented an actual alternative to the masses who had grown up on Van Halen and Whitney Houston and, as a result, Digable Planets found themselves with a Top 20 single in "Rebirth of Slick (Cool Like Dat)." In a lot ways the song paints the picture for the rest of the album with samples that are drenched in cool jazz and interlaced with smart catchy rhymes that move across the hip-hop spectrum of self-aggrandization and political awareness. The widespread appeal of *Reachin'* lies in Doodlebug, Ladybug Mecca, and Butterfly's smooth delivery. Never too excited but always passionate, they keep it going with seemingly lighthearted pieces like "Where I'm From." Here Butterfly almost falls into hip-hop stereotype by tripping on the theme of geographical location (see *Paul's Boutique*); but instead of really letting the listener know where they're from, they go into a chorus of "everywhere, everywhere" and thus really pointing out this record's underlying theme: under the hood of inventive beats and well-placed layered samples are the ideas and attitudes of universal and cosmic spirituality combined with personal-consciousness expansion that crosses geographical and ethnic boundaries. Easily one of the most successful hip-hop records ever made and a must-have selection in most *any* collection.

Jack LV Isles

Blowout Comb
October 1994, Pendulum

Media darlings after the commercial success of their debut, Digable Planets attempted to prove their artistic merit with this second album, and succeeded wildly. A worthy, underrated successor, *Blowout Comb* was just as catchy and memorable as their first, and also offered the perfect response to critics and hip-hop fans who complained they weren't "real" enough. Except for a dark, indecipherable single named "Dial 7 (Axioms of Creamy Spies)," *Blowout Comb* excelled at pushing great grooves over sunny-day party jams, even when the crew was providing deft social commentary—as on "Black Ego" and "Dial 7 (Axioms of Creamy Spies)." The trio used their greater clout to invite instrumentalists instead of relying completely on samples, and the music took on more aspects of the live jam than before. Though *Blowout Comb* still borrowed a host of riffs from great jazz anthems (from Bob James to Bobbi Humphrey), Digable Planets used them well, as beds for their back-and-forth freestyling and solos from guests. The Digables remade Roy Ayers' "We Live in Brooklyn, Baby" into "Borough Check," and invited Guru from Gang Starr to salute Brooklyn's block-parties and barbershops. (The focus on the neighborhood even carried over to the liner notes, laid out like a community newspaper.) The closer, a brassy, seven-minute "For Corners," also captured that fleeting feeling of neighborhood peace. Though *Blowout Comb* lacked the commercial punch of *Reachin'*, Digable Planets made great strides in the two areas they'd previously been criticized: beats and rhymes. The beats were incredible, some of the best *ever* heard on a rap record, a hip-hop version of the classic, off-kilter, New Orleans second-line funk. The productions, all crafted by the group themselves, were laid-back and clearly superior to much hip-hop of the time. The raps, though certainly not hardcore, were just as intelligent as on the debut, and flowed much better. While *Reachin'* came to sound like a moment in time for the jazz-rap crowd, *Blowout Comb* has remained a timeless classic.

John Bush

Digital Underground

Sex Packets
January 1990, Tommy Boy

Sex Packets is a vibrant, wildly funny record that transcends any attempt to dismiss it as mere novelty. Novelty records are throwaways—cheap gags that are funny once, but never pay off with repeat plays, something that *Sex Packets* certainly 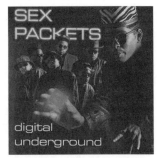 does. *Sex Packets* is layered like any good story. Corny jokes, gross-out tales, flights of fancy, and sheer absurdist humor co-exist comfortably, usually within the course of one song. Take "The Humpty Dance," their breakthrough single and timeless party anthem. Within that one song, Humpty Hump spills out countless jokes, spinning between inspired allusions and thuddingly obvious cut-ups, which are equally funny because of the irrepressible, infectious nature of his rap. And he's so confident in his skills, he's sexy, which is kind of what the album is about—it knows that sex is funny, and sexier because of it. But the very name of the album should be a clear indication that Digital Underground doesn't take any of this stuff all that seriously while creating elaborate, fantastical settings that reveal boundless imagination. The showiest number, of course, is the "Sex Packets" suite that concludes the album, built around their idea for a drug that creates full-blown sexual fantasies (virtual reality before it was in vogue), but their skill at creating distinctive worlds is just as apparent on the endless party of "Doowutchyalike." These are the things that are buried beneath the band's jokes and an enormous amount of George Clinton samples. Much of the music on *Sex Packets* uses the P-Funk canon as their foundation (a notable exception being a swinging interpolation of a Jimi Hendrix *Band of Gypsys* cut on "The New Jazz (One)," a cracking showcase for their team vocal skills). It's so strong an influence, it may seem easy to reduce Digital Underground to the status of mere Clinton imitators, but they take his blueprint, expand it, and personalize it, creating a record that is as loose and funny as anything in the P-Funk empire, and in some ways, easier to access, since the party feels wide open. Few hip-hop albums sound as much like a constant party as this, and years later, it's still impossible to resist.

Stephen Thomas Erlewine

This Is an EP Release
1991, Tommy Boy

Released in the same era of expansive and humorous hip-hop debuts by De La Soul, Digable Planets, Gang Starr, and A Tribe Called Quest, Digital Underground's similarly disposed first album and follow-up EP offered a party-friendly alternative to gangsta rap with a heavy dose of P-funk, jazz, and Prince's electro-funk aesthetic. The Oakland-based crew, featuring Shock-G as alter-ego and frontman Humpty Hump, would continue to ride high with *Sons of the P*, but never really captured the inspired mix of their first forays into the hip-hop arena. That said, curious fans should first check out the group's maiden *Sex Packets* release before diving into this six-song collection; while solid in its own right, the EP does contain two non-essential remixes of tracks off of *Sex Packets*. And even though new cuts like the extended funk jam "Same Song" (featuring a nasty Bernie Worrell-meets-Jimmy Smith synth-organ solo), "Nuttin Nis Funky," "Arguin' on the Funk," and "Tie the Knot" are all impressive, *This Is an EP Release* does not expand on the sound of *Sex Packets*. Still, a very enjoyable selection of cuts full of top-notch rapping, samples, scratches, and elastically funky bass and beats.

Stephen Cook

Sons of the P
October 1991, Tommy Boy

If it ain't broke, don't fix it: *Sons of the P* offers more of the loopy humor and P-Funk fixations that made Digital Underground's debut album, *Sex Packets*, an instant classic. And if *Sons of the P* doesn't quite hit the absurd heights of its predecessor's best tracks, it's still a strong, engaging listen and an entirely worthy follow-up. The group doesn't take the title *Sons of the P* lightly; their George Clinton obsession isn't just manifested in samples, it's everywhere from the extended, chorus-heavy song structures right down to the back-cover art, a P-Funk-style comic strip recasting DU as part of the *Clones of Dr. Funkenstein* concept. Once again, there are two great singles in the affectionate "Kiss You Back" and the Humpty Hump feature "No Nose Job," which rips black celebrities who surgically alter themselves to look less ethnic. In

fact, the group goes in for some overt social commentary on several other tracks as well; "Heartbeat Props" are directed at still-living heroes in the struggle for equality, and "The Higher Heights of Spirituality" is a brief utopian dream. On the other hand, the album closes with "Good Thing We're Rappin'," a full-on pimp rhyme courtesy of Humpty Hump that's a little less genial and a little more Too Short than you might expect from DU. A few tracks don't make much of an impression, but on the whole, *Sons of the P* makes a convincing case for DU as the rightful spiritual heirs to the P-Funk legacy—and George Clinton himself even endorses that idea on the title track.

Steve Huey

The Body-Hat Syndrome
October 1993, Tommy Boy

Rebounding, in the charts anyway, from the relative downturn of 1991's *Sons of the P* LP, Digital Underground continued cultivating its own brand of P-Funk culture on *The Body-Hat Syndrome* two years later, stuffing what had been the  group's first year of silence with a fresh batch of funk-infused rap. Digital Underground's last effort for longtime label Tommy Boy, *The Body-Hat Syndrome* lacked some of the bright spark and humor that informed the band's first two albums. With the edgy grind of the leading single, "The Return of the Crazy One," and its accompanying X-rated video (reworked for public consumption) boosting the band back into the spotlight, the rest of the album unfurled to less than outstanding crossover commercial acclaim—the album's second single, the slightly melancholy and anti-racism cultural awareness politico "Whassup Wit the Love," barely cracked the R&B Top 100. But that's not to say that this set doesn't represent another brilliant feather in the group's cap—it does. Smooth grooves, understated humor, and gentle demonstrations of peace, love, and manifesto continue to drive the Digital Underground style, here sampled across a chunky 20-track set. "Holly Wanstaho" is a fantastic jazz-tripped reinvention of Parliament's "Holly Wants to Go to California," while the completely original big bass beat "Brand Nu Swetta" is the perfect dance groove. The three-part "Body-Hats" breaks up the action. Two bonus tracks, "The Humpty Dance Awards" and "Wheee!, are included on *The Body-Hat Syndrome*'s CD issue. With a smart balance between old-school, new-school, and their own school sonics, Digital Underground has once again brought funk history to life, passing the torch to the next generation and, above all, having one hell of a good time doing it.

Amy Hanson

Playwutchyalike: The Best of Digital Underground
June 2003, Rhino

2003's *Playwutchyalike* differs significantly from 2001's *No Nose Job* in its treatment of Digital Underground's album material, and yet both compilations play to the group's strengths rather well. The only miscue worth truly griping about here is the absence of "The Return of the Crazy One"; aside from that, it comes down to weighing album tracks against one another. This disc smartly includes the album mix of "Underwater Rimes," and it also features a number of other tracks not found on *No Nose Job*: "Sex Packets," "Nuttin' Nis Funky," "Heartbeat Props," and "We Got More." However, the likes of "Carry the Way," "Flowin' On the D-Line," "Doo Woo You," and "Dope-a-Delic"—all of which are present on *No Nose Job*—are sacrificed. Again, some significant singles are found in their truncated radio-edit versions, which is detrimental to songs that are more enjoyable in the loosest form possible. The group's best material has aged extremely well, with "Same Song," "Doowutchyalike," and *especially* "Kiss You Back" proving that the group's most popular hit wasn't even their best. As with *No Nose Job*, *Playwutchyalike* ends the coverage at 1993's *Body-Hat Syndrome*, with none of the group's post-Tommy Boy material (wisely) considered.

Andy Kellman

The Disposable Heroes of Hiphoprisy

Hypocrisy Is the Greatest Luxury
1992, 4th & Broadway

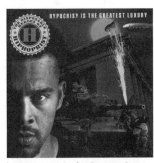

The Disposable Heroes tackled every last big issue possible with one of 1992's most underrated efforts. Dr. Dre and G-funk became all the rage by the end of the year and beyond, but for those looking for at least a little more from hip-hop than that soon-to-be-clichéd style, *Hypocrisy Is the Greatest Luxury* did the business. The group's origins in the Beatnigs aren't hidden at all—besides a stunning, menacing revision of that band's "Television, the Drug of the Nation," the Heroes' first single, the combination of Bomb Squad and industrial music approaches is apparent throughout. Consolidated's Mark Pistel co-produced the album while Meat Beat Manifesto's Jack Dangers helped mix it with the band, creating a stew of deep beats and bass and a constantly busy sonic collage that hits as hard as could be wanted, but not without weirdly tender moments as well. On its own it would be a more than attractive effort, but it's Michael Franti's compelling, rich voice and his chosen subject matter that really make the band something special. Nothing is left unexamined, an analysis of the American community as a whole that embraces questions of African-American identity and commitment ("Famous and Dandy (Like Amos 'n' Andy)") to overall economic and political insanity ("The Winter of the Long Hot Summer," a gripping, quietly threatening flow of a track). There's even a great jazz/funk number, "Music and Politics," with nothing but a guitar and Franti's fine singing voice, ruminating with emotional expression in music and elsewhere with wit and sly anger. Top it off with a brilliant reworking of the Dead Kennedys' anthem "California Uber Alles," lyrics targeting the then-governor of the state, Pete Wilson, and his questionable stances, and revolutions in thought and attitude rarely sounded so good.

Ned Raggett

DJ Jazzy Jeff & the Fresh Prince

Rock the House
1987, Jive

In the 1980s, Philadelphia's hip-hop scene was diverse. At one extreme was the controversial Schoolly D, who was among the founders of gangsta rap even though he wasn't as big as West Coast agitators like N.W.A. and Ice-T. And at the other extreme was DJ Jazzy Jeff & the Fresh Prince, whose fun, lighthearted, often goofy tales were great for comic relief. *Rock the House*, the duo's debut album of 1987, demonstrated that Will Smith, aka the Fresh Prince, was as entertaining and amusing a storyteller as Dana Dane or Slick Rick. But unlike those New York MCs, DJ Jazzy Jeff & the Fresh Prince weren't off-color or controversial—in fact, their unthreatening, clean-cut image led some journalists to dub them "the Cosby kids of rap." And the Philadelphians had no problem with that; in a 1989 interview, Smith asserted that he was proud to be compared to the Cosby kids. You won't find a lot of hard-hitting social commentary on *Rock the House*; Smith and his partner keep things lighthearted on tunes like "Girls Ain't Nothing But Trouble" (the hit single that sampled the *I Dream of Jeannie* theme and put them on the map) and "Just One of Those Days." Equally strong is "Guys Ain't Nothing But Trouble," a sequel to "Girls Ain't Nothing But Trouble" that features female rapper Ice Cream Tee (who had a lot of potential but didn't get very far as a solo artist). Is *Rock the House* pop-rap? Absolutely. But for DJ Jazzy Jeff & the Fresh Prince, lighthearted doesn't mean lightweight. In terms of rapping technique, Smith could hold his own against any of the more hardcore rappers who came out of Philly in the 1980s. This excellent LP is a classic of its kind.

Alex Henderson

He's the DJ, I'm the Rapper
1988, Jive

This is the album on which DJ Jazzy Jeff & the Fresh Prince hit commercial pay dirt, the album that introduced the duo's jokey, benign, and somewhat goofball demeanor to a wide audience. Without *He's the DJ, I'm the Rapper*, in fact, it could be argued that you never would have had Will Smith: Movie Star, as the album afforded him a level and type of exposure he would never thereafter relinquish. Oddly enough, it is DJ Jazzy Jeff who generally was cited as the musical star of the duo, at least in the rap community, on account of his groundbreaking and always-wizardly work on the turntables. That skill is evident ("D.J. on the Wheels"), but often takes a backseat here in deference to the Fresh Prince's whimsical story-songs. To be frank, Smith's rhymes and antics become rather, well, hokey, like Slick Rick with an antiseptic tongue, but they are always good-natured and good fun, admirable qualities in themselves considering rap's growing inclination at the time to drift toward the hardcore and polemical sides of the street. *He's the DJ* is almost cartoonlike by comparison. Painfully corny music videos for the hit singles "Parents Just Don't Understand" and "Nightmare on My Street" underscored the impression to an even greater extent. The reality, though, is slightly more interesting than the caricature. There are songs here ("Brand New Funk," "Pump Up the Bass," the title track) that go straight to the heart of hip-hop's traditional role as sweaty house-party soundtrack and which highlight a more "street" facet of the duo. Still, this is not a consequential album. It is an extremely likable one, however, with a youthful vigor, animateness, and a spirited sense of humor undiminished by the ensuing decades. Compared with some of the strains of rap that were to follow, which often mistook sarcasm or irony for drollery, *He's the DJ* seems a quaint, practically naïve artifact of an era before bling-bling and Benzes became the norm.

Stanton Swihart

Homebase
July 1991, Jive

After the disappointingly uneven *And in This Corner...*, DJ Jazzy Jeff & the Fresh Prince restarted their commercial momentum with *Homebase*, which fitted Will Smith's rhymes with up-to-date, radio-friendly production and a much richer overall sound. For the first time, the album's key single wasn't a comic narrative: "Summertime" was a warm, breezy reminiscence about growing up in Philadelphia and attending barbecues where the whole community showed up to see and be seen. It had all the good vibes of a typical Fresh Prince number, but it was clearly a more mature effort, and that's *Homebase* in a nutshell. The smoothed-out R&B background of "Summertime" provides a template for the record's poppier moments, and there's a thumping new club influence on the dancefloor cuts. Lyrically, when he's not trying to move your butt, Smith paints himself as more of a ladies' man, in keeping with his new young-adult persona. If he's still more innocent than LL Cool J, he's throwing out all his best lines on the single "Ring My Bell" and trying to play the field on "A Dog Is a Dog." And there are a few story songs, like "Who Stole the DJ" and "You Saw My Blinker," that benefit from the fresher-sounding beats. While it doesn't have the youthful, old-school charm of *He's the DJ, I'm the Rapper*, *Homebase* is a successful reinvention that laid the groundwork for Smith's multimedia stardom as an adult.

Steve Huey

The Very Best of DJ Jazzy Jeff & the Fresh Prince
June 2006, Jive

Since it features all the charting singles, *The Very Best of DJ Jazzy Jeff & the Fresh Prince* contains just about everything that any disc jockey played by the duo, including lighthearted smart-ass favorites like "Girls Ain't Nothing But Trouble" and "Parents Just Don't Understand," silly topical fluff like "A Nightmare on My Street" and "I Think I Can Beat Mike Tyson," surprisingly durable minor hits like "Brand New Funk" and "The Things U Do," and even Jazzy Jeff's nimble instrumental flipping of tracks by Bob James, the Mizell Brothers, and Marvin Gaye ("A Touch of Jazz"). One significant track that doesn't appear is "You Saw My Blinker," a rare example of cranky bitterness from the otherwise wise-cracking, punchline-delivering Fresh Prince. The 1998 *Greatest Hits* release and 2003's *Platinum & Gold Collection* aren't much different from this set, so the best route to go is more dependent upon what's available than brain-teasing comparisons of track listings.

Andy Kellman

DJ Kool

The Music Ain't Loud Enuff
1990, Creative Funk

DJ Kool's album debut was an incredibly wide-ranging LP with few similarities to any contemporary hip-hop act, except possibly Mantronix. Including the dancehall ragga track "Raggae Dance," the hip-house track "House Your Body," several crucial sample productions (the title track, "What the Hell You Come in Here For," "How Low Can You Go") and even the touching R&B production "Pressed Against the Glass," Kool proves himself a master of just about every type of party music then circulating.

John Bush

DJ Magic Mike

Bass Is the Name of the Game
1988, Cheetah

For most, DJ Magic Mike's 1988 album *Bass Is the Name of the Game* is remembered for its speaker-ruining low-end and the fact that it went gold, which is some feat for a mostly instrumental Miami bass record. Ask someone who is a bona fide crate crawler and he'll tell you the album is much more, partly responsible for the turntablism explosion along with being a huge influence on cut-up funk folks like Fatboy Slim and most acts signed to the Ninja Tune label. The samples (many of which are lifted off Beastie Boys records) sound nostalgically cheap and the rappers—MC Madness and T-Isaam—are old-school party types who are entirely pre-2Pac, but it's all charming and "dated" in the best sense of the word. What isn't dated at all is Mike's hectic scratching, which uses the turntable as an instrument, adding the human element as robotic drum machines and sequencers hypnotically loop away. The album is also surprisingly diverse for a bass record, ranging from the almost Technotronic, hectic dance of "M&M's Gettin' Off" to the slow bedroom roll of "For the Easy Listeners," which borrows a healthy portion of the Isley Brothers' "Between the Sheets." Topping it all off is the classic "Lower the Dynamite," a track as important to the big beat genre as it is to the second wave of turntable terrorists (Invisibl Skratch Piklz, Rob Swift, the X-Ecutioners, etc.).

David Jeffries

DJ Quik

Quik Is the Name
1991, Profile

The release of DJ Quik's debut album, *Quik Is the Name*, in 1991 begged the question: does rap really need yet another gangsta rapper? Indeed, by that time, rap had become saturated with numerous soundalike gangsta rappers—most of whom weren't even a fraction as interesting as such pioneers of the style as Ice-T, N.W.A, and Schoolly D. Nonetheless, rapper/producer Quik turned out to be more noteworthy than most of the gangsta rappers who debuted that year. Lyrically, the former gang member (who grew up in the same L.A. ghetto as N.W.A, Compton) doesn't provide any major insights. His sex/malt liquor/gang-banging imagery was hardly groundbreaking in 1991. But his hooks, beats, and grooves (many of which owe a debt to '70s soul and funk) are likeable enough.

Alex Henderson

The D.O.C.

No One Can Do It Better
1989, Ruthless

An early landmark of West Coast rap, the D.O.C.'s debut album, *No One Can Do It Better*, remains sorely underheard today, largely because the car crash that destroyed the rapper's voice also cut short his time in the spotlight before he'd had a chance to really cement his reputation among the general public. When *No One Can Do It Better* was released the West Coast had just started to break nationally thanks to the gangsta movement and wasn't known for much outside of N.W.A and Ice-T. In the D.O.C., however, the scene found a new level of credibility: a highly skilled battle rhymer who could hold his own with any East Coast lyrical virtuoso. Though his chops are rarely mentioned in the same breath, the D.O.C. clearly ranks up near the master technicians of the era, Rakim and Big Daddy Kane; while he may not be as smooth as the former or as spectacularly wordy as the latter, he has a distinctively rough, commanding voice and an aggressive, hard-hitting flow all his own. There's another important reason to hear *No One Can Do It Better*: it's where Dr. Dre's legend as a producer really begins. *Straight Outta Compton* notwithstanding, Dre truly comes into his own here, crafting funky, varied tracks that blend synths, drum machines, samples, and live instrumentation. You won't hear anything that resembles a blueprint for *The Chronic*, but sonically, they're as rich as anything around at the time. Both Dre and the D.O.C. are remarkably consistent throughout, so special mention has to go to the rousing N.W.A posse cut "The Grand Finalé," which even features DJ Yella on live drums. It's a shame that the D.O.C. never got the chance for a proper follow-up, but in *No One Can Do It Better*, he at least has one undeniable masterpiece.

Steve Huey

Dr. Dre

The Chronic
December 1992, Death Row

With its stylish, sonically detailed production, Dr. Dre's 1992 solo debut, *The Chronic*, transformed the entire sound of West Coast rap. Here Dre established his patented G-funk sound: fat, blunted Parliament-Funkadelic beats, soulful backing vocals, and live instruments in the rolling basslines and whiny synths. What's impressive is that Dre crafts tighter singles than his inspiration, George Clinton—he's just as effortlessly funky, and he has a better feel for a hook, a knack that improbably landed gangsta rap on the pop charts. But none of *The Chronic*'s legions of imitators were as rich in personality, and that's due in large part to Dre's monumental discovery, Snoop Doggy Dogg. Snoop livens up every track he touches, sometimes just by joining in the chorus—and if *The Chronic* has a flaw, it's that his relative absence from the second half slows the momentum. There was nothing in rap quite like Snoop's singsong, lazy drawl (as it's invariably described), and since Dre's true forte is the producer's chair, Snoop is the signature voice. He sounds utterly unaffected by anything, no matter how extreme, which sets the tone for the album's misogyny, homophobia, and violence. The Rodney King riots are unequivocally celebrated, but the war wasn't just on the streets; Dre enlists his numerous guests in feuds with rivals and ex-bandmates. Yet *The Chronic* is first and foremost a party album, rooted not only in '70s funk and soul, but also that era's blue party comedy, particularly Dolemite. Its comic song intros and skits became prerequisites for rap albums seeking to duplicate its cinematic flow; plus, Snoop and Dre's terrific chemistry ensures that even their foulest insults are cleverly turned. That framework makes *The Chronic* both unreal and all too real, a cartoon and a snapshot. No matter how controversial, it remains one of the greatest and most influential hip-hop albums of all time.

Steve Huey

Domino

Domino
December 1993, OutBurst

The story behind the forgotten rapper Domino is that he found no love among his West Coast brothers. Rumor has it, the whole Left Coast thought he had stolen the up-and-coming Snoop Dogg's style and therefore he was boycotted, prematurely ending his career after just one album. His debut is filled with that laid-back, slippery soul with booming bass that figured heavily into Snoop's early G-funk, and while it does sound a bit like the Doggfather, it's at best an influence. Domino has his own way of leaning, a much jazzier stance that fits perfectly with DJ Battlecat's beats and productions. Flutes, mellow guitars, and plenty of other soul-jazz sounds fill the album and dominate the first hit, the classic "Ghetto Jam," which ends in genuine jam session. The second hit, "Sweet Potato Pie," is even more fondly remembered thanks to Domino's skill at delivering rhymes that "ain't rated PG" with just the right amount of deadpan humor. "Do You Qualify" is a bit creepy since it's Domino's way of asking "Are you jailbait?," but most everything else here goes splendidly with round beds, mirrors on the ceiling, and black-velvet paintings of naked Nubian goddesses.

David Jeffries

Downtown Science

Downtown Science
1991, Def Jam

Downtown Science is not merely an important hip-hop footnote on account of its biracial makeup, which was at the time virtually unprecedented in the rap community, nor is it merely a worthy one-shot wonder from one of genre's most fecund eras; rather it is a shamefully neglected masterwork as forceful and hard-hitting as the albums Public Enemy was making during the same period. In fact, Bosco Money, Downtown Science's wordsmith, is every bit as conscientious and commanding, if not quite as steely and polemical, as Chuck D. (And, as if in homage, the duo does a fine job absorbing the chaotic, kitchen-sink production style of the Bomb Squad on the tensile "Delta Sigma.") His rhyming style is extremely cerebral and exists on a cutting edge off of which few rappers have had the daring to dangle since, and always with a disarming stoicism that injects his words with even more authority, in both a moral and aesthetic regard. Sam Sever, fresh off acclaimed work with 3rd Bass, displayed here the reason that his production skills were in such demand at the time. Even with several nods to rap's past, he steers clear of overused samples and beats, and each track, in addition to providing a backdrop for Bosco Money's meticulous rhymes, is quite forward-looking in its own right. Years before RZA or El-P carved out distinctive sonic niches with their claustrophobic, bloodshot, alien atmospheres, Sam Sever laid down jittery, paranoid sci-fi landscapes on brilliant songs like "This Is a Visit," "Radioactive," and "Room to Breathe." But the duo also broke it down old-school style on "Somethin' Spankin' New," and they spin off some sweaty urban funk with "Down to a Science" and the Big Daddy Kane-like "Keep It On." The role-playing single "If I Was" made a brief appearance on urban play lists; otherwise, *Downtown Science* somehow failed to make much of a dent, and was promptly forgotten. But fans of visionary rap would do themselves a favor in tracking down this gem.

Stanton Swihart

Dream Warriors

And Now, the Legacy Begins
1991, 4th & Broadway

Part of the slew of grand early '90s hip-hop releases that avoided tough criminal posing for inventive, witty lyrics and arrangements, *And Now the Legacy Begins* is a hilarious, entertaining rollercoaster of a record. That the Warriors themselves were Canadian shows that north of the US border isn't all Rush tribute bands, as the duo plays around with any number of inspired samples and grooves, from jazz to harder-edged beats, with style and skill. The most well-known track, "My Definition of a Boombastic Jazz Style," predicts a particular pop trend well in advance, using Quincy Jones' brilliant "Soul Bossa Nova" as its base long before fellow Canuck Mike Myers made the original the Austin Powers theme song. The flow of King Lou and Capital Q, mostly the former, fits the stuttering, dramatic pace of the arrangement to a T, bringing an instant smile to the face and dance to the feet. The lead-off single, "Wash Your Face in My Sink," is an equal winner, a nutty warning to a friend who doesn't have it all together about cleanliness set to a equally playful arrangement. Things aren't always pretty, though—"U Could Get Arrested" is a slamming attack on police racism

delivered with belligerent panache. Throughout the album the Warriors show that they know their pop culture cold. As jazz-inspired producers and arrangers, the Warriors and their various studio assistants may not always be as perfectly smooth as A Tribe Called Quest or Guru, but the results are rarely anything but a joy to hear.

Ned Raggett

Dru Down

Explicit Game
September 1994, Relativity

When *Explicit Game* came out in 1994, numerous West Coast rappers were jumping on the G-funk bandwagon and emulating the recordings that Dr. Dre and Snoop Doggy Dogg were providing for Death Row Records. There is no shortage of Dre/Snoop influence on this CD but, while other Californians were content to be clones of Death Row artists, Oakland's Dru Down was his own man. Definitely a cut above most of the G-funk efforts that came from the West Coast in 1994, *Explicit Game* draws on a variety of gangsta rap influences. In addition to the Dre/Snoop influence, one hears elements of DJ Quik, Eazy-E, and Ice Cube in his rapping style and, at times, Down hints at Cypress Hill, which was a rare example of an L.A. gangsta rap group favoring the sort of complex flow you would have expected from an East Coast group. Down's rapping isn't as consistently complex as Cypress Hill's, but the Cypress Hill influence is still one of the effective tools in his arsenal. By 1994 standards, *Explicit Game* isn't groundbreaking—Down was hardly the first person to rap about inner-city thug life on the West Coast, and this certainly isn't the first gangsta rap CD to be influenced by Dr. Dre's production style. But while Down isn't an innovator, he isn't faceless either. *Explicit Game* doesn't have the historic importance of N.W.A.'s *Straight Outta Compton*, Dre's *The Chronic*, or Ice-T's *Rhyme Pays*, but it's still among 1994's more memorable G-funk/gangsta rap efforts.

Alex Henderson

E-40

The Mail Man
1994, Sick Wid It

Originally issued on the indie Sick Wid It label, E-40's *The Mail Man* EP was blown up into a near album when the Jive label picked it up, added two tracks to it, and began introducing the West Coast slang king to hip-hop fans outside the Bay Area. The timing was right, too, because here the witty and hard rapper is coming into his own and nailing down the quick style that would make him a legend. He sounds ready to rise above of the bargain beats producer Studio Ton was able to afford at the time, but the loose and homegrown feel of the EP has a streetwise charm that wouldn't be heard again once Jive began footing the bill. "Neva Broke" and "Bring the Yellow Tape" make for a killer, lowdown opening ten minutes and the great singles "Captain Save a Hoe" and the title track are both Bay classics, although the Jive bonus remix of "Captain" sounds unfortunately thinner. The other bonus cut, "Ballin' Out of Control," is much better with hand-clapping funk, spacy electro, and E-40's quirky style all coming together in perfect harmony.

David Jeffries

Eazy-E

Eazy-Duz-It
1988, Ruthless

Released shortly after *Straight Outta Compton*, *Eazy-Duz-It* was the first N.W.A spinoff album. Years before Ice Cube went solo with *Amerikkka's Most Wanted* in 1990, before Dr. Dre changed the rap game with *The Chronic* in 1992, before MC Ren struggled to establish himself with *Shock of the Hour* in 1993, and before Yella simply fell into obscurity, Eazy-E rose to immediate superstar status with his solo debut. And for good reason, because *Eazy-Duz-It* has a lot going for it, above all yet more cutting-edge production work from Dr. Dre, who really steals the show here. He melds together samples of P-Funk and Def Jam, along with the leftover electro sounds of mid-'80s Los Angeles and the concurrent hip-hop motifs of New York City, in the end creating a dense, unique, and funky style that sounded absolutely revolutionary in 1988 when Eazy-E rode this album to much success. It helps too that Eazy has an exceptional batch of songs to work with here, including a remix of "Boyz-n-the Hood," which had originally appeared on *N.W.A and the Posse*. Granted, Eazy isn't an especially gifted MC, but his perverse sense of humor compensates, as does the support he gets from his N.W.A associates. Again, Dr. Dre simply steals the show here. Don't be surprised if you find yourself enjoying *Eazy-Duz-It* more for the production than for the rapping, all the more so if you don't share Eazy's sense of humor, which is generally sexist, violent, and unconstructive to society in general (making him the prototypical "gangsta"). In the end, Eazy enjoyed only a brief recording career, with this album standing head and shoulders above anything else he'd ever record apart from N.W.A. When he'd return for his next go-round, *5150 Home 4 tha Sick*, he wouldn't have Dr. Dre on his side, let alone Ice Cube, and the difference couldn't be starker. Very good if not great, *Eazy-Duz-It* was as good as it ever got for Eazy, sadly.

Jason Birchmeier

It's On (Dr. Dre) 187um Killa
November 1993, Ruthless

Released a year after his previous EP (*5150 Home 4 tha Sick*) and a long five years since his one and only album to date (*Eazy-Duz-It*), *It's On (Dr. Dre) 187um Killa* was both a stopgap release for Eazy-E and a response to the runaway success of *The Chronic*. Eazy had been lambasted on that Dr. Dre album (and especially in the "Dre Day" video), so it's no surprise that he returns the favor here on "Real Muthaphuckkin G's" and "It's On," dissing not only Dre but also Snoop Dogg. This ugly, mudslinging conflict aside, Eazy truly shines on these eight songs. Granted, eight songs isn't a lot of music, especially since one of the eight is only a minute-long intro and another is yet another remake of "Boyz-in-the Hood" (and too because Eazy had been so AWOL in previous years—five years and still no follow-up album to *Eazy-*

Duz-It!?!). On the little bit of music that is here, however, Eazy proves that he's still one of the best gangsta rappers out there in the early '90s. Sure, he's not an especially gifted MC, and he's not nearly as witty or perversely humorous as he had been previously on *Eazy-Duz-It*, either, but he has such a singular style and such attitude, he stands out amid the innumerable other gangstas out there at the time. And to elaborate upon his attitude, Eazy seems downright bitter here. The success of Dr. Dre and Ice Cube outside of N.W.A, not to mention the dissolution of that group, seems to have really upset him. So in a way, *It's On* feels cathartic, as if Eazy were venting all his frustrations. It results in a sharp group of songs: there are the Dre disses, of course, but also the murder fantasy of "Any Last Werdz," the f*ck-the-world nihilism of "Still a Nigga," the sexist porno-dance of "Gimmie That Nutt," and the smoke-out of "Down 2 tha Last Roach." In other words, pretty much what you'd expect from Eazy. Yet there's an underlying current of irony here that makes *It's On* all the more poignant in retrospect. For one, Eazy may be dissing Dre to the extreme here, but pretty much all of the production work is straight from the *Chronic* playbook—textbook G-funk, to the point it seems almost parodic. And secondly, the heedless promotion of sexism here is downright haunting in the aftermath of Eazy's subsequent death from AIDS complications little more than a year later. So while on the surface *It's On* may seem like a simple stopgap EP, it's so much more, shedding light on what came of Eazy following his 15 minutes of fame with *Eazy-Duz-It*. In a word, tragic—a tragic downfall that makes Eazy out to be not a martyr, which is how his legacy has often been painted, but instead makes him out to be a casualty of his own professed ideology. Again, tragic.

Jason Birchmeier

Eternal E
December 1995, Ruthless

Eazy-E enjoyed only a brief recording career, but the few albums and EPs he did release—on his own as well as with his group, N.W.A—were tremendously influential, setting the stage for the proliferation of West Coast gangsta rap in the early '90s. Showcasing some of the pioneering gangsta's most influential recordings, *Eternal E* serves as a summary of Eazy's solo highlights, including a couple N.W.A songs but only ones that were solo showcases. You get the standout songs from Eazy's 1988 debut album, *Eazy-Duz-It*, as well as the bulk of his follow-up EP, *5150 Home 4 tha Sick*. But *Eternal E* stops there, unfortunately not including anything from the first-rate *It's On (Dr. Dre) 187um Killa* EP or the third-rate *Str8 off tha Streetz* album. (This presumably is because Eazy's label, Ruthless, left its parent label, Priority, at this point, and *Eternal E* is a Priority release, meaning that post-Priority recordings such as those on *It's On* would have to be licensed for inclusion here—a price the label seems unwilling to pay.) Even if *Eternal E* doesn't round up a full career retrospective, it does feature Eazy's key songs, namely his earliest ones, which boasted cutting-edge production work by Dr. Dre. So this best-of does serve its purpose fairly well, and might be the only Eazy album you'll need. Still, if it's one and only one Eazy album you want, you'd be better off with Priority's *Eazy-Duz-It* reissue from 2002, which includes that entire album plus the entire *5150* EP appended as bonus tracks—giving you mostly everything here and much more. Either way though, you're getting a good portrait of Eazy's best solo music, with the exception of the *It's On* EP, which you will want to hear if you like what you hear here.

Jason Birchmeier

Ed O.G & da Bulldogs

Life of a Kid in the Ghetto
1991, PWL America/Mercury

Life of a Kid in the Ghetto contains a pair of message-oriented singles that sounded like classics in 1991. Neither one peaked inside the Top 50 of Billboard's R&B/Hip-Hop chart, but they did get a little exposure on Yo! MTV Raps and on some of the more adventurous black radio stations. Had they been released a few years later, they wouldn't have stood any kind of chance. "I Got to Have It" touches upon a number of issues (black-on-black crime, drug abuse, inattentive parents), but it's easy to lose in Awesome 2's easy-going, Bohannon-sampling production work. "Be a Father to Your Child," one of sharpest message songs released within any genre, is eternally relevant and replayable, thanks to Ed's plainspoken rhymes and a loping groove assisted by the Roy Ayers Ubiquity's "Searching." Beyond those two songs, there's not quite enough hot material to warrant classic album status, but there's plenty to recommend it. The album is almost evenly split between the addressing topical matters (the agitated but humor-laced "Dedicated to the Right Wingers," the powerful "Speak Upon It") and clowning around ("Bug-A-Boo," "Feel Like a Nut"), and unlike a lot of groups who specialized in one approach but not the other, Ed O.G & da Bulldogs are adept at both.

Andy Kellman

Roxbury 02119
1993, Chemistry/Mercury

The second Ed O.G. album wasn't quite as ambitious or satisfying as his debut. There were no standout singles, and Ed O.G.'s rapping lacked the power, conviction and satirical clout he had previously displayed. The production wasn't as varied, nor were the rhymes and stories as gripping. But it was still much better than much of the prototype "gangsta" material flooding the marketplace.

Ron Wynn

The Egyptian Lover

On the Nile
1984, Egyptian Empire

Before Ice-T, N.W.A., and the late Eazy-E made Los Angeles famous (or infamous) for gangsta rap in the late '80s, the city's rap community was best known for a high-tech, futuristic approach that owed a lot to Afrika Bambaataa's 1982 classic, "Planet Rock." In the early-to-mid '80s, L.A.-based electro-hoppers like the Egyptian Lover, the World Class Wreckin' Cru (the group that Dr. Dre belonged to before N.W.A.), the Arabian Prince, and Uncle Jam's Army didn't get much respect from East Coast hip-hoppers, who insisted that their music wasn't gritty enough. But those artists did enjoy a cult following in Southern California. Besides, the Egyptian Lover never claimed to be a hardcore rapper; *On the Nile*, his debut album of 1984, doesn't pretend to be a Run-D.M.C., L.L. Cool J, or Fat Boys release any more than Grover Washington, Jr. claimed to be a jazz purist. The closest this LP comes to an East Coast hip-hop vibe is the single "What Is a DJ If He Can't Scratch"; all of the other tracks offer a synthesizer-driven blend of rap, dance music, and electro-funk. Though "Planet Rock" is a strong influence on this release, it is hardly the Egyptian Lover's only influence—his sound also owes a debt to Germany's seminal Kraftwerk (whose innovations greatly influenced "Planet Rock"), Prince, Man Parrish, and Giorgio Moroder, as well as Middle Eastern and North African music. The Egyptian Lover never had great rapping skills, but he was definitely an original and imaginative producer/writer—and his risk-taking spirit serves him well on definitive, high-tech tunes like "Egypt Egypt," "My House (On the Nile)," and "Girls." *On the Nile* isn't the only Egyptian Lover LP that is worth owning, but most fans insist that it is his most essential and consistent album—and they're absolutely right.

Alex Henderson

One Track Mind
1986, Egyptian Empire

When the Egyptian Lover's second album, *One Track Mind*, came out in 1986, gangsta rap had yet to become huge. Ice-T's *Rhyme Pays* and N.W.A's *N.W.A. & the Posse*—two landmarks in West Coast gangsta rap—didn't come out until 1987, and East Coast hip-hoppers still associated Southern California with the electro-hop style that the Egyptian Lover is best known for. Anyone who expects to find hardcore rap on *One Track Mind* is bound to be disappointed; this LP isn't for rap purists. But those who appreciated his first album, *On the Nile*, will find this to be a respectable, if imperfect, sophomore effort. Egyptian's influences remain the same; the quirky rapper/producer still combines his appreciation of Afrika Bambaataa's "Planet Rock," Prince, Man Parrish, and Kraftwerk with elements of North African music and Egyptian imagery. It's a strange mixture—Egyptian inhabits a place in which rap, Prince's Minneapolis sound, European synth pop, and North African music come together. But it's a mixture that works well on infectious electro-hop jams like "Livin' on the Nile," the single "Freak-A-Holic," and "A Stranger Place (The Alezby Inn)," which bears a bit of a resemblance to Prince's "Erotic City." As the title *One Track Mind* indicates, the Egyptian Lover shares Prince's love of all things erotic. But this LP is never X-rated; the lyrics are suggestive rather than explicit, which is why some of the tunes on *One Track Mind* had urban radio potential. Egyptian, however, was never a superstar, although he did enjoy an enthusiastic cult following. While *One Track Mind* isn't as essential as *On the Nile*, it's a likable release that fans of the electro-hop sound will enjoy.

Alex Henderson

Eightball & MJG

Comin' Out Hard
August 1993, Suave

Along with OutKast's *Southernplayalisticadillacmuzik* (1994) and Goodie Mob's *Soul Food* (1995), Eightball & MJG's debut, *Comin' Out Hard*, is one of the most influential rap albums to come out of the South. It wasn't as widely heard as those others albums, nor was it as professional-sounding; however, its independent release by Suave House, based in Houston, and its basement-level production were influential in their own way. A generation of underground Southern rappers would arise by the end of the '90s, many of them following the template of *Comin' Out Hard*: underground hardcore rap modeled after West Coast gangsta rap yet delivered in a distinctly Southern manner, released via an indie label with major ambitions. Even the cover artwork of *Comin' Out Hard*, courtesy of Pen & Pixel Graphics, was influential, as the company would go on to design all the bling-blinging No Limit and Cash Money albums of the late '90s. Unfortunately, *Comin' Out Hard* is more historically significant than it is impressive from a strictly musical point of view. The production is admittedly lo-fi, credited to the rappers themselves, and while the raps are effective, the hooks leave room for improvement. Eightball & MJG would indeed improve in the years that followed, ultimately releasing a classic at the end of the decade, *In Our Lifetime, Vol. 1* (1999). *Comin' Out Hard* pales in comparison, yet it's an interesting album to hear from a historical perspective and is certainly noteworthy for its widespread influence, especially throughout the South.

Jason Birchmeier

EPMD

Strictly Business
1988, Priority

EPMD's blueprint for East Coast rap wasn't startlingly different from many others in rap's golden age, but the results were simply amazing, a killer blend of good groove and laid-back flow, plus a populist sense of sampling that had heads nodding from the first listen (and revealed tastes that, like Prince Paul's, tended toward AOR as much as classic soul and funk). A pair from Long Island, EPMD weren't real-life hardcore rappers—it's hard to believe the same voice who talks of spraying a crowd on one track could be name-checking the Hardy Boys later on—but their no-nonsense, monotoned delivery brooked no arguments. With their album debut, *Strictly Business*, Erick Sermon and Parrish Smith really turned rapping on its head; instead of simple lyrics delivered with a hyped, theatrical tone, they dropped the dopest rhymes as though they spoke them all the time. Their debut single, "You Gots to Chill," was a perfect example of the EPMD revolution; two obvious samples, Zapp's "More Bounce to the Ounce" and Kool & the Gang's "Jungle Boogie," doing battle over a high-rolling beat, with the fluid, collaborative raps of Sermon and Smith tying everything together with a mastery that made it all seem deceptively simple. There was really only one theme at work here—the brilliancy of EPMD, or the worthlessness of sucker MCs—but every note of *Strictly Business* proved their claims.

John Bush

Unfinished Business
1989, Priority

EPMD avoided the dreaded sophomore curse and kept its artistic momentum going on its second album, *Unfinished Business*. Once again, the duo triumphed by going against the flow—when MCs ranging from Public Enemy to Sir Mix-A-Lot to N.W.A weren't hesitating to be abrasive and hyper, EPMD still had a sound that was decidedly relaxed by rap standards. For the most part, EPMD's lyrics aren't exactly profound—boasting and attacking sucker MCs is still their favorite activity. However, Erick and Parrish do challenge themselves a bit lyrically on "You Had Too Much to Drink" (a warning against drunk driving) and "Please Listen to My Demo," which recalls the days when they were struggling. But regardless of subject matter, they keep things exciting by having such an appealing, captivating sound.

Alex Henderson

Business as Usual
1990, Def Jam

Business as Usual is an ironic title for EPMD's third album—for in terms of production, it was anything but business as usual for the Strong Island rappers. While *Strictly Business* and *Unfinished Business* favored a very simple and basic approach to production consisting primarily of samples (many of them clever) and drum machines, the production is busier and more involved this time—and even suggests Marley Marl. Unfortunately, the sampling isn't as clever as before. What didn't change was EPMD's relatively laid-back approach to rapping and a preoccupation with sucker MCs. Though not as inspired as its two predecessors, the album does have its moments—including "Rampage" (which unites EPMD with LL Cool J), "Give the People," and "Gold Digger," a candid denunciation of "material girls" who exploit and victimize men financially after a divorce.

Alex Henderson

Business Never Personal
July 1992, Def Jam

Having recorded two undeniable hip-hop classics right out the box, EPMD met with a modicum of disapproval for the first time ever upon the release of its third album, which was graded down by some fans and critics because it seemed to be, yes, more business as usual rather than any sort of musical maturation or progression. Unbowed, Erick Sermon and Parrish Smith returned with what, at the time, was rumored even before it hit shelves to be their final album together. Indeed, the duo broke up not long after *Business Never Personal* came out. It was a perfect way to go out together. The album proved to be both a commercial and artistic triumph at the time, and with each passing year, it sounds more and more like their finest—if not their most historically important—recording. Unapologetically underground throughout its career up to this point, the duo was savvy enough to throw a bone to an ever-growing rap-listening public in a supposed bid for "Crossover" appeal even as it was taking its concluding bow, thereby negating any cries of "sellout" that otherwise might have been tossed at the group's reputation for independence from any commercial concerns. Frankly, though, it would have been a difficult claim to make stick against EPMD anyway. Despite its appealing Zapp sample and hook, "Crossover" is every bit as coated in street soot as the rest of its music. Nevertheless, it is undoubtedly the catchiest thing the pair had ever created. The rest of the album is harder hitting but in every respect as captivating, running from the abrasively metallic "Boon Dox" to the crowd-moving Hit Squad posse cut "Head Banger," and returning the group more often than not to the scowling (though often tongue-in-cheek) intensity and minimalistic aesthetic of its first two records. And if Erick and Parrish hadn't yet made the impending end of their partnership explicit enough, they do so on the final track, where they finally, figuratively kill off Jane, the transvestite prostitute who had hawked them through each of their albums.

Stanton Swihart

Greatest Hits
November 1999, Def Jam

Greatest Hits is a 13-track overview of EPMD's first five albums, culling many of the group's best moments into a fantastic set of loose, flowing grooves. There's a major problem with the compilation, though, and it isn't the fact that a few classics are missing (where are "Let the Funk Flow" and "The Steve Martin"?), though that could be a problem for some. No, the problem is that *Greatest Hits* was released only as a bonus disc that was packaged in a limited-edition issue of the 1999 album *Out of Business*. Which was one of the better albums in the EPMD catalog, but it's doubtful that anyone looking for an overview of the group's career will want to spring for it. As an introduction to the group and an indicator of their accomplishments, *Strictly Business* still can't be beat.

Steve Huey

Eric B. & Rakim

Paid in Full
1987, 4th & Broadway

One of the most influential rap albums of all time, Eric B. & Rakim's *Paid in Full* only continues to grow in stature as the record that ushered in hip-hop's modern era. The stripped-down production might seem a little bare to modern ears, but Rakim's  technique on the mic still sounds utterly contemporary, even state-of-the-art—and that from a record released in 1987, just one year after Run-D.M.C. hit the mainstream. Rakim basically invents modern lyrical technique over the course of *Paid in Full*, with his complex internal rhymes, literate imagery, velvet-smooth flow, and unpredictable, off-the-beat rhythms. The key cuts here are some of the most legendary rap singles ever released, starting with the duo's debut sides, "Eric B. Is President" and "My Melody." "I Know You Got Soul" single-handedly kicked off hip-hop's infatuation with James Brown samples, and Eric B. & Rakim topped it with the similarly inclined "I Ain't No Joke," a stunning display of lyrical virtuosity. The title cut, meanwhile, planted the seeds of hip-hop's material obsessions over a monumental beat. There are also three DJ showcases for Eric B., who like Rakim was among the technical leaders in his field. If sampling is the sincerest form of admiration in hip-hop, *Paid in Full* is positively worshipped. Just to name a few: Rakim's tossed-off

"pump up the volume," from "I Know You Got Soul," became the basis for M/A/R/R/S' groundbreaking dance track; Eminem, a devoted Rakim student, lifted lines from "As the Rhyme Goes On" for the chorus of his own "The Way I Am"; and the percussion track of "Paid in Full" has been sampled so many times it's almost impossible to believe it had a point of origin. *Paid in Full* is essential listening for anyone even remotely interested in the basic musical foundations of hip-hop—this is the form in its purest essence.

Steve Huey

Follow the Leader
1988, UNI

Having already revolutionized hip-hop, Eric B. & Rakim came up with a second straight classic in their sophomore album, *Follow the Leader*, which basically follows the same blueprint for greatness, albeit with subtle refinements. Most noticeably, Eric B.'s production is already moving beyond the minimalism of *Paid in Full*. *Follow the Leader* finds him changing things up more often: dropping in more samples, adding instruments from musician Stevie Blass Griffin, and generally creating a fuller sound over his rock-solid beats. It's still relatively spare, but the extra sonic weight helps keep things fresh. For his part, Rakim wasn't crowned the greatest MC of all time for the variety of his lyrical content, and *Follow the Leader* is no different. Yet even if he rarely deviates from boasting about his microphone prowess (and frankly, he's entitled), he employs uncommonly vivid and elaborate metaphors in doing so. A case in point is "Microphone Fiend," which weaves references to substance addiction throughout in explaining why Rakim can't keep away from the mic. The album-opening title cut is one of his most agile, up-tempo lyrical showcases, demonstrating why he's such a poetic inspiration for so many MCs even today. "Lyrics of Fury" manages to top it in terms of sheer force, using the break from James Brown's "Funky Drummer" before it saturated the airwaves. And, of course, there are several more turntable features for Eric B. *Follow the Leader* may not have broken much new ground, but it captures one of the greatest pure hip-hop acts at the top of its form, and that's enough to make the album a classic.

Steve Huey

Let the Rhythm Hit 'Em
May 1990, MCA

One thing the rap audience will never be accused of is having the world's longest attention span. Even some of the most celebrated hip-hoppers can fade in popularity after only a few albums. Eric B. & Rakim were extremely popular in the mid-to-late '80s, but by 1990, rap buyers were starting to lose interest in them. Not much different from *Paid in Full* or *Follow the Leader*, *Let the Rhythm Hit 'Em* makes rapping technique its number one priority. At time when West Coast MCs like Ice-T and Ice Cube were mainly interested in getting a political message across, Rakim's goal was showing how much technique he had. Rakim may rap in a deadpan tone, but "Step Back," "No Omega," and other tunes leave no doubt that he had sizable chops. There are a few message raps (including "In the Ghetto"), although Rakim spends most of his time finding tongue-twisting ways to boast and brag about his microphone skills. The overall result is a CD that is enjoyable, yet limited.

Alex Henderson

Don't Sweat the Technique
1992, MCA

Starting with their 1986 debut, *Paid in Full*, Eric B. and Rakim earned raves for Eric B.'s often flawless, judicious productions and Rakim's serious yet relentlessly rhythmic rhyming style. This 1992 album finds the duo picking up from where they left off of 1990's *Let the Rhythm Hit 'Em*. "What's on Your Mind" has Rakim with intents to woo under a bubbling track with an adroit interpolation of D Train's 1983 hit of the same name. That track aside, *Don't Sweat the Technique* has Rakim in bleak spirits as thoughts of combat, revenge, and unfortunate "accidents" are not far from his mind. "Casualties of War" has Rakim as an all-purpose psycho with the unsettling hook, "I get a rush when I see blood and dead bodies on the floor." Although it's supposed to be gripping, the thought of a war-ravaged Rakim with his pistols blazing after hearing a truck backfiring is hilarious. All of *Don't Sweat the Technique* would be more disturbing if it wasn't for the brilliant ear of Eric B. who can cut the tension and exact magic out of a going-nowhere track. Although the lyrics and premise of "What's Going On" aren't extremely sharp, the cracking snare drums and low bass riffs are a perfect compliment to Rakim's delivery. The title track is also jazz influenced, but not as potent as the Simon Law and Mr. Lee's Funky Ginger remixes that don't appear here. Like many albums of this type, *Don't Sweat the Technique* ends on tracks of little distinction but it is another strong effort from one of rap's most respected acts.

Jason Elias

ESG

Come Away with ESG
1983, 99

It might have taken two decades, but the true genius of New York's early '80s music being is finally being acknowledged by a much younger generation of fans. And right in the middle of this revolutionary intersection of punk, disco, rap and soul were four sisters: Marie, Valerie, Renee, and Lorraine "Sweet L" Scroggins, and their seminal minifunk outfit, ESG. Recorded live and raw in a small studio located above *Radio City Music Hall*, the band's debut album, *Come Away With ESG* is a lasting document of their unique brand of minimal funk that would influence subsequent postpunk, hip-hop, and dance music acts. Stripped down to the most basic of drum beats and rudimentary basslines, "Come Away" confirms the notion that the real rhythm is what happens between the beats. The staggering gait takes its cues from post-punk outfits P.I.L. and Gang of Four, while the repeated vocal chorus is reminiscent of doo wop's street corner

soul. The more up-tempo "Dance" begins with a beat that could have been lifted from a Motown studio outtake, while "It's Alright" combines primitive single-note guitar lines with equally archaic beats and bongo fills. Most memorable is "Moody and Spaced Out," with its warped electronic sweeps and grooving sixteenth-note hi-hat that propels the beat still favored by well-informed dance music DJs. It is nearly impossible to understate the influence of ESG, who pave the way for acts as diverse as female hip-hop pioneers Salt-N-Pepa, to post-hardcore legends Fugazi. Much in the same way that Marvin Gaye captured the urban plight of Detroit at the turn of the '70s with *What's Going On*, *Come Away With ESG* is a musical snapshot of post-groovy, pre-fresh New York City at the beginning of the '80s.

Joshua Glazer

Esham

Judgement Day, Vol. 1
1992, Reel Life Productions

Esham's ambitious *Judgement Day* double album may not be his most well-crafted work, but it certainly stands as his most inspired work of the '90s, surpassing any of his solo albums or his NATAS albums in sheer scope. Released in 1992, years before the double album became an accepted practice in rap, *Judgement Day* finds the Detroit rapper at his most demented, rapping almost exclusively about horrifying topics such as death, Hell, drugs, ghetto, and straight-up nihilism. While most may not find such disturbing subject matter difficult to enjoy or even stomach, it is hard to deny that Esham's work on this album is precedent setting and to a certain degree influential on subsequent underground rap artists. Besides his nightmarish lyrics, Esham also produces the sample-ridden beats on this album, an accomplishment that rivals his rapping. The production is admittedly lo-fi, yet this is an important element of its appeal; with his taste for fuzzy Funkadelic-styled rock samples, the bedroom studio-sounding production's griminess that results as much from its sampled roots as its quality feels somewhat consistent with Esham's rapping—this is the definition of underground rap. There aren't any of the glossy commercial elements of hip-hop production anywhere to be found here, and also thanks to the album's downright disturbing rapping, this album became and remains an underground cult classic. With this album being as raw as Esham could ever get in terms of both production and rapping, it's no surprise that subsequent releases found him steadily cleaning up both his production and rapping. [Note that *Judgement Day, Vol. 1* and *Judgement Day, Vol. 2* were released separately, though intended as companions.]

Jason Birchmeier

Everlast

Forever Everlasting
March 1990, Warner Bros.

Here's a little known fact of rap history: before Everlast enjoyed recognition as a member of House of Pain, he pursued a career as a solo artist. *Forever Everlasting*, his first and only pre-Pain solo album, is a decent, though not outstanding release proving that he had strong rapping skills long before becoming well known. Ice-T, who serves as this CD's executive producer, once said of Everlast, "Hearing him rap, you'd never know he was white"—and to be sure, the L.A.-based MC is far from a pop rapper. Though most of his lyrics aren't remarkable, this CD definitely has its moments—most notably, "Speak No Evil" (a reflection on injustice in America) and the angry "Fuck Everyone."

Alex Henderson

The Fat Boys

The Fat Boys
1984, Sutra

Because of their comic image, some hip-hoppers dismissed the Fat Boys as a novelty act—some, but not many. The fact is that they were among the best and most popular rappers of the mid-1980s. Along with Run-D.M.C., L.L. Cool J, and Whodini, the Fat Boys were the finest that hip-hop's "Second Generation" (as it was called) had to offer. After making some noise as the Disco Three, the rotund Brooklynites changed their name to the Fat Boys in 1984 and hit big with this excellent debut album, which is humorous, wildly entertaining, and unapologetically funky. Everything from "Fat Boys" to the amusing "Jailhouse Rap" proves that their rapping skills were first-rate. One of the group's strongest assets was Darren Robinson, aka the Human Beat Box, who was known for making percussive sounds with his voice. A celebration of his talent, "Human Beat Box" uses no actual instruments—only Robinson emulating them. This album is a true hip-hop classic.

Alex Henderson

The Fat Boys Are Back
1985, WEA

One of the things that people in the music world have come to fear is the infamous sophomore slump. But there were no signs of a sophomore slump on the Fat Boys' second album, *The Fat Boys Are Back*. The Brooklyn trio showed a great deal of promise on its self-titled debut album of 1984, and this LP is also excellent. Because the Fat Boys acted like buffoons, some people dismissed them as a mere novelty act. But for all their clowning, the Fat Boys had impeccable rapping technique—the skills that they bring to "Yes, Yes Y'all," the title song, and other wildly infectious offerings are first rate. Much to their credit, this album is fairly unpredictable; *The Fat Boys Are Back* finds them rapping to everything from sleek urban contemporary ("Pump It Up") to hard rock ("Rock-N-Roll") and reggae ("Hard Core Reggae"). The latter, in fact, is one of the most impressive examples of hip-hop/reggae fusion to come from rap's second generation. But the Fat Boys don't need real instruments to bust a rhyme; on the a cappella "Human Beat Box, Part II," their only "instrument" is the voice of the late Darren Robinson, aka the Human Beat Box, who used his voice to simulate instruments. Arguably, Robinson and Doug E. Fresh were the closest thing that 1980s hip-hop had to Bobby McFerrin. As time passed, the Fat Boys started sounding like a caricature of themselves. But when *The Fat Boys Are Back* came out in 1985, they were still among the most exciting groups in hip-hop.

Alex Henderson

Crushin'
1987, Mercury

The Fat Boys enjoyed their biggest year in 1987. Their film *Disorderlies* proved much more commercially resilient than anticipated, and this LP earned their only platinum

certification, while becoming the lone Fat Boys album to make the pop Top 10 (peaking at #8). They also landed a Top 20 single with an updated version of "Wipeout."

Ron Wynn

All Meat No Filler: The Best of Fat Boys
March 1997, Rhino

All Meat No Filler: The Best of the Fat Boys is an excellent 18-track compilation of all of the Fat Boys' biggest hits, including "Fat Boys," "Human Beat Box," "Jail House Rap," "Can You Feel It," "The Fat Boys Are Back," "Hard Core Reggae," "Falling  in Love," "Wipeout" (with the Beach Boys), and "The Twist (Yo, Twist!)" (with Chubby Checker). Although some of the latter-day cuts have aged poorly, the Fat Boys' earliest singles are ground-breaking and timeless records, proving that they weren't merely a novelty act.

Stephen Thomas Erlewine

Father MC

Father's Day
1990, Uptown

Before Puffy, Mary J., and the rest of the blingers went off to successful chart domination, there was Father MC. Perfecting the marriage of soul, R&B, and rap into a successful formula, *Father's Day* was not only important, it was a litmus test that launched the careers of both aforementioned artists—as Combs was head producer and Blige made her musical debut as a background singer. Leading off with the new jack classic "I'll Do 4 U," it's immediately apparent that the trio was onto something big. Unfortunately, the rest of the album becomes somewhat formulaic after this point, but the impact of *Father's Day*'s tone and textures would be felt for years to come.

Rob Theakston

Close to You
1992, Uptown

In the 21st century, rap and R&B are seriously joined at the hip. Urban contemporary singers go out of their way to feature major rappers, and even the most hardcore MCs employ R&B singers on their recordings. But it wasn't always that way. In the '80s,  hip-hop encountered a great deal of resistance in R&B circles, and many hardcore rappers wanted nothing to do with

R&B. Father MC did his part to change that. Like Whodini, Salt-N-Pepa, the Fresh Prince, Heavy D, and Young MC before him, Father envisioned a style of hip-hop that was commercial, unthreatening, R&B-drenched, and pop-friendly, but not lightweight or bland; arguably, his new jack swing-minded albums of the early '90s were the rap equivalent of Bobby Brown or Keith Sweat. While *Close to You* is hardly the work of a hip-hop purist, this 1992 release demonstrates that pop-rap can have integrity. Yes, the CD is full of urban contemporary slickness and romantic themes (as opposed to battle rhymes or hard-hitting tales of thug life in the 'hood), but Father's rapping skills are never in doubt; he flows with plenty of confidence, and his East Coast rhyming technique is consistently impressive. *Close to You* underscores the fact that not all pop-rap is created equal. The rhyming skills of some pop-rappers have been limited at best—Vanilla Ice immediately comes to mind—while the more substantial ones (Salt-N-Pepa, the Fresh Prince, Heavy D) have had no problem getting their flow on. Clearly, Father MC falls into the latter category, and his impact was enormous in the early '90s. Father's 1990 debut, *Father's Day*, is widely regarded as his most important and essential release, but *Close to You* was a solid, enjoyable follow-up for the Bronx native.

Alex Henderson

Freestyle Fellowship

To Whom It May Concern...
1991, Beats & Rhymes

Freestyle Fellowship's first album is a potent glimpse into the subcultural, conscientious side of Los Angeles hip-hop, one that would later be eclipsed by gangsta boogie from the likes of Dr. Dre, Snoop Dogg, and all the pretenders who followed in their wake. As such, the joint—like much of the work from De La Soul, the Pharcyde, A Tribe Called Quest, and other equally diverse artists of the period—is a snapshot of a burgeoning art form's purity before it capitulated to the market and rolled out its gripload of Kristal and Bentley worshipers. Not that Freestyle Fellowship ever wandered down that path: they were too busy twisting tongues with blissed-out, stream-of-consciousness rhymes—which is more or less what you'll find, without the hard-hitting beats, on *To Whom It May Concern...* For example, songs like "Jupiter's Journey" and "Sunshine Men" showcase Self-Jupiter and J. Sumbi's respective rhyme flows, but ignore song structure altogether; basically, you're getting the MC without the DJ, which can get boring after a while. But when they pull it all together and work as a collective (as their name implies), things heat up quickly, like on "Convolutions," a breakneck bebop session that is over all too quickly, or "We Will Not Tolerate" and "Dedications," shout sessions that are truncated versions of songs found on their later (and better) album, *Inner City Griots*. Which is not to say that *To Whom It May Concern...* is a snoozer when each rapper works alone. Most of the woefully underrated Aceyalone's tunes are bracing exercises in skill and speed, and Mikah 9 and Self-Jupiter are stellar wordsmiths. But a fellowship functions best when everyone is working together, and there's more evidence of this particular group's promise in its ensuing work.

Scott Thill

Inner City Griots
1993, 4th & Broadway

Freestyle Fellowship emerged on the L.A. rap scene during the early '90s. Given the chance to hone its skills at a health-

food store's open-mic nights, the group quickly earned the attention and respect of the city's hip-hop underground. Their second album, 1993's *Inner City Griots*, is the only completely collaborative album released during the group's career. Surprisingly, each MC (Mikah Nine, Jupiter, Peace, and Aceyalone) seems fully matured at this early stage. On *Inner City Griots*, the production is improved to match the group's vibrant, dexterous wordplay. Swapping rhymes with agility and grace, the Fellowship is a rap tag team par excellence. At times, the lyrics are so dense and the delivery so quick that the words are practically indecipherable. Yet the rappers are just as adept at slowing down the pace without losing a bit of their lyrical energy or creativity. Unrestricted by tired rap themes, the Fellowship strikes at a range of subjects. The abrasive opening one-two of "Blood" and "Bullies of the Block" might throw listeners off guard but as "Everything's Everything" opens, they provide assurances that "It's all right y'all." The guns are dropped and microphones prevail. *Inner City Griots* (a griot is an African storyteller) takes on Aceyalone's twisted nursery rhyme "Cornbread," the positive vibes of "Inner City Boundaries," the locker-room machismo of "Shammy's" (an inevitable ode to the ladies), and "Way Cool," a tale of serial killing horror. On "Park Bench People," the Freestyle Fellowship even asks whether rap music is big enough to take in a sung rumination on homelessness. With live instrumentation provided by the Underground Railroad (whose members appear throughout the album), the song stretches into a section reminiscent of '70s Stevie Wonder. Like all great groups that preceded it, the Fellowship was simply testing the limits of hip-hop and its own capabilities on this multifaceted collection.

Nathan Bush

Doug E. Fresh

Greatest Hits, Vol. 1
August 1996, Bust It

Greatest Hits, Vol. 1 collects all of Doug E. Fresh's biggest hit singles—including "La Di Da Di," "Keep Risin' to the Top," and "The Show," adding a couple of new tracks produced by Sean "Puffy" Combs for good measure. It's a concise and entertaining retrospective that sums up his career very well.

Stephen Thomas Erlewine

Frost

Hispanic Causing Panic
1990, Virgin

Hispanic Causing Panic was an early landmark of Latin hip-hop, simply by virtue of the fact that Kid Frost was one of the first Latino MCs to release an album. Of course, it also doesn't hurt to have a groundbreaking lead single on the order of "La Raza," a smoky, laid-back Latin funk groove with

anthemic Spanglish lyrics about being brown and proud. It's an utterly distinctive, original sound (and miles better than anything Gerardo ever tried). Unfortunately, it isn't explored very much over the rest of *Hispanic Causing Panic*. Kid Frost spends most of his time rhyming in English, which isn't necessarily a bad thing, but he doesn't make as strong a musical statement as he might have if he'd played with the Latin foundations of "La Raza" on more of his additional material. Instead, he sticks with a fairly typical golden-age production style for much of the album, which is accessible without being overly pop-friendly. What's more, his rapping style largely abandons the sly purr of "La Raza," sounding more like your average East Coast MC of the time (with Big Daddy Kane a particular influence). It's as though he wants to prove he can make it on others' terms as well as his own. There are exceptions, of course: "Ya Estuvo (That's It)" puts on a bilingual clinic in MC skills, and the chilling street narratives "Come Together" and "Homicide" return to the ice-cool delivery that marks Frost at his most distinctive. They're good enough to make the remainder of *Hispanic Causing Panic* frustrating—it's good, but it doesn't have enough of what makes Kid Frost so unique.

Steve Huey

Smile Now, Die Later
October 1995, Relativity

Between his first solo album, *Hispanic Causing Panic*, and his second record, *Smile Now, Die Later*, Frost dropped the "Kid" prefix from his name, which is only appropriate—he matured quite a bit between the two records. Where *Hispanci Causing Panic* was a party record infused with the occasional self-aware/socially-conscious vibe, *Smile Now, Die Later* is a politically-charged album, a warning to all of his fellow Latino ghetto denizens to protect themselves. Since Frost's lyrical outlook has grown, it's only appropriate that his music has become richer—now it draws from a variety of sources, from hardcore hip-hop and Latin beats, to deep funk and soul balalds. Like any mid-'90s hip-hop album, *Smile Now, Die Later* runs a bit too long, but if it's boiled down to its essential items, it is one fine listen.

Leo Stanley

Fu-Schnickens

F.U. Don't Take It Personal
February 1992, Jive

Even before they made it to the record bins, three-man New York crew Fu-Schnickens created quite a buzz in the hip-hop community with the oddity of their group name. Once they dropped their debut album, *F.U. Don't Take It Personal*, their music turned out to be every bit as curious and intriguing. The music is inundated with kung fu movie dialogue snippets and all manner of lyrical references to pop culture, both obscure and otherwise; this provides the album with a joyous, tongue-in-cheek, almost cartoonish flair. That sense is countered by the machine-gun-rapid toasting and almost military-like shouts of the three MCs (Poc, Chip, and Moc Fu), who trade off rhymes so telepathically that they seem to finish each other's sentences half the time. In this regard, they fit in perfectly with peers such as Leaders of the New School and Brand Nubian, as part of the early '90s new wave of rap crews that catapulted hip-hop into the future partially by playing up the camaraderie of old-school rap groups. All the peer crews, however, were so progressive because they grew up fully in a hip-hop culture and lifestyle, and knew

where they wanted to take it, thereby developing unique styles and, occasionally, novelties to help them stand out. Fu-Schnickens were no different in this respect, and although their fashion sense (kung fu outfits on the cover) and taste in influences may have initially painted them as a novelty, their approach to music was straight serious on this debut album, and it shows. With production help from A Tribe Called Quest, they create spare, tension-filled, intense soundscapes, and twist reggae and vintage soul samples into unrecognizable, bass-heavy tracks. Even better is the trio's ear for vocal hooks, which stamp each song with an instant appeal.

Stanton Swihart

Nervous Breakdown
October 1994, Jive

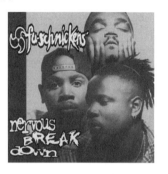

When this Brooklyn trio emerged in 1992 with a unique style that combined high-speed rapping, dancehall chatting, and backward rhymes with *Looney Tunes*-inspired voice impressions and craftily arranged hip-hop grooves, the rap world had never heard anything like it. It took the group several years to follow up its gold debut, *F.U.: Don't Take It Personal*, but *Nervous Breakdown* proved that the Fu-Schnickens could deliver the goods. The album shows an improved lyrical maturity among all three members, but most noticeably Chip Fu, whose hyperactive, onomatopoeic flow has more hilarious, colorful cartoon imagery than anyone this side of the late, great Mel Blanc. While Poc Fu and Moc Fu are both better-than-average MCs with their own unique styles, it is Chip Fu's innovative approach that provides the distinctive personality that sets the group apart from other rap groups of the era. From the opening track, "Breakdown," on, this is a frenzied, fast-paced roller coaster ride of originality that doesn't let up until the last song ends.

Bret Love

Funkdoobiest

Which Doobie U B?
May 1993, Epic

Funkdoobiest's debut album, *Which Doobie U B?*, sounds a lot like their mentors in Cypress Hill—a lot. Not only is DJ Muggs' production very similar, but lead MC Son Doobie's flow often resembles a more robotic version of B Real (that's a compliment, by the way). But it all works anyway—Muggs is in his absolute prime as a producer here, and Son Doobie's rhymes are fittingly surreal and stoner-friendly, albeit more cartoonish than menacing like his Cypress counterpart. The record is front-loaded with its best songs—"The Funkiest," "Bow Wow Wow," and "Freak Mode" were the underground hits, and they're also the first three cuts here. Most of the rest of the album keeps their vibe going with pretty admirable consistency, and stays engaging the whole way through. B Real drops in for a guest spot on the Little Richard-sampling "Wopbabalubop," and there are some nifty echoing drums on "Here I Am." It may not break any new ground, but frankly, *Which Doobie U B?* is better than any latter-day Cypress Hill album.

Steve Huey

The Future Sound

The Whole Shabang, Vol. 1
1992, East West

The "new school" renaissance in hip-hop during the early '90s was so fresh and overflowing with artists approaching the genre in novel and disparate ways that even the fly-by-night and second-tier groups like the Future Sound were capable of terrific and exciting invention, the reason there seems to be an inordinate number of little-known rap albums from the era that now qualify as lost or minor gems. *The Whole Shabang, Vol. 1* is definitely one of those diamonds in the rough, a one-shot, alterna-hop full-length so loopy and breezily entertaining that it seems painted partly in psychedelic colors. It is obvious from the outset—"This Is a Game" samples a cartoon character in its opening bars—that Flashback (aka the Funky Tactitioner) and Relay (aka the Rhythm King Pin) were intent on exploring a plane of existence a few realities removed from the streets. Like a pair of old-school MCs on a new kind of contact high, they vocally teeter-totter back and forth and circle a merry-go-round of rhymes around each other, filling the music with off-the-wall extended metaphors and playful verbal juxtapositions (at times they seem to be speaking their own private language) well above and beyond the hip-hop norm. Producing everything (but for a single Clark Kent track) themselves, the music is an impish match, traipsing through rare and whimsical jazz and soul snippets with spirited aplomb ("The Function," "The Bop Step," "Scriptic Cryptic") when not curling up into drowsy tall tales like "Flashback Relay & the Whole Shabang" and the shimmering "Pixie Groove." Throw brothers and future business moguls Damon and Darien Dash into the mix as executive producers (this was the former's entree into the big leagues of the industry) and you also have a historically intriguing little hip-hop curio. But track it down for the music.

Stanton Swihart

Warren G

Regulate...G Funk Era
June 1994, Def Jam

Anchored by the laid-back G-funk anthem "Regulate," Warren G's appropriately titled *Regulate...G Funk Era* embodies the mid-'90s era of Cali sunshine, endless blunts, and switch-hittin' lowriders with a welcome and somewhat surprising sense of kind-heartedness. Unlike most of his West Coast G-funk peers, Warren doesn't celebrate drive-by gang-bangin', dirty-money stackin', nor G's-up, hoes-down pimpin'. Sure, he says the *F* word once in a while and puffs on the cheeba-cheeba when it's passed his way, but he's essentially a good-natured, all-ages rapper, interested in nothing more than good ol'-fashioned hip-hop. He professes his demeanor succinctly on the catchy hook to "This DJ," the other era-defining highlight here: "It's kinda easy when you're listening to the G-ed-up sound/Pioneer speakers bumpin' as I smoke on a pound/I got the sound fo yo' ass and it's easy to see/That this DJ be Warren G." Like his stepbrother Dr. Dre, Warren is a more talented producer than rapper, and it's his by-the-book

G-funk beat-making that truly shines here. For instance, another album highlight, "Do You See," boasts an elastic bassline and whistling synth hook, capturing the essence of G-funk as only Dre himself could. Warren further compensates for his middling rapping with a couple of guests, a few skits, and a brief running time. Even if "Regulate" and "This DJ" tower far above everything else here, *Regulate...G Funk Era* is nonetheless a minor gem among the myriad G-funk albums of the mid-'90s, and Warren embodies the style itself here with a precision perhaps second only to his older brother and does so with a refreshing air of harmlessness.

Jason Birchmeier

Gang Starr

No More Mr. Nice Guy
1989, Wild Pitch

You don't hear much of *Step in the Arena* on Gang Starr's first album. In fact, aside from some scrupulous lyrical stances by Guru ("Manifest," "Positivity") and some of DJ Premier's hallmark brilliance behind the turntables, this Gang Starr isn't instantly recognizable as the duo who would soon become one of the most respected rap groups of the 1990s. The Gang Starr of *No More Mr. Nice Guy* still has a leg knee-deep in the old-school aesthetic. As a result, Premier's beats are quite a bit simpler and sometimes cruder than fans have come to expect (though they are still several cuts above the rest of the class), and Guru spends considerable energy talking up his own microphone skills and tearing down the next MC's (sometimes electrifying, as on "Gotch U"). That is not the same thing, however, as saying that *No More Mr. Nice Guy* is a subpar album. It is not, by any means. In fact, it's quite good in its own way, but it's also safe to say that the recording is not representative of the Chrysalis-era Gang Starr that devotees would eventually come to revere. Approach this album on its own terms, though, and it has a lot to offer, namely its early, tentative steps into the sampling of jazz. The most conspicuous attempt in this direction is the fine "Jazz Music," which was, nevertheless, reworked to much better effect a few years later for the soundtrack to Spike Lee's *Mo' Better Blues* as "Jazz Thing." The scratching showcase "DJ Premier in Deep Concentration" is an antiquated delight that dips into jazz as well, while the conscientious "Cause and Effect," the steely "2 Steps Ahead," and the uncharacteristic guest production from DJ Mark the 45 King on "Gusto" are all classics waiting to be rediscovered. Indicative or not, fans of the group will want this album, as will those with a jones for the original new-school revolution. More casual fans can probably start their collections with *Step in the Arena*, which *is* a required purchase. [The 2001 Wild Pitch Classics reissue adds three bonus tracks, the strongest of which is "Here's the Proof."]

Stanton Swihart

Step in the Arena
1991, Chrysalis

The album on which DJ Premier and Guru perfected the template that would launch them into underground stardom and a modicum of mainstream success. Guru's deadpan monotone delivery was shockingly different from other early '90s MCs, many of who were either substituting charisma for substance or engaging in hardcore "realism" without really commenting on black inner-city life or offering ways to alter the situation for the better. But it is Guru who sounded like the real clarion call of and to the street on *Step in the Arena*

("Why bring ignorance/where we're inviting you to get advancement," he intones on "Form of Intellect"). *Step in the Arena* was the first real mature flowering of his street-wise sagacity. His voice would grow more assured by the next album, but here Guru imparts urban wisdom of a strikingly visible variety. It's easy to allow yourself to get caught up in the fantasy of hardcore rap, but it is somewhat more involving and disorienting to hear truth that avoids exaggeration or glorification. Guru is not easy on any aspect of the inner city, from the "snakes" that exploit the community ("Execution of a Chump") to those that are a product of it ("Just to Get a Rep"), and the result is a surprising but hard-fought compassion ("Who's Gonna Take the Weight?" pleads for the acceptance of responsibility, for not taking the easy path). He seems to have somehow developed a hopefulness out of the bleak surroundings. DJ Premier was already near the top of his game at this early point. His production seems less jazz-fueled on *Step in the Arena*, opting more for spare guitar lines and tight beats, as well as his unmistakable vocal cut-up style of scratching for a slightly warped and out-of-phase soundscape.

Stanton Swihart

Daily Operation
May 1992, Chrysalis

On *Step in the Arena*, DJ Premier and Guru hit upon their mature sound, characterized by sparse, live jazz samples, Premier's cut-up scratching, and Guru's direct, unwavering street-wise monotone; but, with *Daily Operation*, the duo made their first masterpiece. From beginning to end, Gang Starr's third full-length album cuts with the force and precision of a machete and serves as an ode to and representation of New York and hip-hop underground culture. The genius of *Daily Operation* is that Guru's microphone skills are perfectly married to the best batch of tracks Premier had ever come up with. Guru has more of a presence than he has ever had, slinking and pacing through each song like a man with things on his mind, ready to go off at any second. Premier's production has an unparalleled edge here. He created the minimalist opening track, "The Place Where We Dwell," out of a two-second drum-solo sample and some scratching, but is also able to turn around and create something as lush and melodic as the jazz-tinged "No Shame in My Game" without ever seeming to be out of his element, making every track of the same sonic mind. For an underground crew, Gang Starr has always had a knack for crafting memorable vocal hooks to go with the expert production, and they multiply both aspects on *Daily Operation*. Every song has some attribute that stamps it indelibly into the listener's head, and it marks the album as one of the finest of the decade, rap or otherwise.

Stanton Swihart

Hard to Earn
March 1994, Chrysalis

Gang Starr came out hard on their 1994 album, *Hard to Earn*, an album notably different from its two predecessors: *Step in the Arena* (1991) and *Daily Operation* (1992). While those two classic albums garnered tremendous praise for their thoughtful lyrics and jazzy beats, *Hard to Earn* seems much more reactionary, especially its lyrics. Guru opens the album with a tough, dismissive spoken-word intro: "Yo, all you kids want to get on and sh*t/Just remember this/This sh*t ain't easy/If you ain't got it, you ain't got it, motherf*cker." While this sense of superiority is undoubtedly a long-running convention of not just East Coast rap but rap in general, you don't expect to hear it coming from Gang Starr, particularly with such a bitter tone. Yet this attitude pervades throughout *Hard to Earn*. Songs such as "Suckas Need Bodyguards" and "Mass Appeal" take aim at unnamed peers, and other songs such as "ALONGWAYTOGO" similarly center on "whack crews." The best moments on *Hard to Earn* aren't these songs but instead "Code of the Streets" and "Tonz 'O' Gunz," two songs where Guru offers the type of social commentary that made Gang Starr so admirable in the first place. Yet, even though *Hard to Earn* is a bit short on such thoughtful moments, instead weighed down a bit with harsh attitude, it does offer some of DJ Premier's best productions ever. He's clearly at—or, at least, near—his best here. There isn't a song on the album that's a throwaway, and even the interludes are stunning. Given the subtly bitter tone of this album, it perhaps wasn't surprising then that Guru and Premier took some time to pursue solo opportunities after *Hard to Earn*. You can sense the duo's frustration with the rap scene circa 1994. The two didn't return with another Gang Starr album until four years later when they dropped *Moment of Truth*, a succinct comeback album that reaffirmed their status as one of New York's most thoughtful and artistic rap acts.

Jason Birchmeier

Geto Boys

Grip It! On That Other Level
1990, Rap-A-Lot

A major leap from 1988's clunky and derivative *Making Trouble*, it was this record that gained the attention of Rick Rubin, who would swiftly sign the group to Def American and re-release slightly altered versions of many of these songs for the group's self-titled album. Since ten of the 12 tracks found here would be improved or simply lifted for *The Geto Boys*, there isn't much of a reason why anyone would need this, even though Rap-A-Lot continued to keep it in print. "Seek and Destroy" and "No Sellout" are the only two songs that aren't available elsewhere; the former is a decent, speedy Scarface track, while the latter is a pro-black cut headed by Willie D. The most significant difference between this and the self-titled album can be heard in the versions of "Mind of a Lunatic." The actual backing track was hardly adjusted—if at all—for the self-titled album, but the deliveries from Bushwick Bill, Scarface, and Willie D are much more horrifying and claustrophobic on that later version. Plus, it also sounds much more gut-kicking coming after "Size Ain't Shit." On this disc, it's the final track and seems sequentially out of place.

Andy Kellman

The Geto Boys
1990, Rap-A-Lot

This is a revamped version of *Grip It! On That Other Level*, an album released earlier in the year on Rap-A-Lot. Rick Rubin stepped in, signed the group to Def American, and proceeded to tweak some of the tracks; some other tracks were simply lifted from *Grip It!*, while a couple went so far as to have new vocals recorded. This works like a charm—the album is expertly sequenced, and some songs seem to have twice the impact of their original incarnations. "Mind of a Lunatic" is one such song, and it's one of the primary tracks that caused the Def American-affiliated Geffen to pull the plug on distribution. A horror fantasy of grim, graphic proportions, it's a gangster flick and a psychological thriller rolled into the form of a song. One of its cleanest lines is as follows: "She begged me not to kill her, I gave her a rose—then slit her throat and watched her shake 'til her eyes closed." The rest of the album helped draw the lyrical blueprint that countless groups either mimicked or borrowed from, from the yuks served up by Bushwick in "Size Ain't Shit" to the ridiculously misogynistic rhymes in "Gangster of Love," which are delivered over the guitar lick from Lynyrd Skynyrd's "Sweet Home Alabama." You can also either blame them or thank them for the endless flurry of *Scarface* samples that have littered/adorned so many hip-hop records.

Andy Kellman

We Can't Be Stopped
July 1991, Rap-A-Lot

The cover of the Geto Boys' *We Can't Be Stopped* shows a member with his eye poked out. It's grotesque, but realistic—a realistic cover for an album whose violent, profane lyrics paint a vivid and accurate picture of life as the Geto Boys knew it growing up in Houston's tough ghetto known as the 5th Ward. This CD isn't as thought-provoking as Ice-T's, N.W.A's, or Ice Cube's can be—nor is it the Geto Boys' best offering. But it's an engaging, disturbing effort that comes across as much more heartfelt than the numerous gangsta rap albums by the N.W.A and Cube clones and wannabes who jumped on the gangsta bandwagon in the early '90s. *We Can't Be Stopped* serves as an unsettling reminder of the type of ugly social conditions that were allowed to fester in poor inner-city neighborhoods.

Alex Henderson

Greatest Hits
November 2002, Rap-A-Lot

This is a second and more inclusive package of the Geto Boys' best moments. The first, *Uncut Dope*, covered the group through 1991's *We Can't Be Stopped*; this opens it up to include tracks from 1993's *Till Death Do Us Part*, 1996's *Resurrection*, and 1998's *Da Good da Bad & da Ugly*. Those three albums were more patchy than the ones that came before them—with the exception of *Making Trouble*—and none of the highlights from them are of the caliber of earlier tracks like "Mind of a Lunatic," "My Mind Playing Tricks on Me," and "Trigga Happy Nigga." So, going strictly by pound-for-pound quality, *Uncut Dope* is the better of the two, but it's not as if later tracks like "Six Feet Deep," "The World Is a Geto," and "Gangsta (Put Me Down)" are entirely undeserving of anthology status. Furthermore, this disc has five more tracks and has better sound quality—naturally so since it was released ten years after *Uncut Dope*. Choosing where to go first with this group is a tough call: *The Geto Boys* is the

group's best album, but going with that leaves one without some of the group's best material. And neither *Uncut Dope* nor *Greatest Hits* are clear-cut first stops. Regardless of the choice, some of the most brutally descriptive and alternately funny Southern hip-hop is in well-stocked supply.

Andy Kellman

Grand Puba

Reel to Reel
1992, Elektra

In a sense, Grand Puba really never was a genuine member of Brand Nubian. He was several years older than Lord Jamar and Sadat X, and had already recorded with the old-school crew Masters of Ceremony several years before finally hooking up with his younger mates. And even the mostly collective-minded *One for All* featured a couple Puba solo joints. Based on the sophomore Brand Nubian outing, it is pretty clear that Grand Puba's carefree verbal play, completely unencumbered by ideology, tempered the more in-your-face manifestation of Jamar and Sadat X's radical politics since *In God We Trust* which, as thrillingly polemical as it could be, was also rather severe and uncompromising, even apocalyptic, in its outlook, and therefore off-putting at times. Likewise, based on this debut solo album, it's clear that Brand Nubian created precisely the right context in which Puba's self-reflexive braggadocio could flourish without wearing thin because *Reel to Reel*, as much fun as it is, has little in the way of substance. As a result, the record never becomes more than a pleasing divertissement. Minus any counterweights who can "drop the science," Puba, like some sort of hip-hop Dolemite, proved to be interested mostly in self-puffery, partying, and playing the ladies. While the persona is entertaining as far as it goes, it doesn't have a lot of mileage in it unless you have a high tolerance for tall tales about stunts and blunts. The artist himself had a good time satirizing this penchant at the beginning of the classic "Wake Up" from *One for All*, but seems to have lost sight of some of the possibilities for self-parody here. Having said that, the album really does have a lot to offer, including the irresistible one-two punch of "Check Tha Resume" and "360'," the deep-fried "Honey Don't Front," and the delightfully lazy "Who Makes the Loot?," whipped off with Brand New Heavies when they were at their funkiest. The production (most of it by the artist himself) is universally excellent, and Puba is, without a doubt, one of the cleverest, most cheekily complex MCs to ever pick up a microphone. Just bring your incredulity and sense of humor—the lower the brow the better—and *Reel to Reel* is a real hoot.

Stanton Swihart

Grandmaster Flash

Message from Beat Street: The Best of Grandmaster Flash, Melle Mel & the Furious Five
April 1994, Rhino

A diplomatically titled Rhino compilation, *Message from Beat Street: The Best of Grandmaster Flash, Melle Mel & the Furious Five* is a no-brainer collection featuring the absolute best of the group's four years on Sugar Hill—from the national breakout with 1980's "Freedom" to the beginning of the end, Melle Mel & the Furious Five's rap-on-film classic, "Beat Street." Backed by the party-pleasing productions of Joey and Sylvia Robinson plus gorgeous grooves courtesy of the Sugar Hill house band (guitarist Skip McDonald, bassist Doug Wimbish, drummer Keith LeBlanc), Grandmaster Flash and company recorded most of rap's popular classics from the early '80s, providing a crucial bridge from the street-party aesthetic of the late '70s to Run-D.M.C.'s mid-'80s breakout. Rappers Melle Mel, Scorpio, Cowboy, Kid Creole, and Raheem were tied to old school delivery (carefully and slowly phrased), but they did it better than all the others and had the DJ as well as the tracks to match. Flash & the Five also had the most diversity of any other early rap group, encompassing the refreshing Furious Five/Sugarhill Gang collaboration "Showdown" (more a posse track than a battle), a gritty street-level snapshot of modern life (rap's all-time classic "The Message"), and the vocoder paranoia of "Scorpio." Rhino could've done a better job without too much trouble (simply swapping an ineffective new Megamix with the DJ landmark "Adventures on the Wheels of Steel" would go a long way), but *Message from Beat Street* is still the best introduction to the authors of old school's greatest hits.

John Bush

Adventures of Grandmaster Flash, Melle Mel & the Furious Five: More of the Best
July 1996, Rhino

Although much of Grandmaster Flash's best, biggest, and most groundbreaking work was compiled on *Message From Beat Street: The Best Of, The Adventures of Grandmaster Flash: More of the Best* is necessary for any comprehensive rap collection. The rest of Grandmaster Flash's most important singles, many of which have not appeared on compact disc before, are corralled onto this single-disc. On the whole, the album concentrates on the group's latter-day efforts for Elektra Records, but the cream of the album is the handful of singles for Sugar Hill, including the pioneering "The Adventures of Grandmaster Flash on the Wheels of Steel," which presents the group at its freshest and most innovative. Some of the Elektra recordings are a little rote and by-the-book, but the Sugarhill songs help make this an essential purchase.

Stephen Thomas Erlewine

Adventures on the Wheels of Steel
1999, Sequel

For old-school fanatics who need still more Sugar Hill material, even after Rhino's massive five-disc set *The Sugar Hill Records Story*, Sequel packaged a three-disc box of material recorded by Grandmaster Flash and the Furious Five (plus a few cuts headed by Grandmaster Melle Mel). *Adventures on the Wheels of Steel* spans all the way from their earliest, pre-Sugar Hill recordings (the great singles "Super Rappin' No.

1" and "Flash to the Beat") to the mid-'80s material recorded after Grandmaster Flash split from Sugar Hill (both he and Melle Mel headed collectives composed of former members of the Furious Five). Of course, anyone even vaguely interested in this set is already going to own quite a few of these tracks, from the big Furious Five hits "The Message" and "White Lines" to much-anthologized classics like "Birthday Party," "New York New York," "The Showdown," "Scorpio," and "Message II (Survival)." Where this collection really begins to excel, and attract collectors, is the large number of rarities included. Sure, most old-school fans have "The Adventures of Grandmaster Flash on the Wheels of Steel," but how many have even heard Melle Mel's 1984 update "The New Adventures of Melle Mel"? And the Furious Five were well-known for their social critiques, but after Grandmaster Flash left the fold the group continued to record solid message tracks like "Jesse" (for Jesse Jackson's 1984 presidential campaign), the con-man game "Hustlers Convention," and "Vice." Truth to tell, there are only a pair of unreleased tracks on *Adventures on the Wheels of Steel*, but at least half of these 34 tracks have never been seen on compact disc.

John Bush

The Official Adventures of Grandmaster Flash
January 2002, Strut

Leave it to the archivists at Strut to uncover another facet of the near-legendary New York dance scene of the '70s and '80s. After releases from Larry Levan and Danny Krivit shedding light on what it meant to go clubbing in the late '70s, the label moved to hip-hop—that other musical phenomenon of the era—with *The Official Adventures of Grandmaster Flash*. Half mix album and half history lesson, the compilation cuts back and forth between interviews, vintage or newly recorded turntable sessions, and a few old-school standalones—Babe Ruth's "The Mexican," Kraftwerk's "Trans Europe Express," Yellow Magic Orchestra's "Computer Games"—to get listeners in the mood. Only two of the seven mix sessions are old, though the new mixes were apparently done the same way they would've if he'd been allowed his own mix album in 1982 instead of 2002. (It's a fact obviously hard to prove, but the closest he got at the time, 1981's seven-minutes-of-madness single "The Adventures of Grandmaster Flash on the Wheels of Steel," is still breathtaking.) The new mixes sound just as good, with the master flashing across the spectrum of '70s dance—from Parliament to Thin Lizzy to Cerrone to Spoonie Gee to the Eagles—with deft flicks of the wrist serving as all the transition he needs. The 20-page color liners, produced with Frank Broughton and Bill Brewster (of the mixing history lesson *Last Night a DJ Saved My Life*), are the next best thing to a full video documentary. It's just slightly less revelatory than Strut's crown jewel, Larry Levan's *Live at the Paradise Garage* (mostly because few knew that one existed), but *The Official Adventures of Grandmaster Flash* is still the best look at the best DJ in history.

John Bush

6 Feet Deep
August 1994, V2

6 Feet Deep is a sick joke. A lethally great and a ghoulishly comical one, but a deranged and sadistic prank nonetheless. Eschatological, gruesome, paranoid, and obsessed with death (both imposing and experiencing it), the debut from eeeeevil supergroup Gravediggaz lands somewhere in the nexus at which the bizarro universe of legendary producer Prince Paul—who oversees the whole project while wearing the mask and wielding the shovel of the Undertaker for the occasion—crashes headlong into RZA's dingy, farcical New York City, a haunted, inverse Oz where graffiti meets science fiction meets splatter flick in an unholy alliance that finds Freddy Krueger fiendishly pursuing the turf gangs out of Walter Hill's *The Warriors* down 125th and Elm Streets. Throw in a few crazed variations on Medieval torture techniques, a few too many midnight kung-fu screenings, and a few fantasies of bodily damage so giddily, demonically cartoonish that they would make Wile E. Coyote lick his lips with mischievous envy, and you have this brilliantly strange, whimsically jagged horror film in song (critics unofficially dubbed the style horrorcore) with its maimed and gnawed tongue firmly planted in cheek. If you can stomach the buckets of lyrical blood spilled herein, there is no end to the gory highlights, from the running-in-place nightmare of "Nowhere to Run, Nowhere to Hide" to the psychotically nauseous angel-dust high of "Defective Trip (Trippin')" to the willfully objectionable "1-800 Suicide" and self-destructive "Bang Your Head," all of them terribly catchy. As a bonus, *6 Feet Deep* is sure to offend the sensibilities of all middle-aged family-values crusaders and conservative-type politicians—vampires of a different sort—who aren't in on the joke. Overseas, the album was titled *Niggamortis*. With its combined allusion to mortality and example of wicked wordplay, it would have been even more apropos. Whatever it goes by, though, the album can be resurrected again and again without losing any of its devilishly good potency.

Stanton Swihart

Groove B Chill

Starting from Zero
1990, A&M

In and around 1990, records like these were the order of the day. Carefree and often downright silly rhymes about girls and high school dominated releases by De La Soul, the Jungle Brothers and A Tribe Called Quest. Fortunately, each of these groups as well as Groove B Chill were blessed with great production and ultimately that's what makes *Starting From Zero* even comparable to the classic debuts by the groups listed above. When rhyming over either the Prince Paul or Pete Rock-produced tracks, Groove B Chill give the impression that they can hang with the best of them but on their self-produced numbers it becomes clear that they simply weren't up to the task. To their defense, though, comparing this LP to *3 Feet High and Rising*, *Straight Out the Jungle*, *Done by the Forces of Nature* or *People's Instinctive Travels and the Paths of Rhythm* isn't entirely fair. Not everyone, after all, is capable of making an undisputed hip-hop classic. Inconsistent as it might be, though, with Pete Rock at the controls on "Starting From Zero" and "There It Is" and Prince Paul on "Let It Roll" and "Top of the Hill" one can be assured that at least a handful of jams here could turn a party out. These tracks alone are worth the price of admission while "Let It Roll" in particular is reminiscent of the style Prince Paul employed on De La Soul's stellar debut.

Brandon Burke

Gucci Crew

The Best of Gucci Crew II
August 1994, Hot Productions

Perhaps more than any other strain of rap, bass music is a singles game, since very few groups and producers—save for 2 Live Crew and DJ Magic Mike—have been able to deliver albums that are solid from front to back. Gucci Crew exemplifies this notion, since they released plenty of studio albums with scattered highlights and plenty of fluff. That's why compilations like this one come in very handy—*The Best of Gucci Crew II* pulls from *G4* (1985), *What Time Is It? It's Gucci Time* (1989), *Everybody Wants Some* (1991), and *So Def, So Fresh, So Stupid* (1991). Both "Shirley" and its raunchier successor/update "Sally (That Girl)" are on this disc, as are "Truz 'n' Vogues," "The Cabbage Patch," and "Five Dollar High" (a surprising Top 20 rap hit). Since this contains every noteworthy moment from Gucci Crew's history, there is no need to deal with any of the group's proper albums.

Andy Kellman

Guru

Jazzmatazz, Vol. 1
1993, Chrysalis

Though it can reasonably be argued that rap grew almost directly out of funk and its particular beat, there are a lot of overlaps with jazz, particularly the bop and post-bop eras: the uninhibited expression, the depiction of urban life, just to name two. Jazz samples have also had a large role in hip-hop, but the idea of rapping over actual live jazz wasn't truly fully realized until Gang Starr MC Guru created and released the first in his *Jazzmatazz* series in 1993, with guest musicians who included saxophonist Branford Marsalis (who had previously collaborated with DJ Premier and Guru for the track "Jazz Thing" on the *Mo' Better Blues* soundtrack), trumpeter Donald Byrd, vibraphonist Roy Ayers, guitarist Ronny Jordan, and keyboardist Lonnie Liston Smith, as well as vocalist N'Dea Davenport (also of the acid jazz group the Brand New Heavies) and French rapper MC Solaar. While Guru's rhymes can occasionally be a little weak ("Think they won't harm you? Well they might/And that ain't right, but every day is like a fight" are the lines he chooses to describe kids on the subway in Brooklyn in "Transit Ride"), he delves into a variety of subject matter, from the problems of inner-city life to his own verbal prowess to self-improvement without ever sounding too repetitive, and his well-practiced flow fits well with the overall smooth, sultry, and intelligent feel of the album. From Jordan's solo on "No Time to Play" to Ayers' vibes expertise on "Take a Look (At Yourself)" to MC Solaar's quick and syllabic rhymes on "Le Bien, le Mal," *Jazzmatazz, Vol. 1* (and what turned out to be the best of the series) is a rap album for jazz fans and a jazz album for rap fans, skillful and smart, clean when it needs to be and gritty when that's more effective, helping to legitimize hip-hop to those who doubted it, and making for an altogether important release.

Marisa Brown

Jazzmatazz, Vol. 2: The New Reality
July 1995, Chrysalis

The follow-up to the heavily acclaimed *Jazzmatazz, Vol. 1*. This album might not have quite as much jazz-rap power as the first volume did, but it's still quite good. Some of the big guns of jazz found their way into the album, including Branford Marsalis (who, of course, had already experimented with urban beats a bit with his Buckshot Lefonque project), Freddie Hubbard, Ramsey Lewis, and Kenny Garrett. Underground rapper Kool Keith (at this point still a member of the Ultramagnetics) also makes an appearance. Dancehall reggae princess Patra is included on a track, as are Chaka Khan and Me'Shell N'Degeocello; Jamiroquai helps out in another. In some ways, the personnel on this album may be slightly superior to the first outing, but the music also seems a tiny bit blander. Still, what makes the *Jazzmatazz* albums special is the live synthesis of jazz and rap. With Guru's vocals over the top of live jazz performers (as opposed the usual samples), interplay is facilitated between the two, and thus a whole new dimension is added to the fusion. For someone interested in jazz-rap in general, the first album is a higher priority (as would be Us3's albums, with extensive Blue Note sampling), but this album is still high on the list.

Adam Greenberg

Heavy D

Big Tyme
June 1989, Uptown

Like Whodini, Heavy D. has managed to appeal to both R&B audiences and rap's hardcore. Indeed, Heavy shows strong R&B leanings on *Big Tyme*, his second album, which is definitely softer and more congenial than what one would have expected from Ice-T or Public Enemy that year. But the Long Island MC has a lot of technique—a fact that hardcore hip-hoppers couldn't overlook when hearing him let loose on such numbers as "Here We Go Again, Y'all," "More Bounce" and "You Ain't Heard Nuttin' Yet." Residents of the hood may have viewed the commercial appeal that "Somebody for Me" had suspiciously, but they couldn't ignore Heavy's obvious technique. Although not remarkable, *Big Tyme* is an enjoyable effort that works well as escapist party music.

Alex Henderson

Blue Funk
1992, Uptown

On his fourth release, Heavy D handed over the production duties to three of the hottest underground producers in the business at the time—Tony Dofat, DJ Premier, and his younger cousin Pete Rock—as well as excellent newcomer Jesse West, and the results are outstanding, if completely unlike any previous or subsequent Heavy D & the Boyz recording. Whereas the Heavster's style had always been positive and accessible before, careful not to come across as too confrontational or provocative, he came entirely streetwise on *Blue Funk*, altering (if only for the moment) his straight-laced reputation. Whether it was a deliberate attempt to shift creative

gears and explore different headspace—between each track there is a brief pseudo-therapeutic session—or merely a natural outgrowth of the circles in which the rapper was traveling at the time, the result is one of his least orthodox but most thoroughly satisfying efforts. It takes a moment to register that it is the Overweight Lover who is spitting out lyrics on "Who's the Man?," a song that even liberally quotes the non-upstanding Cypress Hill. He almost could have passed for Notorious B.I.G. (who, indeed, later shows up on the album) in a blind taste test. Of course, he didn't abandon his sensitivity entirely, as "Truthful," with its R&B hook, immediately makes clear, and still tossed several lovey-dovey cuts to the around-the-way girls. But the album decidedly hits with more force, from the smack-talking "Talk Is Cheap" right down to the final "A Buncha Niggas," on which D successfully orchestrates another top-notch posse cut along the lines of *Peaceful Journey*'s uncharacteristic "Don't Curse." Perhaps sonically the album veered too far from the commercial-ready sound that he had successfully mined up to that point, but *Blue Funk* managed only a lackluster reception from critics. (It was a slightly different story with the public, reaching certified gold status.) In any event, it remains a stellar, wholly underrated entry in his discography.

Stanton Swihart

Heavy Hitz
September 2000, MCA

Heavy Hitz is a near-definitive overview of Heavy D & the Boyz' pop-friendly dance-rap style, featuring not only the group's two big hits—"We Got Our Own Thang" and the Top Ten "Now That We Found Love"—but 13 more of their best tracks as well. And that's not as excessive as it might sound to casual observers; Heavy D had not only a good-natured persona and sense of humor, but also a deceptively nimble delivery on the mic, which helps enliven these already infectious party tunes. Heavy D also had a socially conscious side, recording the occasional ode to harmony between genders and races, but that isn't explored very much here; nonetheless, *Heavy Hitz* will likely be perfectly satisfactory for most listeners.

Steve Huey

House of Pain

House of Pain
July 1992, Tommy Boy

It's an album that ushered in an era of a thousand suburban-ites drinking malt liquor, wearing U.S. Postal Service caps, and reawakening their Irish (or in some cases pseudo-Irish) heritage. And it's also the debut album that ushered House of Pain into the forefront of rap culture for a brief period of time. While it's unfair to expect a whole album's worth of quality material like the dynamite classic "Jump Around," there are some strong points on their eponymous debut that emulate the single's strength. Admittedly, there is a significant amount of filler and the topics *du jour* aren't exactly the most original in hip-hop, but the impact of such songs as "Jump Around," "Shamrocks and Shenanigans," and "Put on Your Shit Kickers" more than makes up for the filler. A debut for a group that showed immense promise that sadly wasn't fully realized.

Rob Theakston

Same as It Ever Was
June 1994, Tommy Boy

House of Pain's self-titled album had its moments, but on the whole, wasn't very memorable. However, the Irish-American group really blossomed on its far-superior and much more hardcore second album, *Same as It Ever Was*. With this album, Everlast changed his style of rapping considerably and unveiled a much more distinctive and recognizable approach. Sounding twisted, damaged, and maniacal, Everlast grabs the listener's attention and refuses to let go on such wildly entertaining fare as "Back From the Dead," "Over There Shit," and "Runnin' Up on Ya." House of Pain's subject matter—namely, their superior rapping skills and the threat they pose to sucker MCs—is far from groundbreaking. But an abundance of strong, clever hooks and Everlast's psycho-like rapping make *Same as It Ever Was* consistently appealing.

Alex Henderson

Ice Cube

Kill at Will
1990, Priority

Ice Cube's riveting debut album, *AmeriKKKa's Most Wanted*, was still burning up the charts when Priority Records released this EP, which lacks that album's overall excellence but has its moments. With *Kill at Will*, Cube unveiled his engaging "The Product" and "Dead Homiez," a poignant lament for the victims of black-on-black crime that is among the best songs he's ever written. Enjoyable but not essential are remixes of "Endangered Species (Tales From the Darkside)" and the outrageous "Get Off My Dick and Tell Yo Bitch to Come Here." Clearly, *Kill at Will* was intended for hardcore fans rather than casual listeners. [The EP was later added to a 2003 expanded edition of *AmeriKKKa's Most Wanted*.]

Alex Henderson

AmeriKKKa's Most Wanted
May 1990, Priority

When Ice Cube split from N.W.A after the group's seminal *Straight Outta Compton* album changed the world forever, expectations were high, too high to ever be met by anyone but the most talented of artists, and at his most inspired. At the time Cube was just that. With *AmeriKKKa's Most Wanted* the rapper expanded upon *Compton*, making a more full-bodied album that helped boost the role of the individual in hip-hop. Save the dramatic intro where a mythical Ice Cube is fried in the electric chair, his debut is filled with eye-level views of the inner city that are always vivid, generally frightening, generally personal, and sometimes humorous in the gallows style. Ripping it quickly over a loop from George Clinton's "Atomic Dog," Cube asks the question that would be central to his early career, "Why there more niggas in the pen than in college?," while sticking with the mutual distrust and scare tactics N.W.A used to wipe away any hopes of reconciliation ("They all scared of the Ice Cube/And what I say what I portray and all that/And ain't even seen the gat"). "What I'm kicking to you won't get rotation/Nowhere in the

nation" he spits on the classic "Turn Off the Radio," which when coupled with the intoxicating Bomb Squad production and Cube's cocksure delivery that's just below a shout, makes one think he's the only radio the inner city needs. The Bomb Squad's amazing work on the album proves they've been overly associated with Public Enemy, since their ability to adapt to *AmeriKKKa*'s more violent and quick revolution is underappreciated. Their high point is the intense "Endangered Species," a "live by the trigger" song that offers "It's a shame, that niggas die young/But to the light side it don't matter none." This street knowledge venom with ultra fast funk works splendidly throughout the album, with every track hitting home, although the joyless "You Can't Fade Me" has alienated many a listener since kicking a possibly pregnant woman in the stomach is a very hard one to take. Just to be as confusing as the world he lives in, the supposedly misogynistic Cube introduces female protégé Yo-Yo with "It's a Man's World" before exiting with "The Bomb," a perfectly unforgiving and visceral closer. Save a couple Arsenio Hall disses, *AmeriKKKa's Most Wanted* is a timeless, riveting exercise in anger, honesty, and the sociopolitical possibilities of hip-hop.

David Jeffries

Death Certificate
October 1991, Priority

If Ice Cube's debut was a shocking attack that proved the N.W.A legacy would be stronger divided, his sophomore effort was a new kind of superstar pulling off the miraculous, a follow-up that equals its classic predecessor and tops it in some people's books. With a million copies of *Death Certificate* preordered, Cube was no longer the rock critics' darling. A million people listening was dangerous, especially since he was now slithering his influence into the suburbs. If the black rage didn't get you, the misogyny of "I'm gonna do my thing, with your daughter" probably would. Here, one of rap's greatest storytellers is able to draw hatred in under a minute with the short and direct "Black Korea," an angry protest song concerning Korean grocers that got him dubbed "racist" and "Ice KKKube" by some. The track is an extreme representation of how a much sharper and cutting this album is when compared with his debut, and even though the intro announces the full-length is divided into a "Death Side" and "Life Side," both are equally bleak. With the CD format, the two sides are indistinguishable and run over the listener with fast tales of drug dealing, drive-by shootings, and women who go from "Ms. Thing to Ms. Gonorrhea." This would be numbing if it weren't for the rapper's amazing lyrics, ground-shaking delivery, and insight like when "A Bird in the Hand" deals with the irony of selling crap to buy diapers ("Gotta serve you food that might give you cancer/Cuz my son doesn't take no for answer"). A bit of sweet relief comes with the brightness of the great single "Steady Mobbin'" and with the nostalgia and slow tempo of "Doing Dumb Shit." "True to the Game" ("Ain't that a bitch/They hate to see a young nigga rich") is arguably the quintessential Cube track and if all this weren't enough already, the N.W.A diss "No Vaseline" hangs off the album like a crowd-pleasing, Brick-sampling encore. Although next year's *Predator* would be a bigger hit, *Death Certificate* brings to a close the man's trilogy of perfect albums that began with N.W.A's *Compton* and explodes into a supernova right here.

David Jeffries

The Predator
November 1992, Priority

Released in the aftermath of the 1991 L.A. riots, *The Predator* radiates tension. Ice Cube infuses nearly every song, and certainly every interlude, with the hostile mood of the era. Even the album's most laid-back moment, "It Was a Good Day," emits a quiet sense of violent anxiety. Granted, Ice Cube's previous albums had been far from gentle, but they were filled with a different kind of rage. On both *AmeriK-KKa's Most Wanted* (1990) and *Death Certificate* (1991), he took aim at society in general: women, whites, Koreans, even his former group members in N.W.A. Here, Ice Cube is more focused. He found a relevant episode to magnify with the riots, and he doesn't hold back, beginning with the absolutely crushing "When Will They Shoot?" The song's wall of stomping sound sets the dire tone of *The Predator* and is immediately followed by "I'm Scared," one of the many disturbing interludes comprised of news commentary related to the riots. It's only during the aforementioned "It Was a Good Day" that Ice Cube somewhat alleviates this album's smothering tension. It's a truly beautiful moment, a career highlight for sure. However, the next song, "We Had to Tear This Mothafucka Up," eclipses the relief with yet more calamity. By the time you get to the album-concluding "Say Hi to the Bad Guy" and its mockery of policeman, hopelessness prevails. *The Predator* is a grim album, for sure, more so than anything Ice Cube would ever again record. In fact, the darkness is so pervasive that the wit of previous albums is absolutely gone. Besides the halfhearted wit of "Gangsta's Fairytale, Pt. 2," you won't find any humor here, just tension. Given this, it's not one of Ice Cube's more accessible albums despite boasting a few of his biggest hits. It is his most serious album, though, as well as his last important album of the '90s.

Jason Birchmeier

Ice-T

Rhyme Pays
1987, Sire

Before Ice-T's ascension, L.A. rappers were known primarily for a synthesizer-dominated sound indebted to Kraftwerk's innovations as well as Afrika Bambaataa's 1982 hit, "Planet Rock." While L.A. did have its share of hardcore rappers in the mid-'80s (including Toddy Tee, King Tee, and of course, Ice-T), hardcore rap was dominated by the East Coast. That begin to change in 1987, when Ice-T's debut album, *Rhyme Pays*, was released and sold several hundred thousand copies. Hard-hitting offerings like "409," "Make It Funky," and the title song (which samples Black Sabbath's "War Pigs" and underscores the L.A. resident's love of heavy metal) left no doubt that Ice had very little in common with the Egyptian Lover, the World Class Wreckin' Cru, or the L.A. Dream Team. The album doesn't contain as much gangsta rap as some of his subsequent releases, but it did have enough to stir some controversy. On "Squeeze the Trigger," "Pain," and a new version of "6 'N the Mornin'" (which had been the B-side of Ice's 1986 single "Doggin' the Wax" on Techno-Hop), Ice portrays ruthless felons and raps candidly about

the horrors of the urban ghetto he'd been only too familiar with. With the release of *Rhyme Pays*, the West Coast was well on its way to becoming a crucial part of hip-hop.

Alex Henderson

Power
1988, Sire

As riveting as *Rhyme Pays* was, Ice-T did hold back a little and avoided being too consistently sociopolitical. But with the outstanding *Power*, the gloves came all the way off, and Ice didn't hesitate to speak his mind about the harsh realities of inner-city life. On "Drama," "Soul on Ice" (an homage to his idol Iceberg Slim), "High Rollers," and other gangsta rap gems, Ice embraces a first-person format and raps with brutal honesty about the lives of gang members, players, and hustlers. Ice's detractors took the songs out of context, arguing that he was glorifying crime. But he countered that, in fact, he was sending out an anti-crime message in a subliminal fashion and stressed that the criminals he portrayed ended up dead or behind bars. Another track that some misconstrued was "I'm Your Pusher," an interpretation of Curtis Mayfield's "Pusherman" that doesn't promote the use of drugs, but uses double entendres to make an anti-drug statement. (Ice has always been vehemently outspoken in his opposition to drugs.) In the next few years, gangsta rap would degenerate into nothing more than cheap exploitation and empty clichés, but in Ice's hands, it was as informative as it was captivating.

Alex Henderson

The Iceberg/Freedom of Speech...Just Watch What You Say
October 1989, Sire

Ice-T threw listeners quite a curve ball with his riveting third album, *The Iceberg/Freedom of Speech... Just Watch What You Say*—arguably the closest hip-hop has come to George Orwell's *1984*. Instead of focusing heavily on gangsta rap, Ice-T made First Amendment issues the CD's dominant theme. Setting the album's tone is the opener, "Shut Up, Be Happy," which finds guest Jello Biafra (former leader of punk band Dead Kennedys) envisioning an Orwellian America in which the government controls and dominates every aspect of its citizens' lives. Though there are a few examples of first-rate gangsta rap here—including "The Hunted Child" and the chilling "Peel Their Caps Back"—Ice's main concern this time is censorship and what he views as a widespread attack on free speech in the U.S. As angry and lyrically intense as most of *The Iceberg* is, Ice enjoys fun for its own sake on "My Word Is Bond" and "The Girl Tried to Kill Me"—an insanely funny rap-rock account of an encounter with a dominatrix.

Alex Henderson

O.G. Original Gangster
May 1991, Sire

One of gangsta rap's defining albums, *O.G. Original Gangster* is a sprawling masterpiece that stands far and away as Ice-T's finest hour. Taken track by track, *O.G.* might not seem at first like the product of a unified vision; perspective-wise, it's all over the map. There's perceptive social analysis, chilling violence, psychological storytelling, hair-trigger rage, pleas for solutions to ghetto misery, cautionary morality tales, and cheerfully crude humor in the depictions of sex and defenses of street language. But with a few listens, it's possible to assimilate everything into a complex, detailed portrait of Ice-T's South Central L.A. roots—the album's contradictions reflect the complexities of real life. That's why the more intelligent, nuanced material isn't negated by the violence and sexism—both of which, incidentally, are held relatively in check, with the former having been reshaped into a terrifying but inescapable fact of life. That isn't to say that *O.G. Original Gangster* is designed to appeal to delicate intellectual sensibilities; it's still full of raw, street-level aggression that makes no apologies or concessions. That goes for the music as well as the lyrics. The beats are a little too hard-driving and jittery to really breathe like funk, which only adds to the dark, claustrophobic feel of the production. Ice smoothly keeps up with the music's furious pace and also debuts his soon-to-be-notorious metal band Body Count on one track. That kind of artistic ambition is all over the album, whether in the lean musical attack or the urgent rhymes. *O.G. Original Gangster* is a certifiable gangsta rap classic, and arguably the most realistic, unvarnished representation of a world Ice-T was the first to chronicle on record.

Steve Huey

Greatest Hits: The Evidence
August 2000, Atomic Pop

Ice-T, the self-proclaimed "original gangster" of rap, is one of the few hip-hop artists who truly deserves a greatest-hits compilation. In a genre marked by overnight sensations, rapidly changing trends, and fans with short memories, he put together a long career marked by both consistency and innovation. This 16-track compilation, put together by Ice-T himself, covers 14 years, seven albums, and the title themes for two films (*Colors* and *New Jack City*), but fortunately concentrates primarily on the first five years of his career, when he was at his productive peak. Two more recent songs on this release were not previously domestically available, a U.K. remix of "The Lane," which doesn't add anything to the original, and the unreleased track "Money, Power, Women." Both are decent but should have been left off in favor of older, better classics. Fairly informative liner notes describe the creative process behind each song and each album from Ice-T's perspective. Most of the singles and recognizable songs are included here, with the mysterious exception of "Lifestyles of the Rich and Infamous" and "Gotta Lotta Love," which honored the gang truce in the wake of the L.A. riots. Also excluded are memorably risqué songs, such as "Girls L.G.B.N.A.F." and "Girl Tried to Kill Me," and some of Ice-T's more adventurous collaborations, including Body Count, the forerunner to Limp Bizkit and other rap-metal groups. These exceptions are peripheral, however, and the meat of his career is included here.

Luke Forrest

Jeru the Damaja

The Sun Rises in the East
May 1994, Payday

DJ Premier's first album-length production outside of Gang Starr was his best by far. Where Premier's productions hadn't shone underneath the cracking, over-earnest vocals of Guru, with a superior stylist like Jeru these tracks became brilliant musical investigations with odd hooks (often detuned bells, keys, or vibes), perfectly scratched upchoruses, and the grittiest, funkiest Brooklynese beats pounding away in the background. Of course, the star of the show was Jeru, a cocksure young rapper who brought the dozens from the streets to a metaphysical battleground where he did battle with all manner of foe—the guy around the corner on "D. Original" or an allegorical parade of hip-hop evils on "You Can't Stop the Prophet." The commentary about inner-city plagues arising from spiritual ignorance only continued on "Ain't the Devil Happy," with Jeru preaching knowledge of self as the only rescue from greed and violence. Jeru also courted some controversy with "Da Bichez," at first explaining, "I'm not talkin' 'bout the queens...not the sisters...not the young ladies," but later admitting his thoughts ("most chicks want minks, diamonds, or Benz"). His flow and delivery were natural, his themes were impressive, and he was able to make funky rhymes out of intellectual hyperbole like: "Written on these pages is the ageless wisdom of the sages/Ignorance is contagious." It lacks a landmark track, but *The Sun Rises in the East* stands alongside Nas' *Illmatic* (released the same year, and also boasting the work of Premier) as one of the quintessential East Coast records.

John Bush

J.J. Fad

Supersonic
1988, Ruthless

The ladies of J.J. Fad will forever be remembered for their one and only hit, "Supersonic," and rightfully so, yet their debut album of the same name does have its merits, especially in retrospect. *Supersonic* is very much a product of its time and place, namely 1988 Los Angeles, which, of course, brings to mind *Straight Outta Compton*-era N.W.A, whose production team (Dr. Dre, Yella, and the Arabian Prince) is notably at the helm of this ten-track album. Here, Dre and company don't look to the future of West Coast hardcore rap as they concurrently did on *Straight Outta Compton*; rather, they look back to their respective mid-'80s West Coast electro beginnings. This old-school style of beatmaking suits MC J.B., Baby D, and Sassy C well as that's precisely the style of their rapping, not to mention their lingo ("time to come correct," "cold gettin' stupid," etc.) and fashion sense (peep the wonderful cover photo—spandex, stopwatches, gold chains, big sunglasses, bigger hair, etc.). There unfortunately aren't any lost gems here on *Supersonic* that rival the magnificence of the title track, but there's a great cut-up instrumental remix ("Eeenie Meenie Beats") along with some impressive rhyming and plenty of amazing electro-rap beats. Along the way you'll frustratingly have to endure some awkward pop-isms, chief among them the sung hook of "Way Out" and the entirety of "Is It Love." If you can overlook these moments, or better yet skip over them, there's a bounty of old-school delights here, not to mention the party-starting title track. Not an album to be taken too seriously, *Supersonic* remains a fun novelty that deserves the occasional revival, even if only for the sake of slight amusement.

Jason Birchmeier

The Jonzun Crew

Jonzun Crew
November 1983, Tommy Boy

Despite including most of Jonzun Crew's best tracks, their debut album, *Lost in Space*, wasn't a successful LP. The Boston group with roots in funk were lousy songwriters at this point (more was to come from Maurice Starr), and what's worse, they insisted on writing songs instead of sticking with solid electro parts jams like their singles classics "Pack Jam" and "Space Is the Place." Admittedly, the process did pay minor commercial dividends; "Space Cowboy" became a moderate R&B hit, though its electric interpolation of the trademark whistle from "The Good, the Bad & the Ugly" was hardly the stuff of legend. They sounded appropriately cool on the opener "We Are the Jonzun Crew," but the rest of the non-singles material was stiff and formulaic. Far better to find Jonzun Crew's two landmarks on an old-school/electro compilation. A 2001 reissue on Tommy Boy enticed consumers with two bonus tracks, one of which was Grooverider's drum'n'bass update of "Pack Jam (Look out for the OVC)."

John Bush

Jungle Brothers

Straight Out the Jungle
1988, Warlock

The landmark opening salvo from the Jungle Brothers, *Straight out the Jungle* was also the very first album from the Native Tongues posse, which would utterly transform hip-hop over the next few years. That alone would be enough to make it a groundbreaking release, but *Straight out the Jungle* also contains the musical seeds for a number of soon-to-be-dominant trends. Their taste for jazzy horn samples helped kick-start the entire jazz-rap movement, and their concurrent James Brown fixation was one of the first to follow Eric B. & Rakim's lead. Plus, the group's groundbreaking collaboration with legendary house producer Todd Terry, "I'll House You," is also here; it paved the way for numerous hip-house

hybrids that shot up the dance and pop charts over the next few years. The lyrics were often as cerebral as the music was adventurous and eclectic, appealing to the mind rather than the gut—and the fact that rap didn't necessarily have to sound as though it were straight off the streets was fairly revelatory at the time. "Black Is Black" and the title cut are some of the first flowerings of Afrocentric hip-hop, but the group isn't always so serious; "I'm Gonna Do Yuz," "Behind the Bush," and the sly classic "Jimbrowski" are all playfully sexy without descending into misogyny. To modern ears, *Straight out the Jungle* will likely sound somewhat dated—the raw, basement-level production is pretty rudimentary even compared to their second album, and makes the jazz-rap innovations a bit difficult to fully comprehend, plus the album ends on several throwaways. But it is possible to hear the roots of hip-hop's intellectual wing, not to mention a sense of fun and positivity that hearkened back to the music's earliest Sugar Hill days—and that's why *Straight out the Jungle* ultimately holds up.

Steve Huey

Done by the Forces of Nature
November 1989, Warner Bros.

The follow-up to their groundbreaking debut, *Done By the Forces of Nature* is the point where the Jungle Brothers' production catches up to their musical ambition. There's still a ruddy, lo-fi edge to the record, but the samples are more abundant and intricately woven, and there's an altogether fuller sound that gives the group a greater presence. Moreover, the group's non-musical ideas come into greater focus as well. The Native Tongues' Afrocentric philosophy gets a more extensive airing here than on the debut, filling the record with positive consciousness-raising, both cultural ("Acknowledge Your Own History," "Black Woman," "Beyond This World") and spiritual (the title cut, "In Dayz 2 Come"); there are even the occasional lyrical asides concerning good dietary habits. All of this makes *Done by the Forces of Nature* one of the most intellectual hip-hop albums released up to that point, but as before, the group tempered their cerebral bent with a healthy sense of humor and fun. Thanks to the improved production, the J.Beez are able to take it to the dancefloor better than ever before, and toss in some pure, good-time, booty-shaking grooves in the hits "What U Waitin' For" and "U Make Me Sweat." There's also "Belly Dancin' Dina," a narrative that echoes the playful come-ons of the debut, and proves that progressive thinking and respect for women don't necessarily have to cool the libido. Late in the album, the posse cut "Doin' Our Own Dang" offers the chance to hear most of the Native Tongues—Tribe, De La, *and* Latifah—dropping rhymes all in one place. Through it all, the J.Beez construct an eclectic musical backdrop borrowed from jazz, early R&B, funk, African music, and more. Even if *Straight out the Jungle* was the historical landmark, *Done by the Forces of Nature* feels more realized in many respects, and is arguably the more satisfying listen.

Steve Huey

J. Beez Wit the Remedy
June 1993, Warner Bros.

Willfully difficult, ceaselessly sarcastic and playful, the Jungle Brothers had more talent than virtually all of their contemporaries in alternative rap, but often squandered it taking detours that did little to endear them to hip-hop fans. Four long years after their Native Tongues family had emerged with the success of De La Soul's *3 Feet High and Rising*, the Jungle Brothers finally returned with their third record. Expectations were very high, from fans and their label (Warner

Bros.), but if the JBs didn't exactly bring the remedy with this one, they still featured an obtuse playfulness sorely lacking in hip-hop. Mike Gee and Baby Bam didn't have as much to say as A Tribe Called Quest or even De La Soul; most of the songs here are loved-up sex raps or weed fantasies, and the group deliberately blurs the lines between the two, getting dangerously close to objectifying a woman on "Spark a New Flame," but speaking lovingly of marijuana on "I'm in Love With Indica." The chorus on the hilariously titled satire "My Jimmy Weighs a Ton" (a clear Public Enemy reference) skates back and forth between a sweet diva and a hardcore jam. The productions, virtually all of them by the Jungle Brothers alone, are freewheeling and unpredictable, but vary in quality from intriguing to downright misguided.

John Bush

Just-Ice

Back to the Old School
1986, Sleeping Bag

It's impossible to describe how fresh this album sounded when first released—producer Kurtis Mantronik utilizes the Roland 606 drum machine more potently than any producer before and as its huge beats kick holes beneath Just-Ice's gold-toothed mumble of rhymes, curses, boasts, and yelps, the party gets underway. Back in 1986, this album burned eardrums and if now it sounds less revolutionary it remains a classic early hip-hop album, one that appeared as radical back then as the RZA's production of Wu-Tang Clan did in the late '90s. Neither Mantronik nor Just-Ice were to match it in their subsequent and separate solo work—it's worth reflecting on what might have been created if their partnership had endured. Opening track "Cold Gettin' Dumb" remains one of the most exhilarating tracks from an era when hip-hop was inventing itself day by day. The chauvinistic "Latoya" booms with block-rockin' beats. "Gangster of Hip Hop" and "Little Bad Johnny" lay the seeds for many an ominous rapper to come.

Garth Cartwright

Kool & Deadly
1987, Sleeping Bag

Subtitled "Justicizms," this album boasts one of the ugliest covers ever—a close up of Just-Ice's snarling gold dental work—and the sounds included are equally harsh. Producer KRS-One does not try and emulate Kurtis Mantronic's high-tech polyrhythms and samples, instead he strips the sound right back and keeps things very raw: at times there's little more here than Just-Ice's gruff vocals and the sound of a wheezing drum machine. Some old school fans rate this as the best album by the artist simply because it is so remorseless and raw. Perhaps the trick for newcomers is to check this album first and, if it interests you, then go to *Back to the Old School* for desert. Fans of KRS-One will want to own the record simply to hear him and Just-Ice trading rhymes

on "Moshitup." The standout track is "Going Way Back," where Just-Ice rasps one of the first hip-hop history lessons and dares you to disagree that Brooklyn is where it all began. Ruff stuff.

Garth Cartwright

The Desolate One
1989, Fresh

KRS-One is back at the controls and appears uninterested in changing the stark production formula he employed for *Kool & Deadly*. Of more interest is Just-Ice's rhymes, which have taken on a more detailed and darker worldview—on "Welfare Recipient" he delivers savage ghetto prose of a kind perhaps only the Geto Boys and Ghostface Killah have matched. He's also been listening to Jamaican dancehall records—at the time in New York, there appeared to be a real crossover between the two genres—and he chats in an effective ragamuffin style on "Sleng Teng" and "Na Touch da Just." Not a bad record by any means, but the limitations of Just-Ice's rhyming style and KRS-One's inability to develop his musical soundscape beyond elemental posed real problems for both of them as 1990 dawned and West Coast G-funk was about to sweep all before it.

Garth Cartwright

KC Flightt

In Flightt
1989, RCA

Difficult to categorize and difficult to market, KC Flightt is a unique rapper who has remained in obscurity. Flightt, unlike most rappers, doesn't always rhyme, and can be quite angular and abstract. On his imaginative and visionary debut album, *In Flightt*, he draws on influences ranging from jazz to house music—and is considerably more musical and melodic than most rappers. Not terribly easy to absorb, this cerebral effort must be listened to several times in order to be fully appreciated. In the mid-'90s, Flightt resurfaced in the band of jazz saxophonist Bill Evans (who has been featuring rappers in much the same way jazz artists feature singers) but wasn't nearly as cerebral as he is on *In Flightt*.

Alex Henderson

Kid 'N Play

2 Hype
1988, Select

Kid 'n Play have been unfairly branded as pop sellouts over the years, despite the fact that they really never had a big crossover hit single. It was more their image that crossed over—they had their own unique sense of visual style, yet they were positive, non-threatening, and, well, too gosh-darn *friendly* for the taste of street-level purists. Plus, they were young and clean-cut enough for middle-class teenage audiences to identify with. Accusations of being soft notwithstanding, those qualities are exactly what give their debut album, *2 Hype*, its refreshing charm. There isn't much on the duo's minds other than friendship, dancing, and dating, and everything stays pretty innocent—Kid even confesses to being shy around girls on "Undercover." If all of this seems safe and lightweight, it's also a tremendous amount of good, clean fun. Hurby "Luv Bug" Azor's production keeps things danceable and engaging throughout; the sound is fairly spare, with funky and occasionally club-friendly beats, catchy instrumental hooks behind the choruses, and basic DJ scratching. The whole album is pretty consistent, and the songs that were singles—"Rollin' With Kid 'n Play," "Gittin' Funky," and "2 Hype"—are nearly matched by some of the album tracks, particularly "Brother Man Get Hip," the story songs "Last Night" and "Undercover," and the explanation of the duo's signature dance move, "Do the Kid 'n Play Kick Step." Neither Kid nor Play is a master technician on the mic, but they're both quite respectable, in contrast to some of the would-be pop idols who followed in the years to come. And even if its sound and style are very much of their time, *2 Hype* still holds up surprisingly well, thanks to Kid 'n Play's winning personalities.

Steve Huey

Kid 'n Play's Funhouse
1990, Select

Named after the duo's single from their hit film *House Party*, *Kid 'n Play's Funhouse* has more of the genial dance-rap that made Kid 'n Play's debut album a platinum-selling hit. This time out, the production is fuller and funkier, and the raps are correspondingly more ambitious in terms of tempo and flow—particularly Kid's, which makes sense since he was essentially the focal point. The lyrics are still chiefly about their partnership, their love of rap, and their love of dancing, but there's a distinct battle-MC tone present as well, which seems to indicate that the duo hopes to be taken more seriously as a mature hip-hop act. Individually, both rappers broaden their images based on the characters they played in *House Party*—Kid the reluctant star, Play the ladies' man—yet they're still wholesome at bottom. Their viewpoint crystallizes in "Back to Basics," a lament about hip-hop culture losing its innocent sense of fun and turning violent; it's a more self-aware stance that acknowledges their place in the spectrum. There's also an entertaining guest spot from Salt-N-Pepa on the Play-centered track "I Don't Know," in which Play comes out on the winning end of a love triangle. If *Kid 'n Play's Funhouse* doesn't have quite the same youthful charm as *2 Hype*, it's nonetheless a worthy successor that finds the duo progressing.

Steve Huey

King Tee

Act a Fool
November 1988, Capitol

Defiant, angry, confrontational, and bemused raps from King Tee on this late '80s rap release. While there's some blustering and macho/sexual posturing, there are also many moments where Tee's comments deserve close scrutiny. The production isn't as relentless in the number of fragments, samples, and snippets, or as intricately edited as many other recent hip-hop releases.

Ron Wynn

At Your Own Risk
September 1990, Capitol

Compton rapper King Tee's second album again blended humorous jibes, novelty cuts and some messages, but it was far different from most of what was coming from Compton by 1990. Such songs as "Do Your Thing," "Jay Fay Dray" and "On The Dance Tip" were light years away from N.W.A.-style "gangsta" rap. Even the more serious cuts, like "At Your Own Risk," were more reflective than combative or prophetic, and Tee's rapping was a mix of clowning, taunting and mocking, rather than declaring and challenging.

Ron Wynn

Kool G Rap & DJ Polo

Road to the Riches
March 1989, Cold Chillin'

Kool G Rap & DJ Polo's *Road to the Riches* had been a long time coming when Cold Chillin' released it in 1989. It didn't disappoint. After some successful singles and G Rap's contributions to Marley Marl's Juice Crew, the duo arrived almost fully formed on its debut. Whether boasting (his greatest strength at this point) or spinning tales (which would become his greatest strength), G Rap's knife-edged rhymes—delivered with the hardest-sounding lisp in hip-hop—tear through Marley Marl's productions and DJ Polo's scratching with all the ferocity of a pit bull devouring a piece of meat. Though tracks like "Poison," "It's a Demo," and the title track won this record a lot of respect, there are several other moments that help make this a remarkable debut. On "Men at Work," lines like, "I drop rhymes on paper and then build a skyscraper/When I die scientists will preserve my brain/Donate it to science to answer the unexplained" whip by so fast that it's easy to overlook Marl and Polo's perfectly snarling, densely percussive backdrop. Marl's imaginative sampling gleans from all sorts of unexpected sources, like the harmonica from Area Code 615's "Stone Fox Chase," the odd phasings of Kraftwerk's "Trans-Europe Express" (no one used it like this), and the burbling synths from Gary Numan's "Cars" (remember, this was the late '80s). G Rap's occasional homophobic and woman-hating lyrics, along with some production nuances that haven't aged well, are the only hindrances. Aside from that, *Road to the Riches* showed promise while providing a jolt in its own right.

Andy Kellman

Wanted: Dead or Alive
August 1990, Cold Chillin'

Marley Marl remained on board, and Large Professor and Eric B. also hopped on to help produce Kool G Rap & DJ Polo's second album. With a wider range of sounds and the expansion of G Rap's lyrical range, *Wanted: Dead or Alive* is wholly deserving of classic status. The opening "Streets of New York" remains one of the most thrilling and unique rap singles released; the sparse rhythm, adorned with assured piano runs that complement the song to the point of almost making the song, falls somewhere between a gallop and a strut, and G Rap outlines more vivid scenes than one film could possibly contain. The track cemented Kool G Rap & DJ Polo's role as East Coast legends and showed Kool G Rap's talent as an adept storyteller like nothing before or since. Likewise, "Talk Like Sex" is the nastiest, raunchiest thing he ever recorded, with "I'm pounding you down until your eyeballs pop out" acting as an exemplary claim—as well as one of the few that is printable—made in the song. The boasts, as ever, are in no short supply, but "Erase Racism" takes a break from the normal proceedings with guest spots from Big Daddy Kane and Biz Markie. It's both funny and sobering, with Biz Markie's Three Dog Night chorus providing comic relief after each verse. Adding yet another dimension to the album, DJ Polo throws in a hip-house instrumental that avoids coming off like a throwaway. This album is only part of a major swarm of brilliant rap records from 1990, but it will never be lost in it.

Andy Kellman

Live and Let Die
November 1992, Cold Chillin'

A strong case could be made for *Live and Let Die* as Kool G Rap & DJ Polo's crowning achievement. Who can really say for sure if the controversy surrounding the cover artwork—which shows the duo feeding steaks to a pair of rottweilers, in front of two noose-necked white men—clouded a proper consensus? With across-the-board stellar production help from Sir Jinx and Trakmasterz, G Rap (who also produces) thrives on his no-holds-barred narratives that peaked with *Wanted: Dead or Alive*'s "Streets of New York," but most everything on this album comes close to eclipsing that song. "Ill Street Blues" is practically a sequel to it, and it manages to use more swanky piano vamps and horn blurts without making for a desperate attempt at capitalizing on a past glory. Few tales of growing up in a life of crime hit harder than the title track, in which G Rap displays the traits—unforced frankness, that unmistakable voice, and a flow that drags you involuntarily along—that made him a legend. The album is one story after another that draws you in without fail, and they come at you from several angles. Whether pulling off a train heist, venting sexual frustration, analyzing his psychosis, or lording over the streets, G Rap is a pro at holding a captive audience. All die-hard East Coast rap fans, especially followers of the Notorious B.I.G., owe it to themselves to get real familiar with this album and the two that predated it. If you were to take this duo's best five songs away from them, they'd still be one of the top duos rap music has ever seen.

Andy Kellman

Kool Moe Dee

I'm Kool Moe Dee
1986, Jive

By the time he recorded this self-titled debut solo album, Kool Moe Dee was considered a veteran by hip-hop standards. The graduate of the Treacherous Three made no secret of the fact that he was among the founders of rap's old school—a term

used to describe Kurtis Blow, Grandmaster Flash & the Furious Five, the Sugarhill Gang, Spoonie G, and others who'd been rapping since the late '70s. This engaging album proved that Dee still had considerable technique, and could be a commanding storyteller. Lyrically, he is undeniably blunt, and this bluntness works to his advantage on such gems as "Little John," a reflection on an inner-city youth's life of crime; the anti-cocaine number "Monster Crack"; and the commentary on venereal disease "Go See the Doctor." Kool Moe Dee's infectious hit "Do You Know What Time It Is" was accused of being sexist, but such knee-jerk reactions to the song missed its point—the Harlem native was attacking materialistic women, not women in general. One of this album's producers is Teddy Riley, who went on to enjoy quite a bit of recognition a few years later as a member of the highly influential new jack swing outfit Guy.

Alex Henderson

How Ya Like Me Now
1987, Jive

Kool Moe Dee resented the fact that in the mid-to-late '80s, most of rap's founding fathers were enjoying little attention. But Dee himself was one of the few exceptions, and the old-school survivor had a major hit with his sophomore effort, *How Ya Like Me Now*. He would have done better to devote more time to storytelling and less time to boasting, but he definitely brings plenty of soul and spirit (as well as technique) to this material. Though not as strong as his first album, it definitely has its share of classics, including "Wild Wild West," a reflection on the nitty-gritty environment that surrounded rap during its early years; his denunciation of materialism "No Respect"; and the infectious title song, which was clearly inspired by Dee's feud with L.L. Cool J. A few years later, much of the rap world was sick to death of hearing about the feud, but in 1987, it was a major topic of conversation in hip-hop.

Alex Henderson

Knowledge Is King
May 1989, Jive

What was true of *How Ya Like Me Now* is certainly true of Kool Moe Dee's third solo album, *Knowledge Is King*—the hardcore rapper spends too much time boasting and doesn't devote enough time to his real strength: meaningful storytelling. Nonetheless, his soulful spirit and considerable technique make this effort worthwhile—not remarkable, but certainly engaging. The CD's strongest offerings include "Pump Your Fist," an angry denunciation of social injustice; "The Avenue," a description of a day in the hood; and the controversial attack on materialistic women "They Want Money." The latter was accused of being sexist, but Dee rightly countered that criticizing women who judge men by the size of their wallets rather than the size of their hearts or their brains isn't sexist—it's honest.

Alex Henderson

Greatest Hits
1993, Jive

With a history dating back to the early days of Sugar Hill Records, Kool Moe Dee was able to reinvent himself as a solo artist during the latter half of the '80s, and in the process helped rap transform from an underground party music into a cultural phenomenon. *Greatest Hits* collects 14 of the most essential items from this seminal figure, kicking off with his two best-known songs—the catchy "Wild Wild West" and the influential safe-sex rap "Go See the Doctor." His flow is most definitely old-school—nearly every couplet is squared off at the end—but his technique was in the top of its class for its pre-golden age time period ("Look at Me Now" is impressive by any standard). His chief rival was LL Cool J, and not just in the abstract sense—their on-record feud was the most legendary in early hip-hop, and it's chronicled here on "Let's Go," "Death Blow," and "How Ya Like Me Now." His MC boasts are among the best of their time, but he was also ambitious enough to tackle socially conscious material; apart from the aforementioned "Go See the Doctor," there's "No Respect," a cautionary tale of a street hustler who lost everything, and the Chuck D/KRS-One team-up "Rise 'n' Shine." His production is often heavy on the synths and drum machines, though there are also some James Brown-type samples; a few tracks are produced by new jack swing legend Teddy Riley, and those constitute some of the earliest work in his career. All in all, *Greatest Hits* is an essential look back at one of the greatest talents the old school ever produced.

Steve Huey

Kris Kross

Totally Krossed Out
March 1992, Ruffhouse

Totally Krossed Out, the debut album by kiddie-rap sensations Kris Kross, is so tailored to a particular audience in a particular time period that it's nearly impossible to judge by any objective standard. So let's try anyway. Producer Jermaine Dupri—still a teenager himself—wrote all the songs here, and he delivers a catchy, pop-friendly batch of tracks that manage to stay pretty consistently engaging (perhaps in part because they are short). The album's interview intro disses playground rivals Another Bad Creation (that would have been a *great* hip-hop feud) before segueing into the irresistible smash "Jump" (oh, just try and listen to it without smiling, you heartless grinch). Actually, the miggeda-miggeda-mack bit proves they're not bad rappers, if they're able to borrow technique from Das EFX—though they don't keep it up, if for no other reason than that kids want to understand the words to songs they like. And "Warm It Up" is nearly as good. Some of the album tracks are lyrically generic, but the story song "Party" finds Chris and Chris trying to sneak into a club to meet girlies. There are some surprisingly serious notes struck on "Lil' Boys in da Hood" and "A Real Bad Dream," which paint the duo as knowing street kids who are all too aware of the dangers they could easily fall into. There's nothing terribly frightening, but it's more realistic than the innocent bubblegum you might expect. Of course, then there's the self-explanatory "I Missed the Bus." But overall, *Totally Krossed Out* isn't nearly as obnoxious or cutesy as adults might fear—even if the lads' MC boasts just make you want to pat them on the head.

Steve Huey

KRS-One

Return of the Boom Bap
September 1993, Jive

The reputation of Boogie Down Productions leader KRS-One began to slip in the early '90s as he spent more time educating than performing. He hit back at his critics with the slamming *Return of the Boom Bap*, his first official solo release. Leaving behind the detailed production of the last BDP album, *Sex and Violence*, *Boom Bap* returns the MC to the spare, gritty territory of *Criminal Minded*. KRS-One sounds reinvigorated, as well, spitting out his rhymes with fury and intelligence. Although the record isn't as didactic as *Edutainment* or *Sex and Violence*, KRS-One hasn't made his lyrics simplistic, nor has he abandoned his cutting, intelligent social commentary. The combination of hard, basic beats and exciting rhymes makes *Return of the Boom Bap* a genuine comeback for KRS-One, one of the founding figures of modern hip-hop.

Stephen Thomas Erlewine

Kwamé

Kwamé the Boy Genius: Featuring a New Beginning
1989, Atlantic

Kwamé's debut album, *Kwamé the Boy Genius: Featuring a New Beginning*, is an all-too-brief affair, clocking in at just over half an hour. Although it makes no explicit connection, it's a perfect fit with the Daisy Age revolution being spearheaded by De La Soul around the same time. Positive vibes and offbeat humor abound, and even if producer Hurby "Luv Bug" Azor is no Prince Paul, the music is bright, appealing, and funky. Despite a load of goofy boasts and disses, and an occasional reference to his Islamic faith, Kwamé doesn't take himself too seriously, and he keeps things upbeat and genial the whole way through. The album's centerpiece is the freewheeling narrative "The Man We All Know and Love," which quotes songs from *Sesame Street*, Louis Jordan, and Minnie Riperton (among others) as Kwamé seduces one of his mother's friends and then thinks better of it. It's proof that Kwamé is a sorely neglected figure today, even among fans of playful, intellectual hip-hop.

Steve Huey

A Day in the Life: A Pokadelick Adventure
1990, Atlantic

A Day in the Life: A Pokadelick Adventure is the definitive Kwamé album, a concept record about his life as a high schooler, and also the one where he created his signature visual style with a wardrobe full of polka dots. A self-described "quiet nerd type" who even brags about his excellent grammar on one cut, Kwamé navigates a world of bullies, crushes, immature girls, gossip-mongers, parties, bad report cards, and—of course—sucker MCs. A few songs don't seem to have much to do with the concept, but it hangs together pretty well musically, with buoyant, Daisy Age-flavored production (partly by Kwamé himself). "Ownlee Eue" and "Oneovdabigboiz" are underrated singles, and Kwamé shows off his storytelling talents on album cuts like "Da Man," "Therez a Partee Goinz On," and "Whoz Dat Guy."

A Day in the Life is filled with cartoonish, electronically altered voices commenting on the action and interacting with the bemused hero. It's all good-humored and colorful, if completely non-threatening, and it's too bad that Kwamé seems best-remembered today through disses by hardcore rappers like Tim Dog and the Notorious B.I.G. Sure, the polka dots are goofy, but in light of everything that's happened since then in hip-hop, they also hark back to a simpler, more innocent era, and there's nothing inherently wrong with that.

Steve Huey

L'Trimm

Grab It!
1988, Hot Productions

L'Trimm was the sort of pop-rap group that hip-hop's hardcore loves to hate. Tigra and Bunny D weren't great rappers, and their detractors argued that they made a mockery of rap with their cutesy, girlish image and their frivolous, often silly lyrics. But then, the Miami-based duo wasn't trying to be the female equivalent of Run-D.M.C.—its albums were aimed at dance-pop audiences, and L'Trimm didn't expect to impress fans of hardcore rap any more than Poison expected to be compared to Metallica. *Grab It!*, L'Trimm's debut album, must be taken for what it is: silly, goofy, escapist fun. From "Sexy" and "Better Yet L'Trimm" to the hit "Cars With the Boom," L'Trimm's very pop-minded, club-oriented songs are infectious and entertaining despite the group's obvious limitations. No one who's seriously into hip-hop would think for a minute that Tigra or Bunny have great rapping skills, but for this type of crossover album, you don't need them. You need the right hooks and beats, and this 1988 release succeeds on that level. L'Trimm went on to record a few more albums, but *Grab It!* remains its most consistent and appealing effort.

Alex Henderson

Leaders of the New School

A Future Without a Past...
1991, Elektra

Even in the vibrant early '90s hip-hop scene, *A Future Without a Past...* emerged as a breath of fresh air, simultaneously presenting a throwback to the old-school rhyme tradeoffs and call-and-response rapping styles of crews like the Furious Five and the Funky Four + One, and vaulting rap headlong into its future. Brash and full of youthful energy and exuberance, Leaders of the New School was the perfect meshing of three distinctly different but entirely complementary personalities whose flows flew in the face of conventional MC etiquette, from Dinco D.'s straightforward, intellectual tongue-twisting to Charlie Brown's zany shrieks to Busta Rhymes' viscous, reggae-inspired toasting—skirting the line between seriousness and humor—which, only a few years later, would help him to hit commercial pay dirt as a solo artist. That's not even to mention the DJ and sometime reggae-tinged emcee, DJ Cut Monitor Milo. The result is one of the most infectious rap albums ever created. The songs are, first and foremost, meant to be fun and humorous, and they are certainly that, particularly on Charlie Brown's nonsensical "What's the Pinocchio's Theory," the insistent "Trains, Planes and Automobiles" and "My Ding-A-Ling," and Busta

Rhymes' jovial ode to full-figured women, "Feminine Fatt." The cut-and-paste production is expert throughout, packed with fresh samples, thanks to Bomb Squad member Eric "Vietnam" Sadler, the Stimulated Dummies crew, and the Vibe Chemist Backspin, and the group also show themselves to be quite capable with a sampler, particularly Milo's incredible work on "Case of the P.T.A." and "My Ding-A-Ling." But it would be wrong to simply peg this album as a foray into kinder, gentler, more lighthearted and innocent hip-hop. Firstly, the album has the feel and scope of a loose concept album and is separated into three sections, the first two set in school, the final one following the members after school lets out, and that alone points to a group of young men—mostly still teenagers—trying to move rap into new dimensions. Secondly, the ambience of New York permeates *A Future Without a Past*, but it is simply presented from a younger and far less jaded perspective. Songs such as "Just When You Thought It Was Safe" and "Sound of the Zeekers @#^*?!," if not exactly hard-edged and political, offer far more than throwaway sentiment, and lyrically L.O.N.S. never descend into naiveté. The album portrays a group of young men who are fully emerged in the sometimes less-than-innocent urban life that characterizes hip-hop culture, but are also able to transcend the inherent limits and pitfalls to which that life can lead. In that sense, it is a celebration of all the best aspects of hip-hop culture and youth.

Stanton Swihart

T.I.M.E.
October 1993, Elektra

Far be it for anyone to claim that Leaders of the New School lacked ambition during their fascinating, far too short-lived career, which culminated on this follow-up to their exciting debut album. With *T.I.M.E.* the barely adult-aged members check in with their second loose concept album, this time delving into a sort of urban sci-fi mysticism. Obviously, the group doesn't entirely pull off this concept, and ther point understandably becomes murky or downright opaque. The ambition itself, however, is intriguing in practice, and the album is an endlessly interesting listen. Upon its release, many saw *T.I.M.E.* as a dramatic falloff from the manic, happy-go-lucky charm and vitality of the unit's first album, which had simply combusted in the hop-hop community when it was released two years earlier. In hindsight, *T.I.M.E.* is a much more mature work, both musically and lyrically, pushing forward into territories never hinted at in the first; as a whole, it's also arguably a more interesting album. In its own way, the production here is just as strong as that on the first album. It's far less loopy and idiosyncratic (and less novel) this time around, often just building off a dense beat and an ominous bassline, as on the hypnotic "Syntax Era," instead of pasting together all manner of samples. This approach gives the album much more sonic cohesion and intellectual heft, however. Easily, this is a much more hard-edged venture into the hip-hop underground aesthetic. The entire first half of the album is a dazzling sequence of songs, any of which, regardless of the concept, could have been brilliant singles. Songs such as

"Classic Material" (with an unforgettable horn hook), "Daily Reminder," and "Connections" relentlessly pound their way into your head, and in "A Quarter to Cutthroat," L.O.N.S. comes up with a sensational, gritty New York City and hip-hop anthem. A couple of the pieces on the record's second half don't maintain the same lofty heights as the first—the album is probably ten minutes or so too long—occasionally sounding redundant or flat. They are never complete missteps, however, and the posse cut "Spontaneous (13 MC's Deep)" gives the album its centerpiece. Alas, Busta Rhymes, having already fully reached his distinctive style, seemed a bit confined in the group dynamic here; not long after the album's release, he broke up the group and went solo.

Stanton Swihart

Da Lench Mob

Guerillas in tha Mist
1992, Street Knowledge/Atco

Looking like a cross between the Black Panthers and the Zapatistas on the album cover, Da Lench Mob fully embrace an urban revolutionary rhetoric consistent with their image. Unrepentantly political music of any sort can be difficult to listen to—particularly when it is almost blindly angry and coming from an inherently (though understandably) biased point of view, and also when it sidesteps some of the subtleties of the issues it raises. *Guerillas in tha Mist*, the group's debut album, is guilty of all those things, and yet it is an often brilliant, always invigorating, sometimes infuriating scowl of an album. The album is a relentless onslaught of attitude, but it is not misplaced vehemence or finger-wagging.The final song on the album is titled "Inside tha Head of a Black Man," and that is exactly the psychic and psychological space that *Guerillas in tha Mist* occupies: confused, chaotic, complex, righteous, angry, and turbulent, but also permeated with a sense of braggadocio and looseness. Just because they have trouble on their mind doesn't mean they can't swing, too, and Ice Cube's production does just that, especially on tunes such as "All on My Nut Sac," "Freedom Got an A.K.," and the title track. He loads the songs with rolling fatback bass and funky keyboard riffs, and fills in every empty space with some sort of noise, generally a horn or siren or whistle. When listening to *Guerillas in tha Mist*, it is virtually impossible to catch your breath; in fact, it is so powerfully urgent that it feels as if you've just been punched in the gut. But when experiencing something this significant and consequential, you shouldn't want the blow to be pulled just to increase your comfort level.

Stanton Swihart

Lifer's Group

Lifer's Group
1990, Hollywood

From Ice-T to Eazy-E, numerous gangster rappers have provided chilling narratives about the life of crime they put behind them. The members of the Lifers Group, however, didn't quit before it was too late—they're real-life inmates at New Jersey's infamous Rahway State Penitentiary who recorded this album behind bars. One of the most unsettling recordings in the history of rap, this CD is the hip-hop equivalent of "Scared Straight"—a no-holds-barred audio-documentary of

the horrors of prison life. When these inmates (one of whom had been locked up 14 years in 1990) describe the hell of their day-to-day existences and what led to their incarceration, it's clear that they're actually living the nightmare they document. The Lifers' message to young felons on the outside it clear: change your ways before you end up like us.

Alex Henderson

Lighter Shade of Brown

Brown & Proud
1990, Pump

Latino rappers have ranged from pop-oriented (Gerardo) to hardcore (Cypress Hill, Tha Mexikinz). Debuting with *Brown and Proud*, Lighter Shade of Brown made it clear that they fell into the latter category. The title says it all—the L.A. group wears its Mexican-American heritage like a badge of honor on this promising CD, and in doing so, is usually quite substantial. Most of the material is superb, including "El Varrio" (a no-nonsense description of how tough life can be in L.A.'s working-class Hispanic neighborhoods), "T.J. Nights," and "Pancho Villa" (which salutes the Mexican rebel). *Brown and Proud* wasn't as commercially successful as some of Brown's subsequent work, but in Chicano rap circles, the group commanded some well-deserved respect.

Alex Henderson

LL Cool J

Radio
1985, Def Jam/Columbia

Run-D.M.C. was the first rap act to produce cohesive, fully realized albums, and LL Cool J was the first to follow in their footsteps. LL was a mere 17 years old when he recorded his classic debut album *Radio*, a brash, exuberant celebration of booming beats and B-boy attitude that launched not only the longest career in hip-hop, but also Rick Rubin's seminal Def Jam label. Rubin's back-cover credit ("Reduced by Rick Rubin") is an entirely apt description of his bare-bones production style. *Radio* is just as stripped-down and boisterously aggressive as any Run-D.M.C. album, sometimes even more so; the instrumentation is basically just a cranked-up beatbox, punctuated by DJ scratching. There are occasional brief samples, but few do anything more than emphasize a downbeat. The result is rap at its most skeletal, with a hard-hitting, street-level aggression that perfectly matches LL's cocksure teenage energy. Even the two ballads barely sound like ballads, since they're driven by the same slamming beats. Though they might sound a little squared-off to modern ears, LL's deft lyrics set new standards for MCs at the time; his clever disses and outrageous but playful boasts still hold up poetically. Although even LL himself would go on to more intricate rhyming, it isn't really necessary on such a loud, thumping adrenaline rush of a record. *Radio* was both an expansion of rap's artistic possibilities and a commercial success (for its time), helping attract new multiracial audiences to the music. While it may take a few listens for modern ears to adjust to the minimalist production, the fact that it hews so closely to rap's basic musical foundation means that it still possesses a surprisingly fresh energy, and isn't nearly as dated as many efforts that followed it (including, ironically, some of LL's own).

Steve Huey

Bigger and Deffer
1987, Def Jam

LL Cool J rocketed to the top of the hip-hop world in 1985 with *Radio*, his astonishing debut, but he lost his footing a bit with *Bigger and Deffer*, his mildly disappointing follow-up that proved to be a commercial breakthrough all the same. It's a powerful album that gets underway with a bang, as LL raps, "No rapper can rap quite like I can," and makes his case throughout the album-opening "I'm Bad," a ferocious hardcore rap with a great DJ-scratched hook. While that song ranks among LL's best (and most popular) ever, *Bigger and Deffer* doesn't boast too many other standout moments, with the exception of "I Need Love." Its balladic tenderness comes as a late-album surprise, considering how ferocious LL sounds elsewhere here. Nonetheless, like it or loathe it, the song set the template for a number of such lovers raps that would bring LL much crossover success in the years to come. "I Need Love" aside, *Bigger and Deffer* is consistently solid, produced entirely by the L.A. Posse (Darryl Pierce, Dwayne Simon, and Bobby Erving) and filled with the sort of hard-hitting hip-hop that was Def Jam's staple at the time. But while the album is mostly solid, it does lack the creative spark that had made *Radio* such an invigorating release only a couple years prior (the absence of Rick Rubin here is unfortunate). In those couple years since LL had put out *Radio*, rap music had taken big strides. Now, in 1987, LL had to contend with the likes of Eric B. & Rakim, Kool Moe Dee, Public Enemy, and Boogie Down Productions, with others like EPMD, Big Daddy Kane, Ice-T, and N.W.A on the horizon. When put in such a context, *Bigger and Deffer* pales a bit; in the years since LL's *Radio* rocked the streets of New York, rap had taken leaps and bounds while LL hadn't. So it was no surprise when LL suddenly came under attack by his rivals and a few fans, sending him back to the drawing board for his next effort, the whopping 18-track *Walking with a Panther* (1989).

Jason Birchmeier

Walking With a Panther
1989, Def Jam

Released at a time when hip-hop's anxieties about crossover success were at a fever pitch, *Walking With a Panther* found LL Cool J trying to reinvent his sound while building on the commercial breakthrough of *Bigger and Deffer*. Even though the album succeeded on both counts, it did so in a way that didn't sit well with hip-hop purists, who began to call LL's credibility into question. Their fears about commercialism diluting the art form found a focal point in LL, the man who pioneered the rap ballad—and there are in fact three ballads here, all of them pretty saccharine (and, tellingly, none of them singles). Apart from that, some of the concerns now seem like much ado about nothing, and there are numerous fine moments (and a few great singles) to be found on the album. It is true, though, that *Walking With a Panther* does end up slightly less than the sum of its parts. For one

thing, it's simply too long; moreover, the force of his early recordings is missing, and there's occasionally a sense that his once-peerless technique on the mic is falling behind the times. Nonetheless, *Walking With a Panther* is still a fine outing on which LL proves himself a more-than-capable self-producer. The fuller, more fleshed-out sound helps keep his familiar b-boy boasts sounding fresh, and force or no force, he was in definite need of an update. On the singles—"Going Back to Cali," "I'm That Type of Guy" (inexplicably left off *All World*), "Jingling Baby," and "Big Ole Butt"—LL exudes an effortless cool; he's sly, assured, and in full command of a newfound sexual presence on record. So despite its flaws, *Walking With a Panther* still ranks as one of LL's stronger albums—strong enough to make the weak moments all the more frustrating.

Steve Huey

Mama Said Knock You Out
August 1990, Def Jam

Increasingly dismissed by hip-hop fans as an old-school relic and a slick pop sellout, LL Cool J rang in the '90s with *Mama Said Knock You Out*, a hard-edged artistic renaissance that became his biggest-selling album ever. Part of the credit is due to producer Marley Marl, whose thumping, bass-heavy sound helps LL reclaim the aggression of his early days. *Mama Said Knock You Out* isn't quite as hard as *Radio*, instead striking a balance between attitude and accessibility. But its greater variety and more layered arrangements make it LL's most listenable album, as well as keeping it in line with more contemporary sensibilities. Marl's productions on the slower tracks are smooth and soulful, but still funky; as a result, the ladies'-man side of LL's persona is the most convincing it's ever been, and his ballads don't feel sappy for arguably the first time on record. Even apart from the sympathetic musical settings, LL is at his most lyrically acrobatic, and the testosterone-fueled anthems are delivered with a force not often heard since his debut. The album's hits are a microcosm of its range—"The Boomin' System" is a nod to bass-loving b-boys with car stereos; "Around the Way Girl" is a lush, winning ballad; and the title cut is one of the most blistering statements of purpose in hip-hop. It leaves no doubt that *Mama Said Knock You Out* was intended to be a *tour de force*, to regain LL Cool J's credibility while proving that he was still one of rap's most singular talents. It succeeded mightily, making him an across-the-board superstar and cementing his status as a rap icon beyond any doubt.

Steve Huey

Lord Finesse

Funky Technician
1990, Wild Pitch

It's a simple formula: bring together one of the East Coast's finest rappers with some of the most clever trackmasters in hip-hop, then add in a stellar DJ, and the results are bound to be exciting. *Funky Technician* was just that, an excellent LP of battle rap with Lord Finesse simultaneously claiming *and* proving his immense skills over a set of funky backing tracks that used the familiar James Brown blueprint but delivered it with unobtrusive class and innumerable displays of deft turntable wizardry. DJ Premier, Diamond D, Showbiz, and DJ Mike Smooth himself all contribute classic tracks; surprisingly, though Premier would soon forge a unique style and become one of the most respected producers in rap, it's Diamond D who gets in the best one (the title track), and that with the same sound that Premier would later make his own. Meanwhile, Lord Finesse is dropping rhymes to rank with Rakim and Kane, starting out on "Just a Little Something" with a raft of prize-winning multi-syllables: "Now I'm the constabulary, great in vocabulary/I'm no joke, when up against any adversary." Finesse is fresh and imaginative on nearly every line, and invites A.G. (aka Andre the Giant) for a guest spot on "Back to Back Rhyming." There were a lot of great rap records coming out of New York around the turn of the decade, though, and *Funky Technician* never got the attention it deserved. [The 2007 edition includes one bonus track.]

John Bush

Lords of the Underground

Here Come the Lords
1993, Pendulum

Lords of the Underground rattled off five great singles in a row between 1992-1994, all of which helped make *Here Come the Lords* one of the best rap debuts of 1993. "Psycho," "Chief Rocka," "Flow On," "Here Come the Lords," and "Funky Child" (with that wildly searing horn line) feature spare productions with crisp drum breaks and bone-rattling basslines, most of which glean from the catalogs of Blue Note and James Brown. "Flow On" boasts the inimitable touch of Marley Marl and assistant K-Def, and yet it's hardly the most infectious of the batch. There's nothing lacking about the actual production—it's just that MCs Dupre "Doitall" Kelly and Mr. Funke are on top of their game when they're at their most uninhibited, as heard on "Funky Child." And who could forget the image of a diapered Doitall and a ridiculously afro'd Mr. Funke in that song's video (which played a big role in the album's success)? The remainder of the album has its share of middling moments, but the five singles and some other scattered flashes of greatness are more than enough to make for a record that stands alongside many of the other hallowed rap albums from the era.

Andy Kellman

Keepers of the Funk
1994, Pendulum

After EPMD and the rest of the Hit Squad, Lords of the Underground was the East Coast crew who most frequently utilized the thickest vintage funk samples (look no further than the Parliament-Funkadelic title track, with a cameo by George Clinton himself) and pasted them into the most menacing and bare-bones of contexts. As with the trio's freshman outing, *Keepers of the Funk* features production handiwork straight from the crates of the legendary Marley Marl and his protégé, Kevin "K-Def" Hansford, and again the pair developed backdrops as dense and absorbing—the gritty, rock-solid, low-end grooves, dug six-feet deep, and the crunching

tempos—as they are disorienting and foreboding with their queasy swirl of keyboards and horn loops, but with a few additional nods to jazz this time around. On top of the music, Mr. Funke and Doitall bring it as terse and raw as ever, craftily trading off verses in between gruff, crowd-shouted choruses, a fine approximation of what you might hear in the bowels of the New York/New Jersey underground and given just enough of a spit-shine to bring it street-level. *Keepers* is less consistent on the whole, and less catchy, than the sensational *Here Come the Lords*, but its high points are right up there on the same shelf: the exhilarating late-night chant "Tic Toc," with its Spartan, vibraphone-pocked track; the cool and collected cash-grab "What I'm After"; an unexpected expression of "Faith"; and "Frustrated," another of the Lords' characteristic mental, free-form flows.

Stanton Swihart

Monie Love

Down to Earth
October 1990, Warner Bros.

Few British rappers have enjoyed much recognition among American hip-hop audiences. Perhaps the British MC who has received the most attention in the U.S. is the highly talented Monie Love, whose *Down to Earth* is one of the few British rap efforts released on a major label. With *Earth*, she managed to convert some American hip-hoppers while maintaining the strong respect she enjoyed in British rap circles. If a comparison to Love's American counterparts is needed, she has more in common with Queen Latifah than MC Lyte—Love is aggressive and outspoken, but not quite as hard as Lyte. There are some definite classics here, including "It's a Shame (My Sister)" and the wildly infectious "Monie in the Middle." But like so many American rappers, Love spends too much time boasting and not enough time telling meaningful stories. Nonetheless, her strong and interesting technique and her overall musicality make this album enjoyable, though not outstanding.

Alex Henderson

In a Word or 2
March 1993, Warner Bros.

After the sparkling debut of *Down to Earth*, Monie Love's *In a Word or 2*, arriving three years later in 1993, was hotly anticipated. But despite production and co-writing from Marley Marl, as well as the production contributions of Prince on "Born 2 B.R.E.E.D." and the title track, *In a Word or 2* never seems to go anywhere. Love's musical voice and singsong delivery are still in effect, but her raps are decidedly more aggressive, lacking the playful air of her first record. Where *Down to Earth* was open and honest about its issues, it didn't hit the listener over the head with a giant bat called "FEMINISM." *In a Word or 2* doesn't either necessarily; however, its rattling, crashing beats and aggressive delivery become disorienting after only a few songs. "Full Term Love" just isn't the phrase to build a song around, and the low-key soul of "In a Word or 2" is lost in reverb and not strong enough to break up the dissonance of the rest of the material. The jazzy horns and bassline of "4 da Children" make the song another potential strong point, but it's lost at the very end of the album. Most successful is the sunny "Born 2 B.R.E.E.D." ("Build Relationships where Education and Enlightenment Dominate"), with its funky guitar and ascending chorus. It lets Love's mostly engaging delivery shine, unfettered by the clattering beats that dominate the rest of the album. (A "Hip-Hop Mix" of "Born 2 B.R.E.E.D." is included as a bonus at the end of *In a Word or 2*; it replaces the warm vibe of the original with—no surprise here—clattering, shuffling beats.)

Johnny Loftus

Low Profile

We're in This Thing Together
January 1990, Priority

One of the best hip-hop DJs to come out of Los Angeles in the 1980s, DJ Aladdin teamed up with rapper WC at the end of that decade and formed the short-lived but noteworthy Low Profile. The duo showed some potential on its first and only album, the decent if uneven *We're in This Thing Together*. Especially riveting are "How Ya Livin'" (a commentary on urban violence) and "That's Why They Do It," which explains why some youths resort to drug dealing in the inner city. "Pay Ya Dues" makes a meaningful statement about rappers who get ahead without paying dues, but is marred by a homophobic reference. Though most of songs fall under the heading of decent-but-not-outstanding, the CD offers plenty of proof of Aladdin's impressive technique on the turntables. *We're in This Thing Together* wasn't a big hit, and after Low Profile broke up, WC went on to form WC and the Maad Circle a few years later.

Alex Henderson

Lucas

Lucacentric
1994, Big Beat

"Lucas With the Lid Off" is an irresistible single, full of intoxicating beats, great horn loops, and a supremely confident boast by Lucas. Unfortunately, the rest of the rapper's debut album, *Lucacentric*, fails to ignite, but there are some tracks that will spark the interest of fans of the hit single.

Stephen Thomas Erlewine

Luke

I Got S—t on My Mind
1992, Luke

When Florida attorney Jack Thompson declared war on Luther Campbell, the 2 Live Crew, and Luke Records (formerly Luke Skyywalker Records) in 1989 and claimed that their X-rated rhymes were in violation of American obscenity laws, he didn't put them out of business. All he succeeded in doing

was making Campbell a poster child for the First Amendment and helping him sell even more albums and singles. When Campbell launched his solo career with *I Got Shit on My Mind* in 1992, it was obvious that he wasn't about to clean up his act—this CD is every bit as rude, crude, and X-rated as anything that he had done with the 2 Live Crew. On raunchy, sexually explicit offerings like "Head Head and More Head" and "Menage a Trois," Campbell seems to be thumbing his nose at his adversaries by being as offensive as possible. And those adversaries not only include Thompson and various church groups—they also include other rappers. *I Got Shit on My Mind* finds Campbell attacking everyone from N.W.A. on "Fakin' Like Gangsters" to Kid 'n Play on "Pussy Ass Kid and Hoe Ass Play." Overall, this CD is quite entertaining—that is, if you have a taste for X-rated humor. Campbell has often described himself as a rap version of Richard Pryor or Andrew Dice Clay, and anyone who finds those comedians amusing is likely to see the entertainment value in the rapper's booty rhymes. Those who are don't care for that type of humor won't. *I Got Shit on My Mind* isn't quite as essential as the 2 Live Crew's best releases, but it's a guilty pleasure that Campbell's hardcore fans will enjoy.

Alex Henderson

Mac Dre

The Best of Mac Dre
May 1993, Thizz

Within the span of a decade, Mac Dre released a plethora of albums, not only full-lengths under his own name, but also multiple volumes in the *Rompilation* series. When his best-of finally appeared in 2002, it was about time a collection of this underground West Coast Bay Area rapper's music was compiled. *Tha Best of Mac Dre* goes back all the way to the early '90s, when Dre was recording albums for Strictly Business, compiling several songs from his *Young Black Brotha* (1993) album. There are a total of 32 songs on this best-of, spanning the distance of two discs. This is undoubtedly the place in Dre's huge discography to begin if you're new to his music.

Jason Birchmeier

Craig Mack

Project: Funk da World
1994, Bad Boy

The first hit album released on Sean "Puffy" Combs' Bad Boy label, Craig Mack's *Project: Funk da World* lacks the hardcore edge of Bad Boy's next breakout artist, the Notorious B.I.G., instead gunning for the dancefloor with a slight hint of street attitude. The beats are laid-back, mid-tempo, and effortlessly funky, influenced by the vibe of Dr. Dre's G-funk sound but not slavishly derivative at all. Mack isn't the most skillful rapper who ever lived, but he's game on most of these tracks, with a low, raspy voice and a loose, casual style that's hard to resist when he's on. When he isn't, he strays a little too far off the beat, or lacks enough variety in his flow and surprises in his rhymes to hold the listener's interest. But he's good enough to work a groove, and sometimes that's all you need for a great dance record. The formula gets repetitive over the course of an entire album, especially on the tracks with too many choruses, but there are some definite high points, most notably the smash "Flava in Ya Ear," "Get Down," and "Funk Wit da Style." There's also a clever sample of the *Days of Our Lives* theme song on "Real Raw." In the end, *Project: Funk da World* isn't a bad party record at all, though it's less engaging as a self-contained listen.

Steve Huey

Main Source

Breaking Atoms
1991, Wild Pitch

Main Source's debut album, *Breaking Atoms*, is one of the quintessential cult classics in hip-hop history. Underappreciated compared to peers like A Tribe Called Quest, Gang Starr, or even Brand Nubian, the album probably doesn't get wider acclaim because it was recorded for the ill-fated Wild Pitch label, and thus remained out of print for much of the time its reputation was spreading. Group focal point the Large Professor is a fine rapper, but the album's legend rests more on his production—he debuts one of the most influential styles in hip-hop here, popularizing a number of now widely imitated techniques. Luckily, you don't have to know how to operate an SP-1200, or exactly what panning, chopping, and filtered basslines are, to appreciate the vibrant-sounding results. His intricately constructed tracks are filled with jazz and soul samples, layered percussion, off-kilter sampling effects, and an overall sonic richness. That's doubtlessly enhanced by the presence of two DJs in the group, who contribute lively scratching to the proceedings as well. The album is rather brief, clocking in at around 45 minutes even with a bonus remix, but there's also no wasted space whatsoever. The brightly soulful "Lookin' at the Front Door" is perhaps the best-known single, but there are plenty of other highlights. "Just a Friendly Game of Baseball" is anything but, with its moody backing track and extended lyrical metaphor about police brutality and racial profiling. Meanwhile, "Live at the Barbeque" is one of the most legendary posse cuts ever recorded, featuring guests Joe Fatal, Akinyele, and Nas (the latter two make their recorded debuts here). Aficionados hype *Breaking Atoms* as one of the greatest hip-hop albums of all time, and at least musically speaking, they're not far off. [A Wild Pitch reissue program was underway in the new millennium, but despite rumors, *Breaking Atoms* still hasn't been a beneficiary.]

Steve Huey

Mantronix

Mantronix: The Album
1985, Warlock

Curtis "Mantronik" Khaleel was often quoted as saying that his mission was to "take rap a step beyond the streets," and the innovative producer/mixmaster accomplished that goal on Mantronix's debut album, *Mantronix: The Album*. This excellent 1985 LP was way ahead of its time; while the rapping of Mantronix's partner MC Tee is pure mid-'80s New York hip-hop, the production is anything but conventional. On gems like "Needle to the Groove," "Bassline," and the hit "Fresh Is the Word," you can hear the parallels between Tee's rhyming and the East Coast b-boy rhymes that Run-D.M.C., LL Cool J, and the Fat Boys were providing in 1985. But the album's high-tech, futuristic production sets it apart from other New York hip-hop of the mid-'80s, and even though one of the LP's tracks is titled "Hardcore Hip-Hop," Mantronix had a hard time appealing to hip-hop's hardcore. *Mantronix: The Album* actually fared better in dance music, electro-funk, and club circles than it did among hardcore b-boys. But this is definitely a hip-hop record, and it is also Mantronix's most essential release.

Alex Henderson

Music Madness
1986, Sleeping Bag

Many Mantronix fans will tell you that the group provided its best and most essential work when it was signed to the small Sleeping Bag label and MC Tee was still on board. Listening to *Music Madness*, it's hard to argue with that. This 1986 LP, which was Mantronix's second album and its last album before leaving Sleeping Bag for Capitol, is proof of how fresh-sounding and creative Mantronix was in the beginning. The futuristic outlook that defines "Scream," the single "Who Is It," and other tracks sets *Music Madness* apart from other hip-hop albums that came from New York in 1986; Tee's rapping is very much in the 1980s b-boy tradition, but the club-minded producing and mixing of Curtis "Mantronik" Khaleel is unlike anything you would have heard on a Run-D.M.C. or L.L. Cool J album back then. And that fact wasn't lost on hip-hop's hardcore, which felt that *Music Madness* wasn't street enough. Mantronik was fond of saying that his goal was to "take rap a step beyond the streets," and this album tended to attract dance music and electro-funk lovers and club hounds more than hardcore hip-hoppers. *The Album* remains Mantronix's best album, but this excellent LP runs a close second.

Alex Henderson

That's My Beat
2002, Soul Jazz

As record-store bins began to collapse under the weight of a baffling bumper crop of various-artist compilations put together by everyday artists, free of mixing ("I've never heard of this fellow but I absolutely need two songs on here"), it was pleasantly surprising that room was left for an innovator like Kurtis Mantronik to take his own turn at the game. *That's My Beat* goes way back to the time when Mantronik was coming up as a young buck (most of these tracks were originally released prior to his debut, 1985's *Mantronix: The Album*), and it exemplifies the mixed bag of electro, disco, and rap that helped form the sound of New York during the early '80s. This might as well be the fifth volume of Tommy Boy's phenomenal *Perfect Beats* series. For a record to become popular with party people during this era, it didn't matter who made it and it didn't matter if it was slow or fast—as long as it moved bodies, it got played. On this disc, a rather happy medium is found between scene standards (Yellow Magic Orchestra's kitschy but ever spectacular "Computer Games," the Art of Noise's concrete-bustin' "Beat Box," Funky Four Plus One's undeniably classic "That's the Joint") and less-popular but inspired choices (Machine's "There but for the Grace of God," Unlimited Touch's "I Hear the Music in the Streets," and Suzy-Q's "Get on up and Do It Again" are underground disco gems). While it's true that old jocks and younger trainspotters might groan at the availability of most of these tracks, those who are returning to this music or are finding it for the first time are in for a real good time.

Andy Kellman

Big Daddy Kane and Kool G Rap to freewheeling talents Biz Markie and Masta Ace. As the classic *House of Hits* compilation ably proves over 15 tracks, Marley Marl was a master of tailoring productions to the talents of his varying rappers—from the hardcore intensity of Kool G Rap & DJ Polo on "Poison" to the quick-paced vocal dexterity of Big Daddy Kane on "Set It Off" to the all-in-one classic posse track "Sym-

phony, Vol. 1" (with Masta Ace, Craig G., Kool G Rap, and Big Daddy Kane). Even the same artist could get wildly different tracks; Biz Markie played up the clown prince on "Make the Music With Your Mouth, Biz," but also indulged in some humdrum cynicism for "Vapors" over a production to match. Fans of Cold Chillin' will want to dig deeper with separate volumes on most of the artists here, but few rap compilations match *House of Hits* at illustrating a standard unmatched by any label save Def Jam and Sugarhill.

John Bush

Marley Marl

In Control, Vol. 1
1988, Cold Chillin'

In Control, Vol. 1 is a greatest-hits package (of a sort) featuring singles Marley Marl produced for his stable of artists on the Cold Chillin' label. Mostly though, the album serves to show exactly how important Marley Marl was to the advancement of hip-hop. Before him, hip-hop relied mostly on primitive, artificial sounding 808 drum machine beats. He transformed the genre completely with his stock of drum loops, most lifted from James Brown records. His crisp beats enlivened hip-hop and set the tone for the sample madness that would eventually consume producers. *In Control, Vol. 1* includes some of the best moments from the producer's hip-hop revolution. Rap heavyweights Biz Markie and Heavy D. try their hand at a Barry Manilow impression on their transformation of "We Write the Songs." Master Ace and Action attempt some hip-hop upliftment on "Keep Your Eyes on the Prize," and Master Ace, Craig G., Kool G. Rap, and Big Daddy Kane join forces for one of the best posse cuts in hip-hop history, "The Symphony." While some of these rappers, most notably Heavy D. and Big Daddy Kane, would go on to further success, none ever would sound this tight again. Marley Marl's groundbreaking production and the strength of the various MCs showcased on *In Control, Vol. 1* make the album a must for anyone even remotely interested in hip-hop's history.

Chris Witt

Marley Marl's House of Hits
June 1995, Cold Chillin'

Cold Chillin' certainly deserved the title *House of Hits* during the late '80s, with dozens of the best rappers recording classic tracks that placed high on urban play lists, if not the pop charts themselves. Marley Marl was blessed with a stable boasting immense talents, ranging from hardcore rhymers

Masta Ace

Take a Look Around
July 1990, Cold Chillin'

The debut full-length from Masta Ace, and only one with the Juice Crew (with whom he rapped on "The Symphony"), *Take a Look Around* is as much a testament to Marley Marl and DJ Mister Cee's production as it is to the very able rhyming skills of the collegiate-looking Ace. Though the album never gave the MC the success that other Juice Crew members—including Big Daddy Kane, to whom he is often compared—had, it's still a great representation of what early hip-hop was and could be, both light-hearted ("Can't Stop the Bumrush," "Me and the Biz," which, contrary to popular belief, does not feature Mr. Markie, but instead an impersonation by Masta Ace) and socially aware ("The Other Side of Town," "I Got Ta"), confident without being ridiculous (seen, for example, in "Letter to the Better," which was also the B-side to his first single, "Together," also included here). It's not groundbreaking stuff, but it's consistent and a lot of fun, high-quality rap that shows off the Brooklyn MC's easygoing flow and storytelling skills, a solid hour of music without any filler, and a definite must-have for any fans of old-school hip-hop.

Marisa Brown

SlaughtaHouse
1993, Delicious Vinyl

Five years after making his name as a member in Marley Marl's legendary Juice Crew (he was one of the featured MCs on the classic 1988 posse cut "The Symphony" from Marl's *In Control, Vol. 1*) and three years after recording his buoyant, artistically on-point (though commercially stillborn) debut album, *Take a Look Around*, with its memorable hit "Me and the Biz," battle-scarred Brooklyn underground star Masta Ace returned for his second album with a newly tweaked name and his own supporting crew (Masta Ace Inc.), a new sound and sharply honed style, and a cynical new outlook on the entire rap game. In fact, a disgusted new outlook might be a more appropriate characterization, as a controlled abhorrence oozes from every pore of *SlaughtaHouse*, lashing out not only at easy outside targets (bigoted police, for instance) but also at those shady characters inside the "SlaughtaHouse" whose violence is enacted physically (Ace himself places the part of a mugger on "Who U Jackin?") rather than lyrically, bringing the entire community down in the process. A loose concept album, it is at once an intense exposé and a roughneck paean to the hip-hop lifestyle that broke new ground by merging the grimy lyrical sensibility, scalpel-precise technique, and kitchen-sink beats of East Coast rap with the funk-dripping, anchor-thick low end of West Coast producers. The classic "Jeep Ass Niguh" was one of the quintessential cruising singles of the summer of 1993. Its unlisted remix, "Born to Roll," with its subsonic gangsta bass, is an equally thumping highlight and (with its sample borrowed from N.W.A's "Real Niggas Don't Die") can be seen as the most explicit bridge between East and West. But other hectic, relentless tracks like "The Big East," "Rollin' wit UmDada," and "Saturday Nite Live" are just as excellent, and Ace's crew—particularly Bluez Brothers Lord Digga and Witchdoc—really shines.

Stanton Swihart

Sittin' on Chrome
May 1995, Delicious Vinyl

In the five years that passed between his debut, *Take a Look Around*, and his third full-length, *Sittin' on Chrome*, Brooklyn rapper Masta Ace's sound changed a lot. Angrier lyrics were already starting to show up on his sophomore release, *SlaughtaHouse*, but it was nothing in comparison to *Sittin' on Chrome*. Not that the themes are fueled by testosterone and rage here (and not that they were on *SlaughtaHouse*, either, though there was a great deal more vitriol), but the overall feel of the album—which has by now moved past the boom bap old-school beats into fuller, gloomier production that more aptly represents the mid-'90s East Coast sound—is much darker, with slower, heavier songs that ponder life in the ghetto. But the record's not an attack on the system that has caused the poor conditions of inner-city existence; rather, it's more of a collection of sketches that show it in its entirety, both the good and the bad. The whole Masta Ace Incorporated crew (Lord Digga, Leschea, and Paula Perry) is present here and does a good job—along with Ace, of course, whose flow and lyrics combine to show him off at his best—at adding depth and realism to the album's 16 cuts, interludes and all. It's a formula that clearly works well: *Sittin' on Chrome* boasted the MC's most popular songs, "Born to Roll" (which was also included as a bonus track on *SlaughtaHouse*), "The I.N.C. Ride," and the title track itself, but the other material—"Eastbound," "People in My Hood"—is equally as interesting, and makes the record a very worthwhile addition to a rap collection.

Marisa Brown

Master P

The Ghettos Tryin to Kill Me!
1994, No Limit

Master P's early '90s underground ventures blossomed on *The Ghettos Tryin to Kill Me!*, a wonderfully exploitative album driven by lo-fi G-funk beats and gutter-mentality gangsta rhymes. The album itself doesn't sound too much different from Master P's other early releases, still marred by a spare-change quality production; however, it's the execution that makes *The Ghettos Tryin to Kill Me!* such an impressive step forward for the aspiring kingpin. Rather than simply emulate West Coast gangsta rappers like N.W.A and Above the Law as he had on previous releases, Master P begins to carve out a niche of his own here. The Dirty South motifs still aren't quite yet apparent, but the griminess of the later releases certainly is, as nearly every song here references drug dealing and murder, particularly the standout title track. In fact, like all the other pre-*Ghetto D* albums, Master P is at his rawest here, willing to exploit whatever hardcore motifs he could in order to get a risc from his listeners. He's joined on practically every song by his Cali-era No Limit colleagues, including King George, C-Murder, Big Ed, Cali G, Sonya C, and Silkk the Shocker. Fellow Bay Area hardcore rappers JT the Bigga Figga and San Quinn join the festivities on "Playa Haterz." If you want to hear Master P at his most unapologetically exploitative, this is where to go—if you can find it, that is. [No Limit re-released and repackaged *The Ghettos Tryin to Kill Me!* in 1997 after scoring its distribution deal with Priority. The original version from 1994 is significantly different from the re-release, as Master P unfortunately cut the exceptional "Reverend Do Wrong" because of his beef with then-No Limit soldier King George and added two bonus tracks: the latter-day "Always Look a Man in the Eyes," which features Mystikal and Silkk the Shocker, and "Robbery," which is a C-Murder solo track. The "limited collector's edition" re-release also altered the sequencing and cover art and billed the album misleadingly as "Master P's first underground rap album."]

Jason Birchmeier

MC Breed

MC Breed & DFC
1991, Warlock

Few outside of the Midwest took notice back in 1991 when MC Breed debuted with da Flint Crew (DFC). At the time he was mostly a local phenomenon, stressing the word "phenomenon" because the Midwest didn't have many rappers to call its own at the time, let alone any as talented as Breed. Furthermore, few Midwest rappers had hits as big as "Ain't No Future in Yo' Frontin'," the song that put Breed on the map for years to follow and kept this album on the *Billboard*

R&B charts for a year. With time, however, the Flint, MI, native would become one of the more impressive rappers to emerge in the '90s, eventually moving first to L.A. to hook up with D.O.C. and then Atlanta to hook up with Too $hort. And it's those later efforts with D.O.C. and Too $hort that generally garner the most attention among those who have familiarized themselves with Breed's funk-laced rap. However, it's a shame that so many listeners overlook Breed's debut, which eventually went out of print for many years before finally being remastered and re-released by Warlock in 2002. Yes, it's a relatively lo-fi effort, an independently released album during a time when few rap albums were. But there is a certain sense of novelty that makes *MC Breed & DFC* sound even more special with time. As mentioned, it's one of the first rap albums to come out of the Midwest, merging the then-opposing East and West Coast sounds of the time. For example, "Ain't No Future in Yo' Frontin'" samples Flavor Flav's trademark "to the beat ch'all" for its intro, Zapp's "More Bounce to the Ounce" for its bassline, and uses the whining synth melodies Dr. Dre made famous a year later on his *Chronic* album for its hook (and a snippet of this synth hook would be sampled a year later for Ice Cube's "Wicked"). Breed drew equally from East and West for his sound, being as much influenced by Too $hort and MC Eiht as Chuck D and EPMD. His later albums are no doubt more polished, but none of them are as pure as this, one of the few albums to vividly document the embryonic Midwest rap scene of the time.

Jason Birchmeier

The New Breed
1993, Wrap

MC Breed may have synthesized East and West Coast styles on his debut album, partly explaining why it sounded so novel for its time, but by the time his third album, *The New Breed*, hit the streets in 1993 it was apparent: the Midwestern native had adopted the West Coast sound, which was at its zenith of popularity at the time. Dr. Dre's *The Chronic* was bumping everywhere in 1993, even on the East Coast, so it isn't too surprising that Breed, an artist who's never too far behind the latest trends, headed West and hooked up with D.O.C., the writer/producer who had quietly helped make Dre's *The Chronic* the success that it was. Furthermore, Breed also hooked up with Warren G, who produced some of this album, and a young and delightfully unthuggish 2 Pac, who helped make "Gotta Get Mine," this album's hit single, a career highlight for the former Midwestern and soon to be Dirty South rapper. In fact, Breed's decision to head West for this album proved to be a wise decision. His next album, *Funkafied*, peaked at number nine on *Billboard*'s R&B chart without little to no commercial airplay, a testament to just how impressed the public was by this album.

Jason Birchmeier

The Best of Breed
October 1995, Wrap

Released only a few months after MC Breed's *Big Baller* album in 1995, *The Best of MC Breed* compiled a few of the best tracks from each of his five albums released at the time. All of Breed's best-known songs are here: from *MC Breed & DFC* (1991) you get "Ain't No Future in Yo' Frontin'" and "Just Kickin' It"; from *The New Breed* (1993) "Gotta Get Mine," "Everyday Ho," and "Tight"; from *Funkafied* (1994) "Seven Years" and "Late Nite Creep (Booty Call)"; and from *Big Baller* (1995) "Game for Life" and "Real MC." There are also a few tracks exclusive to this compilation: "Aquapussy," "Well Alright," a remix of "Teach My Kids," and unreleased

versions of "This Is How We Do It" and "Ain't Too Much Worried." Breed's second album, *20 Below*, is practically ignored here, unless you count the unreleased version of "Ain't Too Much Worried," which appeared on that album in its normal version; however, since *20 Below* is perhaps the artist's least remembered and most forgettable album, it's really shouldn't be a major concern. After all, everything you really need is here, including the big hits like "Ain't No Future in Yo' Frontin'" and "Gotta Get Mine," plus a few exclusive tracks as a bonus. Overall, this is a perfect distillation of Breed's first half-decade of work. [Originally released in late 1995, *The Best of MC Breed* was re-released in late 2001 in the wake of Breed's biggest hit in years, "Let's Go to the Club."]

Jason Birchmeier

MC Hammer

Let's Get It Started
1988, Capitol

MC Hammer's double-platinum debut album, *Let's Get It Started*, made him a star in the R&B world even before he crossed over to the pop charts. It isn't as immediately hooky a record as *Please Hammer Don't Hurt 'Em*, in part because Hammer hasn't developed his signature sampling chutzpah. Sure, the hit single "Turn This Mutha Out" samples its title from Parliament's biggest hit, and "That's What I Said" borrows the bassline of "Freddie's Dead," but these aren't the wholesale appropriations that would take Hammer to the top. The main appeal of *Let's Get It Started* is simply that it's well-produced, funky, and danceable, regardless of the quality of the raps. Consider this: By 1988, advancements in lyrical technique were beginning to render even superstars Run-D.M.C. a little outmoded. Just starting out, Hammer sounds slower and less forceful than those old-school legends, and his rhymes are even more squared-off and less fluid in their relationship to the beat. Still, he hollers his simple lyrics with energy and enthusiasm throughout the album, and he does have more power in his delivery here than on *Please Hammer Don't Hurt 'Em*. Plus, this style wasn't *totally* outdated in hip-hop's mainstream quite yet. Still, it isn't what makes the best cuts work. "Turn This Mutha Out" gets by more on its distinctive keyboard riff, and tracks like "They Put Me in the Mix" and "Pump It Up (Here's the News)" are designed more for the dancefloor than the street.

Steve Huey

Please Hammer, Don't Hurt 'Em
January 1990, Capitol

Still the biggest-selling rap album of all time at ten million copies (though the Beastie Boys' *Licensed to Ill* is gaining rapidly), *Please Hammer Don't Hurt 'Em* proved that rap music was no longer just a specialty niche genre, but had the crossover  potential to be a commercial juggernaut. But in an art form so conscious of preserving its integrity, this wasn't the way to go about it—at least not from a creative standpoint. Hammer builds the majority of the songs here on obvious samples from easily recognizable soul and funk hits of the past, relying on the original hooks without twisting them into anything new (or, by implication, his own). That approach confirmed the worst fears of hip-hop purists about how the music might hit the mainstream. Taken on its own terms, *Please Hammer Don't Hurt 'Em* is a pretty slick—if unsubtle—pop confection. Hammer certainly has good taste in source material, if nothing else; the hits "U Can't Touch This" and "Pray" crib from Rick James' "Super Freak" and Prince's "When Doves Cry," respectively, and the ballad "Have You Seen Her" is a flat-out cover of the Chi-Lites' hit (with some updated lyrics). Other tracks sample Marvin Gaye, Earth, Wind & Fire, and the Jackson 5. Throughout the record, choruses are repeated ad infinitum for maximum memorability, which either makes it irresistible or irritating, depending on your taste. Hammer *has* improved as a rapper—his delivery is often more subtle, and he even attempts a little bit of verbal flash here and there. He still isn't technically on a par with the average MC of the time—he's a little too stiff, flowing awkwardly around the beat. Of course, his simple style also makes him easy to understand, and coupled with the highly danceable production and a great set of borrowed hooks, it's easy to see why *Please Hammer Don't Hurt 'Em* was so popular—and why it now functions chiefly as a nostalgia piece.

Steve Huey

MC Lyte

Lyte as a Rock
1988, First Priority

In the earliest years of the hip-hop game, women were quite frequently overlooked until a new breed of female lyricist came along and gave the proverbial middle finger to a male-dominated game. MC Lyte's debut ushered in the era of the female MC—confident, brazen, and not afraid to put male MCs in their misogynist place without flinching. The album starts off with a rather slow introduction before kicking things into high gear with the now classic title track, which put Lyte in the center of a media frenzy. With Lyte reasserting her femininity over and over again without compromising production quality or lyric delivery, *Lyte as a Rock* has aged better than most records that came out during hip-hop's formative years, although at certain moments it has become dated since its release. But what has aged is more than compensated by the classic tunes and the disc's potent historical impact on a generation of women MCs. A classic.

Rob Theakston

Eyes on This
1989, First Priority

A rapper with considerable technique and a fine sense of humor, Lyte was one of the most highly regarded female MCs of the late '80s and early '90s—especially on the East Coast. *Eyes on This*, the Brooklyn native's second album, tends to be one-dimensional lyrically—she spends too much time bragging about how superior her rapping skills are and how inept sucker MCs are. Though it's hard not to admire the technique and strong chops she displays on such boasting fare as "Shut the Eff Up! (Hoe)"—a an attack on Lyte's nemesis Antoinette—and "Slave 2 the Rhythm," she's at her best when telling some type of meaningful story. Undeniably, the CD's standout track is "Cappucino," an imaginative gem in which Lyte stops by a Manhattan cafe and gets caught in the crossfire of rival drug dealers. In the afterlife, she asks herself: "Why, oh why, did I need cappucino?" Were everything on the album in a class with "Cappucino," it would have been an outstanding album instead of simply a good one.

Alex Henderson

Act Like You Know
September 1991, First Priority

Though highly respected in rap's hardcore, MC Lyte was never a platinum seller. Atlantic Records no doubt encouraged her to be more commercial on her third album, *Act like You Know*—a generally softer, more melodic and often R&B-ish effort than either of her first two LPs. But even so, the album is far from a sellout—Lyte's music still has plenty of bite, substance and integrity. Like before, she's at her best when telling some type of story instead of simply boasting about her rapping skills. Especially riveting are "Eyes Are the Soul" (a poignant reflection on the destruction caused by crack cocaine), "Lola at the Copa" (a warning about how a one-night-stand can lead to AIDS); and "Poor Georgie," which describes a young man's life and death in the fast lane. Lyte's change of direction proved to be short-lived—with her next album, *Ain't No Other*, she returned to hardcore rap in a big way.

Alex Henderson

Ain't No Other
1993, First Priority

Whenever a hardcore rapper becomes more commercial, hip-hop's hardcore is likely to cry "sellout." That's exactly what happened to MC Lyte when she increased her R&B/pop appeal with 1991's *Act Like You Know*. The album wasn't without grit or integrity and even had some strong sociopolitical numbers, but hip-hop purists can be every bit as rigid as jazz purists—and they tend to be wary of any attempt to cross over. So in 1993, Lyte ditched the pop elements and emphasized hardcore rap on *Ain't No Other*. The song that did the most to define the album was "Ruffneck," a catchy, inspired single that found Lyte expressing her preference for ragamuffin street kids from the inner city. "Ruffneck" expressed Lyte's allegiance to hip-hop's hardcore, and she's equally rugged and hard-edged on tunes like "Fuck that Motherfucking Bullshit," "Hard Copy," and "Brooklyn." As a bonus track, First Priority includes a remix of "I Cram to Understand U," the song that had put Lyte on the map in 1987. Not earth-shattering but generally decent, *Ain't No Other* will appeal to those who prefer Lyte's more hardcore side.

Alex Henderson

The Very Best of MC Lyte
September 2001, Rhino

Rhino's 2001 collection *The Very Best of MC Lyte* is an excellent summary of MC Lyte's recordings for Atlantic records. The collection balances her career quite nimbly, with four tracks from her 1988 debut *Lyte As a Rock*, five from 1989's *Eyes on This*, three from 1991's *Act Like You Know*, two from *Ain't No Other*, and one from *Bad As I Wanna B*, with her guest appearance on Foster/McElroy's "Dr. Soul," and the Bad Boy remix "Cold Rock a Party" rounding out the compilation for good measure. The decreasing returns from each subsequent album signals that MC Lyte's material did dip as the '90s wore on, but this does contain credible highlights from those records, while her hardcore golden-age recordings—"10% Dis," "I Cram to Understand U," "Kickin' 4 Brooklyn," "Cha Cha Cha," "I Am the Lyte," "Shut the Eff Up! (Hoe)"—still stand as fresh, powerful hip-hop. The first two records still hold their own, but this is a very good sampler and introduction in its own right.

Stephen Thomas Erlewine

MC 900 Ft. Jesus

Hell with the Lid Off
1990, Nettwerk

Aligned more with a rap-informed industrial scene that included Consolidated and Meat Beat Manifesto than with rap itself, MC 900 Ft. Jesus did rhyme, but his delivery was closer to Kerouac's beat poetry than the hardcore poetry of KRS-1. Excellent scratching courtesy of DJ Zero complements the eclectic productions that range from the chop-happy jazz of "Truth Is Out of Style" to the techno-goth funk of "Real Black Angel." The affected irony of his delivery can be distracting, but *Hell With the Lid Off* remains a highly compelling recording, if only for its brash flirtation with so many styles—techno, funk, cool jazz, house—and its refusal to settle for any of them.

Wade Kergan

Welcome to My Dream
1991, Nettwerk

The follow-up to *Hell With the Lid Off* is darker, less cartoonish, and far more influenced by funk and jazz than before (if it weren't for the slightly whiny vocals over top of the opening cut, you might mistake the backing track for something from Miles Davis' fusion period). In a lot of ways, *Welcome to My Dream* was a precursor to trip-hop, layering hip-hop beats over jazzy breaks and dream-like instrumentation. The problem is tracks like "Killer Inside Me" and "Adventures in Failure": the backing tracks are killer and the delivery of the rhymes are top-notch, but they're ultimately a bit silly, which makes it a bit hard to take the rest of the album seriously. That's a shame because there are some great tracks here, like "The City Sleeps'" and "Falling Elevators." As before, DJ Zero scratches with aplomb.

Sean Carruthers

MC Ren

Kizz My Black Azz
June 1992, Priority

Produced with veteran Bobby "Bobcat" Ervin (who was

producing for King Tee and LL Cool J in the mid-'80s) and DJ Train (who also worked with J.J. Fad and Kam), each beat on the *Kizz My Black Azz* EP suits MC Ren's stern, straight-ahead flow and grim lyrics. Sometimes it's difficult to discern whether he's trying to outdo or parody his former group's shock factor, as in the single "The Final Frontier": "I hit a nigga off in the head with a chair/The reason for that, the motherf*cker he was standin' there"; "So when you're at my show, let me see you throw your hands up in the air and slap a ho." With *100 Miles and Runnin'* and Ice Cube's *AmeriKKKa's Most Wanted* two years old, he probably felt the need to hit as hard as possible. Nonetheless, if there is a case to be made for Ren's status as N.W.A.'s best MC—he was undeniably the least appreciated—there's plenty of support to be heard here. The tales, which slightly outnumber the boasts, can be as graphic as a movie rated NC-17, and they're occasionally bold to the point of being tough to digest, but based purely on sound, *Kizz My Black Azz* is halting from start to finish. Never again would he be so fierce. (*Life Sentence*, the follow-up album promised on the back of the EP's original release, developed into 1993's *Shock of the Hour*.)

Andy Kellman

MC Serch

Return of the Product
1992, Def Jam

After putting out two albums as a part of 3rd Bass, MC Serch (born Michael Berrin) set off to work on his own material. Entitled *Return of the Product*, and released in 1992, the record (his only solo release) sits in that transition space of hip-hop, between the Golden Age and the newer East Coast sound that was being shepherded in. Because of this, the beats on *Return of the Product* don't weather as well as some of the other albums that were more firmly grounded in their era (Public Enemy or De La Soul or even 3rd Bass), but Serch's rhymes more than make up for any musical shortcomings (of which there are very few, anyway). The big hit on the album is "Back to the Grill Again," and it's easy to see why. With a bouncy, bassy beat from T-Ray and guest verses from Red Hot Lover Tone, Chubb Rock, and Nas (here shortly after Serch discovered him and two years before his debut, *Illmatic*, would come out), the song is funny and smart, with a catchy hook and intricate flows from all the MCs ("Got crazy game, so no one can stop me/But hey yo, I'm white, I guess my game is hockey," Serch quips). Because the MC's delivery, and his punchlines, are what he's best at, and he's in fine form here: "I can come ghetto and don't have to be a bastard/Hold a conversation and don't have to have the last word/Shoot the gifts swift and not miss the street/Even—umm—and not come off the beat," he rhymes in the quick-paced "Don't Have to Be," while "Hard But True" sees him taking a more discerning look at societal conditions ("Too many times too many crimes get backed up/Case comes up, oops, switch all the facts up/Three kids rape a sister at St. John's/And become graduates, instead of cons.../Probably one of the fathers gave the school a gymnasium"). Serch was one of the few white rappers at this time, and the only one willing to address issues like this, which gives a depth and credibility to his words, and makes *Return of the Product* a pretty interesting release, and absolutely worth listening to.

Marisa Brown

MC Shan

Down by Law
1987, Cold Chillin'

MC Shan's album debut wasn't a success, despite the presence of one justifiable rap classic and several other interesting ideas for songs. Most of the problem lay in Marley Marl's productions, which took the sound of MC Shan no farther than his massive hit, "The Bridge," and seemed to merely duplicate the process with every track. Shan opened with a pair of intriguing project stories, one about a solid student turned junkie ("Jane, Stop This Crazy Thing") and the other about an easy girl ("Project 'Ho"). Admittedly, these tracks weren't quite as exciting as they were compelling, but Marley Marl's constant focus on stuttered-sampling madness soon lapsed into mildness and then simple frustration. Shan got a bit more hardcore on "Kill That Noise," responding again to KRS-One and Boogie Down Productions, and finally returned to the astounding energy level of "The Bridge" with a pair of later tracks, "Down by Law" and "Living in the World of Hip Hop."

John Bush

Play It Again, Shan
June 1989, Cold Chillin'

Along with Big Daddy Kane, Biz Markie and Roxanne Shante, MC Shan was one of the rappers who put Cold Chillin' Records on the map. The New Yorker never had a multi-platinum seller, but he was an entertaining and often clever MC whose solid rhyming skills earned him a medium-sized following in the mid-to-late '80s (especially on the East Coast). While *Play It Again, Shan* isn't outstanding, the CD has quite a few strong points, including "It Don't Mean a Thing" (which draws on the Duke Ellington classic), "Death Was Quite a Surprise" (an account of a youth who gets sick of working for minimum wage, becomes a drug dealer and pays with his life) and the anti-drug commentary "Rock Stuff." The only weak offering is "I Want to Thank You," a cliched Latin freestyle tune that aims for the TKA/Stevie B crowd and proves that Shan should stick to rap.

Alex Henderson

MC Shy D

Got to Be Tough
1987, Luke

Most of the rappers who recorded for Luther Campbell's Luke Skyywalker Records (which later became Luke Records) in the late '80s fell into the Miami bass category. But Peter Jones, aka MC Shy D, was an exception. Originally from the Bronx, Shy D moved to the Atlanta area but never forgot his New York roots. Although the MC's debut album,

Got to Be Tough, was recorded in Ft. Lauderdale, FL, and lists Campbell as its executive producer, none of the material is Florida-sounding. In fact, this 1987 LP is consistently New York-minded. Shy D's rapping style is right out of the Run-D.M.C./LL Cool J school of 1980s New York hip-hop, and his raw, hard-edged producing (which consists mainly of a drum machine, scratching, and samples) leaves no doubt that he was a major admirer of New York turntable wizards like Jam Master Jay and Cut Creator. When this LP came out, other Atlanta-based MCs were opting to project overtly Southern identities. Some were into the sort of fast, hyper bass music and X-rated booty rhymes that Campbell and his Florida colleagues were putting on the map—others favored a sound that was slower than bass but still very Southern-sounding. Shy D, however, was never a Southern-style rapper. He was a native New Yorker who made Atlanta his adopted home, and *Got to Be Tough* sounds like it could have been recorded in Queens, Brooklyn, or the Bronx instead of the South. Occasionally, Shy D gets into social issues; "Paula's on Crack" is a blunt, hard-hitting tune about a young woman who has turned to prostitution to support her crack cocaine addiction. But most of the time, Shy D sticks to boasting lyrics on this LP, which falls short of remarkable but is still an enjoyable and decent slice of 1980s B-boy rhyming.

Alex Henderson

Mellow Man Ace

Escape From Havana
August 1989, Capitol

Cypress Hill, the Mexikinz, Kid Frost and Afro-Rican are among the Latinos who have made valuable contributions to rap—a genre historically dominated by Black males. Like those MCs, the distinctive Mellow Man Ace has used his experiences as a Latino to his artistic advantage when rapping. On his debut album, *Escape From Havana*, the L.A.-based Cuban-American fluctuates between aggressive hardcore rap and more melodic and commercial fare. Ace, who raps in both English and Spanish, had a major hit in "Mentirosa"—an infectious, salsa-influenced gem sampling Santana's "Evil Way." That song and the ballads "B-Boy in Love" and "If You Were Mine" show that even at his most commercial, he still has integrity—while "Rap Guanco," "Mas Pignon" and "River Cubano" demonstrate how hard and forceful he can get. Ace, like a lot of rappers, spends too much time boasting about his microphone skills. Nonetheless, *Escape From Havana* is an individualistic, risk-taking work that's well worth hearing.

Alex Henderson

M.O.P.

To the Death
April 1994, Select

On the success of their first single "How About Some Hardcore," the duo of Lil Fame and Billy Danzenie followed up with their first full-length album, which may as well be called "How About a Lot More Hardcore." The Mash Out Posse bring a level of intensity and energy to the microphone that truly has to be heard to appreciate. Of course, if you're not into that whole guns, thugs, and killing people kind of thing, this isn't for you; as they say on one of the skits on the album, where an interviewer asks them "Can you truly say your music promotes positive outlooks among its listeners?," "Next question!" But, for the gangsta rap aficionado, this album is not to be missed.

Brad Mills

Keith Murray

The Most Beautifullest Thing in This World
November 1994, Jive

Before he managed to get himself locked up for a brief bit later in the decade on an assault charge, Keith Murray was assaulting microphones and thesauruses alike with his ill "Sychosymatic" lyrical skills. Introduced to the rap world at the end of 1993 via a guest spot on the song "Hostile" off Erick Sermon's first solo album, *Double or Nothing*, Murray stepped out on his own at the beginning of the next year with the mellow Sermon-produced hit single "The Most Beautifullest Thing in This World," then backed it up with a full-length debut by the same title. There is nothing new in Sermon's loping music that you couldn't get on EPMD albums or from other recordings by members of the Def Squad, although he did continue to bring the funk hot and viscous as always. The main attraction on *The Most Beautifullest Thing in This World*, then, is Murray's raw, emotionally charged flow and droll (though not as funny as Redman), articulate rhymes, straight out of the battle-rap school of hip-hop. His lyrics, in other words, are often tasty going down (particularly on "How's That" with Sermon and Redman and "Bom Bom Zee" with Paul Hightower and Hurricane G), but won't necessarily stick around to quell any sort of hunger. Still, the album went gold, and is easily recommended for fans of *Double or Nothing* or *Whut? Thee Album*.

Stanton Swihart

Nas

Illmatic
April 1994, Columbia

Often cited as one of the best hip-hop albums of the '90s, *Illmatic* is the undisputed classic upon which Nas' reputation rests. It helped spearhead the artistic renaissance of New York hip-hop in the post-*Chronic* era, leading a return to street aesthetics. Yet even if *Illmatic* marks the beginning of a shift away from Native Tongues-inspired alternative rap, it's strongly rooted in that sensibility. For one, Nas employs some of the most sophisticated jazz-rap producers around: Q-Tip, Pete Rock, DJ Premier, and Large Professor, who underpin their intricate loops with appropriately tough beats. But more importantly, Nas takes his place as one of hip-hop's greatest street poets—his rhymes are highly literate, his raps superbly fluid regardless of the size of his vocabulary. He's able to evoke the bleak reality of ghetto life without losing hope or forgetting the good times, which become all the more precious when any day could be your last. As a narrator, he doesn't get too caught up in the darker side of life—he's simply describing what he sees in the world around him, and trying to live it up while he can. He's thoughtful but ambitious, announcing on "N.Y. State of Mind" that "I never sleep, 'cause sleep is the cousin of death," and that he's "out for dead presidents to represent me" on "The World Is Yours." Elsewhere, he flexes his storytelling muscles on the classic cuts "Life's a Bitch" and "One Love," the latter a detailed report to a close friend in prison about how allegiances within their group have shifted. Hip-hop fans accustomed to 73-minute opuses sometimes complain about *Illmatic*'s brevity, but even if it leaves you wanting more, it's also one of the few '90s rap albums with absolutely no wasted space. *Illmatic* is a great lyricist, in top form, meeting great production, and it remains a perennial favorite among serious hip-hop fans.

Steve Huey

Naughty by Nature

Naughty by Nature
September 1991, Tommy Boy

There was not a bigger, more contagious crossover radio smash in the autumn of 1991 than Naughty by Nature's "O.P.P.," a song that somehow managed the trick of being both audaciously catchy and subversively coy at the same time. Its irrepressible appeal—the Jackson 5 sample, the saucy subject matter, the huge anthemic chorus, Treach's phat rat-a-tat flow—was so widespread, in fact, that it played just as well to the hardcore heads in the hood as it did to the hip-hop dabblers in the suburbs. The beauty of the trio's self-titled full-length debut is that it is every bit as musically accomplished, and every bit as ghetto fabulous, in its entirety as that watershed first single. *Naughty by Nature* is both a pop and a rap classic that chews up stylistic real estate by the block, easily shifting from an old-school rhyme-off between Treach and Vinnie ("Pin the Tail on the Donkey"), the unflappable "Louie Louie" Vega-produced posse cut "1, 2, 3" (with verses from Flavor Unit compadres Lakim Shabazz and Apache), and the teeth-clinching combative dirge "Guard Your Grill," all of which very much come out swinging from the streets, to the more measured, emotionally developed "Ghetto Bastard," which brings an upbeat but nail-tough point of view to a grim tale of parental and societal deprivation without ever asking for an ounce of sympathy. With the assistance of Queen Latifah's makeshift patois, the trio even brought something of the Caribbean to East Orange with "Wickedest Man Alive." All the tracks are as street as they are club astute, trimming the funk loops with live keyboards and saxophone and sanguine, soulful melodies. A must-have album for fans of East Coast rap.

Stanton Swihart

19 Naughty III
February 1993, Tommy Boy

Despite an excellent debut album, Naughty by Nature was pegged as a one-hit wonder by some observers—after all, they'd never duplicate the inescapably catchy "O.P.P.," would they? *19 Naughty III*'s lead single, "Hip Hop Hooray," proved that they could, and the album confirmed that Naughty by Nature were indeed highly underrated in terms of consistency. It's a shade less consistent than the debut, but has all the same strengths: head-nodding beats, Treach's bouncy flow, and a difficult balance between street attitude and accessibility. Naughty by Nature clearly comes from the streets, and have all the aggression of the streets, but they don't glamorize the streets; sure, they'll take care of themselves in a harsh environment, but ultimately they prefer to steer clear of trouble, cops, and jail. It's a refreshingly grounded and realistic perspective, best heard on "Daddy Was a Street Corner," "The Hood Comes First," and "The Only Ones." There are also energized guest appearances from Heavy D ("Ready for Dem") and Queen Latifah ("Sleeping on Jersey"). Kay Gee again shows himself a sorely underappreciated producer, with one foot in the clubs and the other one on the street corner, and that's true of the group as a whole. A few slower moments don't prevent *19 Naughty III* from ranking as Naughty by Nature's second straight triumph.

Steve Huey

Nice & Smooth

Ain't a Damn Thing Changed
September 1991, Ral

Nice & Smooth returned for a second album that injected a much-needed and entirely welcome sense of the absurd into the generally far too austere and sincere New York City underground hip-hop community, which has traditionally sacrificed humor for hardcore technique when it comes to rhyming. Greg Nice and Smooth B., however, are often downright silly and goofball on *Ain't a Damn Thing Changed*. Despite the conscientious-sounding title, there is very little on the album that is concerned with anything other than, first, rocking the microphone, and second, timing the punch line perfectly. There are certainly serious themes tossed out from time to time. The major hit "Sometimes I Rhyme Slow"—which is simply the track of Tracy Chapman's sober, solemn "Fast Car" matched with the duo's superimposed rhyming—makes references to guns, violence, and drug abuse, and several of the other songs contain similar allusions. But far more frequently, the album is characterized by a reckless old-school (think Audio Two) sense of fun, with loony, stream-of-consciousness lyrics that are most interested in dropping the other shoe, shouted sing-along choruses ("Sex, Sex, Sex," "Paranoia"), insanely catchy vocal hooks ("Sometimes," "One, Two and One More Makes Three"), and production filled with bouncy beats and cartoonish, electronic keyboards. The ubiquitous presence of fully harmonized (and occasionally out-of-tune) background vocals is another characteristic that gives the album a jarringly whimsical quality that most rap crews at the time would never have come within earshot of. A Partridge Family sample even plays a substantial role in "Hip Hop Junkies," and the theme song to *Sanford & Son* is the basic track of "Step by Step." Perhaps their sense of humor, to a certain extent, obscures the straight-up rhyming skills that the duo possesses. Greg Nice's abrupt, roughneck dramatics juxtaposed against Smooth B.'s

serene, butter-slick delivery strikes the perfect vocal balance, and the posse cut, "Down the Line," which includes Gang Starr's Guru (perhaps the preeminent underground rapper), proves that they can bring it rugged and raw when they so decide. But because the duo is willing to poke fun at themselves and their craft so unsparingly, the album is completely addictive, in the same way that sugar is, because it is an energy boost and instantly brings into relief an entirely different side of rap: one that doesn't take itself so seriously.

Stanton Swihart

Jewel of the Nile
June 1994, Ral

Years before Puff Daddy found multi-platinum success sampling David Bowie and the Police, Nice and Smooth were perfecting their own unique style of guilty pleasure hip-pop, scoring big hits with the infectious singles "Hip Hop Junkies" and "Sometimes I Rhyme Slow," which sampled the Partridge Family and Tracy Chapman, respectively. The underrated duo's knack for irresistible pop hooks continues on their forth album, beginning with "Return of the Hip Hop Freaks," a jazzy leadoff track so insistently, irritatingly catchy—its chorus is the kind that sticks in your head for weeks at a time—that it makes "Hip Hop Junkies" sound like a tuneless dirge. A mere 11 songs long, including a CD-only remix of "No Bones," *Jewel of the Nile* is an unfairly ignored treasure of '90s hip-pop at its most ingratiatingly mainstream, a nearly perfect little album that proves that hip-pop needn't be a pejorative label. Never the world's greatest lyricists, Greg Nice and Smooth Bee instead excelled at left-field but enormously effective samples (*Jewel of the Nile*'s "Do Watcha Gotta" skillfully jacks the snake-charmer groove from Jefferson Airplane's "White Rabbit"), undeniable chemistry and remarkable pop savvy. Whether mixing it up with a pre-*Whitey Ford* Everlast over crunchy rock & roll guitars on "Save the Children" or holding their own alongside hip-hop royalty Slick Rick, Nice and Smooth are at their infectious, upbeat best throughout *Jewel of the Nile*, one of the most underrated and unfairly overlooked hip-hop albums of the '90s.

Nathan Rabin

The Notorious B.I.G.

Ready to Die
September 1994, Bad Boy

The album that reinvented East Coast rap for the gangsta age, *Ready to Die* made the Notorious B.I.G. a star, and vaulted Sean "Puffy" Combs' Bad Boy label into the spotlight as well. Today it's recognized as one of the greatest hardcore rap albums ever recorded, and that's mostly due to Biggie's skill as a storyteller. His raps are easy to understand, but his skills are hardly lacking—he has a loose, easy flow and a talent for piling multiple rhymes on top of one another in quick succession. He's blessed with a flair for the dramatic, and slips in and out of different contradictory characters with ease. Yet, no matter how much he heightens things for effect, it's always easy to see elements of Biggie in his narrators and of his own experience in the details; everything is firmly rooted in reality, but plays like scenes from a movie. A sense of doom pervades his most involved stories: fierce bandits ("Gimme the Loot"), a hustler's beloved girlfriend ("Me & My Bitch"), and robbers out for Biggie's newfound riches ("Warning") all die in hails of gunfire. The album is also sprinkled with reflections on the soul-draining bleakness of the streets—"Things Done Changed," "Ready to Die," and "Everyday Struggle" are powerfully affecting in their confusion and despair. Not everything is so dark, though; Combs' production collaborations result in some upbeat, commercial moments, and typically cop from recognizable hits: the Jackson 5's "I Want You Back" on the graphic sex rap "One More Chance," Mtume's "Juicy Fruit" on the rags-to-riches chronicle "Juicy," and the Isley Brothers' "Between the Sheets" on the overweight-lover anthem "Big Poppa." Producer Easy Mo Bee's deliberate beats do get a little samey, but it hardly matters: this is Biggie's show, and by the time "Suicidal Thoughts" closes the album on a heartbreaking note, it's clear why he was so revered even prior to his death.

Steve Huey

N.W.A

N.W.A and the Posse
1987, Ruthless

Hip-hop was still very much dominated by New York in 1987 when Macola Records (a company that distributed numerous L.A. rap labels in the 1980s, including Eazy-E's Ruthless Records) distributed N.W.A's groundbreaking debut album, *N.W.A and the Posse*. Ice-T was among the few West Coast rappers enjoying national exposure, and gangsta rap was far from the phenomenon it would become a few years later. A number of the songs—including the brutally honest "Dopeman"—would be reissued on *Straight Outta Compton*, while Eazy-E's first single, "Boyz-n-the Hood" would be included on his 1988 solo album, *Eazy-Duz-It*. And the entire album would be reissued by Priority in 1989. This CD ranges from those early and seminal examples of gangsta rap to songs that are pure, unapologetic fun—such as the outrageously humorous "Fat Girl" and N.W.A associates the Fila Fresh Crew's "Drink It Up," an infectious ode to booze employing the melody from the Isley Brothers' "Twist and Shout." One of the Crew's members was the D.O.C., who Dr. Dre and Eazy-E took to the top of the charts in 1989. Though not quite on a par with *Straight Outta Compton*, this is an engaging and historically important CD that's well worth acquiring.

Alex Henderson

Straight Outta Compton
1989, Priority

Unapologetically frightening, N.W.A's *Straight Outta Compton* is one of the most seminal albums in the history of rap and greatly influenced countless gangsta rappers. N.W.A didn't invent gangsta rap—Ice-T and Schoolly D had already embraced first-person narratives focusing on the harsh realities of ghetto life—but the L.A. group made it even more violent. Portraying gang members and other felons, Dr. Dre,

Ice Cube, MC Ren and Eazy-E took listeners on an arresting journey through L.A.'s tough Compton ghetto. Critics of this highly controversial album contended that N.W.A was glamorizing Black-on-Black crime—the rappers countered that they weren't encouraging violence, but rather were presenting an audio documentary of life as they knew it growing up in Compton. Subsequently, gangsta rap would be plagued by numerous soundalike MCs who lacked even a fraction of N.W.A or Ice-T's originality. But in the innovative hands of N.W.A., it was bold, inspired and arresting. [*Straight Outta Compton* was released in an edited version with all of the profanity removed, and instead changed around so that the album became a parody of edited albums by using hilariously silly replacements for swears and graphic descriptions.]

Alex Henderson

100 Miles and Runnin'
August 1990, Ruthless

Released almost two years after the seminal *Straight Outta Compton* and a little less than a year before the flawed *Niggaz4life*, *100 Miles and Runnin'* effectively accomplishes what an EP should. It both built upon the lingering hype that had surrounded *Straight Outta Compton* and foreshadowed the *Niggaz4life*-era N.W.A, a group that had grown increasingly dissident yet also much wiser after experiencing seemingly endless controversy. This EP's title track remains one of the group's best moments, and with the MTV-aired video picturing them fleeing from police, it was a fitting song for N.W.A to release at the time; furthermore, the song's thick, heavy production showcases rather brilliantly the fact that Dr. Dre had furthered his production talents immensely. Though perhaps hard to stomach for some, "Just Don't Bite It" is anything but forgettable, with Eazy-E's and MC Ren's prerogatives transcending farce and heading into much more potent territory, making this they group's most amusing (in a sense) yet also its most effectively disturbing venture into misogynistic porno rap. The next song, "Sa Prize, Pt. 2," functions as a sequel to "Fuck tha Police" while "Real Niggaz" then provides a sample of the racial belligerence that would fill the first half of *Niggaz4life* and "Kamurshol" promotes the upcoming album over a foreboding beat. Poignantly employing a heavy use of cinematic skits in addition to the songs themselves, *100 Miles and Runnin'* showcases N.W.A's strengths succinctly, balancing them perfectly across just five songs, each representing different aspects of the group's tainted ideology. Any more is almost too much—as would arguably be the case with *Niggaz4life*.

Jason Birchmeier

Niggaz4life
May 1991, Ruthless

It couldn't have been easy for N.W.A to succeed *Straight Outta Compton*, an indisputable landmark moment in rap history. So after three years of enormous controversy, inner strife, and anticipation, it wasn't exactly a surprise when the group's follow-up, *Niggaz4life*, found N.W.A a much different group. The departure of Ice Cube, the group's primary and most talented lyricist, surely made a difference, but there was more. Dr. Dre, Eazy-E, MC Ren, and prolific ghostwriter the D.O.C. weren't out to rouse people anymore à la "Fuck tha Police"; they were out to shock. By mostly devoting the first half of this album to racial belligerence and the second half to merciless misogyny, N.W.A successfully made a truly disturbing, if not horrifying, album. Unfortunately, in its effort to create one of the most shocking albums ever, the group forsook some of its talent. For instance, some of Dre's most ominous productions ever often lie buried beneath nearly inaccessible lyrics. Occasionally, such as in "Automobile" or "I'd Rather Fuck You," Eazy manages to at least integrate some farce, but not everyone will share his twisted sense of humor. Taken as a whole, *Niggaz4life* exemplifies just how distraught the group members were with each other and also why their collaborations would quickly come to an end. They had taken their music as far as it could go with this album—too far for it's own good, perhaps—yet there's a certain vicarious pleasure here if you view *Niggaz4life* as antiestablishment exploitation rather than sincerity. N.W.A pushed the limits of social acceptability here in every way imaginable in hopes of offending everyone. You may not agree with the shocking result, nor advocate it, but you can't help admiring the rebellious (and perhaps even self-parodying) intent, particularly when you keep in mind that this album amazingly debuted atop the *Billboard* album chart.

Jason Birchmeier

The N.W.A Legacy, Vol. 1: 1988–1998
March 1999, Ruthless

Not to be considered an N.W.A best-of (1996's *Greatest Hits* accomplishes that), *The N.W.A Legacy, Vol. 1: 1988–1998* is actually a compilation of some of the better cuts from the group, the group members' solo work, and their collaborations with others. In fact, there are only three actual N.W.A tracks on here, "Fuck tha Police," "Alwayz into Something," and "Straight Outta Compton," with more of the glory going to Eazy-E and Dr. Dre, the latter of whose "Natural Born Killaz," "Keep Their Heads Ringin'," and "Let Me Ride" make up the bulk of the compilation's second disc. It's a nice sampler of early West Coast rap, but it doesn't quite delve into any artist's repertoire enough to give a true taste of any of them. Add this to the fact that the tracks aren't in chronological order, and *The N.W.A Legacy, Vol. 1: 1988-1998* becomes a better option for those who are looking for a broad overview of a scene they don't know much about, but it's a fun collection nonetheless, and shouldn't be thought of any less because of it.

Marisa Brown

Rodney O

Me & Joe
1989, DMSR

When Rodney O. & Joe Cooley's first full-length album, *Me & Joe*, came out in 1988, many hip-hoppers were re-evaluating the Los Angeles rap scene. In the early to mid-'80s, L.A. wasn't famous for hardcore rap; many people associated Southern California with the high-tech, synthesizer-driven electro-hop sounds of the Egyptian Lover, the Arabian

Prince, Uncle Jam's Army, and the World Class Wreckin' Cru (the group that Dr. Dre belonged to before N.W.A.). But in 1987 and 1988, the disturbing gangsta rap of Ice-T and N.W.A. was giving people a different impression of L.A. rap—and all of a sudden, hip-hoppers were expecting hardcore rap to come from Southern California. Although Rodney and Cooley both had electro-hop credentials, *Me & Joe* is essentially a hardcore rap effort. The LP isn't gangsta rap—Rodney doesn't rap in the first person about gang fights or drive-by shootings—but even so, it sent out a message that South-Central L.A. could provide aggressive hip-hop (as opposed to crossover stuff). While some of Cooley's scratching shows an awareness of New York DJs like Jam Master Jay and Cut Creator, *Me & Joe* doesn't sound it was recorded in the Big Apple. Rodney flows like a West Coast rapper—he doesn't sound like he's from Brooklyn, Queens, or the Boogie Down Bronx—and the production tends to be cleaner than what many New York hip-hoppers were favoring at the time. *Me & Joe* isn't a masterpiece; as far as L.A. rap goes, it isn't as important or as challenging a record as Ice-T's *Power* or N.W.A.'s *Straight Outta Compton*. But it's a decent and often catchy, if slightly uneven, footnote in the history of West Coast hip-hop.

Alex Henderson

O.C.

Word...Life
1994, Wild Pitch

O.C.'s auspicious debut announced the arrival of one of modern rap's more gifted storytelling lyricists. The artist dropped his thesis on "Time's Up" a '90s rap benchmark track that served to separate rap's true school from its ever-expanding species of frauds. On that track, O.C. takes umbrage with money-grubbing fake MC's over a combined droning bass guitar and well-plucked sample from Slick Rick's "Hey Young World." The album is drenched in classic, hard-core East Coast B-boyism, but O.C. puts the boasts on the shelf to take up more existential subject matter. On "Born to Live" he spins wistful fables from his childhood in order to discuss life's bittersweet fragility: "born to live/a to die/life's so damn short and I wonder why." The soulful composition lifts a tasteful snippet from Keni Burke's "Keep Rising to the Top." O.C.'s connections to Organized Konfusion shine through on his debut, showcasing a thought-provoking intellectual diversity rarely seen on rap albums. Organized's Pharoah Monche sits in on the album, as do producers Buckwild and Lord Finesse. *Word...Life* saw little commercial success due, in part, to the drained coffers of the failed endeavor that was Wild Pitch Records, but one would be hard-pressed to find a hard-core hip-hop fan without this recording somewhere in their collection

M.F. DiBella

Onyx

Bacdafucup
1993, Def Jam

At the time that *Bacdafucup* hit the record racks and airwaves, Onyx seemed to be inventing a genre all their own: heavy metal rap. Of course, on closer inspection, it is not at all surprising stylistically, given their link to Def Jam and Run DMC, the record company and crew that introduced heavy guitar riffs into hip-hop. Onyx, though, seemed far more threateningly hardcore than Run DMC ever were, and each song on their debut album seems like a quick-triggered, menacing chip set squarely on the shoulders of MCs Big DS, Suavé, Fredro, and Sticky Fingaz. That the entire album from beginning to end circumvents almost any backlash by being so brilliantly catchy as well, is a sterling tribute to how strong a quartet Onyx truly is on this first effort. The group gives the impression that they wanted to spotlight the sort of cartoonish, directionless anger that existed in a lot of hardcore rap, and then funnel that sort of energy into songs full of singalong choruses and joyous, chanted hooks that lend a certain feeling of camaraderie to the whole album. The release is mostly co-produced by Run DMC's Jam Master Jay and newcomer Chyskillz, and its music has a tense, wired edge that amplifies the vividness of the threatening lyrics. Sonically, it has a hardcore East Coast/New York City cast, full of throbbing bass and screeching siren-like effects. The grimy urban vibe is matched by Onyx's narrative thuggery, discharged straight from the streets like pumped-up news dispatches and predating the roughneck rap trend by several years. It's hard to imagine, given the gritty content of the album, that Onyx was aiming for airplay with *Bacdafucup*; nevertheless, almost in spite of itself, it was so good that it earned just that.

Stanton Swihart

Organized Konfusion

Organized Konfusion
1991, Hollywood

The inspired debut album from the duo of Prince Poetry and Pharoahe Monch was arguably *the* underground rap album of the 1990s, at a time when "underground," aside from Ultramagnetic MC's, didn't really yet exist in the coherent manner that it would later in the decade. It most definitely represented an alternative and ran perpendicular to much of what passed for mainstream hip-hop in 1991, with the possible exception of the Native Tongue family, with which Organized Konfusion shared a maverick, sometimes playful, sensibility if not an identifiable sound. The MCs trade rhymes and intertwining, singsong choruses like a pair of old school pros, but their lyrical flows and topical themes were decidedly progressive for the era, and even still manage to sound almost futuristic. Poetry is no slouch as a rapper and, in fact, probably would have been the headliner in almost any other group, but Monch is obviously the breakout star here. His vocal presence is looming and imposing, to an almost apocalyptic degree at times ("Prisoners of War," the title song), as he throws out a relentless jet stream of complex verbiage and knotty images. But each is constantly surprising throughout *Organized Konfusion*, the reason it felt like such a cobweb clearer upon its release, and still feels so today. The duo also handled most of the production chores itself, creating a dense, visceral tapestry of strangely organic sounds, from the syrupy smooth and viscous tones of "Fudge Pudge" and "Audience Pleasers" to "Releasing Hypnotical Gases," all gurgling, alien internal processes, to the first whimsical single, *Who Stole My Last Piece of Chicken?*, presented here in its strikingly disparate original and remix versions. *Organized Konfusion* may be, alongside Main Source's *Breaking Atoms*, the quintessential cult hip-hop album from a decade full of forward-looking efforts.

Stanton Swihart

Stress: The Extinction Agenda
1994, Hollywood

Like a number of ambitious rap artists and groups of the era, Organized Konfusion chose to up the ante on its sophomore effort and use the music as a springboard to explore some associated motifs and collect them together under a loose conceptual frame. Unlike the majority of those artists, OK made it work, and work exceptionally well, by keeping the concepts themselves vague while adding an extra fine-edged intricacy to its verbal licks. Pharoahe Monch and Prince Poetry are even more commanding as lyricists on *Stress*, spinning out stories much closer to the nuts and bolts of the street than on their debut. But in typical fashion for such gifted artists, they probe the psychological implications of urban life rather than merely relaying its superficial qualities. In response, the album's sound is less eccentric without losing any of its innovation. In fact, the duo consistently draped its words in adroit and vibrant sound amalgams, frequently employing electric jazz samples to that end, especially on the Herbie Hancock-sampled "Extinction Agenda" and Buckwild-produced "Why," which brilliantly ties together various strains of the genre. The MCs also plumbed a darker periphery on the portentous "Bring It On," where each raised the level of the lyrical game to unusual heights. Those who prefer the funky-weird Organized of the first album still have plenty to enjoy as well, particularly "3-2-1" and "Let's Organize," a party cut that also bounced off guests Q-Tip and O.C. What *Stress* might have lost in freshness and mirth from its predecessor, though, it gained in cohesiveness, consciousness, resonance, and, most strikingly, vision.

Stanton Swihart

Original Flavor

Beyond Flavor
1993, Atlantic

Veteran jazz drummer Max Roach has often compared rap to bebop, and for all the differences between jazz and rap, there are, in fact, some parallels—especially on the East Coast. Like the beboppers of the 1940s and 1950s, many New York, Philadelphia, and Boston rappers have been obsessed with technique. Anyone who has attended a hip-hop competition in any of those cities knows how technique-obsessed East Coast MCs can be; like bop icon Sonny Stitt, they view music as a form of sportsmanship and want to make sure you know how impressive their chops are. That obsession with technique is impossible to miss on 1993's *Beyond Flavor*, the second album by Original Flavor. This New York group is about flow, flow, and more flow, which is a different mindset from the gangsta rap mindset of many West Coast rappers. If, in 1993, you asked a hip-hop expert what the main differences between East Coast and West Coast rappers were, he/she would have responded that while the West Coast was about beats, hooks, and storytelling, the East Coast was about rhyming technique. There were many exceptions to that generalization, but *Beyond Flavor* does fit that stereotypical view of New York rap; Original Flavor and its allies (including a young, pre-solo career Jay-Z) spend most of this CD bragging about their rapping skills and showing off their considerable technique. When MCs have this much technique, the flow-for-the-sake-of-flow approach can be exhilarating—even if it does wear thin after awhile. Listening to *Beyond Flavor* is a lot of like hearing a group of East Coast hard boppers showing you how fast they can play standards; although chops for the sake of chops has its limitations, you still find yourself admiring and enjoying the display of virtuosity.

Alex Henderson

OutKast

Southernplayalisticadillacmuzik
April 1994, La Face

It is on OutKast's debut album that the fledgling production team Organized Noize began forging one of the most distinctive production sounds in popular music in the '90s: part hip-hop; part live, Southern-fried guitar licks and booty-thick bass runs; and part lazy, early '70s soul. The album was not only artistically successful but also thrived commercially, leaping into the Top 20 album chart on the back of the outstanding hit single "Player's Ball" and eventually going platinum. Although a little bit too dependent on overly simplistic and programmed snare beats, the music is unconditionally excellent, with languid, mellow melodies sliding atop rapid, mechanical drums. Organized Noize already had their distinguishing sound figured out,

down to the last twanged, wah-wahed note. But what makes *Southernplayalisticadillacmuzick* such a wonderful album has even more to do with the presence of its rappers, Dre and Big Boi. No one sounded like OutKast in 1994—a mixture of lyrical acuity, goofball humor, Southern drawl, funky timing, and legitimate offbeat personalities. Few rappers of the '90s have displayed such an inventive sense of rhyme flow either, and few rap artists in general have ears as attuned to creating such catchy melodic and vocal hooks. Almost every song has some sort of tuneful chant or repetitive hook that marks it as instantly memorable. There are occasional dull and mediocre spots, such as "Call of Da Wild" and the overlong "Funky Ride," that can't even be elevated by a head-nodding bassline or a tricky rhyme. Such low points, however, are far outshined by the brilliant moments. Already an extremely strong showing, OutKast would continue to develop into one of the finest, most consistently challenging (not to mention booty-shaking) rap groups of the decade.

Stanton Swihart

Paris

The Devil Made Me Do It
October 1990, Tommy Boy

One listen to *The Devil Made Me Do It* makes one wonder if Paris recorded the album in a cloistered, cold bunker—or at least the kind of abandoned warehouse he and his crew marched through during his videos. As with early Public Enemy (a primary inspiration) and the two X-Clan records, the best moments of Paris' debut work on two levels. Plenty of these tracks have dark, sleek grooves beneath them, built on expert beat programming and vicious claws instead of hooks. In addition to this, there's Paris' scholarly, tightly wound rhymes, which are crammed with pro-black themes—odds are Eldridge Cleaver's *Soul on Ice* and Bobby Seale's *Seize the Time* were committed to memory long before they were written. As one of early '90s Afrocentric rappers, Paris was one of the most unique and most talented in his field, his angered voice cutting and tense enough to make any listener squirm in her or his seat. As often as these tracks are peppered with samples of Chuck D, Black Panthers, and Malcolm X, Paris is never outshone. Poignant tracks like "Break the Grip of Shame," "The Hate That Hate Made," "The Devil Made Me Do It," and "Wretched" ("Mindless music for the masses makes ya think less of the one that hates ya") make for a joyless listen, but it's just as riveting as the most provocative and hedonistic gangsta record.

Andy Kellman

Sleeping with the Enemy
1992, Scarface

The Devil Made Me Do It established Paris as a pro-black radical, a firebrand. The follow-up, 1992's *Sleeping With the Enemy*, saw the MC unleash his most provocative rhymes to such an extent that WEA, Tommy Boy's distributor at the time, opted to have no part in it. This forced Paris to reactivate his Scarface imprint; it delayed the album's release, but attention from the press helped take it to the Top 25 of the top R&B/hip-hop album chart. While Paris spent much of his debut relating his distrust of authority, two inflammatory songs—"Bush Killa" and "Coffee, Donuts & Death"—took that anger into revenge-fantasy territory. The former, formed on a grinding guitar riff and an "Atomic Dog"-based groove, goes into detail about his anger over the then president's neglect of the inner city; though it opens with a mock assassination and features graphic lyrical content, the rationale for Paris' last-resort approach is revealed thusly: "'Cause when I'm violent is the only time the devils hear it." This goes directly into "Coffee, Donuts & Death," in which Paris avenges racist policemen who rape females and abuse power in his community. Lost in all the controversy were some of Paris' most somber and compelling tracks, including "Thinka 'Bout It," "The Days of Old," and "Assata's Song." Worlds apart from the menacing tones of his best-known work, these are introspective, pensive, and frankly beautiful songs that look at the way blacks hurt their own and the value and resilience of black women. The album's production honestly comes close to rivaling the Bomb Squad, with samples—from a young DJ Shadow—and a tense, chaotic mix swirling throughout the more agitated tracks. The only true gripe is the number of lengthy interludes.

Andy Kellman

Man Parrish

The Best of Man Parrish: Heatstroke
December 1996, Hot Productions

Man Parrish, cloaked wizard of the synthesizer, made the artificial appear irresistibly funky. *The Best of Man Parrish: Heatstroke* includes 14 of his best productions, from the seminal electro classics "Hip Hop Be Bop (Don't Stop)" (a John Robie co-production) and "Boogie Down Bronx" (a feature for JVC Force) to his more exploratory dance collages like "Six Simple Synthesizers" and "Techno Trax." Similar to avant turntablist Christian Marclay, Parrish was a figure with more relevance to the disco avant-garde than the hip-hop scene—certainly his collaborators Klaus Nomi and Bowie acolyte Cherry Vanilla wouldn't have shown up on Sugar Hill. Parrish's experimental nature makes for a rocky ride through a "hits" compilation, which takes in mainstream dance ("Heatstroke"), ruddy vocoder electro ("Man Made"), and the type of robot pop that would've made even cut-up popsters Perrey-Kingsley cringe. Still, barring the random old-school/electro compilation that includes a Man Parrish cut, this is the only place to hear what made him stand out.

John Bush

The Pharcyde

Bizarre Ride II the Pharcyde
1992, Delicious Vinyl

The cover shot of a Fat Albert-ized Pharcyde roller coasting their way into a funhouse makes perfect sense, as the L.A.-based quartet introduced listeners to an uproarious vision of earthy hip-hop informed by P-Funk silliness and an everybody-on-the-mic street-corner atmosphere that highlights the incredible rapping skills of each member. With multiple voices freestyling over hilarious story-songs like "Oh Shit," "Soul Flower," the dozens contest "Ya Mama," and even a half-serious driving-while-black critique named "Officer," *Bizarre Ride II the Pharcyde* proved Daisy Age philosophy akin to De La Soul and A Tribe Called Quest wasn't purely an East Coast phenomenon. Skits and interludes with live backing (usually just drums and piano) only enhance the freeform nature of the proceedings, and the group even succeeds when not reliant on humor, as proved by the excellent heartbreak tale "Passing Me By." The production, by J-Sw!ft and the group, is easily some of the tightest and most inventive of any hip-hop record of the era. Though *Bizarre Ride II the Pharcyde* could have used a few more musical hooks to draw in listeners before they begin to appreciate the amazing rapping and gifted productions, the lack of compromise reveals far greater rewards down the line.

John Bush

Labcabincalifornia
November 1995, Delicious Vinyl

LabCabinCalifornia is a more mature record than The Pharcyde's debut. That's not necessarily a good thing, as the group's playful attitude and comic raps were much of what made them so irresistible. True, age has enlightened The Pharcyde on "Moment in Time" and the single "Runnin'," the former a salute to the past and the latter a description of their flight from South Central's Pharcyde Manor to the Hollywood Hills. But the music is much of the problem here. Though the raps are solid, tempos never vary from the usual mid-tempo jam. The keyboard-driven melodies are good—some better than others—but a little variety is needed. The last three tracks ("The Hustle," "Devil Music," "The E.N.D.") do evoke the spirit of the debut, but by that time it's too late—the sophomore jinx has hit.

John Bush

P.M. Dawn

Of the Heart, Of the Soul and of the Cross: The Utopian Experience
August 1991, Gee Street

It may not have been embraced by the entire hip-hop community, but P.M. Dawn's ponderously titled debut *Of the Heart, of the Soul and of the Cross: The Utopian Experience* was a startling reimagination of the music's possibilities. In the post-De La Soul age, hip-hop seemed open to all sorts of eccentrics, but P.M. Dawn was still difficult for purists to accept: They were unabashed hippies whose sound and sensibility held very little street appeal, if any. *Of the Heart...* is soaked in new age spirituality and philosophical introspection, and a song title like "To Serenade a Rainbow" is likely to raise eyebrows among more than just skeptical b-boys. It's true that there's some occasional sappiness and navel-gazing, but it's also true that the group's outlook is an indispensable part of its musical aesthetic, and that's where *Of the Heart...* pushes into the realm of transcendence. It still sounds revolutionary today, although you'd have to call it a Velvet Revolution: it's soft and airy, with ethereal vocal harmonies layered over lush backing tracks and danceable beats. The shimmering ballads "Set Adrift on Memory Bliss" (built on an unlikely sample of Spandau Ballet's "True") and "Paper Doll" were the hits, but they aren't quite representative of the album as a whole. Some tracks, like "Comatose" and "A Watcher's Point of View (Don't 'Cha Think)," are surprisingly funky and driving, and there's also an even more explicit nod to the dancefloor in the Todd Terry hip-house collaboration "Shake." The more reflective raps ("Reality Used to Be a Friend of Mine," "Even After I Die," "In the Presence of Mirrors") strike a fascinating balance between those sensibilities, and there's still little else like them. In the end, *Of the Heart...* is enormously daring in its own way, proving that pop, R&B, and hip-hop could come together for creative, not necessarily commercial, reasons.

Steve Huey

Poison Clan

2 Low Life Muthas
1990, Effect/Luke

Discovered by Luther Campbell, Poison Clan was initially molded similarly to 2 Live Crew, as evidenced by *2 Low Life Muthas*' production—executed by Campbell and 2 Live Crew producer Mr. Mixx—and its mostly lighthearted but occasionally raunchy themes of womanizing, partying, and goofing around. J.T. Money and Debonaire broke out with this album's booming, "Shaft"-sampling "Dance All Night." Not terribly dissimilar from 2 Live Crew tracks like "Move Somethin'," it's one of the few clean songs Poison Clan released—it's easily their most accessible, and it's also one of the best dance-rap singles of the early '90s; some rotation of the video on *Yo! MTV Raps* helped give the group some notice, but the remainder of the album didn't do a great deal to build on its success. The duo proves to be competent on the mic, but they don't go much beyond that, and Mr. Mixx's production work rarely hits the level of his best work for 2 Live Crew. J.T. Money briefly hits upon the gangsta themes that would saturate the remaining PC records; on "Bad Influence," he shows he's most comfortable with hard-edged rhymes. This decent debut comes off as 2 Live lite, an issue that would be rectified right after this.

Andy Kellman

Poisonous Mentality
1992, Effect/Luke

Poisonous Mentality goes to show that J.T. Money wasn't truly in his element on *2 Low Life Muthas*. The departure of his partner, Debonaire, to Home Team ("Pick It Up") brought about a radical shift (a look at the album's cover, depicting J.T. and his droogs escaping with a bag of loot, indicates this) from relatively lighthearted material to harder production and an endless flurry of expletives. Whether relating crude and often cruel sexual exploits or tales of criminal dirty work—often within the same song—it's plain to see that the album has much less to do with J.T.'s desire to keep up with the times, and all to do with him coming into his own. The only full-on sop to the party crowd is "Shake Whatcha Mama Gave Ya"—featuring one of Luther Campbell's delivered-while-on-the-can guest choruses—and it just happens to be one of the best of its kind. This is one of the toughest,

meanest records to have come from the south, from one of the most sick-minded and hilarious MCs of the era. The fact that the album was an anomaly when compared to most of the others coming from Florida at the time has a lot to do with why it isn't widely recognized as such.

Andy Kellman

Poor Righteous Teachers

Holy Intellect
1990, Profile

Holy Intellect was Poor Righteous Teachers' excellent debut, as well as the group's highest charting release, peaking at number 142 on the Billboard 200. Rhymes reflecting the beliefs of the Five Percent Nation never translated to mass appeal, but the group's inability to become more popular is kind of surprising, given that this album can be enjoyed by any fan of Gang Starr, Main Source, the Jungle Brothers, or A Tribe Called Quest. At the very least, it contains some of the era's most undervalued MC'ing. Perhaps it was the group's name, neither as tough-sounding as Public Enemy nor as clever as Brand Nubian. Or maybe they just lacked that one big breakout single. Produced mostly by Tony "Tony D" Depula (YZ, Jazzy Jay, King Sun), *Holy Intellect* contains many examples of late '80s/early '90s rap positing brainy lyrics over energizing productions suited for a party. Having a good time and feeding your mind didn't have to be mutually exclusive events. Take "Butt Naked Booty Bless," which, instrumentally, could be used for any old crowd-goading chatter, rather than Wise Intelligent lines like "Lessons are the key to the style I drop/ Hip-hop, not miscellaneous rhymes." It is worth noting that three tracks were released as singles that hit the Billboard rap chart: the hard-charging "Holy Intellect," the relaxed "Rock Dis Funky Joint," and the tender "Shakiyla," (which sampled Zapp's "Be Alright" before Big Daddy Kane's "Prince of Darkness" and 2Pac's "Keep Ya Head Up."

Andy Kellman

Pure Poverty
1991, Profile

Rappers who take a strong moral stance were beginning to proliferate when the second Poor Righteous Teachers album came out, but this young trio had been "teaching the righteous way" since the beginning, combining hard, funky beats with culture-conscious didacticism. With stage names like Wise Intelligent, Culture Freedom and Father Shaheed, the three may have come across as a bit pretentious, but they really were quite serious; their stated goal was to "teach the blind, deaf and dumb who the real living God is." Okay, maybe a lot pretentious. And if it weren't for the spare, airtight beats and the dexterous samples, their lyrics of cultural awareness, self-sufficiency and religious discipline would probably have fallen flat. But those beats are there and so is the flow—Wise Intelligent's lilting, reggae-influenced speed rap is especially fine, especially on the dancehall-inflected

"Easy Star" and "I'm Comin' Again," an a cappella rap. There are occasional moments of self-contradiction, maybe even hypocrisy: though they solemnly preach respect for "the Black woman," they apparently see nothing wrong with using her orgasmic moans and groans to spice up a track or two. But the album's still a winner overall.

Rick Anderson

Positive K

The Skills Dat Pay Da Bills
November 1992, 4th & Broadway

A duet with MC Lyte on "I'm Not Havin' It" and some underground compilation appearances led to Positive K's 1992 debut for 4th & Broadway, and it features another song where Positive K has female troubles. "I Got a Man" hit the top of the rap singles chart in 1993 and even reached number 14 on the pop chart, giving him the most success he'd ever enjoy. The remainder of the album has more of a hard edge to it, with the Big Daddy Kane-produced "Nightshift" and the downright raw "Carhoppers" and "One 2 the Head" adding dimensions to the album. There's much more to this album than a fluke hit.

Andy Kellman

Powerule

Powerule, Vol. 1
1991, Interscope

Another exceedingly strong album from the copious early '90s hip-hop scene that dropped away virtually unnoticed, Powerule's *Volume One* gave voice to the largely unheard Latino quotient of the late-night, underground New York City community that had always been nearly as essential to the rap world as the African-American community but, up to that point, had rarely made it out of the recording studio. Powerule had dropped a classic underground cut, "Brick in the Wall," in the late '80s, but it wasn't until this 1991 full-length debut that the full extent of their abilities hit wax. It more than delivered on their promise. Most of the album is produced or co-produced by Powerule themselves, and they inject a tough-but-seductive Puerto Rican ambience into the music, in the form of salsafied breaks and samples and shuffle beats and rhythms (especially in songs such as "When the Rhythm Calls," with its unbelievable constantly scratched beat, and "Que Pasa?"). Mixed with the hallucinatory, stop-action, stoned New York vibe of East Coast hip-hop, the album often takes on, to a greater degree than many from its era, the resonance of swaggering nightlife, sweltering summertime block parties, and the cramped, sweaty spaces in which the hip-hop lifestyle has always thrived. From the opening cut, "Back," to the end of the album, *Volume One* characterizes where hip-hop was born and where its beating heart has always remained: musty basements, rooftops, electric after-hours clubs, and hazy studios, with the ever-present thump of low-end pounding at the gut and the tension of the unknown hanging in the air. The trio move from the mellowness of hanging out ("Back," "Que Pasa?") to kicking rhymes with friends ("Rub Off the Wax," featuring Leaders of the New School, and "Young Stars From Nowhere") to doing a show ("5 Minutes 2 Showtime") to hitting the clubs (the buoyant brag-fest "Gots Ta Get This," co-produced by and featuring Large Professor). And on the molasses-thick,

reggae-ish "Premises," MCs Prince Power and E. Ville go beyond simply reflecting the culture, and reflect *on* it as well.

Stanton Swihart

Professor X

Years of the 9, On the Blackhand Side
1991, 4th & Broadway

A New York-based hip-hopper who preached a Black nationalist philosophy, Professor X was the founder of the Black Muslim organization known as the Blackwatch Committee and the leader of the group X-Clan. X's debut solo album, *Years of the 9, on the Blackhand Side*, contrasted sharply with the type of graphic, profane gangster rap that had become incredibly popular. You won't find any gratuitous violence or sexually exploitive material on tunes like "Vanglorious Crib," "The Sleeper Has Awakened," and "Reality," which encourage Black pride, self-respect and cultural awareness. But while some hip-hop writers were quick to praise the Professor's positivity (especially on the East Coast), this enjoyable CD wasn't nearly as big a seller as many of the gangsta rap recordings the West Coast provided in 1991.

Alex Henderson

Public Enemy

Yo! Bum Rush the Show
1987, Def Jam

Sometimes, debut albums present an artist in full bloom, with an assured grasp on their sound and message. Sometimes, debut albums are nothing but promise, pointing toward what the artist could do. Public Enemy's gripping first album, *Yo! Bum Rush the Show*, manages to fill both categories: it's an expert, fully realized record of extraordinary power, but it pales in comparison with what came merely a year later. This is very much a Rick Rubin-directed production, kicking heavy guitars toward the front, honing the loops, rhythms, and samples into a roar with as much in common with rock as rap. The Bomb Squad are apparent, but they're in nascent stage—certain sounds and ideas that would later become trademarks bubble underneath the surface. And the same thing could be said for Chuck D, whose searing, structured rhymes and revolutionary ideas are still being formed. This is still the sound of a group comfortable rocking the neighborhood, but not yet ready to enter the larger national stage. But, damn if they don't sound like they've already conquered the world! Already, there is a tangible, physical excitement to the music, something that hits the gut with relentless force, as the mind races to keep up with Chuck's relentless rhymes or Flavor Flav's spastic outbursts. And if there doesn't seem to be as many classics here—"You're Gonna Get Yours," "Miuzi Weighs a Ton," "Public Enemy No. 1"—that's only in comparison to what came later, since by any other artist an album this furious, visceral, and exciting would unquestionably be heralded as a classic. From Public Enemy, this is simply a shade under classic status.

Stephen Thomas Erlewine

It Takes a Nation of Millions to Hold Us Back
April 1988, Def Jam

Yo! Bum Rush the Show was an invigorating record, but it looks like child's play compared to its monumental sequel, *It Takes a Nation of Millions to Hold Us Back*, a record that rewrote the rules of what hip-hop could do. That's not to say the album is without precedent, since what's particularly ingenious about the album is how it reconfigures things that came before into a startling, fresh, modern sound. Public Enemy used the template Run-D.M.C. created of a rap crew as a rock band, then brought in elements of free jazz, hard funk, even musique concrète, via their producing team, the Bomb Squad, creating a dense, ferocious sound unlike anything that came before. This coincided with a breakthrough in Chuck D's writing, both in his themes and lyrics. It's not that Chuck D was smarter or more ambitious than his contemporaries—certainly, KRS-One tackled many similar sociopolitical tracts, while Rakim had a greater flow—but he marshaled considerable revolutionary force, clear vision, and a boundless vocabulary to create galvanizing, logical arguments that were undeniable in their strength. They only gained strength from Flavor Flav's frenzied jokes, which provided a needed contrast. What's amazing is how the words and music become intertwined, gaining strength from each other. Though this music is certainly a representation of its time, it hasn't dated at all. It set a standard that few could touch then, and even fewer have attempted to meet since.

Stephen Thomas Erlewine

Fear of a Black Planet
March 1990, Def Jam

At the time of its release in March 1990—just a mere two years after *It Takes a Nation of Millions*—nearly all of the attention spent on Public Enemy's third album, *Fear of a Black Planet*, was concentrated on the dying controversy over Profes-

sor Griff's anti-Semitic statements of 1989, and how leader Chuck D bungled the public relations regarding his dismissal. References to the controversy are scattered throughout the album—and it fueled the incendiary lead single, "Welcome to the Terrordome"—but years later, after the furor has died down, what remains is a remarkable piece of modern art, a record that ushered in the '90s in a hail of multi-culturalism and kaleidoscopic confusion. It also easily stands as the Bomb Squad's finest musical moment. Where *Millions* was all about aggression—layered aggression, but aggression nonetheless—*Fear of a Black Planet* encompasses everything, touching on seductive grooves, relentless beats, hard funk, and dub reggae without blinking an eye. All the more impressive is that this is one of the records made during the golden age of sampling, before legal limits were set on sampling, so

this is a wild, endlessly layered record filled with familiar sounds you can't place; it's nearly as heady as the Beastie Boys' magnum opus *Paul's Boutique* in how it pulls from anonymous and familiar sources to create something totally original and modern. While the Bomb Squad was casting a wider net, Chuck D's writing was tighter than ever, with each track tackling a specific topic (apart from the aforementioned "Welcome to the Terrordome," whose careening rhymes and paranoid confusion are all the more effective when surrounded by such detailed arguments), a sentiment that spills over to Flavor Flav, who delivers the pungent black humor of "911 Is a Joke," perhaps the best-known song here. Chuck gets himself into trouble here and there—most notoriously on "Meet the G That Killed Me," where he skirts with anti-homophobia—but by and large, he's never been so eloquent, angry, or persuasive as he is here. This isn't as revolutionary or as potent as *Millions*, but it holds together better, and as a piece of music, this is the best hip-hop has ever had to offer.

Stephen Thomas Erlewine

Apocalypse 91...The Enemy Strikes Black
October 1991, Def Jam

Coming down after the twin highwater marks of *It Takes a Nation of Millions* and *Fear of a Black Planet*, Public Enemy shifted strategy a bit for their fourth album, *Apocalypse 91...The Enemy Strikes Black*. By and large, they abandon the rich,

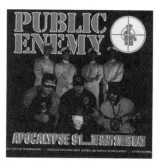

dense musicality of *Planet*, shifting toward a sleek, relentless, aggressive attack—*Yo! Bum Rush the Show* by way of the lessons learned from *Millions*. This is surely a partial reaction to their status as the Great Black Hope of rock & roll; they had been embraced by a white audience almost in greater numbers than black, leading toward rap-rock crossovers epitomized by this album's leaden, pointless remake of "Bring the Noise" as a duet with thrash metallurgists Anthrax. It also signals the biggest change here—the transition of the Bomb Squad to executive-producer status, leaving a great majority of the production to their disciples, the Imperial Grand Ministers of Funk. This isn't a great change, since the Public Enemy sound has firmly been established, giving the new producers a template to work with, but it is a notable change, one that results in a record with a similar sound but a different feel: a harder, angrier, *determined* sound, one that takes its cues from the furious anger surging through Chuck D's sociopolitical screeds. And this is surely PE's most political effort, surpassing *Millions* through the use of focused, targeted anger, a tactic evident on *Planet*. Yet it was buried there, due to the seductiveness of the music. Here, everything is on the surface, with the bluntness of the music hammering home the message. Arriving after two records where the words and music were equally labyrinthine, folding back on each other in dizzying, intoxicating ways, it is a bit of a letdown to have *Apocalypse* be so direct, and there is no denying that the end result is still thrilling and satisfying, and remains one of the great records of the golden age of hip-hop.

Stephen Thomas Erlewine

Queen Latifah

All Hail the Queen
November 1989, Tommy Boy

As strong a buzz as Queen Latifah created with her debut single of 1988, "Wrath of My Madness" and its reggae-influenced B-side "Princess of the Posse," one would have expected the North Jersey rapper/actress' first album, *All Hail the Queen*, to be much stronger. Though not a bad album by any means, it doesn't live up to Latifah's enormous potential. The CD's strongest material includes "Evil That Men Do," a hardhitting duet with KRS-One addressing Black-on-Black crime and other social ills; the infectious hip-house number "Come Into My House"; the rap/reggae duet with Stetsasonic's Daddy-O "The Pros"; and the aforementioned songs. Unfortunately, boasting numbers like "A King and Queen Creation" and "Queen of Royal Badness" aren't terribly memorable. Especially disappointing is "Mama Gave Birth to the Soul Children," a duet with De La Soul that surprisingly, is both musically and lyrically generic. To be sure, Latifah's rapping skills are top-notch—which is why *All Hail the Queen* should have been consistently excellent instead of merely good.

Alex Henderson

Raheem

The Vigilante
1988, A&M

Raheem Bashawn, formerly of the Geto Boys, was only 17 when, in 1988, he recorded his first solo album, *The Vigilante*. Because the infamous, highly controversial Geto Boys are best known for gangsta rap, some people might assume that *The Vigilante* is a gangsta rap album. But it isn't. Although *The Vigilante* is definitely hardcore rap, it doesn't contain any first-person accounts of drive-by shootings, gang bangs, or carjackings. Raheem actually spends most of the album attacking rival MCs and articulating why he believes he's superior; so lyrically, *The Vigilante* is much closer to L.L. Cool J, Run-D.M.C. or Big Daddy Kane than N.W.A., Ice-T, or the Geto Boys. When Raheem raps about getting out the shotgun, it's merely a figure of speech—he's saying that his rhyming skills have the power to make "sucker MCs" get out of hip-hop and find another line of work. A few of the tracks tackle social issues (including "Say No" and "Peace"), but most of the material is apolitical. But while *The Vigilante* is dominated by fairly conventional lyrics, the production of Karl Stephenson and James Smith sets it apart from many of the rap albums that came out in 1988. At the time, a lot of hip-hop producers (especially on the East Coast) went for the drum machine/scratching/sampling formula favored by East Coast residents like Marley Marl. But *The Vigilante* is more musical, and Stephenson uses synthesizers to play real melodies: pop/rock melodies, funk melodies, and reggae melodies.

Musically, this LP is impressive, and like a lot of Dr. Dre's work with N.W.A., Snoop Doggy Dogg, and others, it demonstrates that hip-hop can be hardcore and musical at the same time.

Alex Henderson

Raw Fusion

Live From the Styleetron
November 1991, Hollywood

When Money-B came out with his side project Raw Fusion, it was clear that the Digital Underground member wasn't trying to duplicate Underground's sound. Parts of *Live from Styleetron* are as quirky and eccentric as Underground, but while Underground was heavily influenced by the 1970s funk grooves of George Clinton and Parliament/Funkadelic, Fusion had more in common with jazzy alternative rappers like A Tribe Called Quest, De La Soul and the Jungle Brothers. The production is interesting, and Raw Fusion keeps things unpredictable by sampling everything from jazz and funk to reggae. Humor is an important element of cuts like "Traffic Jam," "Nappy Headed Ninja" and "Ah Nah Go Drip," which pokes fun at the jheri-curl hairstyle that was popular in the 1980s. But the CD takes a more serious turn with "Wild Francis," the tale of an inner-city woman who grows up to be a Marxist revolutionary and is killed in a confrontation with the police. Some of Money's associates from the Underground are on board, including Shock-G and Humpty Hump, but again, no one's going to mistake *Styleetron* for an Underground album. With *Styleetron*, Money saw to it that Raw Fusion was a strong rap act in its own right.

Alex Henderson

Redman

Whut? Thee Album
September 1992, Def Jam

Whut? Thee Album is a terrific debut that established Redman as one of the top MCs on the East Coast. His aggressive delivery is more than hardcore enough for the streets, but *Whut?* is first and foremost a party record. Redman's subject matter centers around his love of funk and his equal love of pot, with some sex and violence thrown in for good measure. He's able to carry it all off with a singular sense of style, thanks to a wild sense of humor that results in some outlandish boasts, surreal threats, and hilarious left-field jokes. In "Blow Your Mind," for example, he announces, "watch me freak it in Korean!," stumbles through part of a verse, and mutters "ah, forget it"; another great moment is "Redman Meets Reggie Noble," a brief duet between himself and his own alter ego in the great Slick Rick tradition. Other offbeat highlights include the genuinely useful instructional track "How to Roll a Blunt" and the hilarious sexcapade story song "A Day With Sooperman Lover." Credit for the album's infectious vibe also has to go to producer Erick Sermon, who fills *Whut?* with deep, loose-limbed beats cribbed from P-Funk and Zapp. Slamming party jams like "Time 4 Sum Aksion," "Rated R," and "Watch Yo Nuggets" are the real meat and potatoes of the record, and Redman's driving, forceful rhyme style makes them all the more invigorating. Still the strongest, most consistent outing in his catalog, *Whut? Thee Album* clearly heralds the arrival of a major talent.

Steve Huey

Dare Iz a Darkside
November 1994, Def Jam

Redman may have become a household name among the rap community by the end of the '90s, but there was a time when he garnered little more than a cult following. Why? Well, *Dare Iz a Darkside* illustrates this better than any of his other '90s albums—nowhere else has Redman ever been this odd, to be quite frank. It's fairly evident here that he'd been listening to his George Clinton records and that he wasn't fronting when he alluded to "A Million and 1 Buddah Spots" that he'd visited. In fact, this album often divides his fans. Many admire it for its eccentricities, while others deride it for being quite simply too inaccessible. It's almost as if Redman is trying to puzzle listeners on *Dare Iz a Darkside* with his continually morphing persona. In fact, there's actually little questioning his motives—it's a matter of fact that Redman's trying to be as crazy as he can without alienating *too* many of those who first knew him for his affiliation with EPMD. And while that affiliation does aid this album, since Erick Sermon plays a large role in production, it's not quite enough. If this album has one unforgivable flaw besides the debatable quirks in Redman's persona, it's the production. Sermon isn't up to his usual standards here, unfortunately, and the album could really use some of his trademark funk. But the reason most fans either feel devotion or disdain for this album isn't the beats, but rather Redman's antics. If you appreciate his wacky sense of insane humor, this album is a gold mine. If you're more into his latter-day Method Man-style rhymes, then this album probably isn't one you want to bother with. After all, though Redman became a household name by the end of the '90s, it surely wasn't because of albums like this.

Jason Birchmeier

Pete Rock & C.L. Smooth

All Souled Out
1991, Elektra

This six-song EP officially introduced Pete Rock & C.L. Smooth to the hip-hop listening community, and it is hard to imagine a stronger or more confident introduction. Pete Rock's unmatched production sound is already in place, fully-formed, drenched in obscure soul music samples and rumbling, cavernous bass. Characterized by his trademark sonic signature, muted and phased trumpet, and flute loops, the songs sound regal with endless depth (with the exception, perhaps, of his own enjoyably buoyant rhyming vehicle, "The Creator"). Of course, C.L. Smooth's lyrics have just as much to do with that regal quality. His vocals are so laid-back and understated—even soothing—that they can be deceptive and difficult to grasp. Once the listener finds a way in, however, there is much to be found in his words; bypassing the normal rap self-involvements, Smooth instead opts to make moral arguments and ask intellectual questions of the urban community, in essence holding a mirror up to that

community without ever devolving into didacticism or soapbox judgment. He is decidedly tough-minded but also sympathetic. Standouts include both versions of "Good Life," the irresistible "Go With the Flow," and the anthemic title track, with rapid-fire rhyming from Smooth and a perfectly funky organ riff, but the whole EP is essential.

Stanton Swihart

Mecca and the Soul Brother
1992, Elektra

It would have been hard to match the artistic success of their debut EP on a full-length recording, but Pete Rock & C.L. Smooth did just that on *Mecca and the Soul Brother*, and they did so in the most unlikely way of all after the succinctness of *All Souled Out*—by coming up with a sprawling, nearly 80-minute-long album on which not a single song or interlude is a throwaway or a superfluous piece. Granted, 80 minutes is a long stretch of time for sustained listening, but the music is completely worthy of that time, allowing the duo to stretch out in ways that their EP rendered impossible. Again, the primary star is Pete Rock's production acumen, and he ups the ante of rock-solid drums, steady cymbal beats, smooth-rolling bass, and fatback organ, not to mention his signature horn loops. C.L. Smooth is the perfect vocal match for the music. He is maybe one of the few MCs capable of rapping a fairly credible love song, as he does on "Lots of Lovin'." "They Reminisce Over You (T.R.O.Y.)," a tribute to friend and Heavy D. dancer Trouble T-Roy, who was accidentally killed, packs a poignant emotional weight, but it is Smooth's more direct and conscientious—and frequently autobiographical—side which ultimately carries the album lyrically. The songs are connected and the album is propelled forward by Rock's quick, soul-tight interludes; these are usually bits of old R&B and soul tunes but sometimes they're spoken pieces or spontaneous, freestyle sessions. These interludes provide a sort of dense spiritual tone and resonance in the album that is not religiously based at all, but fully hip-hop based, emerging from the urban altars that are the basements and rooftops of the city.

Stanton Swihart

The Main Ingredient
1994, Elektra

On their third release overall and second full-length, Pete Rock & C.L. Smooth scaled back on the expansive scope of their sprawling first opus, *Mecca & the Soul Brother*, indeed opting to magnify the main ingredients of their sound: Pete Rock's brilliant production chops and C.L Smooth's complex lyrical delivery. The result is an album that is far more focused, with all the ragged edges and loose threads tied up. It is also just as good as the first record, perhaps an even more satisfying single listen. *The Main Ingredient* is full of rich, resonant, hypnotic songs—the production being among some of the most seductive in hip-hop—that subtly, but absolutely, swing with their lock-step precision. In characteristic Pete Rock fashion, all of the sharp edges have been sanded down, leaving a vibrant and completely lush musical backdrop which seems to have a dreamy nostalgia about it. Old '60s and '70s soul, soul-jazz, and funk samples abound, and the music is dotted with gauzy keyboard washes, hugely echoed bass-drum kicks, milky basslines, and muted horn loops, almost sounding like they are emanating out of water. All of the songs feel immediate, yet they are infused with the sort of roomy ambience that lends to each the impression of a classic tune, evocative of an earlier era, but not one that can be described exactly, and not one to which you can definitively point. As usual, C.L. Smooth is lyrically on point, spitting out intellectual rhymes and narratives that are just as propulsive and engaging as the music. The only negative aspect about the album, then, is that it ended one of the finest hip-hop duos of the first half of the 1990s.

Stanton Swihart

The Roots

Organix
1993, Remedy

The Roots' low-profile debut set out many of the themes they would employ over the course of their successful career. An intro, "The Roots Is Comin'," is barely over a minute long, yet long enough to exemplify the band's funky bassline (here played by Leonard Hubbard), their dreamy and emotional organ chords (thanks to Scott Storch), and their ferociously swift yet clear rhymes from the group's focal MC Black Thought. The song that follows, "Pass the Popcorn" would have been called a "posse cut" in 1993. Everyone could've used a little more practice before stepping up to the mic on this song, but the spirit of the song are not lost in the amateurishness. The creative venture "Writers Block" is an example of just the opposite, as Black Thought flows with spoken word, comically and creatively expressing the experience of a day in the life of a Philadelphian using mass transit. The instrumentation is appropriately frantic and punctuated by [cymbal] crashes (like any mass transit system). Fans of *Do You Want More*, the Roots album released immediately following *Organix*, will recognize the music of "I'm Out Deah," "Leonard I-V," and "Essawhamah?" Another track to note is "The Session (Longest Posse Cut in History),"—no false claim at 12 minutes and 43 seconds. This album should be a part of any Roots fan's collection—not so much because it is an example of their artistry at its best, but because it allows you to see where they came from and how fruitful of a journey it's been.

Qa'id Jacobs

Run-D.M.C.

Run-D.M.C.
1984, Profile

Years after the release of Run-D.M.C.'s eponymous 1984 debut, the group generally was acknowledged to be hip-hop's Beatles—a sentiment that makes a lot of sense, even if *Run-D.M.C.* isn't quite the equivalent of a rap *Please Please Me*. Run-D.M.C. were the Beatles of rap because they signaled a cultural and musical change for the music, ushering it into its accepted form; neither group originated the music, but they gave it the shape known today. But, no matter how true and useful the comparison is, it is also a little misleading, because it implies that Run-D.M.C. also were a melodic, accessible group, bringing in elements from all different strands of popular music. No, Run-D.M.C.'s expanded their music by making it tough and spare, primarily by adapting the sound and attitude of hard rock to hip-hop. Prior to this, rap felt like a block party—the beats were funky and elastic, all about the groove. Run-D.M.C. hit *hard*. The production is tough and minimal, built on relentless drum machines and Jam Master Jay's furious scratching, mixing in a guitar riff or a keyboard hit on occasion. It is brutal urban music, and Run and D.M.C.'s forceful, muscular rhymes match the music. Where other MCs sounded cheerful, Run and D.M.C. prowl

and taunt the listener, sounding as if they were a street gang. And while much of the record is devoted to braggadocio, boasting, and block parties, Run-D.M.C. also addressed grittier realities of urban life, giving this record both context and thematic weight. All of this—the music, the attitude, the words, the themes—marked a turning point for rap, and it's impossible to calculate *Run-D.M.C.*'s influence on all that came afterward. Years later, some of the production may sound a bit of its time, but the music itself does not because music this powerful and original always retains its impact and force as music.

Stephen Thomas Erlewine

King of Rock
1985, Profile

Take the title of Run-D.M.C.'s *King of Rock* somewhat literally. True, the trailblazing rap crew hardly abandoned hip-hop on their second album, but they did follow through on the blueprint of their debut, emphasizing the rock leanings that formed the subtext of *Run-D.M.C.* Nearly every cut surges forward on thundering drum machines and simple power chords, with the tempos picked up a notch and the production hitting like a punch to the stomach. If the debut suggested hard rock, this *feels* like hard rock—over-amplified, brutal, and intoxicating in its sheer sonic force. What really makes *King of Rock* work is that it sounds tougher and is smarter than almost all of the rock and metal records of its time. There is an urgency to the music unheard in the hard rock of the '80s—a sense of inevitability to the riffs and rhythms, balanced by the justified boasting of Run and D.M.C. Most of their rhymes are devoted to party jams or bragging, but nobody was sharper, funnier, or as clever as this duo, nor was there a DJ better than Jam Master Jay, who not just forms the backbone of their music, but also has two great showcases in "Jam-Master Jammin'" and "Darryl and Joe" (the latter one of two exceptions to the rock rules of the album, the other being the genre-pushing "Roots, Rap, Reggae," one of the first rap tracks to make explicit the links between hip-hop and reggae). Even if there a pronounced rock influence throughout *King of Rock*, what makes it so remarkable is that it never sounds like a concession in order to win a larger audience. No matter how many metallic guitar riffs are on the record, this music is as raw and street-level as the debut. It manages to be just as dynamic, exciting, and timeless as that album, as it expands the definition of what both Run-D.M.C. and rap could do.

Stephen Thomas Erlewine

Raising Hell
1986, Profile

By their third album, Run-D.M.C. were primed for a breakthrough into the mainstream, but nobody was prepared for a blockbuster on the level of *Raising Hell*. Run-D.M.C. and *King of Rock* had established the crew's fusion of hip-hop and hard  rock, but that sound didn't blossom until *Raising Hell*, partially due to the presence of Rick Rubin as producer. Rubin loved metal and rap in equal measures and he knew how to play to the strengths of both, while slipping in commercial concessions that seemed sly even when they borrowed from songs as familiar as "My Sharona" (heard on "It's Tricky"). Along with longtime Run-D.M.C. producer Russell Simmons, Rubin blew down the doors of what hip-hop could do with *Raising Hell* because it reached beyond rap-rock and found all sorts of sounds outside of it. Sonically, there is simply more going on in this album than any previous rap record—more hooks, more drum loops (courtesy of ace drum programmer Sam Sever), more scratching, more riffs, more of everything. Where other rap records, including Run-D.M.C.'s, were all about the rhythm, this is layered with sounds and ideas, giving the music a tangible *flow*. But the brilliance of this record is that even with this increased musical depth, it still rocks as hard as hell, and in a manner that brought in a new audience. Of course, the cover of Aerosmith's "Walk This Way," complete with that band's Steven Tyler and Joe Perry, helped matters considerably, since it gave an audience unfamiliar with rap an entry point, but if it were just a novelty record, a one-shot fusion of rap and rock, *Raising Hell* would never have sold three million copies. No, the music was fully realized and thoroughly invigorating, rocking harder and better than any of its rock or rap peers in 1986, and years later, that sense of excitement is still palpable on this towering success story for rap in general and Run-D.M.C. in specific.

Stephen Thomas Erlewine

Tougher Than Leather
1988, Profile

At the end of 1986, *Raising Hell* was rap's best-selling album up to that point, though it would soon be outsold by the Beastie Boys' *Licensed to Ill*. Profile Records hoped that Run-D.M.C.'s fourth album, *Tougher Than Leather*, would exceed the Beastie Boys' quintuple-platinum status, but unfortunately, the group's popularity had decreased by 1988. One of Run-D.M.C.'s strong points—its love of rock & roll—was also its undoing in hip-hop circles. Any type of crossover success tends to be viewed suspiciously in the hood, and hardcore hip-hoppers weren't overly receptive to "Miss Elaine," "Papa Crazy," "Mary, Mary," and other rap-rock delights found on the album. Thanks largely to rock fans, this album did go platinum for sales exceeding one million copies—which ironically, Profile considered a disappointment. But the fact is that while *Tougher Than Leather* isn't quite as strong as Run-D.M.C.'s first three albums, it was one of 1988's best rap releases.

Alex Henderson

Back From Hell
1990, Profile

Longevity isn't a realistic goal for most rappers, who are lucky if they aren't considered played out by their third or fourth album. By 1990, Run-D.M.C.'s popularity had decreased dramatically, and the Queens residents had lost a lot of ground to both West Coast gangster rappers like Ice Cube, Ice-T and Compton's Most Wanted. With its fifth album, *Back From Hell*, Run-D.M.C. set out to regain the support of the hardcore rap audience and pretty much abandoned rock-influenced material in favor of stripped-down, minimalist and consistently street-oriented sounds. Not outstanding but certainly enjoyable, such gritty reflections on urban life as "Livin' in the City," "The Ave.," and "Faces" made it clear that Run-D.M.C. was still well worth hearing. [*Back From Hell* was remastered and reissued in 1999.]

Alex Henderson

Down with the King
May 1993, Profile

After the poor response of *Back from Hell*, Run-D.M.C. decided to make some drastic changes. Their first point of order was to rebuild their dwindling street cred and reiterate their proven track record as the kings by compiling a best-of compilation. Simultaneously, they started work on a fresh and current-sounding album with the help of some of the hottest artists and producers in the rap game. Retreating from the funky new jack swing that overwhelmed *Back from Hell*, they enlisted Pete Rock, Q-Tip, EPMD, Naughty by Nature, the Bomb Squad, and Jermaine Dupri to help produce *Down with the King*. The new sound is decidedly more fashionable, and their fedoras and Adidas are abandoned here for bald heads and baggy black hoodies to match their new gangsta musical direction; which takes an obvious cue from Onyx (signed to Jam Master Jay's label), whose "Slam" was a platinum hit earlier in 1993. Instead of using the intersecting back-and-forth wordplay that launched their career, this new incarnation of Run-D.M.C. incorporates the trendy "grimy" sound with ensemble shouts over specific lyrical parts (think Leaders of the New School). The beats are less corny, less funk-inspired, and more jazzy and sinister, with ominous basslines, organs, and delayed horn samples, and the vocals are more raucous and angry. Longtime fans will wonder why the trio isn't staying true to its past, especially when Run borrow from newcomers Das EFX with "stiggitys" and "riggitys," but the album serves its purpose of winning over a new generation of fans, and old-timers can find solace in the fact that rock is incorporated again in "Big Willie," a throwback to "Rock Box" with a rippin' guitar part from Rage Against the Machine's Tom Morello. While less original than their earlier classic albums, this is an impressive showing from a rap group that's been together ten years, and is pretty damn innovative in its own right.

Jason Lymangrover

Saafir

Boxcar Sessions
1994, Qwest

In the 1990s, the Bay Area rap scene was full of gangsta rappers and G-funksters. But not every rapper who came from Oakland or San Francisco in the 1990s was into gangsta rap; in fact, there were plenty of Bay Area MCs who had nothing to do with that style or G-funk. Take Saafir, for example. *Boxcar Sessions*, the Oakland rapper's first album, favors an abstract, jazz-influenced approach to hip-hop. In terms of complexity and abstraction, Saafir's angular rapping style (which involves a lot of freestyling) is right up there with Digable Planets, A Tribe Called Quest, the Pharcyde, and De La Soul. Saafir is as jazzy as any of those alternative rappers, and he doesn't go for simplicity. But unlike Digable Planets or the Pharcyde, Saafir doesn't embrace a neo-hippie vibe.

Many of the lyrics on *Boxcar Sessions* (which was produced by the Hobo Junction crew) are venomous battle rhymes; Saafir spends much of the album attacking "sucker MCs" and "player haters" in an angry, aggressive fashion. The jazz-minded tracks and the complex, abstract nature of Saafir's rapping style might remind the listener of alternative rap, but the lyrics are not neo-hippie rhymes—*Boxcar Sessions* is, much of the time, a declaration of war on the rappers who Saafir places in the "sucker MC" and "player hater" categories. Obviously, battle rhymes were hardly something new in 1994; Kurtis Blow and other old-school rappers were lambasting sucker MCs 15 years before this CD came out. But Saafir finds clever, interesting ways to boast about his rhyming skills and attack rival MCs. Between Saafir's rapping style and the jazzy production, *Boxcar Sessions* is fairly fresh sounding.

Alex Henderson

Salt-N-Pepa

Hot, Cool & Vicious
1986, Next Plateau

One of the first albums to be released by an all-female rap group, *Hot, Cool & Vicious* is paced by its opening track, "Push It," one of the first rap songs to hit number one on the dance singles charts. Considering how little Salt-N-Pepa actually rap on "Push It," which is all about its instrumental hook, they maintain a surprisingly strong presence over most of *Hot, Cool & Vicious*. No, they aren't technical virtuosos on the mic, but their fairly basic raps are carried off with brash confidence and enthusiasm. Some of the other key tracks borrow ideas from outside sources: the single "Tramp" is a rap remake of the Otis & Carla soul classic, and "The Show Stopper" is an answer record to Doug E. Fresh's "The Show." The duo's sass comes across very well on "My Mic Sounds Nice" and "I'll Take Your Man," and they're equally assertive on "Chick on the Side." In the end, the album needs a little more weight to really come across well, but it's fun and danceable all the same.

Steve Huey

Blacks' Magic
March 1990, London/Next Plateau

Prior to the release of their third album, *Blacks' Magic*, Salt-N-Pepa were viewed as little more than pop crossover artists. Most of their singles had been rap remakes of old R&B songs, and they hadn't even rapped all that much on their biggest hit, "Push It," which got by on its catchy synth hook. But *Blacks' Magic* was where Salt-N-Pepa came into their own. It wasn't that their crossover appeal diminished, but this time they worked from a funkier R&B base that brought them more credibility among hip-hop and urban audiences. More importantly, they displayed a stronger group identity than ever before, projecting a mix of sassy, self-confident feminism and aggressive—but responsible—sexuality. The album's trio of hit singles—"Expression," "Do You Want Me," and the playful safe-sex anthem "Let's Talk About Sex"—summed up this new attitude and got the group plastered all over MTV. But there was more to the album than just the singles—track for track, *Blacks' Magic* was the strongest record Salt-N-Pepa ever released. Even if there's still a bit of filler here and there, *Blacks' Magic* successfully remade Salt-N-Pepa as their own women, and pointed the way to the even more commercially successful R&B/pop/hip-hop fusions of *Very Necessary*.

Steve Huey

Very Necessary
October 1993, London

Salt-N-Pepa exhibited a lot of growth on *Blacks' Magic* (1990), their third album and, by far, best to date. For their follow-up, *Very Necessary*, released a long three and a half years later, in 1993, the ladies delivered a fairly similar album. Like its predecessor, *Very Necessary* boasts a pair of major hits ("Whatta Man," "Shoop") and a lot of fine album tracks. Also like *Blacks' Magic*, *Very Necessary* is filled with strong, prideful rhetoric: femininity, sex, relationships, romance, respect, love—these are the key topics, and they're a world apart from those of the gangsta rap that was so popular circa 1993. And as always, the productions are dance-oriented, with a contemporary R&B edge. Most tracks were produced by Hurby "Luvbug" Azor, though Salt is credited on a few, chief among them "Shoop." *Very Necessary* is just as impressive as *Blacks' Magic*, if not more so. The key difference is, *Blacks' Magic* was a striking leap forward for Salt-N-Pepa, who were somewhat of a novelty act up to that point, whereas *Very Necessary* is a consolidation of everything that had worked so well for the duo previously. Hence the lack of surprises here. Still, the raised expectations don't change the fact that *Very Necessary* is one of the standout—and, for sure, one of the most refreshingly unique—rap albums of its era.

Jason Birchmeier

Scarface

Mr. Scarface Is Back
October 1991, Rap-A-Lot

Fresh from the brilliant success of "Mind Playing Tricks on Me," his breakthrough hit with the Geto Boys, Scarface continues his streak of excellence with his exceptionally creative solo debut, *Mr. Scarface Is Back*. One of the first genuine masterpieces of the gangsta era, the album draws heavily from the densely layered samplescapes of the Bomb Squad and the provocative ghetto-storytelling of Ice Cube. What sets Scarface apart from his New York and Compton peers, though, is his deep-Texas Houston locale, where coke and crime are daily operations. Scarface exploits this reality shockingly and cinematically throughout *Mr. Scarface Is Back*, beginning with the album-opening Al Pacino samples ("All I have in this world..."). From there, Scarface makes an explosive entry ("Ahh yeah, hah/Mr. Scarface is back in the motherf*ckin' house once again!") and tremors through one rhyme after another about the ins and outs of the gangsta life in a loose narrative sequence: drug dealing gone well ("Mr. Scarface"), the joy of recreational sex ("The Pimp"), heedless murder ("Born Killer"), mental unsoundness ("Murder by Reason of Insanity"), further mental unsoundness ("Diary of a Madman"), intoxicating heights of street superiority ("Money and the Power"), drug dealing gone awry ("Good

Girl Gone Bad"), and the consequential last hurrah ("A Minute to Pray and a Second to Die"). The narrative format of *Mr. Scarface Is Back* flows from beginning to end with engaging fluidity, though the album is just as enjoyable in bits and pieces, particularly the ferocious "Mr. Scarface," the remorseful "A Minute to Pray and a Second to Die," and the extensive sampling (Marvin Gaye's "What's Going On," War's "Four Cornered Room," and more, less-obvious source material). Scarface had always been the standout Geto Boy, and he's finally given ample space for his trademark street narratives on *Mr. Scarface Is Back*, one of the first gangsta rap albums to offer as much imagination as it does exploitation.

Jason Birchmeier

The World Is Yours
August 1993, Rap-A-Lot

Scarface once again quickly follows a Geto Boys album, *Till Death Do Us Part*, with a solo release, *The World Is Yours*, just as he'd done two years earlier with his brilliant solo debut, *Mr. Scarface Is Back*. The circumstances are otherwise quite different, though. Scarface had been on a roll in 1991: fresh off the breakthrough success of "Mind Playing Tricks on Me" and its similarly well-received Geto Boys album, *We Can't Be Stopped*, he unveiled a cinematic, somewhat conceptual solo debut that made him a bona fide national superstar. Furthermore, much changed within the rap world between 1991-1993, specifically the end of free-for-all sampling and the widespread proliferation of gangsta rap. Scarface thus delivers a follow-up that's a huge leap forward from his debut, both in terms of production and rhetoric. He works here mostly with producer N.O. Joe, who crafts a G-funk style distinctly modeled after the West Coast sounds of the moment à la *The Chronic*, and he favors personally introspective rhymes rather than his heedful narratives of the past. The heartfelt seven-and-a-half-minute "Now I Feel Ya" showcases this new lyrical approach best, as Scarface rhymes at one point about his new son and how in turn he's had to alter his lifestyle. The significant changes Scarface has made here on *The World Is Yours* showcase his unwillingness to revel in the past, as glorious as his past may have been, yet they at the same time may frustrate fans of his early work, as his new style moves him further into the gangsta rap mainstream.

Jason Birchmeier

The Diary
October 1994, Rap-A-Lot

With the dissolution of the Geto Boys far behind him, Scarface follows the epic overreaching of *The World Is Yours* with *The Diary*, a refreshingly modest album with a few really strong moments and little filler. Never short on ideas, Scarface had nonetheless gone a little too far with the 70-minute *The World Is Yours*. There was plenty of brilliance there, including the stunning "Now I Feel Ya," but you had to do some sifting to find it. That's less the case with the 43-minute *Diary*, which doesn't overextend its ambitions. Scarface

here once again offers a laid-back gangsta ballad, "I Seen a Man Die," that's as thoughtful and somber as the style gets and also perhaps the album highlight. Elsewhere, he teams up with fellow gangsta veteran Ice Cube on "Hand of the Dead Body" and reprises his best-known song, "Mind Playin' Tricks 94." Not counting the interludes, there's only ten songs here, and they're nearly all produced by the team of N.O. Joe and Mike Dean. It may make the album a short listen, yet it also makes *The Diary* one of Scarface's most solid efforts, one where you rarely, if ever, feel inclined to skip a song. And that's something you can't say about the work of most rappers, particularly ones as creative as Scarface.

Jason Birchmeier

Schoolly D

Schoolly D
1986, Jive

From recording some the earliest examples of gangsta rap to becoming one of the first artists signed to the Rykodisc label and then on to scoring Abel Ferrara films and becoming the *Aqua Teen Hunger Force* narrator, the crazy career of rapper Schoolly D begins here. Kicking his homemade debut off with "Rock music is a thing in the past/So all you long-haired people can kiss my ass," Schoolly shamelessly gives the hood people what they want with six tracks of sneakers, skeezers, guns, and money. He may not have set out to create gangsta rap, and his style is much looser than the hardcore baller stance that would later dominate the genre, but letting people know what time it is by giving Joan Jett's "I Love Rock n' Roll" an answer song that mentioned automatic weapons and getting high on "cheeba" set him on the path to becoming one of the earliest poster boys for the evils of rap. While lyrics like "Say it loud/I love rap and I'm proud" were standoffs to one audience, they were "hood lyrics for hood people," direct messages to the inner city delivered, packaged, and distributed by Schoolly himself. From the amateurish but wonderfully alive cover art to the raw beats and scratches provided by DJ Code Money, the rapper's debut is entirely homegrown and cheap in the best way possible. The "gangsta" tag the record has lived with doesn't touch upon the humorous and fun, sleazy subject matter and slang-filled rhymes, which when combined with the D.I.Y. packaging and recording make this something akin to the hip-hop version of the blue humor "party record." Luther Campbell was listening, and began dreaming of 2 Live Crew, but more importantly so was Ice-T, who has cited Schoolly's syncopation on "P.S.K. What Does It Mean?" as one of his—and gangsta rap's in general—biggest inspirations.

David Jeffries

The Adventures of Schoolly D
1987, Rykodisc

Gangster rap is associated primarily with the West Coast, but one of its earliest figures was Philadelphia's Schoolly-D who sent shock waves through hip-hop circles with "Saturday Night," "PSK What Does It Mean?" and other hard-hitting tales of inner-city crime and violence included on this 1987 compilation. Instead of simply examining social problems in the third person, he made things especially jolting by rapping in the first person about life as he knew it growing up in West Philly. Unfortunately, the underrated Schoolly never enjoyed the sales or recognition of Ice-T, Dr. Dre or Ice Cube. But listening to "PSK"'s shocking imagery, it becomes clear just how seminal a figure he was. Though Schoolly isn't nearly as graphic as some of his West Coast counterparts would be, there's no denying his influence. For those interested in hearing some of the earliest examples of gangster rap, *The Adventures of Schoolly-D* is essential listening.

Alex Henderson

Saturday Night! The Album
1987, Jive

Although there are more underground hits on Schoolly D's self-titled debut, his sophomore effort is a better album thanks to higher production values and more direct songs. The song lengths are generally shorter, making for a full-length with greater impact, and DJ Code Money has bought a better drum machine and discovered the joy of dropping quirky samples from cartoons on top of loops off funk records. "We Get Ill" and "Dedication to All B-Boys" are hard anthem highlights, while the underground favorite "Saturday Night" was the kind of sleazy tale of misogyny that put Schoolly in hot water with many critics and community leaders. It didn't help that his delivery had become much colder, sounding a lot less like the ghetto vaudevillian persona on his debut and more like the musclebound menace to society now found in hip-hop history books. Capping off what is otherwise the most representative early Schoolly D release is an odd number that points to his future in soundtracks. "It's Krack" features Schoolly mumbling gibberish in the background as spacy synths and strange scratches create an eerie soundscape. Originally released on Schoolly's own label, the tracks from *Saturday Night! The Album* received wider exposure when the young Rykodisc label released *The Adventures of Schoolly D* compilation, combining all the tracks here with his self-titled debut.

David Jeffries

How a Blackman Feels
October 1991, Capitol

Although one of the founders of gangster rap, Schoolly D never enjoyed the gold or platinum success of the many gangster rappers who reached the top of the charts in the late '80s and early to mid-'90s. The Philadelphian had recorded four albums for Jive/RCA when he resurfaced on Capitol with the uneven and erratic *How a Blackman Feels*. This isn't a bad album, but it isn't one of Schoolly's stronger efforts either. The CD's most engaging offerings include "Die Nigger Die" and "King of New York," both of which are chilling, first-person depictions of a drug dealer's violent world. The album will be of interest primarily to Schoolly's more devoted fans, while those investigating his music for the first time would do better to acquire *Saturday Night: The Album* or *Smoke Some Kill*.

Alex Henderson

2nd II None

2nd II None
September 1991, Profile

Tha D and K.K. once confessed publicly that they were not capable of freestyling in the grand tradition of rap, so it would be quite reasonable if *2nd II None* were not the most groundbreaking album in terms of its concepts and rhymes. And it is, in fact, lacking to some extent in those departments. On this debut album, the duo tended toward conventional gangsta braggadocio and, unfortunately also typical of the form, a rather blatant strain of misogyny. Crews like N.W.A.

and the Geto Boys, while similarly inclined, had nonetheless found ways to undercut or at least give context to the more repugnant, offensive, and sexist themes running through their songs in the way of a trenchant ghetto philosophy that spoke to harrowing issues of the inner-city experience. 2nd II None had little of that insight or ability to tweak gangsta rap clichés. What they did have was their own Dr. Dre sitting behind the boards in the person of DJ Quik, their skilled labelmate, and as a result the album does not lack in the least in the vitality of its sound, a deep, organic funk. His skilled way with a sampler and, frequently, live instruments make it entirely possible to listen to wonderful tracks like "Underground Terror" and the smoked-out blaxploitation porno of "Mystic" without noticing the trite words at all. Still, Tha D and K.K. deserve credit for breaking gangsta rap out of its aversion to the more melodious aspects of urban music. The duo had a tendency to slip into smooth R&B crooning during choruses, a novel technique at the time, previously seen as an affront to street authenticity but since quite commonplace in hip-hop. It helped the album break into the mainstream, and the singles "Be True to Yourself" and the horny "If You Want It" remain minor old-school classics by consequence.

Stanton Swihart

The Sequence

Sugarhill Presents the Sequence
1980, Sugar Hill

No doubt, Salt-N-Pepa emulated the Sequence, who preceded them as tough rap divas. The lineups and attitudes are similar, and none of the curvy rappers comes off as passive, unliberated women. Gwendolyn (Blondie) Chisholm, Cheryl (Cheryl the Pearl) Cook, and Angela (Angie B) Brown, b.k.a. Sequence were street-wise, gritty and butter-bred. "Simon Says" has a contagious, comical beat that's made for disco. Showing they do more than rap, they break off in "The Times When We're Alone," a slow and sensual winner. The nursery rhyme raps on "We Don't Rap the Rap," with its energetic beats, are like dancing pills. *Sesame Street*-like sounds continue, lyrically anyway, on "Funk a Doodle Rock Jam," infants must have loved this one, they could pronounce some lyrics, particularly "doodle." Heavy beats and well-spaced horns, married with Sequence's three part harmonies and leads, keeps you rocking until the end. The group borrowed from Parliament's "Give Up the Funk" and came up with "Funky Sound" where Blondie, Angie B and Cheryl the Pearl take turns busting bodacious raps.

Andrew Hamilton

The Sequence
1982, Sugar Hill

The Sequence's second album contains all of the same funky, soulful grooves they busted on *Sugar Hill Presents the Sequence*. It's almost an even split between the ballads and hip-hop numbers: "I Don't Need Your Love," a wailing beauty, pulled up lame at number 40 on Billboards' R&B chart in May of 1982, a poor showing for one of their best performances; "Love Changes," led by Angie B, is seven plus minutes of gut-wrenching soul searching; "Unaddressed Letter" is an unexpected piece of traditional soul that works like a charm; James Brown's "Cold Sweat" gets a makeover and a new feel; and finally, "Funk That (You Mothers)" and "Get It Together" are hip-hoppers accented with hot raps.

Andrew Hamilton

Erick Sermon

No Pressure
1993, Def Jam

When EPMD finally unravelled after months of rumors and internal turmoil, Erick Sermon wasted no time grabbing the mike. He's quite obsessed with proving he can cut it alone, although his self-titled debut didn't move far from EPMD's trademarks: fat, crunching basslines, neatly inserted samples lifted mainly from Zapp, tight vocal edits, and Sermon's mush-mouthed, deadpan raps. His targets included condoms, sexual warfare, hip-hop groupies, and would-be rap challengers. While this contains the obligatory "bitches" and "niggas" references, there's not as much gun worship as you might expect. *No Pressure* is as much, if not more, EPMD's final release as Erick Sermon's debut.

Ron Wynn

Lakim Shabazz

Pure Righteousness
1988, Tuff City

The first of two unjustly swept-to-the-side albums cut by Flavor Unit member Lakim Shabazz and his primary producer, DJ Mark the 45 King—who featured the young and energetic MC on releases like *Master of the Game*, *Rhythmical Madness*, and "The 900 Number"—*Pure Righteousness* is equal parts brash boasting and shouts to the Five Percent Nation of Islam, supported by dusty funk and jazz breaks, a little scratching, and some occasional drum-machine-driven boom bap. There's even a hip-house instrumental, "Adding On," based around D-Train's "You're the One for Me." That one hasn't aged too well, and the album isn't quite a classic, but it is essential for anyone into late '80s and early '90s rap that paid serious due to the Five Percent Nation, from Paris' *The Devil Made Me Do It* to X Clan's *To the East, Blackwards*. The album is front-loaded with its two best tracks, both lyrically and musically, with Shabazz voice at its most potent and inciting. And yeah, the second track, "Black Is Back," was quite possibly a major inspiration behind the "I'm Black, Y'all" (aka "I'm blackedy black black b-black black, yo, 'cause I'm black and I'm back") spoof in *CB4*. Still, it's hard not to get caught in its racing rush of electric piano, "Funky Drummer" loop, and proud rhymes, which do go well beyond pointing out the color of Shabazz's skin.

Andy Kellman

Shanté

Bitch Is Back
1992, Livin' Large

It's hard to believe that Roxanne Shante was only 16 when she recorded "Roxanne's Revenge" with legendary NY producer Marley Marl, and perhaps even more difficult to believe that she still sounds 16. Even as hip-hop evolves into a more vulgar, in-your-face style of music, Shante adapts and delivers the goods. Her latest effort proves that she can still rhyme among the best in the business, even going head to head with Kool G Rap with the track "Deadly Rhymes." A battle record to the end, this album should go down in history as one of the best ever created by a female rap artist.

Brad Mills

The Best of Cold Chillin'
October 2001, Landspeed

Most hip-hop fans wouldn't recognize a single track from Roxanne Shanté *other* than "Roxanne's Revenge," making some wonder whether *The Best of Cold Chillin'* is worth it when compared to all the great compilations that include her lone rap classic. There's a case to be made, though, since "Roxanne's Revenge" was her first single and she greatly improved over five years of recording. She found her niche quite soon, as evidenced by tough, no-nonsense beats-and-rhymes tracks like "Bite This" and "The Payback." Also, Shanté's "Def Fresh Crew" featured a lovable human beatbox named Biz Markie, and the future commercial king of Cold Chillin' makes a great appearance on "Def Fresh Crew." (Another all-time rapper, Kool G Rap, stops by for "Deadly Rhymes.") Listeners might be surprised at the quality of material here, but all in all *The Best of Cold Chillin'* definitely works best for golden-age fans who want to get back in the mood with a few period tracks they haven't heard before.

John Bush

Shinehead

The Real Rock
June 1990, Elektra

In the late 1980s and early '90s, New Yorkers ranging from Boogie Down Productions to Heavy D were combining rap with dancehall reggae. Another key player in this rap/reggae experimentation was Shinehead, who keeps things very positive and uplifting on his sophomore effort *The Real Rock*. However, much of the CD isn't reggae-influenced, and the East Coast resident wisely avoids being predicable. Ranging from such fun, lighthearted material as "World of the Video Game" and "Musical Madness" to the more serious messages of "Family Affair" (which draws on the Sly Stone classic and stresses the importance of a cohesive family unit), the anti-smoking tune "Cigarette Breath" and the spiritual title song, *The Real Rock* was one of the best rap releases of 1990. It's unfortunate that Shinehead's popularity was so short-lived.

Alex Henderson

Showbiz & A.G.

Runaway Slave
1992, PolyGram

A product of the tightknit Bronx underground posse D.I.T.C., *Runaway Slave* is a cornerstone album of hip-hop's middle school phase. Building on and borrowing from the layered, jazz-influenced sound of such contemporaries as Gang Starr and Pete Rock & C.L. Smooth, Showbiz & A.G. affixed a gangster mentality to grainy, fortified beats, etching their own unique style. While the crossover "Soul Clap" and "Party Groove" are club cuts, the rest of the album is more densely expressive. Showbiz and his talented peer Diamond shape their beats around simple, deep drum tracks—but add subtle loops of chaotic horns, loose strings, or abrupt piano notes to create concise and hard-hitting overtures. Tasteful flute swatches light up "Silence of the Lambs," an ear-ringing saxophone buzzes on "Still Diggin'," and the motor mouthed late legend Big L introduced himself on the classic down-the-line jam "Represent," pulling such punchlines as "MCs be braggin' about cash they collect/But them chumps is like Ray Charles 'cause they ain't seen no money yet." The young A.G. (aka Andre the Giant) flows effortlessly throughout this album, an MC whose skill and unique voice would only mature in the future. While some of the import of this album is muted by modern-day technological sound booth advancements, Showbiz & A.G. did it raw and undiluted and the resulting sound was fresh, innovative, and most of all satisfying for hip-hop heads.

M.F. DiBella

Sir Mix-A-Lot

Swass
1988, American

Sir Mix-A-Lot is one of greatest ironies in the history of rap. His occasional sociopolitical statements show he can be every bit as intelligent a commentator as KRS-One or Chuck D, but Mix's forte has always been the type of fun, escapist, even goofy fare that dominates his debut album, *Swass*. Though forceful and aggressive at times, the distinctive Seattle native never considered himself a hardcore rapper and is quick to point out that his influences range from quirky new waver Gary Numan to metal bands to George Clinton. Ranging from aggressive rap/metal like "Hip-Hop Soldier" and an inspired interpretation of Black Sabbath's "Iron Man" (which employs headbangers Metal Church) to his enjoyably silly impression of hillbillies on "Square Dance Rap" and "Buttermilk Biscuits," *Swass* set the tone for Mix's career by appealing to pop fans more than hardcore rap listeners. His strongest sociopolitical raps (including "Society's Creation" and "Jack Back") would come later.

Alex Henderson

Seminar
1989, American

With his second album, Sir Mix-A-Lot continued focusing primarily on the type of material that made his first reach gold status: escapist, lighthearted pop/rap that fared well among pop, R&B and dance-music circles, but generally wasn't well received in "the hood." What few sociopolitical songs the CD does contain are first-rate, including "The

(Peek-A-Boo) Game" (which uses Siouxsie & the Banshees as a reference point) and "National Anthem." An angry number addressing the Iran-contra scandal, the drug plague and the plight of Vietnam vets, the latter is as powerful as anything Public Enemy, KRS-One or Ice-T has done. Nonetheless, what made *Seminar* a hit weren't those gems, but odes to cars, gold chains and "fly girls." As enjoyable as such escapist fare as "My Hooptie" and "Beepers" is, Mix sells himself short by not including more message songs.

Alex Henderson

Mack Daddy
February 1992, American

The massive success of "Baby Got Back" may have earned Sir Mix-a-Lot the dreaded "one-hit wonder" label, as well as an appearance on VH1's "Where Are They Now?," but the Seattle native has always been a much more interesting and important figure than his reputation would suggest. One of the first rappers outside of New York and L.A. to score significant chart success, Mix-a-Lot's music is generally a lot more irreverent and tongue-in-cheek than people give him credit for, the work of a chubby studio geek living out his most ridiculous playboy fantasies on wax. "Baby Got Back" may be the song that put Sir Mix-a-Lot on the map, but it's actually one of the album's weaker tracks. Far better is *Mack Daddy*'s first single, "One Time's Got No Case," a song that finds Mix-a-Lot addressing standard hip-hop subject matter in a novel fashion, striking out against racist police officers not through gunplay or violence but by handing the guilty parties a righteous legal smackdown in a court of law. The rest of *Mack Daddy* charts a similarly cheeky cruise through the not-so-mean streets of Seattle, with Mix-a-Lot addressing such vital subject matters as the nefarious proprietors of fake designer merchandise at swap meets ("Swap Meet Louie") and the importance of not getting whipped by opportunistic females ("Sprung on the Cat"). It's all extremely silly stuff, made even more so by Mix-a-Lot's nasal flow and knack for ridiculous double entendres: "Yo baby, I got a big snake, all you gotta do is make it dance" is a typically subtle Mix-a-Lot come-on. But damn if isn't infectious, funky, and downright fun, making *Mack Daddy* one of the premiere hip-hop guilty pleasures of the '90s.

Nathan Rabin

Slick Rick

The Great Adventures of Slick Rick
1988, Def Jam

Slick Rick's reputation as hip-hop's greatest storyteller hangs on his classic debut, *The Great Adventures of Slick Rick*, one of the most influential rap records of the late '80s—for better and worse. Most of the production is standard early Def Jam, but Rick's style on the mic is like no one else's. His half-British accent and odd, singsong cadences often overshadow the smoothness of his delivery, but there's no overlooking the cleverness of his lyrics. His carefully constructed narratives are filled with vivid detail and witty asides, and his cartoonish sense of humor influenced countless other rappers. He'll adopt a high voice for his female characters, and even duets with his old alter ego MC Ricky D on "Mona Lisa." But there's also a dark side to *The Great Adventures*—namely its vulgarity and off-handed misogyny. No MC had ever dared go as far on record as Rick, and the tracks in question haven't really lost much of their power to offend, or at least raise eyebrows. The notorious "Treat Her Like a Prostitute" is the prime suspect, undermining well-intentioned advice (don't trust too quickly) with cynical, often degrading portrayals of women. "Indian Girl (Adult Story)," meanwhile, is an X-rated yarn with a barely comprehensible payoff. Yet this material is as much a part of Rick's legacy as his more admirable traits, and he was far from the last MC to put seemingly contradictory sides of his personality on the same record. And it's worth noting that most of his *Great Adventures*, no matter how dubious, end up as cautionary tales with definite consequences. That's especially true on the tragic "Children's Story," in which a teenage robber's increasingly desperate blunders lead to his destruction. In the end, *The Great Adventures* is simply too good not to deserve the countless samples and homages by everyone from Snoop Dogg to Black Star.

Steve Huey

The Ruler's Back
July 1991, Def Jam

It was easy to dismiss *The Ruler's Back* before it was even released, or to assume that there was no way it could live up to *The Great Adventures of Slick Rick*. Of course, it did not attain the same level of artistic success as that debut, and it certainly did not equal that album's commercial success, in fact seemingly passing beneath the radar of the whole hip-hop community, for the most part. At the time of its release, the album received mixed reviews and indifferent reactions even from fans of Slick Rick. That's another unfortunate, ill-fated aspect of *The Ruler's Back*, because, in truth, it is a strong, albeit uneven, progression from the debut and occasionally strikes a flawless note. To think of the album as anything other than a confused, transitional effort would be inaccurate, but it does not follow that it isn't an intriguing record. The messiness of its execution perfectly encapsulates the sort of turmoil Slick Rick was experiencing in his life at the time, and the music pulls the listener into that sort of tangled experience. Both Vance Wright's production and Slick Rick's rapping sound pressed for time, and they rush through the songs with a whip-lashing intensity. It can be a disorienting listen, but it is also a pure adrenaline rush. Slick Rick was going through a time of hurtling change, and the hurried breathlessness of the music captures that. *The Ruler's Back* is all over the map, lacking the thematic focus that held the first album together, but its frayed-threads, seams-showing immediacy is part of what makes it such an underrated album in the hip-hop canon.

Stanton Swihart

Snoop Dogg

Doggystyle
November 1993, Death Row

If Snoop Dogg's debut, *Doggystyle*, doesn't *seem* like a debut, it's because in many ways it's not. Snoop had already debuted as a featured rapper on Dr. Dre's 1992 album, *The Chronic*, rapping on half of the 16 tracks, including all the hit singles, so it wasn't like he was an unknown force when *Doggystyle* was released in late 1993. If anything, he was the biggest star in hip-hop, with legions of fans anxiously awaiting new material, and they were the ones who snapped up the album, making it the first debut album to enter the *Billboard* charts at number one. It wasn't like they were buying an unknown quantity. They knew that the album would essentially be the de facto sequel to *The Chronic*, providing another round of P-Funk-inspired grooves and languid gangsta and ganja tales, just like Dre's album. Which is exactly what *Doggystyle* is—a continuation of *The Chronic*, with the same production, same aesthetic and themes, and same reliance on guest rappers. The miracle is, it's as good as that record. There are two keys to its success, one belonging to Dre, the other to Snoop. Dre realized that it wasn't time to push the limits of G-funk, and instead decided to deepen it musically, creating easy-rolling productions that have more layers than they appear. They're laid-back funky, continuing to resonate after many listens, but their greatest strength is that they never overshadow the laconic drawl of Snoop, who confirms that he's one of hip-hop's greatest vocal stylists with this record. Other gangsta rappers were all about aggression and anger—even Dre, as a rapper, is as blunt as a thug—but Snoop takes his time, playing with the flow of his words, giving his rhymes a nearly melodic eloquence. Compare his delivery to many guest rappers here: Nate Dogg, Kurupt, and Dat Nigga Daz are all good rappers, but they're good in a conventional sense, where Snoop is something special, with unpredictable turns of phrase, evocative imagery, and a distinctive, addictive flow. If *Doggystyle* doesn't surprise or offer anything that wasn't already on *The Chronic*, it nevertheless is the best showcase for Snoop's prodigious talents, not just because he's given the room to run wild, but because he knows what to do with that freedom and Dre presents it all with imagination and a narrative thrust. If it doesn't have the shock of the new, the way that *The Chronic* did, so be it: Over the years, the pervasive influence of that record and its countless ripoffs has dulled its innovations, so it doesn't have the shock of the new either. Now, *Doggystyle* and *The Chronic* stand proudly together as the twin pinnacles of West Coast G-funk hip-hop of the early '90s.

Stephen Thomas Erlewine

Son of Bazerk

Bazerk Bazerk Bazerk
May 1991, Soul/MCA

One of the rowdiest, craziest, noisiest, most animated records the rap world has seen, *Bazerk Bazerk Bazerk* recalls everything from James Brown to Bad Brains to the Time to King Tubby to... well, a great number of things—occasionally within the span of one track. With the Bomb Squad producing their singular brand of controlled chaos, Son of Bazerk's commanding, amped-up Bobby Byrd-like barks and

grunts take center stage, while the four-member No Self Control & the Band—who often pipe in vocally—act as support. Energizing lead single "Change the Style" gained the most attention for good reason; its multiple tempo shifts constantly revert to a hyperactive funk arrangement, with its diversions dipping into doo wop, dub, and thrash. "Sex, Sex and More Sex" is less about Bazerk's sexual prowess and more about the complications of a night out ("So kill all that noise about your crackhead boyfriend—you three ladies grab your coats we five thousand."). A major change of pitch occurs in "N-41," when the whole crew shares the mike over little more than a skeletal, propulsive machine beat. Similar to most Bomb Squad productions, the album has a merciless up-down-up-down sequence, with tracks continually flowing directly into each other. This only intensifies the breathless mania of the album. The only gripe with the record is that not enough room is left for squeaky MC Halfpint; every single one of her exultations, shrieks, and background vocals is priceless.

Andy Kellman

Souls of Mischief

93 'Til Infinity
September 1993, Jive

One of hip-hop's great lost masterpieces, 93 'Til Infinity is the best single album to come out of Oakland's Hieroglyphics camp, and ranks as a seminal early classic of the West Coast underground. The Souls of Mischief weren't even out of their teens when they completely redefined the art of lyrical technique for the West Coast, along with fellow standard-bearers Freestyle Fellowship, the Pharcyde, and Hiero founder Del tha Funkee Homosapien. The Souls come off as four brash young MCs who are too smart for their own good, yet they're so full of youthful exuberance that it's impossible to dislike them for it. They're also excellent storytellers, punctuating their tales with a wry wit and clever asides; still, they're able to take on the grittier subjects of violence and death with a worldliness beyond their years. The production—all by various core Hieroglyphics members—is just as good as the raps, driven by complex beats, unpredictable basslines, and samples drawn from spacy fusion records and East Coast jazz-rap crews. Main Source and Gang Starr both provide track foundations here, and it's possible to hear the intricately constructed loops of the former and the lean attack of the latter (circa *Step in the Arena*) in the record's overall style. A better comparison, though, would be to the effortless flow and telepathic trade-offs of A Tribe Called Quest. In fact, 93 'Til Infinity seems to actively aspire to the fluidity of the best Tribe albums; tracks often segue directly into one another without pause—and the transitions are seamless. Although the title cut is an underappreciated classic, 93 'Til Infinity

makes its greatest impression through its stunning consistency, not individual highlights. Put it all together, and you've got one of the most slept-on records of the '90s.

Steve Huey

Spearhead

Home
September 1994, Capitol

Former Disposable Hero of Hiphoprisy Michael Franti takes his ideas even further with his debut record, covering a wide range of topics addressing the social conditions not only relevant to the African-American community, but to society in general. Immediate comparisons to other artists such as A Tribe Called Quest and Arrested Development are inevitable. They were all socially conscious and chose to have a message in their music, an angle decidedly different from the other two avenues of hip-hop of the time that focused on either gangster material or good-time, mindless commercial fodder. With a dark, brooding voice that could easily place him as the heir to Isaac Hayes or Barry White, *Home* greatly stressed consciousness and social thought over material value, but not at the expense of cheapening any other aspect of production. The whole vibe brought forth by employing a live band and backing singers easily paved the way for many nu-soul artists who continue to seek this path of influence. In the annals of hip-hop history, *Home* is an essential cornerstone to bringing socially conscious soul music and hip-hop close together.

Rob Theakston

Special Ed

Youngest in Charge
1989, Profile

In 1989, at the tender age of 16, Brooklynite Special Ed burst on the scene with enough talent and swagger to stake his claim among hip-hop's big boys. For Special Ed, M.C. stands for master of cleverness, and *Youngest In Charge* is replete with it. The gifted manchild boasts a versatile repertoire, using various lyrical styles and rhymes spiked with punchlines and metaphors that indicate wisdom beyond his 16 years. The meat of the album lies in its first three tracks. The opening cut, "Taxing," is Ed's coming-out party as he kicks entertaining verses over a slickly produced, squealing guitar-riff-laced track produced by Howie Tee. The following track is a masterpiece, Ed's claim to hip-hop immortality, "I Got It Made." It's four-plus minutes of artful arrogance, an instant hip-hop classic and anthem for all precocious hip-hop-heads of the era. To round out the trio came "I'm the Magnificent," a continuation of Ed's bragging rights over a sample from "Shantytown" (off Jimmy Cliff's *The Harder They Come* soundtrack). Because the first three tracks are so stellar, the rest of the album seems to be something of an afterthought; however, the remainder of the album does contain a few jewels. "The Bush," Ed's ode to his stomping grounds of Flatbush, features a sample of Al Green's "Love and Happiness," while "Think About It" is Ed's warning to those who wish to test his supremacy on the mic. On "Heds and Dreds," Ed flips a dancehall cadence to show his West Indian heritage. *Youngest In Charge* is a delightful release from a young hip-hop pioneer, a demonstration of the Edenic age of hip-hop when youthful exuberance and expression were highly valued.

M.F. DiBella

Legal
1990, Profile

If you asked most hip-hoppers of the late '80s or early '90s what main the difference between East Coast and West Coast rappers was, they would have explained that while West Coast rappers were primarily concerned with beats and lyrics, the top priority of East Coast rappers was their rapping technique. Having interesting lyrics *à la* Ice-T and Ice Cube or impressive tracks *à la* Dr. Dre would get you respect in L.A., San Diego or Oakland, but if you were an aspiring MC in Queens, Philadelphia or Atlantic City, the best way to earn the respect of your homeboys and homegirls was showing off your flow or rhyming technique. Around 1989-91, Special Ed was among the East Coast's most respected rappers, and the thing that earned him so much respect was the type of excellent technique he brings to his second album, *Legal* (so named because he had turned 18). Produced by Hitman Howie Tee, the main purpose of this CD is showing off Ed's rapping skills—and, to be sure, they're quite solid. That said, the album's best moments come when he tells some type of story instead of simply boasting and displaying his technique. "Livin' Like a Star" and "The Mission" demonstrate that the Flatbush, Brooklyn native can be a funny and clever storyteller when he puts his mind to it; the problem is that he doesn't do nearly enough storytelling. This is a generally likable effort, although it certainly isn't without its limitations.

Alex Henderson

Spice 1

Spice 1
May 1992, Jive

The sheer vulgarity, anger, coarseness, sexism and horror unveiled, celebrated and presented on Oakland rapper Spice 1's debut release can be frustrating and saddening. But more importantly, it should not be ignored. Spice 1 has done what "gangsta" rap's detractors should want; he's stripped away even the slightest veneer of glamour around the atmosphere of casual violence, sexual exploitation and drug selling he examines. His style, an appropriate mix of irony, disdain, acceptance and confusion, never succumbs to the situation or seeks to justify or downplay the sense of impending doom.

Ron Wynn

Spoonie Gee

Godfather of Hip Hop
June 1996, Ol Skool Flava

As a forefather of rap and one of the few rappers ever to release a record in the '70s, Spoonie Gee dropped expansive storytelling rhymes nearly a decade before Slick Rick ever did, masterfully boasting his abilities as a lover through poetry like an over-caffeinated Cyrano de Bergerac. He was undoubtedly one of the fastest and smoothest rappers of the Sugarhill era, and on *The Godfather of Hip Hop* he proves capable of freestyling on and on, sometimes flowing past the seven- or eight-minute mark, in the vein of an '80s block party freestyle session. This seems perfectly appropriate, considering he got his chops passing the mike in situations like these in Manhattan with Kool Moe Dee, L.A. Sunshine, and Special K (the Treacherous Three). The production quality of Spoonie's first couple songs are a lot like those released with his first crew: minimal drum-heavy jams with funk bass, cowbell, and claps, accented with encouragements to participate in the fun by rockin', freakin', and yellin' "yes, yes y'all." Such is the case with his most legendary cut, "Love Rap," in which he spins line after line over a simple drum-and-congo beat, all the while explaining the trials and tribulations of wooing the ladies. He's got a one-track mind: even on the battle-rhyme track "That's My Style," where he reprimands Schooly D for biting his style of delivery, he eventually ends up on a tangent about romancing his girl. You can't blame him; Spoonie's a lover, not a fighter. He makes that abundantly clear. But even though the themes of his raps are one-dimensional (girls, partying, and more girls), he's charismatic and engaging enough to keep the simple topic of female persuasion entertaining, which is quite impressive considering that his career lasted nearly ten years. The evolution of rap is clearly illustrated as the disc progresses, and listeners can trace the time line from early '80s Sugar Hill Records joints ("Spoonin' Rap") to mid-'80s Tuff City Records songs with Marley Marl ("The Godfather") all the way up to the new jack-ish songs he recorded with Teddy Riley ("Did You Come to Party"). While the latter tracks are lackluster in comparison to the bigger hits at the beginning of the album, ultimately this is a solid compilation, and the only disc of entirely Spoonie Gee material that's still available.

Jason Lymangrover

Steady B

Bring the Beat Back
1986, Jive

Half engaging freestyles and battle raps, and half album filler, *Bring the Beat Back* was 17-year-old Steady B's debut release. Standout tracks like "Get Physical," "Stupid Fresh" and, most notably, the title song itself, established Steady as an up-and-coming lyricist. But with its corny dance tunes ("Do the Fila") and lightweight novelty songs ("Yo Mutha" and "Cheatin' Girl"), *Bring the Beat Back* is a mixed bag.

Mtume Salaam

What's My Name
1987, Jive

Steady B's second album continued in the style of his first—it was solid, if unexceptional, '80s-era hip-hop. Producer Lawrence Goodman and Steady's DJ Tat Money were becoming a little more adventurous, adding brief samples, scratched breaks and even a live drum or two to accent the straightforward rhythm tracks. Less gimmick laden than the previous *Bring the Beat Back*, *What's My Name* was Steady's most satisfying album.

Mtume Salaam

Stetsasonic

On Fire
1986, Tommy Boy

There weren't many bands utilizing a hip-hop format in the mid-'80s, making Stetasonic quite unique on the pop front in 1986. While their subject matter was invariably light and their raps now hopelessly tame and effete, they were ground-breaking at the time and retain a certain charm.

Ron Wynn

In Full Gear
1988, Tommy Boy

Stetsasonic's ac-knowledged clas-sic, *In Full Gear* greatly expanded the musical ap-proach of their debut, making full use of new sam-pling technology as well as their unique live-band format. It's an ambitious double-LP set that seemingly aims for nothing less than to encompass every stylistic branch of hip-hop circa 1988. Over the course of 17 tracks, the group runs through state-of-the-art street-level hip-hop, an R&B crossover ballad, human beatboxing, Afrocentric spoken word poetry, Def Jam-style minimal-ism, DJ cuts, James Brown and Sly Stone samples, proto-Daisy Age sounds courtesy of Prince Paul, early jazz-rap, dancehall reggae, slamming Run-D.M.C.-style rap-rock, and Miami bass. It all makes for a staggering *tour de force* and a highly individual record that really doesn't sound quite like anything else—whether before, after, or during its time. The group makes no secret of its desire to help hip-hop push music forward, calling hip-hop "the most progressive form of music since jazz" in the liner notes, and launch-ing a spirited defense of sampling as an art on the ground-breaking single "Talkin' All That Jazz." Yet no matter how progressive-minded things get, Stet keeps a warm, genial block-party vibe going throughout the record, which holds all the experimentation together. Prince Paul fans tracing his career backward might initially be disappointed that his warped humor isn't much in evidence here, since he was an equal member of a multi-talented six-man crew, and gets (or shares) production credit on only six tracks. But, even if it isn't wholly a product of his vision, the vibrant eclecticism of *In Full Gear* is very much in keeping with his aesthetic anyway. This album doesn't always quite get its due, partly because of the flurry of hip-hop classics released around the same time, but it's certainly up near the head of the class of 1988.

Steve Huey

Blood, Sweat & No Tears
July 1991, Tommy Boy

What turned out to be Stetsasonic's parting long-player, *Blood, Sweat & No Tears* may have disappointed those ex-pecting another *In Full Gear*, but there was much to love here despite a long-winded, partially deflating running time. Starting out with a devastating instrumental, "The Hip

Hop Band," Stetsa sounded fresher than ever on "No B.S. Allowed" and the funky groupie tribute, "Speaking of a Girl Named Suzy." "Go Brooklyn 3" sounded surprisingly reminiscent of West Coast hardcore, but the very next track, "Walkin' in the Rain," was a smooth ballad that sampled the 1972 Love Unlimited hit (and re-created the oh-so-sexy Barry White phone conversation). As a band, Stetsasonic still had plenty of ties to funk, dropping expressive party jams like "So Let the Fun Begin" and the P-Funk name-dropping "Don't Let Your Mouth Write a Check That Your Ass Can't Cash." Prince Paul, then coming off the success of De la Soul's *3 Feet High and Rising*, hardly dominated this record; Bobby Simmons and Daddy O each produced as many (or more) tracks as he did (most of them great), while DBC and Wise also contributed. If it lacks the classic status that *In Full Gear* instantly commanded, *Blood, Sweat & No Tears* was still a fitting last hurrah to one of the golden age's most diversely talented combos.

John Bush

The Sugarhill Gang

The Sugarhill Gang
1980, Sugar Hill

Although the Sug-arhill Gang didn't invent hip-hop, they were the first rap act to have a huge international hit. Released in 1979, "Rapper's Delight" was mil-lions of listeners' first exposure to hip-hop—before that, very few peo-ple outside of New York even knew what hip-hop was. The Sugarhill Gang were also among the first rap acts to record a full-length LP; when this self-titled debut album came out in 1980, the vast majority of old-school MCs were only providing 12" singles. So *The Sugarhill Gang* is a historically important album even though it is a bit uneven. While "Rapper's Delight" and "Rapper's Reprise" (which features the Sequence, hip-hop's first all-female group) are excellent, most of the material is merely decent. And the ironic thing is that half of the songs aren't even rap. "Bad News Don't Bother Me" and "Here I Am," both of which find the Sugarhill Gang singing instead of rap-ping, are romantic R&B slow jams—and "Sugarhill Groove" is a sleek disco-funk number that hints at Roy Ayers. So this LP can hardly be called the work of hip-hop purists; in 1980, Sugarhill Records leader Sylvia Robinson (herself a veteran R&B singer) evidently felt that putting out an all-rap album would be risky. But, while *The Sugarhill Gang* isn't a masterpiece, it's still an album that hip-hop historians will find interesting.

Alex Henderson

8th Wonder
1982, Sugar Hill

While they didn't garner the critical praise of their label co-horts, Grandmaster Flash & the Furious Five, the Sugarhill

Gang still produced their share of memorable slices of early hip-hop. Helping to bring Sylvia Robinson's Sugar Hill Records into the limelight, the label's namesake group erred more on the funk side of the hip-hop equation, plying a steamy, all-night mix of go-go grooves, straight funk singing, and rapping. *8th Wonder* features the hits "Apache" and the title track, as well as such slick funk burners as "Hot Hot Summer Day" and the incredible bit of uptown dance alchemy "Funk Box" (shades of Prince here). *8th Wonder* may not be as good a starting point for newcomers as roundups on Rhino and Sequel, but it certainly will be one fans won't want to miss.

Stephen Cook

The Best of Sugarhill Gang
July 1996, Rhino

Sugarhill Gang's biggest hits are collected on this single-disc compilation. In addition to "Rapper's Delight"—the first rap single to reach the pop Top Ten—the group's seven other R&B hits are included on the disc, plus three other singles that never made the charts. All of the songs are presented in their original 12" versions. Not all of the material is first-rate—in retrospect, the group's old-school groove tended to be a little simplistic, monotonous, and too polished, while their rhymes were frequently stilted and sometimes just outright silly—but this music, especially "Rapper's Delight," is important historically. Most casual fans of old-school hip-hop will be content with purchasing "Rapper's Delight" on a various-artists collection, but for those wanting to dig deeper into the trio's history, *The Best of Sugarhill Gang* is a definitive retrospective.

Stephen Thomas Erlewine

Terminator X

Terminator X & the Valley of the Jeep Beets
May 1991, Def Jam

For hardcore Public Enemy fans, the release of Terminator X's debut solo album, *Terminator X & the Valley of the Jeep Beets*, in 1991 was a major event. Terminator X, of course, is best-known for his work as Public Enemy's DJ; his cutting and scratching added a lot to five-star albums like *Fear of a Black Planet* and *It Takes a Nation of Millions to Hold Us Back*, and he has a well-deserved reputation for being one of hip-hop's most creative turntable manipulators. When you're talking about great hip-hop DJs, Terminator's name deserves to be mentioned along with the likes of Grandmaster Flash, Jam Master Jay, Cut Creator, and the seminal Kool DJ Herc. Not surprisingly, Public Enemy's influence is quite strong on this album, and yet *Terminator X & the Valley of the Jeep Beets* is hardly a carbon copy of PE's releases. Public Enemy leader Chuck D has a cameo on "Buck Whylin'," but ultimately this album is about Terminator's skills as a DJ/producer. Various producers are featured—including Juvenile Delinquintz, Andreas 13, the Interrogators, and the controversial Sister Souljah—and the album detours into R&B singing when Section 8 is employed on "No Further." Overall, the raps are decent without being remarkable; most of the rapping isn't on a par with what Chuck D and Flavor Flav gave us on PE gems like "Fight the Power" and "Don't Believe the Hype." Terminator's turntable skills are what, more than anything, make this CD worth the price of admission. Even if a particular rap is merely adequate, Terminator maintains one's attention with his consistently imaginative deejaying. Not perfect but generally enjoyable, *Terminator X*

& the Valley of the Jeep Beets is worth checking out if you're an admirer of his work with Public Enemy.

Alex Henderson

Tha Alkaholiks

21 & Over
April 1993, Loud

Ohio natives turned West Coast underground kings, Tha Alkaholiks have long been one of hip-hop's best-kept secrets: hilarious lyrical acrobats who have never received the critical or commercial support they deserve. Assembled by gangsta rapper

King Tee, they offer a witty, anarchic, and party-friendly alternative to the stone-faced, largely humorless gangsta rap that ruled the West Coast throughout much of the early '90s. With the punch lines and comic timing of comedians and undeniable skills and killer delivery of topnotch MCs, rappers J-Ro and Tash have more than enough talent and energy to back up their endlessly clever boasting. Producer, DJ, and occasional MC, E-Swift is the group's secret weapon, an unjustly underrated beatsmith whose rubbery grooves and infectious production help make Tha Alkaholiks perhaps the greatest party group in hip-hop history. With titles like "Last Call," "Mary Jane," and "Only When I'm Drunk," Tha Alkaholiks will never be mistaken for members of some sort of latter-day temperance movement, but their music, rhymes, and beats are so irreverent, infectious, and just plain fun that their booze-loving shtick never gets old. Brief (only ten songs) and filler-free, *21 & Over* is perhaps the quintessential West Coast party album, as well as one of the most promising debut albums of the '90s, regardless of genre.

Nathan Rabin

Coast II Coast
February 1995, Loud

Tha Alkaholiks' wonderfully assured 1993 debut, *21 & Over*, established the group as the closest thing hip-hop has to the Marx Brothers—a trio of inspired comic anarchists devoted to, in their own immortal words, "hoes, flows, and 40 oz." But while *21 & Over* won Tha Alkaholiks (who eventually changed their name to Tha Liks) a sizable cult following, it failed to win the group the sort of attention and sales that Likwit Crew affiliate protégé Xzibit eventually snagged by hooking up with super-producer Dr. Dre. Undeterred, Tha Liks released *Coast II Coast* in 1995, a solid, consistent, and hilarious follow-up that sticks to the group's winning formula while offering enough variation, stylistically and sonically, to keep things interesting. Alkaholik DJ E-Swift still handles the bulk of the production, but he's joined behind the boards by Lootpack's Madlib (also known as Quasimoto) and East Coast heavyweight Diamond D, who provides the hypnotic *Enter the Dragon* sample that propels "Let It Out." Then-newcomer Xzibit makes his present felt throughout, ripping snidely misogynistic rhymes on "Hit And Run" and getting in touch with his inner Big

Bank Hank on the hilarious old-school parody "Flashback." The rest of *Coast II Coast* nicely balances J-Ro and Tash's lyrical acrobatics with E-Swift's rubbery grooves, resulting in an album that's jazzier and more laid-back than Tha Liks' debut—Q-Tip of A Tribe Called Quest even pops up on "All the Way Live"—but no less winning. *Coast II Coast* failed to net Tha Liks gold or platinum sales, but it otherwise succeeds smashingly, effortlessly satisfying Liks diehards while still leaving them thirsty for more.

Nathan Rabin

3rd Bass

The Cactus Album
October 1989, Def Jam

Besides the upper-middle-class frat-punks-in-rap-clothing shtick of the Beastie Boys and emissary/producer Rick Rubin, who both gained a legitimate, earned respect in the rap community, there were very few white kids in rap's first decade who spoke the poetry of the street with compassion and veneration for the form. That is, until *The Cactus Album*. Matching MC Serch's bombastic, goofy good nature and Prime Minister Pete Nice's gritty, English-trained wordsmithery (sounding like a young Don in training), 3rd Bass' debut album is revelatory in its way. For one, it is full of great songs, alternately upbeat rollers ("Sons of 3rd Bass"), casual-but-sincere disses ("The Gas Face"), razor-sharp street didacticism ("Triple Stage Darkness," "Wordz of Wizdom"), and sweaty city anthems ("Brooklyn Queens," "Steppin' to the A.M.," odes to day and night, respectively), with A-plus production by heavyweights Prince Paul and Bomb Squad, as well as the surprising, overshadowing work of Sam Sever. The duo may not have come from the streets, but their hearts were there, and it shows. The album embodies New York life. Not every single idea plays out successfully—Serch's Louis Armstrong impression on "Flippin' Off the Wall..." is on the wrong side of the taste line, and "Desert Boots" is a puzzling Western-themed insertion—but they are at least interesting stretches that add to the dense, layered texture of the album. *The Cactus Album* was also important because it proved to the hip-hop heads that white kids could play along without appropriating or bastardizing the culture. It may not have completely integrated rap, but it was a precursor to a culture that became more inclusive and widespread after its arrival.

Stanton Swihart

Derelicts of Dialect
June 1991, Def Jam

Although 3rd Bass didn't fully realize their tremendous potential, the Brooklyn rappers offered enjoyable, if uneven, albums. Like the group's 1989 debut, their second and final album, *Derelicts of Dialect*, makes it clear that the MCs weren't aiming for the pop charts—and were loyal only to the hip-hop hardcore. When MC Serch and Pete Nice tear into such aggressive and forceful declarations as "Pop Goes the Weasel" (an inflammatory attack on Vanilla Ice), "Portrait of the Artist as a Hood," and "Ace in the Hole," it's clear why they were among the few white MCs who were successful in the young black community—someone who heard their rapping without seeing their picture could easily assume they were black. Although the goofy "Herbalz in Your Mouth" shows some De La Soul and Tribe Called Quest influence, 3rd Bass don't allow themselves to be nearly as lighthearted, and keep things hardcore and intense.

Alex Henderson

Tone-Loc

Loc-ed After Dark
1989, Delicious Vinyl

A forgotten man in the rise of West Coast rap, Tone-Loc was effectively cut off from his hometown scene in Los Angeles by his unexpected pop success. Paced by the singles "Wild Thing" and "Funky Cold Medina"—both co-written by a  pre-fame Young MC, and some of the earliest productions by the legendary Dust Brothers—Loc's debut album, *Loc-ed After Dark*, became the second rap album to top the pop charts, following the Beastie Boys' *Licensed to Ill*. Loc's distinctively rough, raspy voice and easygoing delivery made him an appealing storyteller, but he was aiming for the streets more than the pop charts. So there's the occasional profanity, the stalker-tinged title track, and "Cheeba Cheeba," which made waves at the time as one of the earliest pro-marijuana raps on record (of course, this was before Cypress Hill, and Nancy Reagan's "Just Say No" campaign was still fresh in the public's mind). The minor singles "I Got It Goin' On" and "On Fire" (the latter the first record ever released on Delicious Vinyl) are both pretty good, but some of the album's momentum is wasted on some fairly standard MC boasts (Loc has much more personality than he does lyrical technique). Even if *Loc-ed After Dark* is erratic, though, it still deserves more respect than it's generally accorded.

Steve Huey

Cool Hand Loc
November 1991, Delicious Vinyl

Aiming for credibility among hardcore hip-hoppers, Delicious Vinyl was careful not to include a lot of pop-influenced material on Tone-Loc's second album, *Cool Hand Loc*. But sadly, the inventiveness he displayed on "Wild Thing" continued working against Loc among b-boys and hip-hop's hardcore, who still resented the success he'd enjoyed in the pop market. Though not quite as strong as the triple platinum *Loc-ed After Dark*—either commercially or artistically—the album is a respectable and satisfying effort. The former L.A. gang member tends to overdo it with boasting lyrics—a problem he shares with quite a few other rappers—but his boasts are often quite clever. Sadly, Tone-Loc didn't have much longevity; after *Cool Hand Loc*, little was heard about him.

Alex Henderson

Too Short

Life Is...Too Short
1988, Jive

Too Short never had the skills or technique of LL Cool J or Big Daddy Kane, but what the Oakland rapper lacks in technique, he's always more than made up for with irresistible, '70s-inspired funk grooves that simply won't quit. When

Short—after enjoying a small cult following for a few years in Northern California—joined a major label with *Life Is... Too Short*'s predecessor, *Born to Mack*, too many East Coast MCs were inundating hip-hop with clichéd tracks consisting of only James Brown samples and a drum machine. Too Short, however, presented an attractive alternative with highly melodic, danceable tracks that made no secret of his love of '70s funk heroes like Parliament, the Ohio Players, and Cameo. This CD's X-rated, sexually explicit lyrics received their share of vehement criticism, and the MC responded that Too Short is an outrageous character who shouldn't be taken too seriously. Be that as it may, his commanding reflection on the drug plague, "City of Dope," underscores the fact that he's cheating himself artistically by not devoting more time to social commentary and less time to exploiting sex.

Alex Henderson

Born to Mack
August 1989, Jive

By the time Jive Records released *Born to Mack*, Too Short's major-label debut, the young rapper was already a music industry veteran, having released several albums on the independent 75 Girls label. With *Born to Mack* Too Short continued the formula that had already made him a regional star—sexually explicit lyrics over sparse, bass-heavy rhythm tracks. What is missing from this album, though, is any levity, humor, or musical exploration. Without the benefit of a lyrical wink or nod, and without any sign of his future head-nodding, funk workouts, Too Short's trademark "pimp" tales are stripped bare, revealing themselves too misogynist to be enjoyable. Even so, due to the success of the nearly ten-minute, underground smash "Freaky Tales," *Born to Mack* expanded Too Short's fan base past his Oakland, CA, hometown, eventually selling past gold status. Many of Short's later efforts, such as *Life Is...Too Short* and *Shorty the Pimp* were funnier, funkier, and plain better, but *Born to Mack* stands as most of the world's introduction to one of rap's most enduring, and best-selling, artists ever.

Mtume Salaam

Short Dog's in the House
August 1990, Jive

With *Short Dog's in the House*, Oakland's most sexually explicit MC gave his followers more of what he was known for—X-rated lyrics, a relaxed style of rapping, and addictive, melodic tracks recalling the splendor of '70s funk. R&B fans who complained that rap on the whole wasn't sufficiently melodic couldn't make that complaint about the distinctive Too Short. When his raunchy lyrics continued to come under fire, he maintained that he was simply portraying a character—and that he wasn't really the ghetto pimp he portrayed. As entertaining as his albums are, Short's inspired interpretation of Donny Hathaway's "The Ghetto" makes it crystal clear that he would do well to be more lyrically challenging more often.

Alex Henderson

Shorty the Pimp
July 1992, Jive

Shorty the Pimp was Too Short's seventh album. As one would expect from an entertainer with six albums behind him, Too Short had by now perfected his craft. Though his focus was still on womanizing and pimping, by 1992 the rest of the rap world had "caught up" with the Oakland rapper's

explicit brand of boasting and bragging. Aware of this, Too Short had gradually begun adding battle rhymes ("In the Trunk"), social commentary ("I Want to Be Free"), and cautionary tales ("So You Want to Be a Gangster") to the mix. Never particularly gifted as a rapper, Too Short's proved himself a wily veteran in his ability to squeeze every bit of effect out of his relatively simple style. But what separated *Shorty the Pimp* from the rest of the now-crowded rap field was the music. Producer Ant Banks, multi-instrumentalist Shorty B, and Too Short himself created a satisfying blend of funk samples augmented by live drums and deftly played basslines. Many of the backing tracks are composed well enough to be successful on their own.

Mtume Salaam

Cocktails
January 1995, Jive

Album number nine from Too Short carries on his tradition of lyrics about the joys of pimping, rapped moderately to groovy, funky, jazzy beats. Delete the raps from Too Short's tales, and you still have a commercial product. Spacy Bootsy  Collins-influenced vocals appear on some cuts, giving the funk an eerie feel. Too Short likes naked, foxy ladies on his covers, and *Cocktails* is no exception; he picked a beauty pictured with a snake coiled around her curvaceous brown body. Homie Ant Banks appears on "Can I Get a Bitch," and 2Pac, MC Breed, and Father Dom join him on "We Do This"—some nice rappin' on this one. "Coming Up Short" catches Too Short at his pimpingest best, spitting out mack lyrics to a funky-azz beat like an ol'-skool Chicago pimp. A female vocalist changes the pace on "Things Changes," adding some emotive vocal runs; Baby D, who sounds like he's seven, appears like a regular and gets off a tight rap that belies his age. Too Short is all geeked on "Paystyle," a mini macking fable and his best rap on the set. On the last track, "Sample the Funk," he acknowledges the creators of funk: James Brown, George Clinton, Bootsy Collins, Johnny "Guitar" Watson, the Ohio Players, and so on. According to Too Short and his homies, pimping is an all-American game, and they praise the nefarious endeavor on every track.

Andrew Hamilton

Tragedy Khadafi

Intelligent Hoodlum
1990, A&M

Intelligent Hoodlum's 1990 debut. The one-time Riker's Island inmate raps of black politics and culture, while finding plenty of room for whimsical observations and some fine vocal flow. Producer Marley Marl of Biz Markie and Big Daddy Kane fame provides the beats and production in fine style: layered, lean, and dope. If you like you old school cuts in the sophisticated Gang Starr and Markie mode, then this collection of hip-hop gold will no doubt be welcome. Add a little De La Soul humor, and you have a solid album.

Stephen Cook

Treacherous Three

Turn It Up
July 2000, Sequel

Sequel's winning wrap-up of one of the best old-school crews does have a major miscue (not including their debut, "The New Rap Language"), but it certainly overwhelms all the other poor excuses for Treacherous Three compilations. From Kool Moe Dee's blistering speed rap to open "Whip It," Treacherous Three proved that hip-hop was soon going to transcend the block-party aesthetic to become a phenomenon focused on MCs testing each other in dramatic rap battles, more akin to jazz blowing contests. Still, for all the party jams and braggadocio exercises ("At the Party," "The Body Rock," the title track, "Bad Mutha"), *Turn It Up* also illustrates that these three were already looking to the emergence of message tracks; "Yes We Can Can" is an example of classic empowerment hip-hop years before it became popular, and "Dumb Dick" preaches (albeit rather crudely) about the benefits of staying in school and staying away from promiscuity—a prelude to Kool Moe Dee's own solo hit "Go See the Doctor." Though most of these had the sound of Sugar Hill in full effect ("Feel the Heartbeat" is the classic Treacherous Three track from the label), "Get Up" was an imaginative detour into electro, while Sequel wisely chose the rarer X-rated version of "Xmas Rap" (one that barely would've prompted a parental advisory 15 years later).

John Bush

A Tribe Called Quest

People's Instinctive Travels and the Paths of Rhythm
April 1990, Jive

One year after De la Soul re-drew the map for alternative rap, fellow Native Tongues brothers A Tribe Called Quest released their debut, the quiet beginning of a revolution in non-commercial hip-hop. *People's Instinctive Travels and the Paths of Rhythm* floated a few familiar hooks, but it wasn't a sampladelic record. Rappers Q-Tip and Phife Dawg dropped a few clunky rhymes, but their lyrics were packed with ideas, while their flow and interplay were among the most original in hip-hop. From the beginning, Tribe focused on intelligent message tracks but rarely sounded over-serious about

them. With "Pubic Enemy," they put a humorous spin on the touchy subject of venereal disease (including a special award for the most inventive use of the classic "scratchin'" sample), and moved right into a love rap, "Bonita Applebum," which alternated a sitar sample with the type of jazzy keys often heard on later Tribe tracks. "Description of a Fool" took to task those with violent tendencies, while "Youthful Expression" spoke wisely of the power yet growing responsibility of teenagers. Next to important message tracks with great productions, A Tribe Called Quest could also be deliciously playful (or frustratingly unserious, depending on your opinion). "I Left My Wallet in El Segundo" describes a vacation gone hilariously wrong, while "Ham 'n' Eggs" may be the oddest topic for a rap track ever heard up to that point ("I don't eat no ham and eggs, cuz they're high in cholesterol"). Contrary to the message in the track titles, the opener "Push It Along" and "Rhythm (Dedicated to the Art of Moving Butts)" were fusions of atmospheric samples with tough beats, special attention being paid to a pair of later Tribe sample favorites, jazz guitar and '70s fusion synth. Restless and ceaselessly imaginative, Tribe perhaps experimented too much on their debut, but they succeeded at much of it, certainly enough to show much promise as a new decade dawned.

John Bush

The Low End Theory
September 1991, Jive

While most of the players in the jazz-rap movement never quite escaped the pasted-on qualities of their vintage samples, with *The Low End Theory*, A Tribe Called Quest created one of the closest and most brilliant fusions of jazz atmosphere and hip-hop attitude ever recorded. The rapping by Q-Tip and Phife Dawg could be the smoothest of any rap record ever heard; the pair are so in tune with each other, they sound like flip sides of the same personality, fluidly trading off on rhymes, with the former earning his nickname (the Abstract) and Phife concerning himself with the more concrete issues of being young, gifted, and black. The trio also takes on the rap game with a pair of hard-hitting tracks: "Rap Promoter" and "Show Business," the latter a lyrical soundclash with Q-Tip and Phife plus Brand Nubian's Diamond D, Lord Jamar, and Sadat X. The woman problem gets investigated as well, on two realistic yet sensitive tracks, "Butter" and "The Infamous Date Rape." The productions behind these tracks aren't quite skeletal, but they're certainly not complex. Instead, Tribe weaves little more than a stand-up bass (sampled or, on one track, jazz luminary Ron Carter) and crisp, live-sounding drum programs with a few deftly placed samples or electric keyboards. It's a tribute to their unerring production sense that, with just those few tools, Tribe produced one of the best hip-hop albums in history, a record that sounds better with each listen. *The Low End Theory* is an unqualified success, the perfect marriage of intelligent, flowing raps to nuanced, groove-centered productions.

John Bush

Midnight Marauders
November 1993, Jive

Though the abstract rappers finally betrayed a few commercial ambitions for *Midnight Marauders*, the happy result was a smart, hooky record that may not have furthered the jazz-rap fusions of *The Low End Theory*, but did merge Tribe-style intelligence and reflection with some of the most inviting grooves heard on any early '90s rap record. The productions, more funky than jazzy, were tighter overall—but the big improvement, four years after their debut, came with Q-Tip's and Phife Dawg's raps. Focused yet funky, polished but raw, the duo was practically telepathic on "Steve Biko (Stir It Up)" and "The Chase, Pt. 2," though the mammoth track here was the pop hit "Award Tour." A worldwide call-out record with a killer riff and a great pair of individual raps from the pair, it assured that *Midnight Marauders* would become A Tribe Called Quest's biggest seller. The album didn't feature as many topical tracks as Tribe was known for, though the group did include an excellent, sympathetic commentary on the question of *that* word ("Sucka Nigga," with a key phrase: "being as we use it as a term of endearment"). Most of the time, A Tribe Called Quest was indulging in impeccably produced, next-generation games of the dozens ("We Can Get Down," "Oh My God," "Lyrics to Go"), but also took the time to illustrate sensitivity and spirituality ("God Lives Through"). A Tribe Called Quest's *Midnight Marauders* was commercially successful, artistically adept, and lyrically inventive; the album cemented their status as alternative rap's prime sound merchants, authors of the most original style since the Bomb Squad first exploded on wax.

John Bush

Beats, Rhymes and Life
July 1996, Jive

With each of its first three albums, A Tribe Called Quest seemed to be on its way to bigger and better things, artistically and commercially. *Beats, Rhymes and Life* promptly ended that streak and still ranks as the group's most disappointing listen. Amplifying the bare beats-and-bliss of *The Low End Theory* but erasing the hooks of *Midnight Marauders*, *Beats, Rhymes and Life* simply wasn't a compelling record. In fact, A Tribe Called Quest sounded bored through most of it—and, to put it bluntly, there wasn't much to get excited about either. Previously so invigorating and idea-driven, Q-Tip and Phife strutted through their verses, often sounding confused, hostile, and occasionally paranoid (check out the battle tracks, "Phony Rappers" and "Mind Power"). Meanwhile, the skeletal productions offered little incentive to decode the lyrics and messages, most of which were complex as expected. Though several other tracks had solid productions (like the spry, bass-driven backing to "Phony Rappers"), *Beats, Rhymes and Life* saw A Tribe Called Quest making its first (and only) significant misstep. (Constant touring off the success of *Midnight Marauders* may have been a factor.) Yes, they were still much better than the vast majority of alternative rappers, but it seemed they'd lost their power to excite. One of the few successes was a surprising R&B crossover called "1nce Again" (featuring Tammy Lucas).

John Bush

Two Kings in a Cipher

From Pyramids to Projects
August 1991, RCA

In the early '90s, an abundance of Afrocentric rappers came from the Northeastern corridor—the region of the U.S. that gave fans Brand Nubian, X-Clan, Professor X, Isis, Queen Mother Rage, and quite a few similar artists. These hip-hoppers showed no awareness of either the gangsta rap that was coming from the West Coast or the bass music and booty rhymes that were inescapable in the Deep South; instead of rapping about thug life or being sexually explicit, Afrocentric MCs were more likely to talk about African history or the Islamic faith. One of the lesser-known acts that came out of hip-hop's Afrocentric school was the East Coast duo Two Kings in a Cipher, whose debut album, *From Pyramids to Projects*, is competent but not remarkable. The rappers had an intriguing name and an interesting image—D.O.P. dressed very b-boy and sported baseball caps, whereas the Noble Amen-Ra wore a fez and dressed like an Islamic scholar from Egypt or Morocco. But, unfortunately, the material isn't as interesting as the group's image. That isn't to say that *From Pyramids to Projects* is a bad album. D.O.P. and Amen-Ra are capable rappers, and their rhymes aren't weak—but they aren't mind-blowing either. Most of the time, D.O.P. and Amen-Ra sound undeveloped; one hears their potential, but they settle for adequate instead of excelling. With the right guidance, support, and direction from a record company, perhaps Two Kings in a Cipher could have developed into a group that was exceptional instead of merely competent. But that's only speculation. The duo never recorded a second album, and this little-known CD is only a small footnote in the history of East Coast Afrocentric rap.

Alex Henderson

2 Live Crew

2 Live Crew Is What We Are
1986, Luke

There was a time when many New York hip-hoppers refused to believe that rappers from Miami could record a gold or platinum album or give them any real competition. That was before 1986, when the 2 Live Crew's debut album, *2 Live Is What We Are*, came out on Luther Campbell's Miami-based Luke Skyywalker Records (later renamed Luke Records). This LP did a lot to popularize Florida-style bass music, and like the gangsta rap that was coming from California, it demonstrated that rappers didn't have to be from New York to sell a lot of records. Musically, *2 Live Is What We Are* was a definite departure from New York rap—the grooves are much faster—and lyrically, the album put booty rhymes on the map. The 2 Live Crew wasn't the first rap group to talk about sex, but this album did take sexually explicit rap lyrics to a new level of nastiness. With X-rated offerings like "Throw the D" and "We Want Some Pussy," Campbell and his colleagues popularized a style of rap that thrives on decadence for the sake of decadence. These tunes are as humorous as they are raunchy; Campbell has often compared the 2 Live Crew's booty rhymes to the off-color humor of Richard Pryor, Andrew Dice Clay, and Rudy Ray Moore—and, to be sure, there are some parallels. Like those comedians, the 2 Live Crew is genuinely funny—but only if you have a taste for X-rated humor. Anyone who finds Moore, Pryor, and Clay offensive should avoid the 2 Live Crew as well. But for those who do appreciate that type of humor, *2 Live Is What We Are* is a classic of its kind.

Alex Henderson

Move Somethin'
1987, Luke

Although the 2 Live Crew's debut album, *2 Live Is What We Are*, went gold and sold more than 500,000 copies in the U.S., the LP wasn't without its detractors. Some New York hip-hoppers argued that Luther Campbell and his associates were pandering to the lowest common denominator, and everyone from church groups to feminists argued that their X-rated booty rhymes were nothing more than pornography with a beat. But the Crew's fans didn't care what their critics had to say, which is why their second album, *Move Somthin'*, was also a big seller. Anyone who found *2 Live Is What We Are* offensive was unlikely to be converted by *Move Somthin'*; booty rhymes like "HBC," "One and One" (an X-rated interpretation of the Kinks' "All Day and All of the Night") and "S&M" are as crude and sexually explicit as anything on the group's previous album. "S&M," as its title indicates, is an ode to kinky sex. The 2 Live Crew was hardly the first group to address the subject of bondage and sado-masochism—back in 1967, the Velvet Underground's "Venus in Furs" was among the kinkier rock songs of its day. Some of the Ohio Players' pre-Mercury album covers employed S&M/bondage imagery, and the 1980s heavy metal band Bitch had a female lead vocalist who loved to sing about the pleasures of being a whip-toting dominatrix. But kinky sex hasn't been a prominent subject in hip-hop, and "S&M" is unusually kinky for rap. Of course, the Crew didn't need to rap about whips and chains to offend people; even without "S&M," this LP would have been X-rated. *Move Somthin'* was trashed by the Crew's critics, but those who aren't offended by X-rated humor will find it to be a thoroughly entertaining sophomore effort.

Alex Henderson

As Nasty as They Wanna Be
1989, Luke

2 Live Crew's infamous—record store clerks were actually arrested for selling the album—and double platinum—a great example of how being banned can increase sales—*As Nasty As They Wanna Be* may be more talked about than listened to, but it's actually a thoroughly entertaining effort and as solid a album as the trashy party rap genre could have hoped for. In the first moments a sampled voice asks, "What do we get for ten dollars?" In a sleazy slow tone that might make Ron Jeremy blush, a hooker answers, "Everything you want" as the album begins to deliver on this street corner promise with the legendary "Me So Horny" ("me love you long time"). With a sample of *Full Metal Jacket*'s

Vietnamese hooker, a cheap drum machine, a fat bassline, and a simple set of rhymes that are filled with every cuss word, innuendo, and misogynist, knuckle-dragging reference to women imaginable, "Me So Horny" is the reason 2 Live Crew should exist. Nothing they or their leader Luke (Luther) Campbell recorded afterwards sounded as lean, as hook filled, and so instantly grabbing as the single. From the inner city strip clubs to the headphones of teenagers in the suburbs, the track was a massive guilty pleasure, one that could also fill the dancefloor in a second. The album that follows repeats and repeats this cheap and silly porno formula and miraculously stretches it as far as it can go. Divided into four sides—one for each member, the only reason anyone remembers their names—*Nasty* keeps it rolling with tracks that capture "Horny"'s energy, ("Put Her in the Buck"), its cleverness ("Dirty Nursery Rhymes"), and a whole bunch that are just as hooky. "The F**k Shop" is the best example of the latter with its easy to grasp chorus and wicked use of a loop from Van Halen's "Ain't Talkin' 'Bout Love." Other smart samples like Kraftwerk for "Dick Almighty" and Jimi Hendrix for "My Seven Bizzos" keep the album alive, while interludes lifted from Andrew Dice Clay, Rudy Ray Moore, Eddie Murphy, and Richard Pryor give away its true inspirations. A couple amusing left turns—the 12-bar "2 Live Blues" and the dancehall party "Reggae Joint"—round out the album, and suddenly the full-length that doesn't seem like it could ever suffer an injustice gets sold short by history, at least when it comes to remembering what a grand porno achievement Luke and his crew created.

David Jeffries

Banned in the USA
July 1990, Little Joe

When Florida attorney Jack Thompson did everything he could to have the X-rated music of 2 Live Crew outlawed, his assault on the First Amendment led many free-speech advocates to take up the group's cause. Thompson's actions inspired  quite a bit of anger from both white liberals and African-American rappers, who saw something obscene about a prosperous lawyer declaring war on a young black entrepreneur who had avoided the pitfalls of Miami's Liberty City ghetto. Luke was under attack for doing the very thing Republicans consistently advocate—using free enterprise to pull himself up by the bootstraps. Ironically, many of those who defended his First Amendment rights had little or no use for his lyrics. *Banned in the USA*, the Crew's first album for a major label and its first after the battle with Thompson, is for many, a guilty pleasure. Say what you will about Luke's high-school locker-room lyrics; the Crew's Miami bass rap can be quite catchy, infectious and amusing. Many New York hip-hoppers were quick to criticize the fast tempos employed by Miami rappers like Luke, but the fact that they did it their own way instead of emulating Northeastern MCs is something to admire instead of lambast.

Alex Henderson

2Pac

2Pacalypse Now
November 1991, Interscope

When 2Pac's full-length debut, *2Pacalypse Now*, came out in 1991, it didn't have the same immediate impact, didn't instantly throw him into the upper echelons of rap's elite, as Nas', Jay-Z's, or even his biggest rival, Notorious B.I.G.'s did, but the album certainly set him up for his illustrious and sadly short-lived career. Part of its initial problem, what held it back from extensive radio play, is that there's not an obvious single. The closest thing to it, and what ended up being the best-known track from *2Pacalypse Now*, is "Brenda's Got a Baby," which discusses teenage pregnancy in true Pac fashion, sympathetically explaining a situation without condoning it, but it doesn't even have a hook, and most of the other pieces follow suit, more poetry than song. The album is significantly more political than the rapper's subsequent releases, showing an intelligent, talented, and angry young man (he was only 20 when it came out) who wanted desperately to express and reveal the problems in the urban black community, from racism to police brutality to the seemingly near impossibility of escaping from the ghetto. He pays tribute to artists like KRS-One, N.W.A, and Public Enemy, all of whom he also considered to be provoking discussion and reaction, but he also has cleanly carved out an image for himself: articulate and smart, not overtly boastful, and concerned about societal problems, both small and large (and though he discusses these less and less as career progresses, he never leaves them behind). Yes, the edges of *2Pacalypse Now* can be a bit rough, yes the beats aren't always outstanding, and yes, the MC's flow can be a little choppy, even for him, but it's still a great look at what 2Pac could offer, and a must-have for any fan of his, or hip-hop in general.

Marisa Brown

Strictly 4 My N.I.G.G.A.Z.
February 1993, Jive

On 2Pac's debut album, *2Pacalypse Now*, the rapper showed himself to be a supremely passionate man, brimming over with ideas and anger and ready to voice his political and social opinions, call things like he saw them. This same kind of energy and  lyrical acumen is found on his sophomore release, *Strictly 4 My N.I.G.G.A.Z.*, a record that, while it begins exploring the MC's more gangsta side ("Last Wordz," for example, which features verses from Ice Cube and Ice-T), still includes the provocative, reflective lines on which he first made his name as a solo artist, and which he continued even as he became more and more popular (and, for some, more and more frightening). "Keep Ya Head Up," one of his biggest hits, and his tribute to black women, especially single mothers, is deeply thoughtful and poignant ("And since we all came from a woman, got our name from a woman, and our game from a woman/I wonder why we take from our women, why we rape our women, do we hate our women?"), expressing opinions that aren't often equated with hardcore rappers, while tracks like "I Get Around" brags about his sexual conquests. But this was what 2Pac was, anyway, a juxtaposition between tough and sensitive, social consciousness and misogynistic boasting, and *Strictly 4 My N.I.G.G.A.Z.* shows this. The angry protest songs calling out police and politicians, reminiscent of Public Enemy—and with Bomb Squad-esque beats to boot (albeit a lesser version of)—the screw-the-world mentality, the soft introspection, the preaching-but-not-proselytizing, and the party anthems are all here, and though the production sometimes suffers, especially in the middle of the album, where it's utterly forgettable, the record shows a continually developing MC, with increasingly complex lyrical themes, well on his way to becoming nearly unstoppable.

Marisa Brown

Me Against the World
March 1995, Interscope

Recorded following his near-fatal shooting in New York, and released while he was in prison, *Me Against the World* is the point where 2Pac really became a legendary figure. Having stared death in the face and survived, he was a changed man on record, 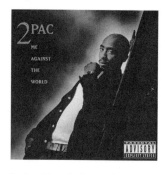 displaying a new confessional bent and a consistent emotional depth. By and large, this isn't the sort of material that made him a gangsta icon; this is 2Pac the soul-baring *artist*, the foundation of the immense respect he commanded in the hip-hop community. It's his most thematically consistent, least-self-contradicting work, full of genuine reflection about how he's gotten where he is—and dread of the consequences. Even the more combative tracks ("Me Against the World," "Fuck the World") acknowledge the high-risk life he's living, and pause to wonder how things ever went this far. He battles occasional self-loathing, is haunted by the friends he's already lost to violence, and can't escape the desperate paranoia that his own death isn't far in the future. These tracks—most notably "So Many Tears," "Lord Knows," and "Death Around the Corner"—are all the more powerful in hindsight with the chilling knowledge that he was right. Even romance takes on a new meaning as an escape from the hellish pressure of everyday life ("Temptations," "Can U Get Away"), and when that's not available, getting high or drunk is almost a necessity. He longs for the innocence of childhood ("Young Niggaz," "Old School"), and remembers how quickly it disappeared, yet he still pays loving, clear-eyed tribute to his drug-addicted mother on the touching "Dear Mama." Overall, *Me Against the World* paints a bleak, nihilistic picture, but there's such an honest, self-revealing quality to it that it can't help conveying a certain hope simply through its humanity. It's the best place to go to understand why 2Pac is so revered; it may not be his definitive album, but it just might be his best.

Steve Huey

All Eyez on Me
February 1996, Death Row

Maybe it was his time in prison, or maybe it was simply his signing with Suge Knight's Death Row label. Whatever the case, 2Pac re-emerged hardened and hungry with *All Eyez on Me*, the first double-disc album of original material in hip-hop history. With all the controversy surrounding him, 2Pac seemingly wanted to throw down a monumental epic whose sheer scope would make it an achievement of itself. But more than that, it's also an unabashed embrace of the gangsta lifestyle, backing off the sober self-recognition of *Me Against the World*. Sure, there are a few reflective numbers and dead-homiez tributes, but they're much more romanticized this time around. *All Eyez on Me* is 2Pac the thug icon in all his brazen excess, throwing off all self-control and letting it all hang out—even if some of it would have been better kept to himself. In that sense, it's an accurate depiction of what made him such a volatile and compelling personality, despite some undeniable filler. On the plus side, this is easily the best production he's ever had on record, handled mostly by Johnny J (notably on the smash "How Do U Want It") and Dat Nigga Daz; Dr. Dre also contributes another surefire single in "California Love" (which, unfortunately, is present only as a remix, not the original hit version). Both hits are on the front-loaded first disc, which would be a gangsta classic in itself; other highlights include the anthemic Snoop Dogg duet "2 of Amerikaz Most Wanted," "All About U" (with the required Nate Dogg-sung hook), and "I Ain't Mad at Cha," a tribute to old friends who've gotten off the streets. Despite some good moments, the second disc is slowed by filler and countless guest appearances, plus a few too many thug-lovin' divas crooning their loyalty. Erratic though it may be, *All Eyez on Me* is nonetheless carried off with the assurance of a legend in his own time, and it stands as 2Pac's magnum opus.

Steve Huey

UGK

Too Hard to Swallow
November 1992, Jive

Truth in advertising, *Too Hard to Swallow* is UGK before they got funked up, grinding over some minimal, hard beats that aren't as complementary to their delivery as the smoother production they would later favor. Still, thanks to members Bun B and Pimp C's ability to write memorable rhymes, the album—which repeats some tracks from their impossible to find indie release *The Southern Way*—is a winner with three mammoth singles so important to the UGK story. "Something Good" puts a crooked beat under Rufus' most popular number, "Use Me Up" tells its pissed-off tale over a Bill Withers sample, and "Pocket Full of Stones" is a classic tale of crack rocks, Cadillacs, and making bail. The mucho macho "Cramping My Style" is a fan favorite with "hump and dump" lyrics that didn't really play nice with radio, and the snide "I'm So Bad" is a great example of how well Pimp C can offend and amuse at the same time. While most will prefer the Kingz' later sound, this is some fans' favorite album thanks to its unforgiving punch and visceral, controversial, cop-killer lyrics.

David Jeffries

Super Tight...
August 1994, Jive

UGK's third release smoothed out some of the rough edges of their earlier efforts without even coming close to selling out, something that not only landed them in the *Billboard* 200 album chart for the first time but solidified their status as the leaders of Texas hip-hop. Well aware they were going to earn a new audience with the album, *Super Tight...* reprises one of *Too Hard to Swallow*'s best tracks as "Pocket Full of Stones, Pt. 2" and adds an anthem for the duo with "Underground," a track that marries a George Clinton-styled chorus with stone-cold rhymes. The Bun B showcase "Feds in Town" is the fondly remembered gangsta track of the album, "Front, Back & Side to Side" gave both Mike Jones and Paul Wall their blueprints for success ten years later, and Pimp C's slow and funky beats reached maturity right here, but if there's one reason UGK arrived with *Super Tight...*, it's "It's Supposed to Bubble." The snide swagger so key to the duo is captured in two lines—"It's Dom Perignon/It's supposed to bubble"—as laid-back funk, deep bass, and jazzy guitar loops all come together in perfect harmony. It's the sound of UGK finding the perfect formula to take Texas hip-hop to another level, two years before their next album, *Ridin' Dirty*, would make them the undisputed champions of Lone Star rap.

David Jeffries

Ultramagnetic MC's

Critical Beatdown
1988, Next Plateau

Besides being an undeniable hip-hop classic, the first album by the cult crew Ultra-magnetic MC's introduced to the world the larger-than-life, one-of-a-kind personality of Kool Keith. That alone would make this some sort of landmark recording, but it also happens to be one of the finest rap albums from the mid-to-late '80s "new school" in hip-hop that numbered among its contributors Run-D.M.C., Public Enemy, and Boogie Down Productions. *Critical Beatdown* easily stands with the classic recordings made by those giants, and it is, in some ways, more intriguing because of how short-lived Ultramagnetic turned out to be. It would be wrong to assume that the finest thing about the album is its lyrical invention. Lyrically the group is inspired, to be sure, but the production is equally forward-looking. *Critical Beatdown* is full of the sort of gritty cuts that would define hip-hop's underground scene, with almost every song sounding like an instant classic. Although he turns in a brilliant performance, Kool Keith had not yet taken completely off into the stratosphere at this early point. He still has at least one foot planted on the street and gives the album a viscerally real feel and accessibility that his later work sometimes lacks. His viewpoint is still uniquely and oddly individual, though, and he already shows signs of the freakish conceptualizing persona that would eventually surface fully under the guise of Dr. Octagon. If Kool Keith gives the album its progressive mentality and adrenaline rush, Ced-Gee gives it its street-level heft and is, in many ways, the album's core. Somewhere in the nexus between the two stylistic extremes, brilliant music emanated. *Critical Beatdown* maintains all its sharpness and every ounce of its power, and it has not aged one second since 1988.

Stanton Swihart

B-Side Companion
October 1997, Next Plateau

The Ultramagnetic MC's belong in the groundbreaking rap category (along with the likes of Run-D.M.C., Grandmaster Flash, etc.). Formed in the mid-'80s, the group rejected the fun rap style popular at the time (i.e., the Fat Boys and early Beastie Boys) and set out to create their own serious, funky, and bass-heavy groove style. The group definitely succeeded, but like many early rap artists, they did not meet with the commercial success they deserved for their trailblazing efforts. Back in the '80s, the 12" single was the main format for rappers to show their stuff (few rappers were granted full-length albums). So the Ultramagnetic MC's made the most of the 12", releasing many before their 1988 full-length *Critical Beatdown* appeared. An abundance of B-sides amassed after a while (with many as strong, if not better than, the featured A-side), so Next Plateau Records compiled the *crème de la crème* of these hard-to-find tracks on *The B-Side Companion*, remixing most to give them a more contemporary feel. Their first-ever release, "Ego Trippin'," is featured here as "Ego Trippin' 2000" and sets the tone for the rest of the album. You can't go wrong with tracks like "Watch Me Now," "MC's Ultra Part 2," and "Funky," all equally strong old-school rap that deserves to be heard. The seeds for today's rap stars were planted on the tracks included on *The B-Side Companion*.

Greg Prato

The U.M.C.'s

Fruits of Nature
October 1991, Wild Pitch

On their debut album, *Fruits of Nature*, the UMC's—Hass G and Kool Kim—are endlessly imaginative, witty, and effervescent by disposition and lyrical flow, and always intelligent. When it came to the music, co-producers Hass G and RNS decked it out in vintage soul and old Blue Note-styled tracks, with reams of obscure, idiosyncratic vocal samples tossed in as hooks, breaks, and bridges. The resulting effort is yet another vastly underrated rap album out of those banner years in hip-hop, 1991 and 1992, when commercial and economic instincts had yet to turn the music formulaic. The ironic thing is that nearly everything on *Fruits of Nature* is sing-along catchy and so ebullient that it would have sounded great bounding out of radios or from MTV. Unfortunately, it is also the sort of hip-hop that is too idiosyncratic and brainy to garner a widespread audience. Instead of alchemizing their jazz-tinged sensibility into a more earnest and reverent underground hip-hop extension of the jazz tradition, UMC's twist their jazzy inclinations into what are essentially pop songs that, even while generating a singular style all their own, cover the full range of the catchiness spectrum: ingratiating melodic tunes ("One to Grow On"), carbonated word play ("Blue Cheese"), cleverly disguised boasts and straight rhyming ("Kraftworks," "Swing It to the Area," "Any Way the Wind Blows"), loping urban anthems ("You Got My Back," "Jive Talk"), and more serious-minded cuts ("Morals"). There's even an urban take on storybook tales ("Never Never Land") and a sort of ballad ("Feelings"). The commercial failure of the UMC's and groups like them opened up hip-hop to the same sort of Top 40-ready and cookie-cutter artistry in the latter part of the decade that had previously swallowed rock and pop music. For a brief couple years, though, rap as uniquely excellent as *Fruits of Nature* could be found around every urban corner.

Stanton Swihart

Us3

Hand on the Torch
November 1993, Blue Note

Hip-hop/jazz fusionisters Us3 have forged the most elaborate union between the styles since the early days of Gang Starr and A Tribe Called Quest. Blue Note's vast catalog gives them a huge advantage over several similar groups in terms of source material, and classic sounds by Art Blakey, Horace Silver, and Herbie Hancock provide zest and fiber to their narratives. Indeed, when things falter, it's because the raps aren't always that creative. They are serviceable and sometimes catchy, but too often delivered without the snazzy touches or distinctive skills that make Quest and Gang Starr's material top-notch. But when words and music mesh, as on "Cantaloop" or "The Darkside," Us3 show how effectively hip-hop and jazz can blend.

Ron Wynn

U.T.F.O.

The Best of U.T.F.O.
December 1996, Select

U.T.F.O. never had many hits. During the mid-'80s, the rap group released a series of singles, but only one stood out, and for good reason, because that song, "Roxanne, Roxanne," is one of the classic rap singles of all time. Though "Roxanne, Roxanne" only hit number ten on the R&B charts, it was far more popular than its chart position suggests, spawning a craze of answer records that ran for nearly two years. Unfortunately, U.T.F.O. never released anything else that quite matched the quality of "Roxanne, Roxanne," though their follow-up, "The Real Roxanne," was entertaining in its own right. Since the group had an uneven track record, *The Best of U.T.F.O.* is the best way to get acquainted with the group, even though it has a number of weak spots itself. Nevertheless, it has all the necessary items U.T.F.O. ever recorded, and

"Roxanne, Roxanne" is a single that should be heard by all rap and hip-hop fans.

Leo Stanley

Vanilla Ice

To the Extreme
1990, SBK

An enormous hit in its time, with sales of over seven million copies, *To the Extreme* proved that a white rapper could be made into a mainstream pop idol. It also proved that traditional pop-idol marketing tactics wouldn't work for very long on rap audiences. Ice's undoing wasn't so much his actual music as it was his fabricated credibility—his wholly imaginary street-gang background, his ridiculous claims that "Ice Ice Baby" was not built on an obvious sample of Queen and David Bowie's "Under Pressure." It's hard to listen to *To the Extreme* now and believe a word he's saying; the posturing just doesn't ring true at all. The odd thing is, not all of the record is as awful as it's cracked up to be. Ice's mic technique is actually stronger and more nimble than MC Hammer's, and he really tries earnestly to show off the skills he does have. Unfortunately, even if he can keep a mid-tempo pace, his flow is rhythmically stiff, and his voice has an odd timbre; plus, he never seems sure of the proper accent to adopt. He's able to overcome those flaws somewhat in isolated moments, but they become all too apparent over the course of an entire album. Outside of "Ice Ice Baby" and the not-as-good "Play That Funky Music" ("steppin' so hard like a German Nazi"), there are some decent dance tracks and a few forgettable mediocrities. There are also a few inexcusable low points: the poorly rapped sexcapade "Life Is a Fantasy," the awkward reggae toasting of "Rosta Man" [sic], and "I Love You," a lyrically simplistic, overemoted ballad that makes LL Cool J's "I Need Love" sound like "Straight Outta Compton." Overall, *To the Extreme* might technically be better than *Please Hammer Don't Hurt 'Em*, but its hubris isn't quite as much fun.

Steve Huey

Volume 10

Hip-Hopera
March 1994, RCA

With the release of "Pistolgrip-Pump" as his debut single in 1993, Volume 10 set quite an ambitious precedent for himself. As the song and its off-centered interpretation of "More Bounce to the Ounce" captured anthem status across the States, no one quite knew what to expect next from the self-proclaimed lyrical Heavyweight. When his full-length album *Hip-Hopera* hit stores in 1994 it sure enough put a schizophrenic spin on what was quickly becoming typical Los Angeles gangsta rap. As a product of the *Goodlife* open mic sessions, Volume 10 utilized psychedelic-tinged beats provided by the likes of the Baka Boyz, Fat Jack, and Bosco Kante to cover almost every topic under the South Central sun. While hood warfare gets the flamboyant treatment on tracks such as "Knockoutchaskull" and "Flow Wood," a more introspective approach is taken on "Where's the Sniper" and "First Born," which respectively tackle the topics of alcoholism and fatherhood. As a second single, "Sunbeams" didn't even come close to matching the reach of "Pistolgrip-Pump," but it did prove that a touch of nature could still be enjoyed among even the most tense of urban situations.

Robert Gabriel

Watts Prophets

Things Gonna Get Greater: The Watts Prophets 1969–1971
September 2005, Water

The Watts Prophets
Things Gonna Get Greater: The Watts Prophets 1969-1971

Water Records— the incomparable, mysterious reissue label—has outdone themselves this time by reissuing the first two albums by the Watts Prophets, a spoken-word poetry group that grew out of the Watts Writers' Workshop. The Prophets—Anthony "Amde" Hamilton, Richard Dedeaux, Otis O'Solomon and later Dee Dee McNeil—were not as well-known nationally as their East Coast contemporaries the Last Poets, but they have influenced and have been sampled by countless hip-hop artists. The two recordings featured here, the 1969's *Black Voices: On the Streets in Watts* and 1971's *Rappin' Black in a White World*, are seminal documents of the Black Power struggle that was wiped out by the FBI's Cointelpro operation, incarceration, death, poverty and other persecutions from the power culture. The albums are presented here in reverse order—as Water is wont to do—and, aesthetically, it makes sense. *Rappin' Black in a White World* features McNeil's bluesed-out piano, her deeply influential proto-feminist poem "There's a Difference Between a Black Man and a Nigger," and the wonderfully haunting yet poignant "Sell Your Soul." Her voice and piano textures the suit on the first side of the disc. Dedeaux's "Amerikkka" is the highlight of the set with its righteous anger and deep rhythmic heartbeat. On *Black Voices: On the Streets in Watts* it is Hamilton's voice that startles, exhorts and occasionally frightens the listener. It's immediate, direct from the street and in your face. The album is rawer, less connected track for track, more slice of life, from the gut. Ragged, wailing saxophones and hand drums color the poetic proceedings that insist on revolution and a holistic approach to living while being suffocated and eaten alive in the white America. These records are not for everybody, but then, they never were. They are for those who can handle the truth that is still the truth. The game and its rules haven't changed; only the adornments and surfaces have changed. This is rap, hard, immediate and angry; it's a heart full of soul and a belly full of hard beauty that rings like a cry from the wilderness. Welcome to the real hardcore.

Thom Jurek

WC and the Maad Circle

Curb Servin'
October 1995, Payday

Musically, WC & the Maad Circle's *Curb Servin'* is by-the-books West Coast gangsta rap, with deep funk grooves and lazy, rolling beats. Coolio, who used to be a member of the crew in the early '90s, and Ice Cube make guest appearances, but what distinguishes it from others of the genre is the lyrical flair of WC, who spices up his rhymes with surreal, original imagery, even on the standard boasting tracks.

Stephen Thomas Erlewine

Whodini

Escape
1984, Jive

A vast improvement over the previous year's debut, *Escape* is the second album from the seminal no-nonsense New York rappers. Unlike many rappers, Whodini got their beats and musical backing from synthesizers. While this isn't a conceptual masterpiece and really is nothing more than sure-shot singles and sound-alike single, "Five Minutes of Funk" was an instant classic. The just-as-good "Freaks Come Out at Night" has the guys talking about nocturnal freaks with vivid lyrics and a little too much inside information. Listening to *Escape*, one has to be struck with the minimalism offered here. On "Big Mouth" and "Friends," producer Larry Smith provides clutter-free tracks for the guys to rap over. In contrast, the fast-paced "Escape (I Need a Break)" brings in ambulance sounds and ends up being a great instance of unconsciously danceable rap. Better yet, the closer "We Are Whodini" distills the essence of the group more than the other groundbreaking tracks here, and still retains a sense of freshness. The real unsung hero on *Escape* is the DJ, Grandmaster Dee, who provides deft work. Recorded at Battery Studios in England, *Escape* has a countless amount of memorable lines and productions, and has held up over time better than the debut.

Jason Elias

Back in Black
1986, Jive

As one of the first successful rap acts, Whodini albums quickly became standard bearers and necessary purchases for fans. The Brooklyn-raised trio of Jalil Hutchins, Ecstasy, and DJ Grandmaster Dee first came to national attention with the single "The Haunted House of Rock." Their third record, *Back in Black*, is the follow-up to a multi-platinum album, 1984's *Escape*. Those expecting a by-the-numbers sequel of sorts to that effort won't be too let down here. Although *Back in Black* does revisit lyrical and musical themes of previous efforts, it also offers a few new tricks or two. The first track (and a single release), "Funky Beat" features monster bass and drums, the one-two punch of Hutchins and Ecstasy, as well as a rare rap from Grandmaster Dee. The well-produced "One Love" has great synth signatures and the

guys dispensing their brand of pithy and pragmatic advice. They seem to unlearn those lessons by the time the hilarious "I'm a Ho" rolls around. The slow, scratch-laden track has a boastful chorus ("I rock three different freaks after every show") and some great rhymes from Hutchins. Despite the group's best efforts, *Back in Black* does often seem to be style over substance. Luckily the producer Larry Smith knew how to keep things sonically interesting. On the lyrically foggy "Fugitive," the hard rock guitars and clanging cymbals mesh especially well with Ecstasy's droll and abrupt delivery. "Echo Scratch" is also all over the road, but it was a great chance for Grandmaster Dee to show off his turntable skills. Also recorded at Battery Studios in London (as was *Escape*), *Back in Black* wasn't as influential as its predecessor, but it's nearly as enjoyable.

Jason Elias

Funky Beat: The Best of Whodini
June 2006, Jive/Legacy

Nearly identical to 1990's *Greatest Hits* and 1995's *The Jive Collection*, *Funky Beat: The Best of Whodini* contains all but one of Whodini's charting singles (including "One Love," "Friends," "Funky Beat," "Freaks Come Out at Night," "Five Minutes of Funk," and "Magic's Wand") and a couple better-known—and radio-unfriendly, lyrically—album cuts ("I'm a Ho," "Judy"). Any hip-hop fan who came of age after the '80s is likely to think of all this as very primitive and inextricably linked to its era, but he or she will certainly find out that Whodini were one of the primary groups to set the precedent for the fusion of hip-hop and R&B that would begin to dominate radio during the early '90s.

Andy Kellman

The World Class Wreckin' Cru

Turn off the Lights: Greatest Hits Plus
November 2001, Thump

Noted as the first group blessed with Dr. Dre's production expertise, the World Class Wreckin' Cru recorded some solid West Coast electro singles, more energetic than the style's other prime production act (Egyptian Lover), if not as revolutionary. Dre certainly rated with the prime electro producers across the nation—New York's Arthur Baker (Afrika Bambaataa) and Detroit's Juan Atkins (Cybotron)—and his best work ("Surgery," "Juice") was a big influence on bass music as well as West Coast rap. *Turn off the Lights: Greatest Hits Plus* has all of the best World Class Wreckin' Cru tracks, but there's still plenty of samey filler. The single "Turn off the Lights" is bland enough to have sounded totally innocuous on the charts during 1988, while dance tracks like "Cabbage Patch" and "The Fly" are tired novelties. The only other interesting inclusions are a pair of tracks that point toward Dre's work in N.W.A.—the surprisingly hardcore "Mission Possible" and "B.S." (the first a Public Enemy sound-alike, but the last one a completely original gangster fantasy). Still, unless you're very curious about Dr. Dre's origins in the Compton clubs, it's far better to seek out an old-school compilation that includes "Surgery" or "House Calls."

John Bush

Wu-Tang Clan

Enter the Wu-Tang (36 Chambers)
November 1993, Loud

Along with Dr. Dre's *The Chronic*, the Wu-Tang Clan's debut, *Enter the Wu-Tang (36 Chambers)*, was one of the most influential rap albums of the '90s. Its spare yet atmospheric production—courtesy of RZA—mapped out the sonic blueprint that countless other hardcore rappers would follow for years to come. It laid the groundwork for the rebirth of New York hip-hop in the hardcore age, paving the way for everybody from Biggie and Jay-Z to Nas and Mobb Deep. Moreover, it introduced a colorful cast of hugely talented MCs, some of whom ranked among the best and most unique individual rappers of the decade. Some were outsized, theatrical personalities, others were cerebral storytellers and lyrical technicians, but each had his own distinctive style, which made for an album of tremendous variety and consistency. Every track on *Enter the Wu-Tang* is packed with fresh, inventive rhymes, which are filled with martial arts metaphors, pop culture references (everything from Voltron to Lucky Charms cereal commercials to Barbra Streisand's "The Way We Were"), bizarre threats of violence, and a truly twisted sense of humor. Their off-kilter menace is really brought to life, however, by the eerie, lo-fi production, which helped bring the raw sound of the underground into mainstream hip-hop. Starting with a foundation of hard, gritty beats and dialogue samples from kung fu movies, RZA kept things minimalistic, but added just enough minor-key piano, strings, or muted horns to create a background ambience that works like the soundtrack to a surreal nightmare. There was nothing like it in the hip-hop world at the time, and even after years of imitation, *Enter the Wu-Tang* still sounds fresh and original. Subsequent group and solo projects would refine and deepen this template, but collectively, the Wu have never been quite this tight again.

Steve Huey

X Clan

To the East, Blackwards
April 1990, 4th & Broadway

The self-sufficient X Clan should've made a bigger splash with *To the East, Blackwards*, the group's debut album for 4th & Broadway. Name-dropping Nat Turner and Marcus Garvey and dressing in red, black, and green instead of black and silver didn't exactly lend itself to marketability in 1990, but there's

no evidence to the contrary that this Afrocentric group released one of the best rap records that year—which is saying a great deal. Yes, plenty of groups had already swiped liberally from Funkadelic, and true, "Grand Verbalizer"'s instrumental backdrop is nearly identical to "Microphone Fiend," but there's an infectious vigor with the way each track is fired off that makes those points moot. Brother J's bookish, caramel-smooth delivery is like no other, and Professor X's jolting appearances after nearly every verse ("This is protected by the red, the black, and the green—*with a key*! Sissy!") add even more character to the album. X Clan relentlessly pushes its pro-black motives and beliefs, and though the points are vague at times, at no point does it ever grow tiring. This isn't just a testament to the skills of the MCs—it also stands as a testament to the group members as producers. Like the best work of BDP and PE, a thorough listen to *To the East, Blackwards* is more likely to provoke deep thought than an entire chapter of the average American school's history book. And history books simply don't provide this kind of electric charge.

Andy Kellman

Xodus
May 1992, Polydor

More of the same is hardly a bad thing when considering X Clan's second album. They're still jacking beats—from Special Ed, D-Nice, and Main Source, for instance—and they're still spreading their knowledge with righteous, if occasionally vague, verve. The most significant change in the group's sound is the decreased reliance upon Funkadelic and George Clinton samples. This serves them well and shows that they had more going for them than most people gave X Clan credit for. Furthermore, expecting them to come out with some form of party jam or anything less serious than their typical material was just plain wrongheaded—they wouldn't've worn it well at all. And so, they stick to what they do best: railing against racism and the other issues that hold blacks down ("F.T.P.," which refers once again to Yusef Hawkins' 1989 beating at the hands of a white mob) and bolstering their doctrine with tight, detailed productions. The normally relaxed and somewhat reserved Brother J breaks from his usual playbook on "Rhythem of God" with a blitzing, forceful delivery. On "Cosmic Ark," he rhymes with such authority and momentum that the end of the track seems to make him stop prematurely; the track lasts five and a half minutes but could've gone on into double digits. Not quite as excellent as the debut, *Xodus* is nonetheless another album lacking dull moments. Unfortunately, the group split before it was able to make a third.

Andy Kellman

Yo-Yo

Make Way for the Motherlode
March 1991, East West

As positive as Queen Latifah but as abrasive in her delivery as MC Lyte, Yo-Yo showed some potential on her debut album, *Make Way for the Motherlode*. The decent, if uneven, CD (which Ice Cube produced with Sir Jinx and Del Tha Funkee Homosapien) was more of a critical success than a commercial success. The hip-hop press was quick to praise Yo-Yo, who urges young women to practice responsible sexuality, respect themselves and demand respect from men. On "Girl, Don't Be No Fool," Yo-Yo stresses that women shouldn't allow men to physically abuse them under *any* circumstances—a message that definitely needed to be heard, although regrettably, the song doesn't distinguish between the "dogs" and "good guys." Cube has memorable cameos on "What Can I Do?" and "You Can't Play With My Yo-Yo," but his presence wasn't enough to make *Motherlode* anything more than a moderate hit.

Alex Henderson

Young Black Teenagers

Young Black Teenagers
February 1991, Soul

In the early 1990s, a rap group stirred some controversy by calling itself Young Black Teenagers. The name wouldn't have made a difference if they really were Black, but in fact, the Teenagers were actually White. Some MCs were angry and resentful, while others realized that YBT was actually making a pro-Black statement. Among the quintet's supporters were Public Enemy, and in fact, this impressive CD (which had a cover modeled after *Meet the Beatles*) was produced by the team that had been producing PE and Ice Cube, the Bomb Squad. Anyone who dismissed YBT as a mere novelty didn't seriously listen to "Punks, Lies & Videotape," "Mack Daddy Don of the Underworld" or "Daddy Kalled Me Niga Cause I Liked to Rhyme," all of which prove that their rapping skills were quite strong. Like House of Pain and 3rd Bass, YBT was a white group that rejected pop-rap, and it is the hardcore approach that wins out on this rewarding and provocative disc.

Alex Henderson

Young MC

Stone Cold Rhymin'
1989, Delicious Vinyl

Young MC wasn't given props at the time and he wasn't respected in the years following the release of his debut *Stone*

Cold Rhymin', largely because he worked entirely in the pop-rap/crossover vein. All the same, that's what's great about his debut, since it's exceptionally clever and effective, a wonderful combination of deft rhymes and skillful production. And there's no discounting Matt Dike, Michael Ross, the Dust Brothers, and engineer Mario Caldato, Jr. (the latter two names

are members of the Beastie Boys' inner circle), who make this record easily accessible, without a trace of guilt, even if it does sample from familiar sources. And, really, Young MC is a gifted rapper, spinning out rhymes with a deft touch and turning out rhymes much more clever than they should be. Yes, *Stone Cold Rhymin'* is a product of its time, particularly in its sound and lyrical references, but divorced from the Bush era, it comes off as one of the catchiest, friendliest pop-rap records and it's still an infectious party record years after its release.

Stephen Thomas Erlewine

Zimbabwe Legit

Zimbabwe Legit
March 1992, Hollywood

The odds that a record of this type would work had to be pretty low; the whole project smacked of a novelty, and one that would probably result in an overly poppy crossover. Surprisingly, the only two tracks put out by Zimbabwe Legit prove that the Ndlovu brothers had skills right in line with some of the best alternative East Coasters working then. Over a hard-hitting, jazzy production, the rappers switch deftly between languages on "Doin' Damage in My Native Language," betraying little of a foreign account and indulging in rhymes much better than could be expected for *anyoneís* debut. (Indeed, their profile was so low that Zimbabwe Legit could well have been an alias for a pair of American rappers.) Of the remixes, Mista Lawnge's is pretty solid, but DJ Shadow's is in another league altogether—one of the seminal productions in hip-hop history, his sprawling, six-minute "Legitimate Remix" remade the original into a late-night, back-to-Africa sample symphony.

John Bush

PART II: DIGGING IN THE CRATES

Rap didn't come from nowhere, although it might have sounded that way at the dawn of the '80s. It had deep roots that stretched back through disco, back through the funk, fusion, and reggae of the '70s, back through the soul and jazz of the '60s. It's easy to argue that the roots of rap started even before that. Surely, there are talking blues and raucous R&B records of the '50s that are not dissimilar to some of the grooves and attitude that appeared in hip-hop during the '80s—but during the prime days of the golden age, it was the music of the '60s and '70s that provided the key inspiration for hip-hop.

In this part, we've pulled together a cross-section of pivotal sounds and albums from the '60s and '70s, ranging from hard-driving funk to laid-back soul-jazz. We've included such titans as James Brown, Miles Davis, George Clinton, Donald Byrd, and Sly Stone. Some of these albums were sampled heavily on rap records. Some merely provided a touchstone for the sound and spirit of old-school hip-hop, but all are worth seeking out, whether they're found on CD or deep in the stacks of a used-record store.

ALBUM DIRECTORY

Cannonball Adderley

Black Messiah
1972, Capitol

Still immersed in the burgeoning electronic jazz-rock explosion of the times, Cannonball Adderley goes further toward a rapprochement with the rock and soul audiences than ever before on this fascinating, overlooked double album. For starters, he recorded it live at West Hollywood's *Troubadour* club, then known as a showcase for folk and rock acts. He also imported additional players into his quintet, expanding into exotic percussion effects with Airto Moreira (whom Miles Davis had previously featured), hard rock guitar with sessionman Mike Deasy, fiery tenor sax from the young Ernie Watts, and occasional seasoning from conguero Buck Clarke and clarinetist Alvin Batiste. "Now I don't give a damn whether you can count or not, we still are the Cannonball Adderley Quintet!," quoth the leader, who is in loose, loquacious form throughout the set (the jazz world badly misses his witty verbal intros). With Joe Zawinul now flying off to Weather Report, his replacement is an even more electronically minded pianist, George Duke, who levitates into the outer limits with his Echoplex and ring modulator and proves to be a solid comper. But Zawinul is not forgotten, for the band pursues a long, probing, atmospheric excursion on his tune, "Dr. Honouris Causa." Adderley generously gives Deasy two contrasting feature numbers—"Little Benny Hen," a raucous, amateurishly sung blues/rock piece, and "Zanek," a great countrified tune with an avant-garde freakout at the climax—and all of the other guests save Clarke get single solo features. Brother Nat Adderley gamely visits the outside on cornet, not always convincingly, while Cannonball doubles with increasing adventurousness on soprano and alto and bassist Walter Booker and drummer Roy McCurdy deftly handle all of the changes of style. Cannonball adeptly keeps pace with Miles Davis, his former boss—the driving "The Chocolate Nuisance" could easily be a first cousin of "Pharoah's Dance" on *Bitches Brew*—while not abandoning his funky soul-jazz base nor the special audience-friendly ambience of his concerts. Unlike Adderley's other two-for-one-priced double albums of the '70s, this one was inexplicably sold at full price, which probably limited its sales and might partly explain why it remains surprisingly hard to find in used LP bins. But interest in the early jazz-rock period ought to provoke a CD reissue.

Richard S. Ginell

The Average White Band

AWB
August 1974, Rhino

After debuting with 1973's excellent but neglected *Show Your Hand* (later reissued as *Put It Where You Want It*), the Average White Band switched from MCA to Atlantic and hit big with this self-titled gem. Upon first hearing gutsy, Tower of Power-influenced funk like "Person to Person" and the instrumental "Pick Up the Pieces" (a number one R&B hit), many soul fans were shocked to learn that not only were the band members white—they were whites from Scotland. Like Teena Marie five years later, AWB embraced soul and funk with so much conviction that it was clear this was anything but an "average" white band. This album is full of treasures that weren't big hits but should have been—including the addictive "You Got It," the ominous "There's Always Someone Waiting," and a gutsy remake of the Isley Brothers' "Work to Do." [When Rhino reissued *AWB* on CD in 1995, an edited live version of "Pick Up the Pieces" recorded at the 1977 *Montreux Jazz Festival* was added. (The full-length version had been included on Rhino's 1994 reissue of *Warmer Communications*.)]

Alex Henderson

Cut the Cake
June 1975, Rhino

In the informative liner notes that he wrote for Rhino's early '90s reissue of *Cut the Cake*, writer A. Scott Galloway explains that this excellent album was recorded under less-than-ideal circumstances. The Average White Band's original drummer, Robbie McIntosh, died of a heroin overdose in 1974, and the surviving members were still in mourning when they started working on their third album, *Cut the Cake* (which originally came out on LP in 1975). Steve Ferrone, a black drummer from London, England, was hired as a replacement—ironically, he became the first black member of a Scottish soul/funk band that had a very African-American sound and a largely African-American following. Despite the fact that AWB's members still had McIntosh's death on their minds when they were writing and recording *Cut the Cake*, this isn't a depressing or consistently melancholy album; far from it. In fact, parts of the album are downright fun, especially up-tempo funk gems like "School Boy Crush," "Groovin' the Night Away" and the hit title song (which made it to number seven on *Billboard*'s R&B singles chart). *Cut the Cake* is also the album that gave us the ballad "Cloudy" (one of the more melancholy tracks) and AWB's version of "If I Ever Lose This Heaven," a smooth soul classic that was originally recorded by Quincy Jones in 1973. The song wasn't a chart-buster—it peaked at number 25 on *Billboard*'s R&B singles chart—but it did become a favorite among AWB fans and enjoyed a lot of exposure on quiet storm formats. AWB's members certainly don't sound like they're in mourning on *Cut the Cake*. If anything, they honor McIntosh's memory by showing their resilience and delivering one of their finest, most engaging albums.

Alex Henderson

David Axelrod

Song of Innocence
1968, Capitol

Producer, arranger, and engineer David Axelrod made his mark with Cannonball Adderley, Lou Rawls, and the Electric Prunes. He created recording dates—both live and in the studio—with crisp innovative production, forward-looking arrangements, and killer sound effects (the Prunes' weird "Mass in F Minor" is a case in point). No one, however, expected him to make his own records. Nonetheless, in 1968 his first concept work was issued under the EMI imprint. His inspiration was *Songs of Innocence*, English poet William Blake's watershed collection of poems; Axelrod set seven of them to music using a bevy of studio musicians and a lot of clout at the label. Using a rock orchestra, Axelrod created a suite that blended pop, rock, jazz, theater music, and R&B that has withstood the test of time, and has been revisited and sampled by electronica pioneers such as DJ Shadow and DJ Cam. Perhaps the best known tune of this mystical mixture is the jazzed out, slow groove of "Holy Thursday," with its bluesy bop piano lines and huger than huge string section playing a vamp from a Count Basie tune. Meanwhile, the rhythm section floats a steady, swinging rhythm to the guitars and brass who answer with dramatic harmonics centered around a complex yet elegant melodic, and the guitar itself screams overhead. It's a jazz boogaloo with classical overtones. And yes, it, and the rest of the album, sound as if it would be excessive and awful. This was visionary work in 1968, and, to commit heresy, withstands the test of time better than the Beatles *Sgt. Pepper's Lonely Hearts Club Band* album that allegedly inspired it. Axelrod's psychedelia is implied; its compositional form and feeling that drive him to celebrate the wildness and folly of youth with celebration and verve. And as a result, the music here sounds fresh, free of cynicism and hipper-than-thou posturing, remaining new each time it is heard. *Song of Innocence* made critics turn their heads in its day, regarding it as a visionary curiosity piece; today it's simply a great, timeless work of pop art that continues to inspire over three decades after its initial release.

Thom Jurek

Songs of Experience
1969, Capitol

After the modicum of success he'd experienced with his debut, *Song of Innocence*, set to William Blake's epic suite of poems, composer, arranger, and producer David Axelrod turned to the British poet's *Songs of Experience* for inspiration in creating his follow-up album. Using eight of Blake's poems, Axelrod composed a suite that was less rock in its aim and more pop- and jazz-oriented in places, but overall a more orchestral work. Texturizing a symphony with percussive elements and the use of British and Irish folk song, as well as the stylistic inventions of fellow arranger Gerald Wilson for effect, Axelrod created a sobering, and, in places, even melancholy collage of song and lyrical styles that slid rather than drove home its point: that experience is a good but bittersweet teacher. Axelrod's compositions are positively literary here, lush and varied, using as much space as they do sound for dramatic and dynamic effect. His complex use of the various colors of the horn section was capable of producing allowed him to create new palettes for the rock instrumentation. The centerpiece of the album is "The Human Abstract," a gently swinging, funky, bass-driven work that juxtaposes a strummed electric guitar playing augmented sevenths against

an acoustic piano and a muted drone of horns. By the time the guitar enters for its solo, the strings have erected a space out of the ether for themselves to further shore up the orchestra's time-honored body against the wail of unrepentant youth. The tension in the tune is dramatic, colorful, and hued with as much red and yellow as there is blue and black. When the French horns and tuba state their case against the high-flying impetuousness of the restless spirit, a piano bridges the gap, whispering the melody's main theme in the center channel, whispering them both out into silence. Other notables are the positively majestic "The Divine Image," and the pastoral sadness in "A Little Girl Lost." Axelrod's meditations were getting darker with the times in 1969, but they hadn't yet reached the horrific potential for darkness that they would on 1971's *Earth Rot*. In 1969, Axelrod was still a musical contemplative searching for a sound that best exemplified not only his feelings but also the heady text he sought to sonically illustrate. He succeeded in spades.

Thom Jurek

Roy Ayers

Coffy
1973, Polydor

A blaxploitation masterpiece on par with Curtis Mayfield's *Superfly* and Isaac Hayes' *Shaft*, Roy Ayers' soundtrack for the 1973 Pam Grier vehicle *Coffy* remains one of the most intriguing and evocative film scores of its era or any other. Ayers' signature vibes create atmospheres and textures quite distinct from your average blaxploitation effort, embracing both heavy, tripped-out funk ("Brawling Broads") and vividly nuanced soul-jazz ("Aragon"). The vocal numbers are no less impressive, in particular the rapturous opening cut, "Coffy Is the Color." Richly cinematic grooves, as inventive and cohesive as any of Ayers' vintage Ubiquity LPs. Highly recommended.

Jason Ankeny

Change Up the Groove
1974, Polydor

Its misleading title notwithstanding, *Change Up the Groove* does little to alter the inimitable jazz-funk aesthetic Roy Ayers perfected on earlier LPs like *He's Coming* and *Virgo Red*. The record simply offers more of a very, very good thing, as a result remaining somewhat overlooked in the vibraphonist's large catalog. What's impressive about *Change Up the Groove* is the seeming effortlessness of it all. Ayers' command of the almighty groove is absolute, and he divines the funk even in left-field material like the theme from the television hit *M.A.S.H.* More traditional fare like the scorching "Fikisha (To Help Someone to Arrive)," the measured "When Is Real, Real?," and a shimmering cover of Stevie Wonder's rapturous "Don't You Worry 'Bout a Thing" proves no less impressive, and even if there's no obvious standout, Ayers makes no missteps, either—tremendous stuff from top to bottom.

Jason Ankeny

Everybody Loves the Sunshine
1976, Polydor

Roy Ayers's had long made his shift into R&B/soul by 1976's *Everybody Loves the Sunshine*. His recordings of this period can be very hit and miss, and in this particular record, you get both. The title track, "Everybody Loves the Sunshine," is a quintessential song from the mid-'70s. While it might not have slammed the charts like Wild Cherry's "Play That Funky Music," it's still a revered classic. It evokes that feeling of sweltering concrete in Brooklyn where the only relief is the local fire hydrant. Entirely sung by a choir repeating the same lines throughout, the rhythm section rolls along with a perfectly looped laid-back groove. It moves along lazily, hypnotically, and sluggishly as the sun slows things down to the right speed and "folks get down in the sunshine." The rest of the album can be considered incidental, but still mildly interesting.

Jack LV Isles

Evolution: The Polydor Anthology
1995, Polydor

Evolution charts Roy Ayers' 12 years and 20 LPs with Polydor, a rich time where his gliding, loose-groove jazz-funk gained many fans—though perhaps fewer than it did 20 years later in the midst of the rare groove/acid jazz revival. During the 1970s, Ayers and his band, Ubiquity, progressed from political- and social-commentary funk to blaxploitation to disco to some surprisingly touching R&B ballads, and this two-disc set covers it all with grace and a smooth flow. Fans of hip-hop, groove music, funk, and jazz will all be able to find something to enjoy on the collection. Highlights include "We Live in Brooklyn Baby," "Evolution," "Running Away," and "Get on up, Get on Down," among others.

John Bush

Baby Huey

The Baby Huey Story: The Living Legend
1971, Water

Baby Huey's only album, released after his untimely death, is titled *The Living Legend* with good reason. He was legendary in his appearance, a 400-pound man with a penchant for flamboyant clothing and crowned by a woolly Afro, a look that is best illustrated by one of several rare photos included in the Water Records edition that shows our man in a wide-lapeled polka-dot shirt with a lime-green jacket. Beyond his unusual appearance, though, he was graced with a stunning, fierce voice on par with Otis Redding and Howard Tate, wailing and howling one moment

and oddly tender and sentimental the next. Nowhere on *Living Legend* is his range more apparent than on the opening track, "Listen to Me," where listeners are introduced to both the enigma of Baby Huey and his diamond-tough psychedelic funk backing band, the Baby Sitters. The high-energy instrumental workout "Mama Get Yourself Together" is worthy of the J.B.'s and a hazy, spiraling ten-minute rendition of Sam Cooke's chestnut "A Change Is Going to Come" confirms that the Baby Sitters could hold their own with Blood, Sweat & Tears. Further lore that catapults *The Living Legend* from good to great: the production was helmed by Curtis Mayfield, reason enough to make it near essential, and is highlighted by three of his compositions, "Mighty Mighty," which Mayfield and the Impressions recorded a few years earlier; "Running," a classic Mayfield cut that can only be heard here ripped to glorious bits by a band that is trying to let every member solo; and "Hard Times," which Mayfield himself would revisit on his 1975 album *There's No Place Like America Today*, although Baby Huey's razor-edged reading remains the definitive version—no small caveat considering Mayfield not only wrote the tune, but could rightfully be considered one of the architects of soul to boot.

Wade Kergan

The Bar-Kays

Gotta Groove
1969, Stax

In the wake of the tragic plane crash that claimed the lives of four of their bandmates and soul legend Otis Redding, trumpeter Ben Cauley and bassist James Alexander formed a new edition of the Bar-Kays to cut *Gotta Groove*, a celebration of life and music that ranks among the funkiest, hardest-driving LPs ever released under the Stax aegis. The record's immense debt to Sly & the Family Stone is repaid via the two-part "Don't Stop Dancing (To the Music)," which galvanizes the Bar-Kays' trademark deep-fried soul grooves with an infusion of psychedelia. Even further out is the blistering "Street Walker," with its shrieking guitar licks and organ fills. But most of all *Gotta Groove* serves as a showcase for the ferocious drumming of Roy Cunningham and Willie Hall, whose relentlessly funky rhythms push cuts like "Humpin'" and "Jiving 'Round" well past their somewhat pedestrian melodies—little wonder the album's proven a fecund source of samples for acts including Cypress Hill, Ice Cube, and GZA.

Jason Ankeny

Money Talks
October 1978, Stax

Although the Bar-Kays stuck with the Stax Records until its demise in 1976, the label stopped releasing the group's recordings after 1973. However, when they re-emerged as a success on the Mercury label with hits like "Shake Your

Rump to the Funk," some unreleased recordings they made between 1974 and 1976 were released as an album entitled *Money Talks*. Although this repackaging was obviously designed to cash in on the group's success, *Money Talks* stands up as a solid and consistent album in its own right. This material lays the groundwork for the Bar-Kays' post-Stax style by trading live-in-the-studio jams for a carefully produced sound and blending in standout pop hooks into the funky grooves. The best example is "Holy Ghost," a hard-grooving monster of a jam where elaborate horn arrangements dance around a thick synthesizer bassline as Larry Dodson lays down a salacious vocal about his lover's otherworldly romantic skills. It became a big R&B hit when released as a single in 1978 and was later sampled by M/A/R/R/S on their club classic "Pump Up the Volume." Other memorable tracks include the title track, a high-stepping tune that showcases the chops of the horn players, and "Mean Mistreater," an unlikely but effective Grand Funk Railroad cover that transforms the minimalist original tune into a spooky yet sexy mood piece built on some languid keyboard work. None of the other tracks are as strong as "Holy Ghost" (which is so good that it bookends the album in two versions), but they are all listenable and flow together surprisingly well as an album. All in all, *Money Talks* is a fine slab of vintage funk that will please anyone who loves old-school grooves.

Donald A. Guarisco

The Best of the Bar-Kays
1988, Stax

While curiously overlooking the group's earliest hits ("Soul Finger" and "Knucklehead"), *The Best of the Bar-Kays* offers a worthwhile thumbnail portrait of the Bar-Kays' evolution from a neo-Booker T. & the MG's soul instrumental combo into one of the wilder funk ensembles of the 1970s. Focusing on the years 1968 (when the group's second lineup came together following the death of four members of the band in the same airplane crash that claimed Otis Redding) through 1975 (when the band left Stax to sign with Mercury), *The Best of the Bar-Kays* finds them bridging the gap between the R&B sounds of the 1960s and the 1970s, and gaining more than their share of attitude along the way. Highlights include a very Booker T.-influenced cover of "Midnight Cowboy," the funky and funny Isaac Hayes pastiche "Son of Shaft," a revved-up take on "Montego Bay," and the tight groove of "A.J. the Housefly." While not a complete overview of the Bar-Kays' career, *The Best of the Bar-Kays* is at least a strong starter, and should ideally be followed up by *The Best of Bar-Kays*, which concentrates on their work for Mercury.

Mark Deming

Gary Bartz

The Shadow Do!
1975, Prestige

Not as known as the later *Music Is My Sanctuary*—which was an even further departure, in its increased smoothness, from his Ntu Troop dates, and more popular by virtue of being released on Blue Note—*The Shadow Do!* was the first time Gary Bartz sought assistance from Fonce and Larry Mizell, the sibling duo who enlivened many sessions throughout the '70s with their soaring fusion of soul, funk, and (as Bartz would say) "the j-word." At this point, some j-word purists were hip to the Mizell program, what with dates from Bobbi Humphrey, Donald Byrd, and Johnny Hammond

already in circulation. Checking the back of this Prestige release supplied all the info they needed to know: production by the Mizells, and four people credited with playing some form of synthesizer. Keyboardist Hubert Eaves, bassist Michael Henderson, guitarist Reggie Lucas, percussionist Mtume, and drummer Howard King help lend a sound that is a little funkier and heavier than most Mizell-guided sessions, but it's no less sweet. The second through fourth songs of side one exude joy and love, anchoring the album in a sense of contentedness so infectious that it might've even won over a few cold souls expecting straight jazz. Bartz's saxophones are at their melodic best, dancing, skipping, and trilling through the arrangements. He also sings lead, present on most of the songs, and though he probably didn't win any publication's best vocalist award, no one sounds like him, and the Mizells' own background harmonies are on-point as ever. (Reissued on CD at least twice in Japan, in 1993 and 2007.)

Andy Kellman

Archie Bell

Tightening It Up: The Best of Archie Bell & the Drells
August 1994, Rhino

It could be assumed that Archie Bell & the Drells essentially did the same thing over and over again, since "Tighten Up" almost consigns them to the level of one-hit wonders, but that's not an accurate assessment of their gifts. True, they often followed the same stylish, sunny, utterly infectious sound, but there was a lot more depth and variety there, as Rhino's terrific 20-track collection *Tightening It Up: The Best of Archie Bell & the Drells* illustrates. What it reveals to those that weren't playing close attention is that the group was one of the first great Philly soul outfits, recording a number of Gamble & Huff's early songs and providing a training ground for the seminal duo. Though the hits didn't come fast and furious, like they would later, they, Bell & the Drells, created some wonderful singles, highlighted by "(There's Gonna Be A) Showdown" and "A World Without Music." There's plenty of other terrific moments throughout this collection, which proves that Bell & the Drells were far more than a one-hit wonder—they were one of the great under appreciated soul outfits of their time.

Stephen Thomas Erlewine

The Blackbyrds

The Blackbyrds
October 1973–October 1974, A&M

This amazing album is the product of six full-time Howard University students taking the direction of department head and jazz great Donald Byrd into the Fantasy Studios along with the aid of production wizard Larry Mizell. The result is some of the finest groove-oriented jazz music ever recorded. The rhythm section of Joe Hall on bass and Keith Killgo on drums provides a tight foundation for the Blackbyrds to enhance any dancefloor with their soulful explorations. With Kevin Toney supplying beautiful keyboard work and Barney Perry hitting listeners up with his chicken-scratch guitar, the skeletal framework for what could be called optimistic funk was firmly established by this debut record. Recommended songs include "Do It, Fluid," "Reggins," and "Summer Love," although the overall consistency of quality tracks on *The Blackbyrds* is reason enough to give the album a complete listen.

Robert Gabriel

City Life
November 1975, Fantasy

The Blackbyrds—a jazz-funk outfit formed in a university class taught by jazz trumpeter Donald Byrd, who produced the albums and wrote most of the tunes—were more of an Earth, Wind & Fire-style horn band than a purist jazz crew, but few groups were better in their chosen style, and 1975's *City Life* is probably their best album. It's certainly their most successful, including the pop hit "Happy Music" and what has become their signature tune, a percolating Latin-flavored jam called "Rock Creek Park" that's one of the pinnacles of '70s jazz-funk. As on the bouncy title track, the lyrical content is minimal, a simple hypnotic chant, but the fluid interplay of the musicians, who are masters of the unison horn section and the polyrhythmic groove, is what's important about this music. Other highlights include the funky southern-style soul of "Hash and Eggs" and the lyrical ballad "Love So Fine." This is often-sublime stuff ripe for rediscovery by fans of '70s funk, soul, and fusion.

Stewart Mason

Blowfly

Weird World of Blowfly
1971, Henry Stone

Recorded live in the studio, *The Weird World of Blowfly* has the ambience of an after-hours party. In the tradition of older albums by similar (though tamer) acts like Doug Clark & Hot Nuts, *The Weird World of Blowfly* starts with his theme song, "Weird World," and then moves through 14 sexual and scatological parodies of popular soul and pop hits of the time, interspersed with good-humored, rambling introductions. So is it funny? Some will undoubtedly find the whole enterprise juvenile and distasteful, and frankly, a couple of the parodies are a little too obvious to be clever (surely sixth graders around the world have written songs like "Shittin'

on the Dock of the Bay"), but most of the album is really very funny, for those who like this sort of thing. The 1995 reissue adds three tracks to the original LP (first released on Clarence Reid's own Weird World label), including both sides of a celebrated mid-'70s holiday single, "Jingle Fuckin' Bells" and "Queer for the New Year," along with, oddly enough, a clean single released under Reid's own name in 1974, "Fonky Party."

Stewart Mason

Hamilton Bohannon

Stop and Go
1973, Dakar

Hamilton Bohannon's finest record concocts sensuous funk grooves from daring arrangements boasting tripped-out wah-wah guitars, punishing basslines, and massive drum breaks. In short, a sampler's wet dream. While later Bohannon discs would veer too far into the realm of up-tempo disco, *Stop and Go* favors slower, sexier rhythms. Add in the chorus vocals of the Haywood Sisters on tracks like "Run It on Down, Mr. D.J." and the remarkable "Singing a Song for My Father," and the end result is the kind of uncommonly lush and tactile funk album R. Kelly would skip recess to make.

Jason Ankeny

Booker T. & the MG's

Green Onions
October 1962, Atlantic

There's not a note or a nuance out of place anywhere on this record, which was 35 of the most exciting minutes of instrumental music in any category that one could purchase in 1962 (and it's no slouch four decades out, either). "I Got a Woman" is the single best indicator of how superb this record is and this band was—listening to this track, it's easy to forget that the song ever had lyrics or ever needed them, Booker T. Jones' organ and Steve Cropper's guitar serving as more-than-adequate substitutes for any singer. Their version of "Twist and Shout" is every bit as satisfying. Even "Mo' Onions," an effort to repeat the success of "Green Onions," doesn't repeat anything from the earlier track except the tempo, and Jones and Cropper both come up with fresh sounds within the same framework. "Behave Yourself" is a beautifully wrought piece of organ-based blues that gives Jones a chance to show off some surprisingly nimble-fingered playing, while "Stranger on the Shore" is transformed into a piece of prime soul music in the group's hands. "Lonely Avenue" is another showcase for Jones' keyboard dexterity, and then there's the group's cover of Smokey Robinson's "One Who Really Loves You," with a ravishing lead performance by Jones on organ and Cropper's guitar handling the choruses. Just when it seems like the album has turned in all of the surprises in repertory that it could reasonably deliver, it ends with "Comin' Home Baby," a killer jazz piece on which Steve Cropper gets to shine, his guitar suddenly animated around Jones' playing, his quietly trilled notes at the crescendo some of the most elegant guitar heard on an R&B record up to that time.

Bruce Eder

Hip Hug-Her
June 1967, Rhino

Still riding high years after the success of "Green Onions," *Hip Hug-Her* is another 11-song solid session of Southern soul delivered by one of the best bands in the business. In an attempt to appeal to the up-and-coming mod movement, the cover features an alluring model flanked by fashionable faceless people. But not to judge the album by its cover, *Hip Hug-Her* finds the group diving deeper into soulful territories, no doubt aided by the addition of bassist Duck Dunn to the fold. The title track is clearly one of the stronger cuts on the album, but other tunes such as the midtempo Motown anthem "Get Ready" and the group's interpretation of "Groovin'" make this one of the strongest full-lengths in the Booker T. & the MG's catalog.

Rob Theakston

Brass Construction

Brass Construction
April 1975, United Artists

Some bands enjoy their greatest success with their first release, and this Brooklyn-based funk ensemble is a good example. Their first single was the chart-topping "Movin'." Aside from the verse being chanted in unison, this aggressively paced dance number, with its catchy, melodious hook line, utilizes reeds and brass, complemented by keyboard and synthesizer solos from bandleader Randy Muller. The single moved its way to the number one spot on the R&B charts, the group's only chart-topper out of 17 singles that reached the charts, and one of two to ever crack the Top Ten. The follow-up single, "Changin'," has a similar arrangement at a slightly slower tempo. The melody is not seductive like its predecessor. Seeming to be more of a musical exhibition and less dance-oriented, it still managed to peak at number 24 on the charts. While the group's music is centered around its horns, the majority of the songs from this album feature vocals throughout the verses and choruses. Adding their social awareness to the mix on a couple tracks, all numbers are consistent with the album's dance/funk appeal.

Craig Lytle

The Brothers Johnson

Right on Time
1977, A&M

Potentially viewed as something of a warm-up for Quincy Jones before producing Michael Jackson's wildly successful *Off the Wall* and *Thriller* albums, the Brothers Johnson's first two releases spawned hits like "I'll Be Good to You" and brought  George and Louis Johnson to a mass audience of their own. (Louis, in fact, would go on to play bass on those first two sessions by the King of Pop.) As with the Jackson discs, Jones creates a seamless mix of pop and funk on the Brothers sophomore release *Right on Time*, helping to create the group's second chart-topper "Strawberry Letter 23" as well the equally effervescent, minor R&B hit "Runnin' for Your Lovin'." With Earth, Wind & Fire's airy dancefloor hits in mind, the Brothers also deliver polished funk tracks like "Right on Time" and "Never Leave You Lonely," as well as more pop-friendly material like "Free Yourself, Be Yourself" and "Love Is." And with one of the best jazz arrangers in the business behind the board, the Brothers couldn't forgo some instrumentals here as well, specifically the breezy, funk-in-a-quiet-storm number "Q" and the less intriguing, synthesizer jam "Brother Man." An enjoyable and even infectious collection that, in its sophistication, certainly avoids being just some sort of dry run for Jones.

Stephen Cook

Chuck Brown

Bustin' Loose
1979, Valley Vue

In the 1980s many of go-go's supporters insisted that it was going to become as big as rap. Regrettably, that never happened. Go-go was huge in Washington, D.C., where a Chuck Brown or Rare Essence show was as big a deal as a George Clinton concert, and a go-go release could be as impressive a seller as the latest Rick James record. But nationally, only a few go-go songs became major hits: E.U.'s "Da Butt" was huge in 1988, and Chuck Brown soared to the top of the R&B charts in 1978 with the insanely funky "Bustin' Loose." Brown and his band, the Soul Searchers, showed a great deal of promise on this debut album, which James Purdie produced at the famous Sigma Sound Studios in Philadelphia. The title song is one of go-go's all-time classics, and anyone with a taste for sweaty, hard-driving funk will also find a lot to love about "If It Ain't Funky" and "I Gotcha Now." But not everything on the album is aggressive. Even though Brown is best known for his gutbucket funk grooves, "Could It Be Love" and an inspired cover of the Jerry Butler/Gamble & Huff pearl "Never Gonna Give You Up" demonstrate that he has no problem handling romantic ballads and slow jams. It isn't surprising that the album's slower tracks are so heavily influenced by Philly soul. After all, Sigma Sound is where the O'Jays, the Intruders, Blue Magic, Teddy Pendergrass, the Stylistics, Billy Paul, and countless others recorded their biggest hits. Most of *Bustin' Loose*, however, isn't typical of recordings made at Sigma; the majority of the material is pure go-go, and *Bustin' Loose* went down in history as one of go-go's most essential releases.

Alex Henderson

James Brown

There It Is
June 1972, Polydor

Brown's Polydor debut, *Hot Pants*, was nothing more than an inferior remake of the title track baited with a batch of half-baked vamps. *There It Is*, his second Polydor studio album, was a marked improvement. Not that he put much into this one either. This 1972 effort collected five of his best early '70s tracks and mixed in minimal filler. "Talkin' Loud and Sayin' Nothing" and "There It Is (Parts 1 and 2)," with its bebop-style horns, were both innovative and hard driving to a fault. The hilarious "I'm a Greedy Man," with its hypnotic bass and help from Bobby Byrd, has Brown firing off such witticisms as "I'm a greedy man / yes I are" and "Taking care of my business / now run tell that." Brown wasn't all fun and games on this one. "King Heroin," an eerie, laid-back jazz offering, has him reciting chilling poetry about the ills of the drug. "Public Enemy #1 (Pt. 1)" attempts to re-create the same message. By "Public Enemy #2 (Pt. 2)" he is doing nothing but connecting the same dots and screaming himself hoarse to little effect. Although by this point Brown was best known for his dance tracks, he still had a way with a ballad. "Who am I," a song that had been kicking around his oeuvre for aeons, gets a strong arrangement and has Brown giving an impassioned performance. Like many of his '70s albums, *There It Is* was out of circulation for close to 20 years until it was reissued on CD in mid-'90s. It's well worth picking up.

Jason Elias

Black Caesar
February 1973, Polydor

After Isaac Hayes kicked his career into high gear with the popular and influential score for *Shaft*, and Curtis Mayfield managed the same feat with *Superfly*, seemingly every major soul star of the early 1970's ended up doing music for a blaxploitation film, and James Brown was certainly no exception. Brown sang the title tune for Larry Cohen's idiosyncratic black crime film *Black Caesar*, as well as performing ten other pieces for the movie's soundtrack (most written by Brown in collaboration with Fred Wesley); Barry Devorzon's lead-off cut, "Down and Out In New York City," sets up the picture's story, while most of the other five vocal cuts reflect the film's narrative in one way or another (although "Make It Good To Yourself" seems to be here mainly because of it's high funk quotient, and on "Mama Feelgood," Brown appropriately hands the vocal chores over to Lynn Collins). Like most soundtrack albums of the period, *Black Caesar* sounds rather scattershot, especially when the music is divorced from the film's narrative, and this isn't one of Brown's stellar albums of the 1970's; however, there are several top-notch tracks, especially the much-sampled "The Boss," the potent "Make It Good To Yourself," and the melodramatic "Mama's Dead," and Fred Wesley's superb horn charts, Jimmy Nolen's percussive guitar, and Jabo Starks' dead-on-the-one drumming make even the weaker instrumental cuts worth a quick listen (though just try to imagine a chase scene cut to something with the power of "Mother Popcorn"—now THAT would be a movie!).

Mark Deming

The Payback
December 1973, Polydor

Originally released in 1973 as a sprawling two-LP set, *The*

Payback was one of James Brown's most ambitious albums of the 1970's, and also one of his best, with Brown and his band (which in 1974 still included Fred Wesley, Maceo Parker, St. Clair Pinckney, Jimmy Nolen, and Jabo Starks) relentlessly exploring the outer possibilities of the James Brown groove. Stretching eight cuts out over the space of nearly 73 minutes, *The Payback* is long on extended rhythmic jamming, and by this time Brown and his band had become such a potent and nearly telepathic combination that the musicians were able pull out lengthy solos while still maintaining some of the most hypnotic funk to be found anywhere, and on the album's best songs—the jazzy "Time Is Running Out Fast," the relentless "Shoot Your Shot," the tight-wound "Mind Power," and the bitter revenge fantasy of the title cut—the tough, sinuous rhythms and the precise interplay between the players is nothing short of a wonder to behold. And even the album's lower-key cuts (such as the lovelorn "Doing The Best That I Can" and "Forever Suffering") sink their hooks into the listener and pull you in; quite simply, this is remarkable stuff, and even Brown's attempts at lyrical relevance (which were frankly getting a bit shaky at this point in his career) are firmly rooted enough to sound convincing. *The Payback* turned out to be one of James Brown's last inarguably great albums before he hit a long fallow streak in the mid-to-late 70's, but no one listening to this set would ever imagine that this was the work of an artist (or a band) about to run out of gas.

Mark Deming

Ain't That a Groove 1966–1969 (James Brown Story)
1984, Polydor

In the first few years after James Brown left Polydor Records at the start of the '80s, the label did little with his catalog, issuing a perfunctory best-of and licensing early material to Solid Smoke. But in 1984, Polydor began looking for ways to repackage and reissue its treasure trove of material (which included not only Brown's '70s work for them, but also his Federal/King sides of the '50s and '60s). The initial result was two albums, *Ain't That a Groove* and *Doing It to Death*, both produced by British Brown expert Cliff White (who had compiled the well-regarded U.K. compilations *Solid Gold* and *Roots of a Revolution*). *Ain't That a Groove* presented Brown's hits from the second half of the '60s that hadn't turned up on *The Best of James Brown*, including such classics as "Don't Be a Drop Out," "I Can't Stand Myself (When You Touch Me)," "Licking Stick—Licking Stick," "Give It up or Turnit a Loose," and "I Don't Want Nobody to Give Me Nothing (Open the Door, I'll Get It Myself)." These were the defining tracks in Brown's '60s funk revolution, irresistible dance songs that, as often as not, also contained potent social messages. The music's immediacy made it hard to think of in the retrospective sense the album implied, but with much of Brown's catalog out of print, it was good to hear these songs again.

William Ruhlmann

In the Jungle Groove
1986, Polydor

In the Jungle Groove was one of the first (and still one of the best) collections of James Brown's transitional and hard-hitting soul/funk workouts from 1969–1971. While the first few numbers here feature Brown sidemen who were in on his mid-'60s hits, the majority feature the original J.B.'s outfit that helped the singer forge several extended and funk-defining sides during 1970. Faced with a walkout by his old band, Brown partially formed the J.B.'s out of the New Dapps from Cincinnati, taking aboard brothers Phelps "Catfish" Collins on guitar and William "Bootsy" Collins on bass; many of those ex-band members, namely drummer Clyde Stubblefield, guitarist Clair St. Pinckney, and trombonist Fred Wesley, would eventually return to flesh out the J.B.'s lineup. The one constant was vocalist and organist Bobby Byrd, who had been with Brown since the singer's start in 1956. The incredible grooves Bootsy Collins and Stubblefield laid down here would become manna for hip-hop DJs over 15 years later, with the album's "Funky Drummer (Bonus Beat Reprise)" becoming one of the supreme breakbeats of all time. Filling out the collection are the very soulful pre-J.B.'s tracks "It's a Brand New Day" (tenor saxophonist Maceo Parker's only appearance on the disc) and the original "Funky Drummer," as well as the post-Bootsy cut "Hot Pants (She's Got to Use What She's Got to Get What She Wants)." All the numbers here are as in the pocket as you will ever hear in soul and funk. And while many of these tracks are found on various packages like Polydor's *Funk Power* and *Foundations of Funk*, *In the Jungle Groove* has the upper hand with its unequaled coverage of Brown's transformation from soul brother number one to funk originator.

Stephen Cook

Star Time
May 1991, Polydor

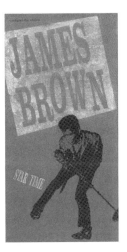

When the four-disc *Star Time* box was released in 1991, James Brown's catalog sorely needed an overhaul; much of it was out of print, and what was available was hardly befitting of his magnitude. *Star Time* got everything right: it put Brown's hugely influential career into striking perspective, helping to complete his critical renaissance, and the richness of its music set a standard for box sets in general. It was no easy task to balance Brown's lengthy, multi-part funk workouts with the need to include all of his most significant tracks, and the compilers did an excellent job in deciding when and when not to truncate ("Cold Sweat," for example, *must* be heard in its entirety). There's nothing from *Live at the Apollo* (which should be experienced start to finish), and his last hurrah on the pop charts, "Living in America," is missing, but these 71 tracks cover all the other high points, and make an eloquent case for Brown as the greatest R&B artist of all time. Disc One covers Brown's early R&B years, when his pleading intensity helped lay the groundwork for soul music. Disc Two, however, is where his genius truly crystallizes—it basically chronicles the birth of funk, as Brown gradually discards song structure in favor of working hard grooves; it also offers a picture of Brown's emergence as a bandleader and spokesman for black pride. Disc Three features Brown's hardest funk, including his much-revered material with the Bootsy Collins band. Disc Four traces Brown's later creative decline, yet he duplicated his former glories often enough to make this disc a surprisingly solid listen; plus, his massive impact on hip-hop

is underlined on the last track, the Afrika Bambaataa duet "Unity." *Star Time* paved the way for several other excellent compilations which highlighted different parts of Brown's vast legacy, but as the definitive retrospective of one of the most important musicians of the 20th century (black or otherwise), it has yet to be equaled.

Steve Huey

Soul Pride: The Instrumentals (1960–1969)
March 1993, Polydor

Everyone knows how hot James Brown's bands were, but not everyone's aware that he and his sidemen recorded lots of instrumental sides in the '60s. Originally scattered haphazardly over many out-of-print singles and albums, *Soul Pride* brings together the best of this work into one cohesive and chronological package. These cuts are nearly equal in power to J.B.'s vocal performances. Not only does the band cook on most of these insinuating vamps, but you can also hear the evolution of the man's sound from gritty R&B to tight-as-a-drum soul to free-form funk. Soul Brother number one himself plays organ and adds unpredictable shouts and screams on most of these tracks. But the chief stars are sidemen like Maceo Parker, Fred Wesley, and Pee Wee Ellis, who broke new ground in laying their compulsive counterpoint riffs. This fiery two-disc, 36-track box set contains over two hours of music, as well as a few non-LP B-sides and previously unreleased tracks.

Richie Unterberger

Foundations of Funk—A Brand New Bag: 1964–1969
March 1996, Polydor

There are several worthy James Brown compilations. But this is the one, more than any other, that presents his most fertile and innovative soul and funk material. From 1964's "Out of Sight" through 1969's "Mother Popcorn," this was

Brown at the apex of his creativity, turning soul into funk in the mid-'60s, then pushing the rhythm even more to the forefront. Most of his hit singles from this five-year explosion of white heat are on this 27-track, two-CD set, including "Out of Sight," "Papa's Got a Brand New Bag," "I Got You (I Feel Good)," "Say It Loud—I'm Black and I'm Proud," and "Cold Sweat." There are some minor omissions that could be questioned (the absence of the studio version of "Bring It Up," for instance), and big James Brown fans will already have the lion's share of tracks, on the *Star Time* box and other releases. It does, however, contain minor but significant bonuses: an alternate take of "Cold Sweat," a previously unreleased live medley of "Out of Sight" and "Bring It Up," and a previously unreleased live version of "Licking Stick—Licking Stick." There are also longer versions of "I Don't Want Nobody to Give Me Nothing" (ten minutes!), "I Got the Feelin'," "The Popcorn," and "Brother Rapp" that were edited when they were prepared for official release.

Richie Unterberger

Funk Power 1970: A Brand New Thang
June 1996, Polydor

The period during which Brown was backed by the original J.B.'s (with Bootsy and Catfish Collins) was extremely brief, lasting only a year. But it was also an extremely important and influential phase of Brown's career, when he moved from soul-funk to hard funk, stretching out the grooves and putting more stress on the bottom than ever before. This 78-minute disc is the cream of his recordings from the Bootsy Collins era. The nine tracks (the tenth is a brief public-service annoncement) include some of his core funk workouts— "Get Up I Feel Like Being a Sex Machine" (two versions), "Super Bad," "Give It Up or Turn It Loose," "Talkin' Loud and Sayin' Nothing," "Get Up, Get Into It, Get Involved," and "Soul Power." It's not for those who find Brown's funk phase too monotonous, and indeed the grooves do get a bit similar when experienced all at once. But it's unquestionably the best of Brown's '70s recordings, and indeed some of the hardest funk ever waxed by anyone at any time. As a bonus, the CD has previously unreleased complete versions of "Soul Power" (12 minutes) and "Talkin' Loud and Sayin' Nothing" (14 minutes), as well as a previously unreleased version of "There Was a Time."

Richie Unterberger

Make It Funky—The Big Payback: 1971–1975
July 1996, Polydor

While the first half of the 1970s saw James Brown's sales and art start to slowly decline, at their best he and the J.B.'s remained capable of generating a lot of heat. Record-wise it was a very erratic period, especially on his albums, which makes this two-and-a-half-hour double-disc compilation of his best material from the era especially welcome. Besides his biggest hits from the time ("Make It Funky," "Get on the Good Foot," "The Payback," "Funky President"), it has a number of high-charting R&B 45s that didn't make it onto the *Star Time* box. Familiar hits are sometimes presented in their full unedited mega-versions (12 minutes of "Make It Funky," 14 of "Papa Don't Take No Mess"), and there are also a few previously unreleased outtakes and alternate versions. It's only a disappointment relative to the towering accomplishments of his 1960s and early '70s classics. On its own terms, it's excellent funk, if rather homogenous taken all at once, with occasional departures from the formula, like "Down and Out in New York City," with its poppy woodwinds.

Richie Unterberger

B.T. Express

Do It ('Til You're Satisfied)
November 1974, Roadshow

Do It ('Til You're Satisfied) features two million sellers by the New York natives; the title track and "Express" are funky, irresistible disco gems. Produced by Jeff Lane and mixed by Tom Moulton, the two dancefloor classics features hypnotic basslines, handclaps on alternate beats, and the coolest congas on the planet, all combined with masterfully mixed guitars, saxophones, flutes, strings, Barbara Joyce Lomas' blaring lead, Louis Risbrooks' bass vocal retorts, and

Richard Thompson's support vocals. Lane was never able to repeat the tightness of the two tracks on subsequent albums or even on this one. "If I Don't Turn You On" and "Do You Like It" come close, but "Once You Get It," "Do It," "This House Is Smoking," and "Mental Telepathy" do not. Good, because of the two classics, but a greatest-hits collection would be even better.

Andrew Hamilton

Jerry Butler

The Iceman Cometh
November 1968, Mercury

The Ice Man Cometh, Jerry Butler's most successful LP, was the first full-album work from the production team Kenneth Gamble and Leon Huff. It marks an excellent collaboration, the first time R&B production techniques reached a level of maturity and elegance capable of fully complementing one of the smoothest vocalists in soul history. The Top Ten singles "Hey, Western Union Man" and "Only the Strong Survive" weren't just popular radio hits, but great performances displaying how far the R&B/soul crowd had progressed from the novelty-laden '50s. Thanks to Butler and Gamble/Huff, the sound proved incredibly influential, both in the short term (Elvis Presley was definitely listening and cut a very similar "Only the Strong Survive" one year later) and the long term (Gamble and Huff's Philly Intl. label ruled the mid-'70s R&B world with the same sound). Here's where it coalesced.

John Bush

Bobby Byrd

The Bobby Byrd Got Soul: The Best of Bobby Byrd
August 1995, Polydor

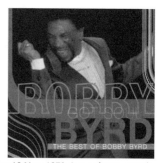

As is the case with the JB's and other James Brown protégés, Bobby Byrd's legacy is spread over numerous out-of-print, difficult-to-find vinyl records. So this 22-song retrospective, which gathers numerous singles, and a couple of previously unreleased tracks spanning 1964 to 1973, is a welcome consolidation of his most significant work into one package. Solid stuff, covering both standard soul from the '60s and hard funk (usually featuring the JB's) from the early '70s, though it sounds a lot more like a James Brown record with a different vocalist than a Bobby Byrd record that happens to benefit from James Brown's backing crew. Brown produced (and occasionally contributed to) all of the recordings here, and duets with Bobby on the 1968 single "You've Got to Change Your Mind."

Richie Unterberger

Donald Byrd

Stepping into Tomorrow
November–December 1974, Blue Note

Beginning with a crack of thunder, like it was made to trail Gary Bartz's "Mother Nature" (actually recorded at a slightly later date), *Stepping into Tomorrow* contains almost all of the Mizell trademarks within its title track's first 30 seconds: a soft and easy (yet still funky) electric-bass-and-drums foundation, silken rhythm guitar, organ and piano gently bouncing off one another, light synthesizer shading, and co-ed group vocals to ensure true lift-off. It's only one in a line of many magnetic '70s sessions led by Fonce and Larry Mizell, and it differs from their two previous Donald Byrd dates—the polarizing and groundbreaking *Black Byrd* and the deceptively excellent *Street Lady*—by not featuring any of Roger Glenn's flute, and focusing on heavily melodic and laid-back arrangements. Even the speedy "You Are the World," by some distance the most energetic song, seems more suited for relaxing in a hammock than shooting down a freeway. Many of the musicians present on the previous Byrd-Mizell meetings are here, including drummer Harvey Mason, bassist Chuck Rainey, keyboardist Jerry Peters, and guitarist David T. Walker. As ever, those who pined for the approach of Byrd's '60s dates would tune out a sublime set of material, but maybe some of those who sniffed at the straightforward nature of some of the rhythms and riffing were won over by the supreme layering of the many components (the way in which "Think Twice" lurches forward, peels back, and gathers steam is nothing short of heavenly), not to mention some deeply evocative playing from Byrd himself.

Andy Kellman

Places and Spaces
August 1975, Blue Note

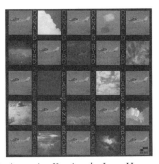

Reuniting with Larry Mizell, the man behind his last three LPs, Donald Byrd continues to explore contemporary soul, funk, and R&B with *Places and Spaces*. In fact, the record sounds more urban than its predecessor, which often played like a Hollywood version of the inner city. Keeping the Isaac Hayes, Curtis Mayfield, and Sly Stone influences of *Street Lady*, *Places and Spaces* adds elements of Marvin Gaye, Earth, Wind & Fire, and Stevie Wonder, which immediately makes the album funkier and more soulful. Boasting sweeping string arrangements, sultry rhythm guitars, rubbery bass, murmuring flügelhorns, and punchy horn charts, the music falls halfway between the cinematic neo-funk of *Street Lady* and the proto-disco soul of Earth, Wind & Fire. Also, the title *Places and Spaces* does mean something—there are more open spaces within the music, which automatically makes it funkier. Of course, it also means that there isn't much of interest on *Places and Spaces* for jazz purists, but the album would appeal to most fans of Philly soul, lite funk, and proto-disco.

Stephen Thomas Erlewine

Cameo

Cardiac Arrest
1977, Chocolate City

In 1977, one of funk's most promising debuts came from Cameo, whose first album, *Cardiac Arrest*, made it crystal clear that Larry Blackmon's outfit was a force to be reckoned with. If you were into hard, tough funk in 1977, it was impossible not to be excited by Cameo's debut. This excellent LP contains a romantic soul ballad ("Stay By My Side") as well as the original version of "Find My Way," which is the sort of smooth yet funky disco-soul that groups like the Trammps and Double Exposure were known for in the late '70s. But for the most part, this is an album of aggressive, unapologetically gritty funk. On classics like "Rigor Mortis," "Funk, Funk," and "Post Mortem," one can pinpoint Cameo's influences—namely, Parliament/Funkadelic, the Ohio Players, and the Bar-Kays. But at the same time, these gems demonstrate that even in 1977, Cameo had a recognizable sound of its own. And ultimately, Cameo would become quite influential itself. For funk lovers, *Cardiac Arrest* is essential listening. Period.

Alex Henderson

Jimmy Castor

16 Slabs of Funk
March 2002, RCA

BMG Heritage's 2002 collection of The Jimmy Castor Bunch, *16 Slabs of Funk*, doesn't cover as much ground as Rhino's 1995 set *The Everything Man*, but concentrates instead on Jimmy Castor's early '70s work for RCA Records. This means there are crucial tracks missing—no "Hey Leroy, Your Mama's Callin' You"; no "Bertha Butt Boogie"; no "Supersound" (to mention the most obvious tunes missing in action, and this isn't even counting a sampling of his earlier doo wop material tacked onto the Rhino set). So this really isn't the first place to turn if you want to hear The Jimmy Castor Bunch, especially if you want all the best stuff on one disc. However, if you want to dig deeper into his funky prime, this collection *is* a necessity, since it contains just three tracks from the Rhino comp; with the remaining 13 tracks being wildly funny, wildly funky, jams that may be silly; but for sheer enjoyment, The Jimmy Castor Bunch falls just below Parliament in their flamboyant goofiness.

Stephen Thomas Erlewine

Chic

Risqué
1979, Atlantic

Chic was very much in its prime when it recorded its third album, *Risqué*, which contained hits that ranged from "My Feet Keep Dancing" and "My Forbidden Lover" to the influential "Good Times." That feel-good manifesto is one of the first songs that comes to mind when one thinks of the disco era and the Jimmy Carter years, but Chic's popularity certainly wasn't limited to the disco crowd. The fact that

"Good Times" became the foundation for both the Sugarhill Gang's "Rapper's Delight" and Queen's "Another One Bites the Dust" tells you a lot—it underscores the fact that Chic was influencing everyone from early rappers to art rockers. A group that many rock critics were so quick to dismiss was having an impact in many different areas. From hip-hoppers to new wavers in London and Manchester, *Risqué* was considered primary listening. And *Risqué* is impressive not only because of its up-tempo cuts, but also because of slow material that includes the lush "A Warm Summer Night" and the dramatic ballad "Will You Cry (When You Hear This Song)." *Risqué* is definitely among Chic's essential albums.

Alex Henderson

George Clinton

Computer Games
November 1982, Capitol

In the late '70s George Clinton helmed a massive empire bound to eventually decline—which it did, rather suddenly. Once he distanced himself in the early '80s from the massive kinetic force that was Parliament/Funkadelic and signed a solo contract with Capitol, he suddenly seemed rejuvenated in terms of creativity and enthusiasm. This freewheeling disposition comes across clearly on *Computer Games*, his first solo album. Of course, calling this a true solo album isn't exactly accurate, since Bootsy, Gary Shider, and Walter "Junie" Morrison all play a role in the album's success. Still, you get the sense that Clinton is firmly in control of this album, something you can't honestly say about the latter-day Parliament and Funkadelic records, and this sense makes the album quite revealing. Above anything, Clinton turns here to the early '80s vogue for synthesizers and drum machines that would later become staples of hip-hop and techno production. This taste for new studio technology still in its primitive stage gives the album a slightly stiff feeling, as the humans are replaced by machines, a very different style of funk. It's this proto-techno funk that colors the album's better moments, particularly "Atomic Dog," "Loopzilla," and the title track. If you're expecting the freewheeling style of his earlier work, you may be disappointed by the confined feeling of Clinton's '80s work. Ultimately, this album ends up being by far the best of Clinton's solo career, with nearly every song having its own character and its own strengths, while latter albums struggled to come up with anything as inventive or effective. Furthermore, no successive album has anything remotely as catchy as "Atomic Dog," a song that Clinton himself could never duplicate no matter how hard he tried on his next three albums.

Jason Birchmeier

Dennis Coffey

Evolution
1971, Sussex

Dennis Coffey's Sussex label debut remains his most consistent and rewarding LP, not to mention his most commercially successful. *Evolution* delivers precisely what its title promises, spotlighting Coffey's growth as a guitarist and as a composer. Its infectious centerpiece "Scorpio" reached the R&B Top Ten, buoyed by Coffey's ear-grabbing guitar intro and a Hall of Fame drum break that is the source for an endless number of samples. The leadoff cut, "Getting It On," has proven no less fecund, its opening guitars and Andrew Smith's drums bit off by both the Beastie Boys and Public Enemy. But *Evolution* also charts the development of Coffey's skills as an arranger, cherry-picking elements of rock, funk, and soul to create a unique sound not too far removed from jazz fusion. Somehow he even transforms Led Zeppelin's blues-rock behemoth "Whole Lotta Love" into a vacuum-packed funk groove.

Jason Ankeny

Bootsy Collins

Stretchin' Out in Bootsy's Rubber Band
April 1976, Warner Bros.

Arguably, William "Bootsy" Collins was to 1970s P-funk what Snoop Doggy Dogg was to 1990s gangsta rap—a quirky, goofy, highly colorful figure who was as funky as he was entertaining. The very sound of Snoop's voice is amusing, and the same goes for Collins. But for all their eccentricity, neither Snoop nor Collins are mere novelty artists. If you removed all the humorous banter from *Stretchin' Out in Bootsy's Rubber Band*, it would still be an album of ultra-funky grooves. Released in 1976, this LP found a 24-year-old Collins launching his solo career after having been employed by James Brown and George Clinton. Collins produced his solo debut with Clinton, and not surprisingly, the Parliament/Funkadelic influence is impossible to miss on P-funk gems like "Psychoticbumpschool" and the hits "I'd Rather Be With You" and "Stretchin' Out (In a Rubber Band)." But this album also made it clear that Collins was very much his own man; in fact, he was Clinton's most distinctive disciple and inevitably became influential himself. All of the albums that Collins provided in the late '70s are worth owning, but *Stretchin' Out in Bootsy's Rubber Band* is among his most consistent and his most essential.

Alex Henderson

Ahh...The Name Is Bootsy, Baby!
January 1977, Warner Bros.

Bootsy Collins' debut solo album, *Stretchin' Out in Bootsy's Rubber Band*, was an extremely tough act to follow, but thankfully, there are no signs of a sophomore slump (either creatively or commercially) on his second album, *Ahh...The Name Is Bootsy, Baby!* Most P-funk addicts consider this 1977 LP essential listening, and it isn't hard to see why they feel that way. Everything on the album is excellent; that is true of up-tempo smokers like "The Pinocchio Theory" and the title song as well as slow, moody, eerie offerings such as

"What's a Telephone Bill?" and "Munchies for Your Love." The lyrics are consistently humorous and clever, the grooves are consistently infectious. You can think of *Ahh...The Name Is Bootsy, Baby!* as a meeting of the funk minds—Collins produced this record with his mentor, George Clinton, who co-wrote all of the material. So Clinton has a lot of input and gives *Ahh...The Name Is Bootsy, Baby!* the distinctive P-funk sound that Parliament/Funkadelic was known for. But at the same time, he encourages Collins' originality—Bootsy's Rubber Band sounds like a Parliament/Funkadelic spin-off (which is exactly what it was), but not a Parliament/Funkadelic clone. Without question, *Ahh...The Name Is Bootsy, Baby!* is essential listening for lovers of hard 1970s funk.

Alex Henderson

Bootsy? Player of the Year
February 1978, Warner Bros.

Released in 1978 at the height of Parliament-Funkadelic mania, *Bootsy? Player of the Year* finds Bootsy far from short of quality material despite his affiliation with the numerous P-Funk-affiliated projects being churned out at this time. In fact, this album finds Bootsy at his peak; his previous two albums may have their share of brilliant moments and were no doubt filled with great ideas, melodies, and funk, but here he seems to have perfected his songwriting. There really isn't a dull song on *Bootsy? Player of the Year*. The up-tempo songs—"Bootsy?," "Bootzilla," and "Roto-Rooter"—rate as some of the most exciting P-Funk material ever released, each song clocking in over five minutes and chock-full of elastic basslines. On the other hand, the abundance of slow jams—"May the Force Be With You," "Very Yes," and "As In (I Love You)"—helps maintain a good balance, providing a breather from the sweatier moments. Then there is "Hollywood Squares," a song that teeters somewhere between a dance song and a ballad, sometimes picking up the pace, other times slowing it down to a strut. Along with *Stretchin' Out in Bootsy's Rubber Band* (1976) and *Ahh...The Name Is Bootsy, Baby!* (1977), *Bootsy? Player of the Year* rates among the most enjoyable P-Funk albums ever. Unfortunately, it also marks the end of a glorious run. By the following year, 1979, it was clear that the P-Funk army was running out of fresh ideas, and Bootsy was no exception, as he'd struggle creatively for a couple years to come. This makes *Bootsy? Player of the Year* seem all the more special in retrospect, because it was among the last of the great P-Funk releases.

Jason Birchmeier

Lyn Collins

Think (About It)
1972, Polydor

At the time of the release of *Think (About It)* in 1972, Lyn

Collins had been a member of James Brown's performing revue for about two years. Her full-throated voice had earned her the nickname "the Female Preacher" and a shot to record her own album. Of course, the Godfather was in the producer's chair, writing four of the nine tracks, directing the J.B.'s as they laid down their usual funky grooves, and liberally adding vocals throughout. The title track is the main point of interest here; from Collins' throat-ripping vocals to the track's nasty groove to Brown's background interjections, this is a killer. (Rob Base & DJ E-Z Rock later sampled the track for their rap classic "It Takes Two.") The rest of the record is a little uneven: "Just Won't Do Right" is a good doo wop-ish ballad with some churchy organ and great vocals by Collins and Brown, "Wheels of Life" is a nice little groover that sounds like vintage Aretha Franklin, and "Women's Lib" is a very slow ballad that lets Collins show off her anguished yowl of a vocal to its fullest. Where the album stumbles is on the covers of familiar songs. Her versions of Bill Withers' "Ain't No Sunshine" and the Gamble & Huff classic "Never Gonna Give You Up" are mediocre, and worst of all is her leaden take on "Fly Me to the Moon." Still, the record is worth tracking down for hardcore James Brown or funky soul fans. The less devoted should look for "Think (About It)" on one of the many compilations on which it appears.

Tim Sendra

The Commodores

Machine Gun
July 1974, Motown

Before the Commodores started having major adult contemporary hits like "Three Times a Lady," "Easy," and "Still," they were happy to be a full-time funk/soul band. The Southerners became increasingly pop-minded in the late '70s, but when their debut album, *Machine Gun*, came out in 1974, their music was unapologetically gritty. This was, without question, a very promising debut—Lionel Richie and his allies really hit the ground running on sweaty funk items like "Young Girls Are My Weakness," "The Bump," "Gonna Blow Your Mind," and the single "I Feel Sanctified." These songs aren't funk-pop or sophisticated funk—they're hardcore funk. What you *won't* find on *Machine Gun* are a lot of sentimental love ballads. In the late '70s, the Commodores became as famous for their ballads as they were for their funk and dance material, but believe it or not, there are no ballads to be found on this consistently funky, mostly up-tempo debut. As much as this LP has going for it, *Machine Gun* isn't the Commodores' best or most essential album. *Machine Gun* is rewarding, but their subsequent albums *Caught in the Act* (1975), *Movin' On* (1975), and *Hot on the Tracks* (1976) are even stronger.

Alex Henderson

The Crusaders

Southern Comfort
1974, MCA

The follow-up to 1973's *Unsung Heroes* was the first of the group's Blue Thumb efforts to be distributed by ABC Records. The label switch also coincided with the inclusion of lyrical guitarist Larry Carlton as a full-fledged member. Although much of *Southern Comfort* puts a gloss on ideas made definitive on earlier efforts, the complaints are minimal and this remains the most appealing, multi-faceted incarnation of the band. The first track, "Stomp and Buck Dance," is an offhanded and skilled approach to the group's patently earthy style. The insistent "The Well's Gone Dry" has the edginess of some of the better tracks on *Unsung Heroes*, and has Carlton doing great work on the bridge. Not surprisingly, it is Carlton's presence here that adjusts the band chemistry and makes the best of *Southern Comfort* even more so. The best track here, the poignant "When There's Love Around," has Carlton's guitar attaining the perfect sense of longing that meshes well with Joe Sample's trademark Fender Rhodes tones. The last tracks here are also in a thoughtful ballad vein: "Lilies of the Nile" has great horn work from Wilton Felder and Wayne Henderson, and the last track, "A Ballad for Joe (Louis)," is a heartfelt rumination on the death of the famed boxer, featuring Sample's inherent sense of melody. A good representation of the Crusaders' tasteful and intelligent playing, *Southern Comfort* is more than recommended to their fans.

Jason Elias

Cymande

Cymande
1973, Collectables

Invigorating head music done Rastafarian style by Cymande. "Zion I" is a spiritual chant put to music, setting the mood for *Cymande*. A laid-back "One More" lulls you into subliminal meditation before "Getting It Back" jolts you into some scintillating Jamaican funk-fusion. There's a message in many of Cymande's cuts, with "Listen," and "Bra" (a recognition of the women's lib movement), the most inspiring. Both are sung with passion, and are skillfully executed; the former is slow and painstaking in its message, while "Bra" slaps you upside the head with a stirring sax solo and bass-fueled vamp. An air of supreme coolness permeates *Cymande*, unusual for a first effort written by members of the band. Cymande sound like they have done this before; nowhere is this more evident than on the beautiful "Dove," a gorgeous concoction of lead guitar, tambourines, haunting backing vocals, and percussion, with the horns used as sparingly as table-seasoning on a gourmet dish. Along with "Bra," the group's most popular cut is "The Message"—it's difficult keeping body parts still on this grooving mutha. All in all, *Cymande* is a marvelous collection that premiered a fine funk band.

Andrew Hamilton

Betty Davis

Betty Davis
May 2007, Light in the Attic

Betty Davis' debut was an outstanding funk record, driven by her aggressive, no-nonsense songs and a set of howling performances from a crack band. Listeners wouldn't know it from the song's title, but for the opener, "If I'm in Luck I Might Get Picked Up," Davis certainly doesn't play the wallflower; she's a woman on the prowl, positively luring the men in and, best of all, explaining exactly how she does it: "I said I'm wigglin' my fanny, I'm raunchy dancing, I'm-a-doing it doing it/This is my night out." "Game Is My Middle Name" begins at a midtempo lope, but really breaks through on the chorus, with the Pointer Sisters and Sylvester backing up each of her assertions. As overwhelming as Davis' performances are, it's as much the backing group as Davis herself that makes her material so powerful (and believable). Reams of underground cred allowed her to recruit one of the tightest rhythm sections ever heard on record (bassist Larry Graham and drummer Greg Errico, both veterans of Sly & the Family Stone), plus fellow San Francisco luminaries like master keyboardist Merl Saunders and guitarists Neal Schon or Douglas Rodriguez (both associated with Santana at the time). Graham's popping bass and the raw, flamboyant, hooky guitar lines of Schon or Rodriguez make the perfect accompaniment to these songs; Graham's slinky bass is the instrumental equivalent of Davis' vocal gymnastics, and Rodriguez makes his guitar scream during "Your Man My Man." It's hard to tell whether the musicians are pushing so hard because of Davis' performances or if they're egging each other, but it's an unnecessary question. Everything about Betty Davis' self-titled debut album speaks to Davis the lean-and-mean sexual predator, from songs to performance to backing, and so much the better for it. All of which should've been expected from the woman who was too wild for Miles Davis. [The 2007 Light in the Attic edition includes bonus tracks.]

John Bush

They Say I'm Different
May 2007, Light in the Attic

Betty Davis' second full-length featured a similar set of songs as her debut, though with Davis herself in the production chair and a radically different lineup. The openers, "Shoo-B-Doop and Cop Him" and "He Was a Big Freak," are big, blowsy tunes with stop-start funk rhythms and Davis in her usual persona as the aggressive sexual predator. On the title track, she reminisces about her childhood and compares herself to kindred spirits of the past, a succession of blues legends she holds fond—including special time for Bessie Smith, Chuck Berry, and Robert Johnson. A pair of unknowns, guitarist Cordell Dudley and bassist Larry Johnson, do a fair job of replacing the stars from her first record. As a result,

They Say I'm Different is more keyboard-dominated than her debut, with prominent electric piano, clavinet, and organ from Merl Saunders, Hershall Kennedy, and Tony Vaughn. The material was even more extreme than on her debut; "He Was a Big Freak" featured a prominent bondage theme, while "Your Mama Wants Ya Back" and "Don't Call Her No Tramp" dealt with prostitution, or at least inferred it. With the exception of the two openers, though, *They Say I'm Different* lacked the excellent songs and strong playing of her debut; an explosive and outré record, but more a variation on the same theme she'd explored before. [The 2007 Light in the Attic edition includes bonus tracks.]

John Bush

Miles Davis

Bitches Brew
August 1969–January 1970, Columbia/Legacy

Thought by many to be the most revolutionary album in jazz history, having virtually created the genre known as jazz-rock fusion (for better or worse) and being the jazz album to most influence rock and funk musicians, *Bitches Brew* is, by its very nature, mercurial. The original double LP included only six cuts and featured up to 12 musicians at any given time, most of whom would go on to be high-level players in their own right: Joe Zawinul, Wayne Shorter, Airto, John McLaughlin, Chick Corea, Jack DeJohnette, Dave Holland, Don Alias, Benny Maupin, Larry Young, Lenny White, and others. Originally thought to be a series of long jams locked into grooves around one or two keyboard, bass, or guitar figures, *Bitches Brew* is anything but. Producer Teo Macero had as much to do with the end product on *Bitches Brew* as Davis. Macero and Davis assembled, from splice to splice, section to section, much of the music recorded over three days in August 1969. First, there's the slow, modal, opening grooves of "Pharaoh's Dance," with its slippery trumpet lines to McLaughlin's snaky guitar figures skirting the edge of the rhythm section and Don Alias' conga slipping through the middle. The keyboards of Corea and Zawinul create a haunting, riffing groove echoed and accented by the two basses of Harvey Brooks and Dave Holland. The title cut was originally composed as a five-part suite, though only three were used. Here the keyboards punch through the mix, big chords and distorted harmonics ring up a racket for Davis to solo over rhythmically outside the mode. McLaughlin is comping on fat chords, creating the groove, and the bass and drums carry the rest for a small taste of deep-voodoo funk. Side three opens with McLaughlin and Davis trading funky fours and eights over the lock-step groove of hypnotic proportion that is "Spanish Key." Zawinul's trademark melodic sensibility provides a kind of chorus for Corea to flat around, and the congas and drummers working in complement *against* the basslines.

This nearly segues into the four-and-a-half minute "John McLaughlin," with its signature organ mode and arpeggiated blues guitar runs. The end of *Bitches Brew*, signified by the stellar "Miles Runs the Voodoo Down," echoes the influence of Jimi Hendrix; with its chuck-and-slip chords and lead figures and Davis playing a ghostly melody through the shimmering funkiness of the rhythm section, it literally dances and becomes increasingly more chaotic until about nine minutes in, where it falls apart. Yet one doesn't know it until near the end, when it simmers down into smoke-and-ice fog once more. The disc closes with "Sanctuary," a previously recorded Davis tune that is completely redone here as an electric moody ballad reworked for this band, but keeping enough of its modal integrity to be outside the rest of *Bitches Brew*'s retinue. The CD reissue adds "Feio," a track recorded early in 1970 with the same band. Unreleased—except on the box set of the complete sessions—"Feio" has more in common with the exploratory music of the previous August than with later, more structured Davis music in the jazz-rock vein. A three-note bass vamp centers the entire thing as three different modes entwine one another, seeking a groove to bolt onto. It never finds it, but becomes its own nocturnal beast, offering ethereal dark tones and textures to slide the album out the door on. Thus *Bitches Brew* retains its freshness and mystery long after its original issue.

Thom Jurek

On the Corner
June 1972, Columbia/Legacy

Could there be any more confrontational sound in Miles Davis' vast catalog than the distorted guitars and tinny double-timing drums reacting to a two-note bass riff funking it up on the first track from *On the Corner*? Before the trumpet even enters the picture, the story has been broken off somewhere in the middle, with deep street music melding with a secret language held within the band and those who can actually hear this music—certainly not the majority of Miles' fan base built up over the past 25 years. They heard this as a huge "f*ck you." Miles just shrugged and told them it wasn't personal, but they could take it that way if they wanted to, and he blew on his trumpet. Here are killer groove riffs that barely hold on as bleating trumpet and soprano sax lines (courtesy of Dave Liebman on track one) interact with John McLaughlin's distortion-box frenzy. Michael Henderson's bass keeps the basic so basic it hypnotizes; keyboards slowly enter the picture, a pair of them handled by Herbie Hancock and Chick Corea, as well as Ivory Williams' synthesizer. Finally, Colin Walcott jumps in with an electric sitar and there are no less than five drummers—three kits (Al Foster, Billy Hart, and Jack DeJohnette), a tabla player, and Mtume. It's a four-tune suite, "On the Corner" is, but the separations hardly matter, just the shifts in groove that alter the time/space continuum. After 20 minutes, the set feels over and a form of Miles' strange lyricism returns in "Black Satin." Though a tabla kicks the tune off, there's a recognizable eight-note melody that runs throughout. Carlos Garnett and Bennie Maupin replace Liebman, Dave Creamer replaces McLaughlin, and the groove rides a bit easier—except for those hand bells shimmering in the background off the beat just enough to make the squares crazy. The respite is short-lived, however. Davis and band move the music way over to the funk side of the street—though the street funkers thought these cats were too weird with their stranded time signatures and modal fugues that begin and end nowhere and live for the way the riff breaks down into emptiness. "One and One" begins the new tale, so jazz breaks down and gets polished off and resurrected as a far blacker, deeper-than-blue character in the form of "Helen Butte/Mr. Freedom X," where guitars and horns careen off Henderson's cracking bass and Foster's skittering hi-hats. It may sound weird even today, but *On the Corner* is the most street record ever recorded by a jazz musician. And it still kicks.

Thom Jurek

Deodato

Prelude
September 1972, CTI

Prior to *Prelude*, Eumir Deodato was primarily known, if at all, as a tasteful, lyrical, bossa nova-based sometime arranger for the likes of Antonio Carlos Jobim, Frank Sinatra, Wes Montgomery, and others. Enter Creed Taylor, who gave Deodato a chance to step out on his own as a pianist/leader, doing a few tunes of his own plus a healthy quota of CTI-patented jazz interpretations of classical pieces by Richard Strauss ("Also Sprach Zarathustra (2001)"), Debussy ("Prelude to the Afternoon of a Faun"), and bowdlerized Borodin ("Baubles, Bangles and Beads"). Well, "2001"—a clever, up-tempo Latin-groove takeoff on the opening measures of Strauss' tone poem suddenly exploded and became an improbable hit single. In its wake, *Prelude* soared to number three on the pop LP charts, and Deodato was propelled out of the arranger-for-hire business. Though overshadowed by "2001," the other tracks also hold up well today, being mostly medium-tempo, sometimes lushly orchestrated, conga-accented affairs that provide velvety showcases for Deodato's lyrical electric piano solos. The record also made a temporary star out of John Tropea, whose electric guitar has a lot of rock & rolling zip and fire, and Hubert Laws, Stanley Clarke, and Marvin Stamm each get a little solo room too. This would be the biggest hit Deodato and CTI ever had, and though short on playing time (32 minutes), it still makes enjoyable listening.

Richard S. Ginell

Deodato 2
1973, Epic

Deodato's debut for CTI, *Prelude*, earned him a genuine reputation for funky fusion with its groove-tight cover of "Thus Spake Zarathustra," the theme from Stanley Kubrick's *2001: A Space Odyssey*. The rest of the album isn't quite as memorable, but it fit the bill and got nice reviews for its innovative read of Borodin and Debussy's "Prelude to the Afternoon of a Faun." On *2*, the Brazilian composer and arranger dips into the funked-up fusion formula tank once again, and comes out with a more consistent disc than its predecessor. Arranged, conducted, and keyboarded by Deodato

himself instead of CTI house arrangers Don Sebesky or Bob James, the maestro enlisted a fusion who's who of sidemen including drummer Billy Cobham, bassist Stanley Clarke, and flutist Hubert Laws, as well as rockers like John Tropea on guitar. The larger ensemble that provides brass, woodwind, and string support includes trumpeter Jon Faddis and Jim Buffington. "Super Strut" kicks it off. Deep-grooved lines of accented angular riffing and rim-shot syncopation by Cobham turn this simply notated four-stepper into a burning ball of greasy rock and souled-out jazz. This is followed by a wildly campy but nonetheless wondrous read of "Rhapsody in Blue" done Stevie Wonder-style. Deodato's keyboard work never lets the groove drop; he pulls the rhythm section down around him and hunkers his phrasing to punch up the long, sweeping horns and string lines. Less successful is a read of "Nights in White Satin," with its overwrought strings, and a "Pavane for a Dead Princess" that's a snore. The album officially closes with "Skyscrapers," another jazz-rock rave-up that blasts holes in the sonic sky with its dueling keyboard and guitar lines. [The remastered version of the CD includes three bonus tracks that include a steamy little bossa nova number, "Latin Flute," with Laws tearing up the solo spot, and a lounge lizard's dream of a cover version in Steely Dan's "Do It Again," with flutes and keys trading the melody lines and Tropea's wah-wah guitars chunking up the backbeat. Why this wasn't on the original album or a follow-up is a mystery.]

Thom Jurek

Lou Donaldson

Mr. Shing-a-Ling
October 1967, Blue Note

Lou Donaldson does attempt to loosen up a bit with *Mr. Shing-A-Ling*, but the whole affair is a bit stilted and misconceived. Not quite the full-fledged electric funk workout that was becoming commonplace for old-guard soul-jazz musicians in the late '60s, but not quite the bop-inflected soul-jazz of the early '60s either, *Mr. Shing-A-Ling* falls into a netherworld that won't connect either with jazz purists or fans of grooving jazz-funk. When the group does try to get funky on the record, the results just sound lazy—there's no spark to the rhythms, or to Donaldson's melody lines, especially on the embarrassing cover of the pop hit "Ode to Billie Joe." When the quintet settles into a mid-tempo vamp, Donaldson, trumpeter Blue Mitchell and organist Lonnie Smith do spin out some good solos, but the lack of energy and enthusiasm the group has for the material makes *Mr. Shing-A-Ling* a bit of a tiring listen.

Stephen Thomas Erlewine

Hot Dog
April 1969, Blue Note

A wildly erratic slice of funky soul-jazz in keeping with Lou Donaldson's late '60s commercial accessibility, *Hot Dog* isn't a total washout, but it's just as hit-and-miss as many of Donaldson's albums from the era (even if you are a fan of the style). The main sticking points are the contemporary R&B covers that open and close the album. "Who's Making Love" has an out-of-tune group vocal that fails to be charming in its amateurishness, and the funk of "It's Your Thing" sounds leaden and lifeless despite the best efforts of breakbeat legend

Leo Morris (later Idris Muhammad) on drums. Take those away and *Hot Dog* would be a fairly decent effort. Also featuring guitarist Melvin Sparks, organist Charles Earland, and trumpeter Ed Williams, the ensemble really catches fire on "Turtle Walk," a Donaldson original where the groove sounds natural and helps push the soloists. The Donaldson-penned title cut also gets pretty funky, though the underlying vamp is a little insubstantial to stretch out over ten minutes. The Tommy Turrentine ballad "Bonnie" returns Donaldson to the sweet, romantic territory he's mined so well over the years. So *Hot Dog* does have some worthwhile moments; it's just a pity the overall finished product isn't more consistent—the cover photo is great.

Steve Huey

The Dramatics

Whatcha See Is Whatcha Get
1972, Stax

The Dramatics had been around in one form or another for nine years before the members got to release their first LP, and the result was a pair of breakthrough hits over the spring and summer of 1971, beginning with the title track, a Top Ten single that boasted not only extraordinary singing from bass to falsetto, but a soaring, punchy horn arrangement and some of the best fuzztone guitar heard on a hit record since the Rolling Stones' "Satisfaction." The Afro-Cuban-flavored "Get up and Get Down" followed it into the R&B Top 20, and the *Whatcha See Is Whatcha Get* album followed them both. It was the third hit off of the album, "In the Rain," a delicate ballad that was issued separately as a single in early 1972, topping the R&B charts and reaching number five on the pop charts, that solidified the group's reputation and elevated them to the front rank of '70s soul acts. The album showcased the group equally well doing up-tempo dance numbers ("Mary Don't Cha Wanna") and ballads ("Thank You for Your Love," "Fall in Love, Lady Love"), melding very attractive vocals to arrangements that instantly grabbed the listener, all of it pulled together by songwriter/producer Tony Hester. Even the lesser material, such as "Gimme Some (Good Soul Music)"—on which Hester knew that one minute and 34 seconds was all that was needed to make its point—were so attractive and rousing that they easily carried their portion of the album, whose short running time was its only flaw. All of the members, from Willie Ford's powerful bass to Ron Banks' airy falsetto, were presented to best advantage, but none more so than William "Wee Gee" Howard's lead vocals; ironically, this would be Howard's only completed album with the group, and their only album for two years to come because of the accompanying personnel problems. Still, it's a match for any soul album of its era. In 2002, ZYX Records of Germany issued a new CD edition of *Whatcha*

See Is Whatcha Get with its original cover art re-created and remastered in 24-bit digital audio, which is so crisp that it has to be heard to be believed.

Bruce Eder

Earth, Wind & Fire

Earth Wind and Fire
February 1971, Warner Bros.

The debut for the nine-member Earth, Wind & Fire was as assured as that of any rock band from the '60s and early '70s. Already fluent with the close harmonies of the classiest soul groups, the deep funk of James Brown, and the progressive social concerns and multiple vocal features of Sly & the Family Stone, the group added (courtesy of auteur Maurice White) a set of freewheeling arrangements, heavy on the horns, that made *Earth Wind and Fire* one of their finest albums—the artistic equal of their later hits, if not on the same level commercially. Unlike the work of most early funk bands, the songwriting was as strong and focused as the musicianship; the record boasts a set of unerringly positive compositions, reflecting the influence of the civil rights movement with nearly every song urging love, community, and knowledge as alternatives to the increasing hopelessness plaguing American society. The stop-start opener "Help Somebody," the deep funk extravaganza "Moment of Truth," and the sweet ballad "Love Is Life" were unified in their pursuit of positivity, while even the potentially incendiary title "Fan the Fire" was revealed in a peaceful context: "The flame of love is about to die/Somebody fan the fire." And the instrumental closer, "Bad Tune," is hardly a cast-off; the furious kalimba work of Maurice White and wordless backing vocals combine to create an excellent piece of impressionist funk.

John Bush

All 'N All
November 1977, Columbia

Earth, Wind & Fire's artistic and commercial winning streak continued with its ninth album, *All 'N All*, the diverse jewel that spawned major hits like "Serpentine Fire" and the dreamy "Fantasy." Whether the visionary soul men are tearing into the hardest of funk on "Jupiter" or the most sentimental of ballads on "I'll Write a Song for You" (which boasts one of Philip Bailey's many soaring, five-star performances), *All 'N All* was a highly rewarding addition to EWF's catalog. Because EWF had such a clean-cut image and fared so well among pop audiences, some may have forgotten just how sweaty its funk could be. But "Jupiter"—like "Mighty, Mighty," "Shining Star," and "Getaway"—underscores the fact that EWF delivered some of the most intense and gutsy funk of the 1970s.

Alex Henderson

The Emotions

Untouched
1972, Volt

Jeanette Hutchinson was replaced by fellow Chicagoan Theresa Davis for the group's second album. But there was little change in the kind of sweet gospel-soul the trio sang—perhaps it was a shade poppier than the first LP, but barely. Includes the small hit "Show Me How," and "Blind Alley," which was sampled in 1988 for Big Daddy Kane's 1988 hit "Ain't No Half-Steppin'," and then again by Mariah Carey on her hit "Dream Lover." *Untouched* and the Emotions debut LP (*So I Can Love You*) were combined onto one CD on a 1996 reissue.

Richie Unterberger

ESG

A South Bronx Story
May 2000, Universal Sound

With their limited resources, the Scroggins sisters put the boogie down in the Boogie Down Bronx. Major kudos to Universal Sound for compiling ESG's best works for *A South Bronx Story*, a crucial document of sparse, old school funk. Until 2000, the group's scant material had been nearly impossible to find. The most legendary inclusion is the Martin Hannett-produced 7" EP that was originally released on Factory (later released as a 12" in the U.S. by 99 with live tracks backing it). This release featured their trademark "Moody," which ended up being listed as a Top 50 classic by nearly all of New York's dance clubs; it was also immortalized on a volume of Tommy Boy's excellent *Perfect Beats* series, lodged between Liquid Liquid and Strafe. Like the remainder of their recorded output, it featured the three "R"s: rhythm, rhythm, and more rhythm. Also on the debut EP was their most sampled "UFO"; the nauseous siren trills at the beginning found sped-up use in at least half a dozen rap tracks in the late '80s and early '90s. Big Daddy Kane and LL Cool J used it, and the Bomb Squad slyly swiped it for Public Enemy's "Night of the Living Baseheads." But arguably their best moment was "Dance" with its jumpy Motown rhythm, post-punk bass, and narrative/old school vocals. It sounds like a wild mix of the Supremes and *Metal Box*-era Public Image Limited. Deborah's bass, though not as musicianly, captures the spirit of PiL's Jah Wobble copping Motown session bassist James Jamerson. It's that sort of sprited, unconscious hybrid that made ESG so unique. After all, they played the opening night of Manchester's Factory club and the closing night of Larry Levan's Paradise Garage.

Andy Kellman

The Fatback Band

Raising Hell
1975, Southbound

Fatback's second album of 1975 is a serious improvement over *Yum Yum*: the arrangements are tighter, the hooks are stronger, and the grooves keep the listener riveted from start to finish. It downplays the live feel of previous albums like *Keep on Steppin'* in favor of a more carefully arranged feel

that highlights the tasty keyboard and synthesizer work of Gerry Thomas. *Raising Hell* also produced two major hits for the group: "(Are You Ready) Do the Bus Stop" capitalizes on the dance craze of the title with a steady bass-driven groove that works in layers of keyboards, guitars, and horns to keep things interesting, and "Spanish Hustle" is a propulsive dance jam that alternates synthesizer flights of fancy with intense Latin percussion breaks guaranteed to make the listeners shake their hips. The album tracks that back up these singles don't make their presence felt as strongly, but none ever descend to the level of filler: "Groovy Kind of Day" alternates smooth harmony vocals with jazzy electric-piano riffs to create a smooth mid-tempo track and the group's cover of the Four Tops' classic "I Can't Help Myself" is cleverly re-arranged to fit Fatback's dance floor format. The result is a fine collection of funky dance music that helped Fatback solidify their reputation as one of New York's foremost disco groups. It remains just as listenable and is worth a spin for disco and funk fans alike.

Donald A. Guarisco

Hustle! The Ultimate Fatback 1969–84
August 2004, Ace

For those looking for a compilation with about twice as much music as the best previous Fatback best-of (Rhino's 1997 single-CD *The Fattest of Fatback*) offered, the double-CD *Hustle! The Ultimate Fatback 1969–84* does the trick. It's actually missing a few songs that appeared on the Rhino comp, but there's no arguing with the good value it supplies, with 31 songs and about two hours of music. It also includes a number of items from their early, more soul-funk-oriented career in particular that escaped inclusion on the Rhino release, which covered the narrower era of 1975–1983. That leaves room for quite interesting items like the 1974 single "Wicki-Wacky" (with its delightful jazzy scat vocals), Fatback Brother Bill Curtis' 1973 single "Dance Girl" (which benefits from similar jazzy singing), the seriously boogalooing 1973 instrumental "Soul March," and the James Brown-Jackson 5-influenced 1971 Johnny King & the Fatback Band single "Peace, Love Not War"/"Keep On Brother Keep On." But the major hits and misses that most fans would regard as essential are here, including "Spanish Hustle," "(Are You Ready) Do the Bus Stop," "I Found Loving," "Backstrokin'," "I Like Girls," "Gotta Get My Hands on Some Money," "Is This the Future?," and the seminal 1979 proto-rap track "King Tim III (Personality Jock)" (actually issued as a B-side). You could offer a couple of minor complaints about the packaging: the track sequencing follows a random chronology rather than a straight progression, and although the title indicates a 1969–1984 time span, actually the first cuts here are from the aforementioned 1971 Johnny King & the Fatback Band single. Otherwise, it's a well-annotated march through the act's history as Fatback journeyed from soul and funk to disco and rap, never breaking through to the top tier of R&B acts, but always reflecting the mutations black popular music itself was going through from the early '70s to the mid-'80s.

Richie Unterberger

The Five Stairsteps

Love's Happening
1968, Curtom

Producer Curtis Mayfield gives the revamped Five Stairsteps a bouncy, younger sound on their sophomore release. Member Clarence Burke Jr. composed most of the songs on their first album; this time, Mayfield has the biggest say. Clarence sounded like he was crying on the first LP; on this release, Mayfield has eliminated most of the pain in his voice. Three Impression remakes get a half-hearted treatment by the Stairsteps. However, they excel on Mayfield's "Stay Close to Me" and the gorgeous, floating, testimonial "Baby Make Me Feel So Good." The backing vocals on "Baby" are unique to the Stairsteps; the chorus is sung in staccato blips with voices bouncing around the lead like pinballs. Unlike the remakes, these Mayfield compositions seemed tailored for the group. A common misconception with this LP is that Cubie played a major role—he didn't. Cubie was only four or five years old when they waxed this; that's Cubie babbling on "New Dance Craze."

Andrew Hamilton

Roberta Flack

First Take
June 1969, Atlantic

Roberta Flack's debut album, titled *First Take* in true underachiever fashion, introduced a singer who'd assimilated the powerful interpretive talents of Nina Simone and Sarah Vaughan, the earthy power of Aretha Franklin, and the crystal purity and emotional resonance of folksingers like Judy Collins. Indeed, the album often sounded more like vocal jazz or folk than soul, beginning with the credits: a core quartet of Flack on piano, John Pizzarelli on guitar, Ron Carter on bass, and Ray Lucas on drums, as fine a lineup as any pop singer could hope to recruit. With only one exception—the bluesy, grooving opener "Compared to What," during which Flack proves her chops as a soul belter—she concentrates on readings of soft, meditative material. A pair of folk covers, "The First Time Ever I Saw Your Face" and "Hey, That's No Way to Say Goodbye," are heart-wrenching standouts; the first even became a surprise hit two years later, when its appearance in the Clint Eastwood film *Play Misty for Me* pushed it to the top of the pop charts and earned Flack her first Grammy award for Record of the Year. Her arrangement of the traditional "I Told Jesus" has a simmering power, while "Ballad of the Sad Young Men" summons a stately sense of melancholy. Flack also included two songs from her college friend and future duet partner, Donny Hathaway, including a tender examination of the classic May–December romance titled "Our Ages or Our Hearts." The string arrangements of William Fischer wisely keep to the background, lending an added emotional

weight to all of Flack's pronouncements. No soul artist had ever recorded a record like this, making *First Take* one of the most fascinating soul debuts of the era.

John Bush

Aretha Franklin

Young, Gifted and Black
1971, Rhino

It's nearly impossible to single out any of Aretha Franklin's early '70s albums for Atlantic as being her best, particularly given the breadth of her output during this era. In terms of albums rather than singles, it's probably her strongest era, and if you count live albums like *Amazing Grace*, choosing a standout or a favorite record isn't any easier. Yet of this stunning era, *Young, Gifted and Black* certainly ranks highly among her studio efforts, with many arguing that it may be her greatest. And with songs like "Rock Steady," that may be a valid argument. But there's much more here than just a few highlights. If you really want to go song by song, you'd be hard-pressed to find any throwaways here—this is quite honestly an album that merits play from beginning to end. You have upbeat songs like the aforementioned "Rock Steady" that will get you up out of your seat moving and grooving, yet then you also have a number of more introspective songs that slow down the tempo and are more likely to relax than rouse. And if that wide spectrum of moods isn't enough reason to celebrate this album, you get some unlikely songs like a take on "The Long and Winding Road." Plus, you also have to keep in mind that Franklin was in her prime here, not only in terms of voice but also in terms of confidence—you can just feel her exuding her status as the best of the best. Furthermore, her ensemble of musicians competes with any that she had worked with on previous albums. So even if this isn't *the* greatest Aretha Franklin album of the early '70s, it's certainly a contender, the sort of album that you can't go wrong with.

Jason Birchmeier

Funkadelic

Funkadelic
1970, Westbound

Funkadelic's self-titled 1970 debut is one of the group's best early-to-mid '70s albums. Not only is it laden with great songs—"I'll Bet You" and "I Got a Thing..." are obvious highlights—but it retains perhaps a greater sense of classic '60s soul and R&B than any successive George Clinton-affiliated album. Recording for the Detroit-based Westbound label, at the time Funkadelic were in the same boat as psychedelic soul groups such as the Temptations, who had just recorded their landmark *Cloud Nine* album across town at Motown, and other similar groups. Yet no group had managed to effectively balance big, gnarly rock guitars with crooning, heartfelt soul at this point in time quite like Funkadelic. Clinton's songs are essentially conventional soul songs in the spirit of Motown or Stax—steady rhythms, dense arrangements, choruses of vocals—but with a loud, overdriven, fuzzy guitar lurking high in the mix. And when Clinton's songs went into their chaotic moments of jamming, there was no mistaking the Hendrix influence. Furthermore, Clinton's half-quirky, half-trippy ad libs during "Mommy, What's a Funkadelic?" and "What Is Soul" can be mistaken for no one else—they're pure-cut P-Funk. Successive albums portray Funkadelic drifting further toward rock, funk, and eventually disco, especially once Bernie Worrell began playing a larger role in the group. Never again would the band be this attuned to its '60s roots, making self-titled release a revealing and unique record that's certainly not short on significance, clearly marking the crossroads between '60s soul and '70s funk.

Jason Birchmeier

Free Your Mind...And Your Ass Will Follow
1970, Westbound

It's one of the best titles in modern musical history, for song and for album, and as a call to arms mentally and physically the promise of funk was never so perfectly stated. If it were just a title then there'd be little more to say, but happily, *Free Your Mind* lives up to it throughout as another example of Funkadelic getting busy and taking everyone with it. The title track itself kicks things off with rumbling industrial noises and space alien sound effects, before a call-and-response chant between deep and chirpy voices brings the concept to full life. As the response voices say, "The kingdom of heaven is within!" The low and dirty groove rumbles along for ten minutes of dark fun, with Bernie Worrell turning in a great keyboard solo toward the end—listening to it, one gets the feeling that if Can were this naturally funky, they'd end up sounding like this. From there the band makes its way through a total of six songs, ranging from the good to astoundingly great. "Funky Dollar Bill" is the other standout track from the proceedings, with a great, throw-it-down chorus and rhythm and a sharp, cutting lyric that's as good to think about as it is to sing out loud. The closing "Eulogy and Light," meanwhile, predates Prince with its backward masking and somewhat altered version of the Lord's Prayer and Psalm 23. At other points, even if the song is a little more straightforward, there's something worthwhile about it, like the random stereo panning and Eddie Hazel's insane guitar soloing on "I Wanna Know If It's Good for You," with more zoned and stoned keyboard work from Worrell to top things off. The amount of drugs going down for these sessions in particular must have been notable, but the end results make it worthy.

Ned Raggett

Cosmic Slop
1973, Westbound

With a much more stripped-down version of the band, if the credits are to be believed (five regular members total, not counting any vocalists), Funkadelic continued its way through life with *Cosmic Slop*. A slightly more scattershot album than the group's other early efforts, with generally short tracks (only two break the five-minute barrier) and some go-nowhere ballads, *Cosmic Slop* still has plenty to like about it, not least because of the monstrous title track. A bitter,

heartbreaking portrait of a family on the edge, made all the more haunting and sad by the sweet vocal work—imagine an even more mournful "Papa Was a Rollin' Stone"—the chorus is a killer, with the devil invited to the dance while the band collectively fires up the funk. Elsewhere, the band sounds like it's more interested in simply hitting a good groove and enjoying it, and why not? If introductory track "Nappy Dug-out" relies more on duck calls and whistles than anything else to give it identity, it's still a clap-your-hands/stomp-your-feet experience, speeding up just a little toward the end. As for the bandmembers themselves, Bernie Worrell still takes the general lead thanks to his peerless keyboard work, but the guitar team of Gary Shider and Ron Bykowski and the rhythm duo of Tyrone Lampkin and Cordell Mosson aren't any slouches, either. George Clinton again seems to rely on the role of ringleader more than anything else, but likely that's him behind touches like distorted vocals. Certainly it's a trip to hear the deep, spaced-out spoken word tale on "March to the Witch's Castle," a harrowing picture of vets returning from Vietnam—and then realizing that Rush ripped off that approach for a song on its *Caress of Steel* album a year or two later!

Ned Raggett

Standing on the Verge of Getting It On
1974, Westbound

Expanding back out to a more all-over-the-place line-up—about 15 or so people this time out—Funkadelic got a bit more back on track with *Standing on the Verge*. Admittedly, George Clinton repeats a trick from *America Eats Its Young* via another re-recording of an *Osmium* track, namely leadoff cut "Red Hot Mama." However, starting as it does with a hilarious double soliloquy (with the first voice sounding like the happier brother of Sir Nose d'Voidoffunk) and coming across with a fierce new take, it's a good omen for *Standing on the Verge* as a whole. Eddie Hazel's guitar work in particular is just plain bad-ass; after his absence from *Cosmic Slop*, it's good to hear him fully back in action with Bernie Worrell, Cordell Mosson, Gary Shider, and the rest. In general, compared to the sometimes too polite *Cosmic Slop*, *Standing on the Verge* is a full-bodied, crazy mess in the best possible way, with heavy funk jams that still smoke today while making a lot of supposedly loud and dangerous rock sound anemic. Check out "Alice in My Fantasies" if a good example is needed—the whole thing is psychotic from the get-go, with vocals as much on the edge as the music—or the wacky, wonderful title track. There are quieter moments as well, but this time around with a little more bite to them, like the woozy slow jam of "I'll Stay," which trips out along the edges just enough while the song makes its steady way along. In an unlikely but effective turn, meanwhile, "Jimmy's Got a Little Bit of Bitch in Him" is a friendly, humorous song about a gay friend; given the rote homophobia of so much later hip-hop, it's good to hear some founding fathers have a more open-minded view.

Ned Raggett

Let's Take It to the Stage
April 1975, Westbound

One of Funkadelic's goofiest releases, *Let's Take It to the Stage* also contains more P-Funk all-time greats as well, making for a grand balance of the serious and silly. Perhaps the silliest is at the end—there's not much else one can call the extended oompah/icing rink start of "Atmosphere." The title track is as much a call to arms as "Free Your Mind and Your Ass Will Follow" is, but with a more direct musical performance and a more open nod to party atmospheres (not to mention the source of one of Andrew Dice Clay's longest-running bits). The targets of the band's good-natured wrath are, in fact, other groups—"Hey, Fool and the Gang! Let's take it to the stage!" There's no mistaking the track that immediately follows makes it even more intense—"Get off Your Ass and Jam" kicks in with one bad-ass drum roll and then scorches the damn place down, from guitar solo to the insanely funky bass from Bootsy Collins. It may only be two and a half minutes long, but it alone makes the album a classic. Hearing Collins' unmistakable tones is usually enough to get anything on the crazy tip, but "Be My Beach" just makes it all the more fun, as does the overall air of silly romance getting nuttier as it goes. "Good to Your Earhole" sets the outrageous mood just right—it's one of the band's tightest monsters of funk, guitars sprawling all over the place even as the heavy-hitting rhythm doesn't let one second of groove get lost. Of course, there's also one totally notorious number to go with it, but "No Head No Backstage Pass" has one of the craziest rhythms on the whole album, not to mention lip-smackingly nutty lines delivered with the appropriate leer.

Ned Raggett

Hardcore Jollies
1976, Priority

Funkadelic's major-label jump brought its version of life more into line with Parliament, though the crucial difference between the two—Funkadelic's guitars vs. Parliament's horns—remains intact. Eddie Hazel is missed, as always, but Gary Shider and Mike Hampton do fine work. Whoever peels off the concluding solo at the end of "Comin' Round the Mountain" deserves credit, even if it's sometimes flash for flash's sake. Similar exercises in feedback can be found on the title track and elsewhere, sometimes great, sometimes time-keeping. Still, after all, the album itself is dedicated "to the guitar players of the world," so it can't be said that George Clinton and company aren't keeping the proper focus on things. Generally, things are fairly light on *Hardcore Jollies*, though a remake of earlier highlight "Cosmic Slop" retains the sharp sentiments, even if it's not quite as strongly delivered as before (musically it's much more centered around the bass and drums, though things get duly crazed all around toward the end). Otherwise, the emphasis is on fairly clean jams and rhythms, with more lower-key goofiness than before but still merrily out there. If it's not truly gone and great like *Maggot Brain* or *Let's Take It to the Stage*, it's still good listening at its best moments. "If You Got Fun, You Got Style" makes for a better chat-up dancefloor appreciation than most, while "Soul Mate" balances out obvious "want you bad" sentiments with squirrelly lead vocals that don't quite fit the subject at hand. And who could knock the use of the "there's a place in France/where the ladies wear no pants" melody in "You Scared the Lovin' Outta Me"? Pedro Bell does some of his best work ever for the cover and inside art, while the accompanying short story is hilarious.

Ned Raggett

One Nation Under a Groove
1978, Priority

One Nation Under a Groove was not only Funkadelic's greatest moment, it was their most popular album, bringing them an unprecedented commercial breakthrough by going platinum and spawning a number one R&B smash in the title track. It was a landmark LP for the so-called "black rock" movement, best-typified in the statement of purpose "Who Says a Funk Band Can't Play Rock?!"; more than that, though, the whole album is full of fuzzed-out, Hendrix-style guitar licks, even when the music is clearly meant for the dancefloor. This may not have been a new concept for Funkadelic, but it's executed here with the greatest clarity and accessibility in their catalog. Furthermore, out of George Clinton's many conceptual albums (serious and otherwise), *One Nation Under a Groove* is the pinnacle of his political consciousness. It's unified by a refusal to acknowledge boundaries—social, sexual, or musical—and, by extension, the uptight society that created them. The tone is positive, not militant—this funk is about community, freedom, and independence, and you can hear it in every cut (even the bizarre, outrageously scatological "P.E. Squad"). The title cut is one of funk's greatest anthems, and "Grooval-legiance" and the terrific "Cholly" both dovetail nicely with its concerns. The aforementioned "Who Says a Funk Band Can't Play Rock?!" is a seamless hybrid that perfectly encapsulates the band's musical agenda, while "Into You" is one of their few truly successful slow numbers. The original LP included a three-song bonus EP featuring the heavy riff rock of "Lunchmeataphobia," an unnecessary instrumental version of "P.E. Squad," and a live "Maggot Brain"; these tracks were appended to the CD reissue. In any form, *One Nation Under a Groove* is the best realization of Funkadelic's ambitions, and one of the best funk albums ever released.

Steve Huey

Uncle Jam Wants You
1979, Priority

Almost as if Clinton and company wanted to atone for parts of *One Nation Under a Groove*, *Uncle Jam Wants You* takes not merely a more daring musical approach but a more forth-right political stance. The cover art alone is brilliant, front and back showing Clinton in Huey P. Newton's famous Black Panther pose. The main goal is the cover subtitle's stated claim to "rescue dance music 'from the blahs,'" and "Uncle Jam" itself does a pretty funny job at doing that, starting out like a parody of patriotic recruitment ads before hitting its full, funky stride. It's still very much a disco effort, but one overtly spiking the brew even more than before with P-Funk's own particular recipe, mock drill instructors calling out dance commands and so forth. The absolute winner and most famous track, without question, is the 15-minute deep groove of "(Not Just) Knee Deep." It'd be legend alone for being the musical basis for De La Soul's astonishing break-through a decade later with "Me, Myself and I," but on its own it predates the mutation of disco into electro thanks to the stiff beat and Worrell's crazy keyboards. Elsewhere there are pleasant enough jams like "Field Maneuvers," kicking around some good guitar work amidst the hop-and-skip beat, and the weepy ballad "Holly Wants to Go to California," intentionally undercut by all the cheering and noise deep in the mix. It's not to say that Funkadelic hasn't left the entire world of coke spoons and pointing to the sky behind them, as "Freak of the Week" shows, which isn't entirely far off from the early Sugar Hill party/zodiac aesthetic. Then again, lines like "disco-sadistic, that one beat up and down, it just won't do" amidst the whistles and screams have their own impact.

Ned Raggett

The Electric Spanking of War Babies
1981, Priority

With George Clinton, a humorous phrase could be nothing more than playful tomfoolery, or it could be a double entendre with a deep political meaning. The phrase "electric spanking of war babies" falls into the latter category—it referred to what the funk innovator saw as the U.S. government using the media to promote imperialistic wars. To Clinton, the American media functioned as a propaganda machine during wartime. But whether or not one cares to examine its hidden political messages, *Electric Spanking* is an above-average party album. *Spanking* falls short of the excellence of *One Nation Under a Groove* and *Uncle Jam Wants You* and didn't boast a major hit single, but amusing funk smokers like "Electro-Cuties" and "Funk Gets Stronger" aren't anything to sneeze at, nor is the reggae-influenced "Shockwaves." *Spanking* turned out to be the last album Clinton would produce under the name Funkadelic—when he hit the charts again in 1983, Mr. P-Funk was billing himself as a "solo artist."

Alex Henderson

Music for Your Mother
March 1993, Westbound

Though *Tales of Kidd Funkadelic* brought together some oddballs and rarities from Funkadelic's early-to-mid '70s existence, it wasn't until *Music for Your Mother* came out that there was a full compilation of all the band's singles from birth to the mid-decade switch to Warner Bros. And what a compilation it is: Bringing together some of the band's best material as well as some of its craziest, *Music for Your Mother* does the business for any self-respecting P-Funk clone. Given that the focus is on A- and B-sides rather than album cuts, it isn't a truly exhaustive overview—that would require the inclusion of songs like "Maggot Brain" and "Free Your Mind and Your Ass Will Follow," for a start. It's a small quibble in context, though, especially given the inclusion of a number of songs that never made it onto the original eight albums. Most notable is a curious rarity, the semi-smooth soul "I Miss My Baby" single, which was credited to U.S., with music by Funkadelic (U.S. being a group led by eventual P-Funk guitarist Gary Shider).

As for the other B-sides and uncollected numbers, they're an understandably mixed but often interesting bunch, including alternate instrumental takes of "Music for Your Mother" and "I Wanna Know if It's Good to You," the unreleased "Can't Shake It Loose" single, the gospel/feedback freakout "Open Our Eyes," and the hilariously titled "Fish, Chips and Sweat." The amazing bonus to the whole collection is the exhaustive 24-page booklet, reviewing the entire early history of Funkadelic via archival photos and a slew of interviews with the surviving participants. Plenty of fun tales are told, but George Clinton didn't participate—not surprising, given the unflattering picture eventually painted of him—while the depressing fates of Eddie Hazel and Tawl Ross get deserved attention.

Ned Raggett

Motor City Madness: The Ultimate Funkadelic Westbound Compilation
October 2003, Westbound

Some Funkadelic fans might be disappointed that the two-CD *Motor City Madness: The Ultimate Collection* compilation has nothing from the records the group did in the late '70s and early '80s after leaving the Westbound label. But it *does* most certainly live up to its title: it's the best anthology of the band's work from the first half of the 1970s that's likely to be produced. Crammed with two and a half hours of music, it includes both popular and lesser-known cuts from their 1970–1976 releases, among them several of the songs most associated with the group. "Cosmic Slop," "Free Your Mind and Your Ass Will Follow," "Maggot Brain," "Loose Booty," and "America Eats Its Young" are all here, but so are a bunch of things that won't necessarily be familiar to the man or woman who's only heard Funkadelic records at other people's houses. And though the Westbound singles collection *Music for Your Mother* is also necessary to get a full view of early Funkadelic at their best, *Motor City Madness* also puts some of those singles in a different light, since some songs (like "Loose Booty," "Cosmic Slop," and "Standing on the Verge of Getting It On") are presented here in LP versions that are noticeably longer than the 45 versions on *Music for Your Mother*. Long liner notes also do their part to put the legendarily confusing early history of Funkadelic into some kind of understandable order. It's arguable whether, however, the non-chronological track sequencing was a good decision: it's hard enough to keep the Funkadelic story straight without the dates of the songs jumping back and forth too. You can always fiddle with the sequencing with your CD programmer if you want, of course, and however it's sliced, the range of progressive soul and funk is tremendous, from nearly psychedelic freakouts and spaced-out makeout music to quasi-Temptations soul with a goofy spin and near-disco.

Richie Unterberger

The Gap Band

Gap Band IV
1982, Mercury

Gap Band IV featured a complete lineup of up-tempo, mid-tempo, and alluring ballads. The feature releases, in order, were "Early in the Morning," "You Dropped a Bomb on Me," and "Outstanding." The first two are energized numbers seasoned around horrific bass lines and Charlie Wilson's dazzling vocals. Respectively, they peaked at number one and two on the *Billboard* R&B chart. Not as aggressive, the latter is a festive number paced an unorthodox percussive beat. It claimed the number one spot on the *Billboard* R&B chart as well. There were no other official selections to grace *Billboard*. However, every song visited radio, and rightly so. The sentimental numbers "Stay With Me," "Seasons No Reason to Change," and "I Can't Get Over You" have become standard among R&B radio. The latter features a sentimental flügelhorn exhibition by Ronnie Wilson. Mellow numbers always seem to retain that timeless appeal whereas up-tempo numbers fade with time. This album is different; the up-tempo numbers remain inviting as well. This is a great album.

Craig Lytle

Marvin Gaye

What's Going On
May 1971, Motown

What's Going On is not only Marvin Gaye's masterpiece, it's the most important and passionate record to come out of soul music, delivered by one of its finest voices, a man finally free to speak his mind and so move from R&B sex symbol to true recording artist. With *What's Going On*, Gaye meditated on what had happened to the American dream of the past—as it related to urban decay, environmental woes, military turbulence, police brutality, unemployment, and poverty. These feelings had been bubbling up between 1967 and 1970, during which he felt increasingly caged by Motown's behind-the-times hit machine and restrained from expressing himself seriously through his music. Finally, late in 1970, Gaye decided to record a song that the Four Tops' Obie Benson had brought him, "What's Going On." When Berry Gordy decided not to issue the single, deeming it uncommercial, Gaye refused to record any more material until he relented. Confirmed by its tremendous commercial success in January 1971, he recorded the rest of the album over ten days in March, and Motown released it in late May. Besides cementing Marvin Gaye as one of the most important artists in pop music, *What's Going On* was far and away the best full-length to issue from the singles-dominated Motown factory, and arguably the best soul album of all time. Conceived as a statement from the viewpoint of a Vietnam veteran (Gaye's brother Frankie had returned from a three-year hitch in 1967), *What's Going On* isn't just the question of a baffled soldier returning home to a strange place, but a promise that listeners would be informed by what they heard (that missing question mark in the title certainly wasn't a typo). Instead of releasing listeners from their troubles, as so many of his singles had in the past, Gaye used the album to reflect on the climate of the early '70s, rife with civil unrest, drug abuse, abandoned children, and the spectre of riots in the near past. Alternately depressed and hopeful, angry and jubilant, Gaye saved the most sublime, deeply inspired performances of his career for "Mercy Mercy Me (The Ecology)," "Inner City Blues (Make Me Wanna Holler)," and "Save the Children." The songs and performances, however, furnished only half of a revolution; little could've been accomplished with the Motown sound of previous Marvin Gaye hits like "Stubborn Kind of Fellow" and "Hitch Hike" or even "I Heard It Through the Grapevine." *What's Going On*, as he conceived and produced it, was like no other record heard before it: languid, dark and jazzy, a series of relaxed grooves with a heavy bottom, filled by thick basslines along with bongos, conga, and other percussion. Fortunately, this aesthetic fit in perfectly with the style of long-time Motown sessionmen like bassist James Jamerson and guitarist Joe Messina. When the Funk Brothers were, for once, allowed the opportunity to work in relaxed, open proceedings, they produced the best work of their careers (and indeed, they recognized its importance before any of the Motown executives). Jamerson's playing on "Inner City Blues (Make Me Wanna Holler)" functions as the low-end foundation but also its melodic hook, while an improvisatory jam by Eli Fountain on alto sax furnished the album's opening flourish. (Much credit goes to Gaye himself for seizing on these often tossed-off lines as precious; indeed, he spent more time down in the Snakepit than he did in the control room.) Just as he'd hoped it would be, *What's Going On* was Marvin Gaye's masterwork, the most perfect expression of an artist's hope, anger, and concern ever recorded.

John Bush

Trouble Man
December 1972, Motown

Marvin Gaye turned to soundtracks in the early '70s, and came out with one that ranked right alongside the epic scores done by Curtis Mayfield and Isaac Hayes. The film itself was a typical '70s "blaxploitation" effort, but Gaye's vocals, seamless production, and a nice mix of up-tempo funk, light ballads, and pseudo-macho camp were brilliant.

Ron Wynn

I Want You
March 1976, Motown

I Want You, while it was a Top Ten smash for Marvin Gaye in 1976, is not as generally well-known as its predecessors for a number of reasons. First, it marked a sharp change in direction, leaving his trademark Motown soul for lush, funky, light disco. Secondly, its subject matter is as close to explicit as pop records got in 1976. Third, Gaye hadn't recorded in nearly three years and critics were onto something else—exactly what is now anybody's guess. From the amazing Ernie Barnes cover painting "Back to Sugar Shack" to the Coleridge-Taylor Perkinson string and horn arrangements to Leon Ware's exotic production that relied on keyboards as well as drums and basses as rhythm instruments, *I Want You* was a giant leap for Gaye. The feel of the album was one of late-night parties in basements and small clubs, and the intimacy of the music evokes the image of people getting closer as every hour of a steamy night wears on. But the most astonishing things about *I Want You* are its intimacy (it was dedicated to and recorded in front of Gaye's future second wife, Jan), silky elegance, and seamless textures. Gaye worked with producer Leon Ware, who wrote all of the original songs on the album and worked with Gaye to revise them, thus lending Gaye a co-writing credit. The title track is a monster two-step groover with hand percussion playing counterpoint to the strings and horns layered in against a spare electric guitar solo, all before Gaye begins to sing on top of the funky backbeat. It's a party anthem to be sure, and one that evokes the vulnerability that a man in love displays when the object of his affection is in plain sight. Art Stewart's engineering rounds off all the edges and makes Gaye's already sweet crooning instrument into the true grain in the voice of seductive need. "Feel All My Love Inside" and "I Want to Be Where You Are" are anthems to sensuality with strings creeping up under Gaye's voice as the guitars move through a series of chunky changes and drums punctuate his every syllable. In all, the original album is a suite to the bedroom, one in which a man tells his woman all of his sexual aspirations because of his love for her. The entire album has been referenced by everyone from Mary J. Blige to D'Angelo to Chico DeBarge and even Todd Rundgren, who performed the title track live regularly. By the time it is over, the listener should be a blissed-out container of amorous vibes. *I Want You* and its companion, Ware's *Musical Massage*, are the pre-eminent early disco concept albums. They are adult albums about intimacy, sensuality, and commitment, and decades later they still reverberate with class, sincerity, grace, intense focus, and astonishingly good taste. *I Want You* is as necessary as anything Gaye ever recorded.

Thom Jurek

Graham Central Station

Ain't No 'Bout-A-Doubt It
1975, Warner Bros.

On their third album, Graham Central Station created an album full of trademark infectious pop-soul grooves, but one that lacked the consistently strong work that defines a true classic. However, that doesn't mean that *Ain't No 'Bout-A-Doubt It* is less than listenable: in fact, it contains some of the group's finest songs. The album's all-time funk classic is the opening track "The Jam," a "Dance to the Music"-styled funk workout that intersperses a dazzling group groove with individual solos for each player. "Water" is another strong funk tune, an insistently rhythmic song that blends thump-popping basslines with backwards tape loops to create an intriguing blend of funk and psychedelia. *Ain't No 'Bout-A-Doubt It* also produced a number one R&B smash in "Your Love," which marries the group's talent for funky grooves to an old-fashioned love song with a melody that harkens back to doo wop. However, not everything on *Ain't No 'Bout-A-Doubt It* is as strong as these highlights: "It Ain't Nothing but a Warner Bros. Party" is a lightweight jam with throwaway lyrics, and the group's rote version of the Ann Peebles classic "I Can't Stand the Rain" fails to add anything memorable to the song. All in all, *Ain't No 'Bout-A-Doubt It* lacks the strong material to make it memorable, but its high points make it a worthwhile listen for funk enthusiasts.

Donald A. Guarisco

Larry Graham

The Best of Larry Graham and Graham Central Station, Vol. 1
April 1996, Warner Bros.

Although Sly Stone was the musical genius of the legendary Sly & the Family Stone, bassist Larry Graham was their heart and soul. Graham proved to be a master of the bass while with the Family Stone, singlehandedly inventing the slap and pop technique of funk bass, which is now commonplace in popular music. Following his departure from the band after the 1971 classic *There's a Riot Going On* (due to Sly's unpredictable behavior and drug abuse), Graham set out to form his own band, Graham Central Station. And soon it became apparent that the party had moved—Graham and company kept racking up the hits, while the Family Stone hit the skids. *The Best of Larry Graham and Graham Central Station* does an excellent job of collecting highlights from their 1974 debut all the way up to their softer early '80s period. By far the best track on the compilation is the hard funk of "Hair," and a down-and-dirty number about equality not being based on appearance. Graham Central Station also had a knack for writing some infectious, up-tempo numbers that, once put on your turntable, turn the room into an instant party ("It's Alright," "The Jam," and especially "Now D-U-Wanta Dance"). Also included is the group's biggest hit, the soulful ballad "One In a Million You," which skyrocketed to number one on the R&B chart and hit number nine on the pop charts in 1980. *The Best of Larry Graham and Graham Central Station Vol. 1* is essential funk.

Greg Prato

Al Green

I'm Still in Love With You
December 1972, The Right Stuff

I'm Still in Love With You shares many surface similarities with its predecessor, *Let's Stay Together*; from Al Green and Willie Mitchell's distinctive, sexy style to the pacing and song selection. Despite those shared traits, *I'm Still in Love With You* distinguishes itself with its suave, romantic tone and its subtly ambitious choice of material. Green began exploring country music with this album by performing a startling version of Kris Kristofferson's "For the Good Times," as well as a wonderful, slow reinterpretation of Roy Orbison's "Oh Pretty Woman." And the soul numbers are more complex than they would appear—listen to how the beat falls together at the beginning of "Love and Happiness," or the sly melody of the title track. There isn't a wasted track on *I'm Still in Love With You*, and in many ways it rivals its follow-up, *Call Me*, as Green's masterpiece.

Stephen Thomas Erlewine

Call Me
July 1973, The Right Stuff

Al Green reached his creative peak with the brilliant *Call Me*, the most inventive and assured album of his career. So silky and fluid as to sound almost effortless, Green's vocals revel in the lush strings and evocative horns of Willie Mitchell's superbly intimate production, barely rising above an angelic whisper for the gossamer "Have You Been Making Out O.K." With barely perceptible changes in mood, *Call Me* covers remarkable ground, spanning from "Stand Up"—a call to arms delivered with characteristic understatement—to renditions of Hank Williams' "I'm So Lonesome I Could Cry" and Willie Nelson's "Funny How Time Slips Away," both of them exemplary fusions of country and soul. Equally compelling are the album's three Top Ten hits—"You Ought to Be With Me," "Here I Am (Come and Take Me)," and the shimmering title cut. A classic.

Jason Ankeny

Al Green's Greatest Hits
April 1975, The Right Stuff

Upon its original release in 1975, *Al Green's Greatest Hits* pretty much summed up everything about Green, containing his ten biggest hits up to that point. A few years later, it was followed by a second volume, which contained hit singles that had charted since the release of the first collection. In 1995, The Right Stuff reissued *Al Green's Greatest Hits*, adding five of the highlights from the second volume of greatest hits as bonus tracks. The result was a definitive single-disc compilation, featuring 15 of Green's absolute best songs, including "Tired of Being Alone," "Let's Stay Together," "I'm Still in Love With You," "Call Me," "Here I Am," "Sha-La-La (Make Me Happy)," and "L-O-V-E (Love)." The original version of *Greatest Hits* was great, but the revision made it nearly perfect.

Stephen Thomas Erlewine

Herbie Hancock

Head Hunters
1973, Columbia/Legacy

Head Hunters was a pivotal point in Herbie Hancock's career, bringing him into the vanguard of jazz fusion. Hancock had pushed avant-garde boundaries on his own albums and with Miles Davis, but he had never devoted himself to the groove as he did on *Head Hunters*. Drawing heavily from Sly Stone, Curtis Mayfield, and James Brown, Hancock developed deeply funky, even gritty, rhythms over which he soloed on electric synthesizers, bringing the instrument to the forefront in jazz. It had all of the sensibilities of jazz, particularly in the way it wound off into long improvisations, but its rhythms were firmly planted in funk, soul, and R&B, giving it a mass appeal that made it the biggest-selling jazz album of all time (a record which was later broken). Jazz purists, of course, decried the experiments at the time, but *Head Hunters* still sounds fresh and vital decades after its initial release, and its genre-bending proved vastly influential on not only jazz, but funk, soul, and hip-hop.

Stephen Thomas Erlewine

Future Shock
1983, Columbia

Herbie Hancock completely overhauled his sound and conquered MTV with his most radical step forward since the sextet days. He brought in Bill Laswell of Material as producer, along with Grand Mixer D.ST on turntables—and the immediate result was "Rockit," which makes quite a post-industrial metallic racket. Frankly, the whole record is an enigma; for all of its dehumanized, mechanized textures and rigid rhythms, it has a vitality and sense of humor that make it difficult to turn off. Moreover, Herbie can't help but inject a subversive funk element when he comps along to the techno beat—and yes, some real, honest-to-goodness jazz licks on a grand piano show up in the middle of "Auto Drive."

Richard S. Ginell

Donny Hathaway

Everything Is Everything
July 1970, Atlantic

Already a respected arranger and pianist who'd contributed to dozens of records (by artists ranging from the Impressions to Carla Thomas to Woody Herman), with this debut LP Donny Hathaway revealed yet another facet of his genius— his smoky, pleading voice, one of the best to ever grace a soul record. *Everything Is Everything* sounded like nothing before it, based in smooth uptown soul but boasting a set of excellent, open-ended arrangements gained from Hathaway's background in classical and gospel music. (Before going to Howard University in 1964, his knowledge of popular music was practically non-existent.) After gaining a contract with Atco through King Curtis, Hathaway wrote and recorded during 1969 and 1970 with friends including drummer Ric Powell and guitarist Phil Upchurch, both of whom lent a grooving feel to the album that Hathaway may not have been able to summon on his own (check out Upchurch's unforgettable bassline on the opener, "Voices Inside (Everything Is Everything)"). All of the musical brilliance on display, though, is merely the framework for Hathaway's rich, emotive voice, testifying to the power of love and religion with few, if any, concessions to pop music. Like none other, he gets to the raw, churchy emotion underlying Ray Charles' "I Believe to My Soul" and Nina Simone's "To Be Young, Gifted and Black," the former with a call-and-response horn chart and his own glorious vocal, the latter with his own organ lines. "Thank You Master (For My Soul)" brings the Stax horns onto sanctified ground, while Hathaway praises God and sneaks in an excellent piano solo. *Everything Is Everything* was one of the first soul records to comment directly on an unstable period; "Tryin' Times" speaks to the importance of peace and community with an earthy groove, while the most familiar track here, a swinging jam known as "The Ghetto," places listeners right in the middle of urban America. Donny Hathaway's debut introduced a brilliant talent into the world of soul, one who promised to take R&B farther than it had been taken since Ray Charles debuted on Atlantic.

John Bush

Isaac Hayes

Hot Buttered Soul
1969, Stax

Released at the tail end of the '60s, *Hot Buttered Soul* set the precedent for how soul would evolve in the early '70s, simultaneously establishing Isaac Hayes and the Bar-Kays as major forces within black music. Though not quite as definitive as *Black Moses* or as well-known as *Shaft*, *Hot Buttered Soul* remains an undeniably seminal record; it stretched its songs far beyond the traditional three-to-four-minute industry norm, featured long instrumental stretches where the Bar-Kays stole the spotlight, and it introduced a new, iconic persona for soul with Hayes' tough yet sensual image. With the release of this album, Motown suddenly seemed manufactured and James Brown a bit too theatrical. Surprising many, the album features only four songs. The first, "Walk on By," is an epic 12-minute moment of true perfection, its trademark string-laden intro just dripping with syrupy sentiment, and the thumping mid-tempo drum beat and accompanying bassline instilling a complementary sense of nasty funk to the song; if that isn't enough to make it an amazing song, Hayes' almost painful performance brings yet more feeling to the song, with the guitar's heavy vibrato and the female background singers taking the song to even further heights. The following three songs aren't quite as stunning but are still no doubt impressive: "Hyperbolicsyllabicsequedalymistic" trades in sappy sentiment for straight-ahead funk, highlighted by a stomping piano halfway through the song; "One Woman" is the least epic moment, clocking in at only five minutes, but stands as a straightforward, well-executed love ballad; and finally, there's the infamous 18-minute "By the Time I Get to Phoenix" and its lengthy monologue which slowly eases you toward the climactic, almost-orchestral finale, a beautiful way to end one of soul's timeless, landmark albums, the album that transformed Hayes into a lifelong icon.

Jason Birchmeier

...To Be Continued
1970, Stax

Released in late 1970 on the heels of two chart-topping albums, *Hot Buttered Soul* (1969) and *The Isaac Hayes Movement* (also 1970), Isaac Hayes and the Bar-Kays retain their successful approach on those landmark albums for *To Be Continued*, another number one album. Again, the album features four songs that span far beyond traditional radio-friendly length, featuring important mood-establishing instrumental segments just as emotive and striking as Hayes'

crooning. Nothing here is quite as perfect as "Walk on By," and the album feels a bit churned out, but *To Be Continued* no doubt has its share of highlights, the most notable being "You've Lost That Lovin' Feelin'." The album's most epic moment opens with light strings and horns, vamping poetically for several minutes before Hayes even utters a breath; then, once the singer delivers the song's orchestral chorus, the album hits its sentimental peak—Hayes elevating a common standard to heavenly heights once again. Elsewhere, "Our Day Will Come" features a nice concluding instrumental segment driven by a proto-hip-hop beat that proves just how ahead of his time Hayes was during his early '70s cycle of Enterprise albums. It's tempting to slight this album when holding it up against Hayes' best albums from this same era, but a comparison such as this is unfair. Even if Ike isn't doing anything here that he didn't do on his two preceding albums—*Hot Buttered Soul*, *The Isaac Hayes Movement*—and isn't quite as daring as he is on his two successive albums—*Black Moses*, *Shaft*—*To Be Continued* still topples any Hayes album that came after 1971. It didn't top the R&B album chart for 11 weeks on accident—this is quintessential early '70s Isaac Hayes, and that alone makes it a classic soul album.

Jason Birchmeier

Black Moses
1971, Stax

The sheer tenacity—albeit undeniably fitting—of this double-disc set has made *Black Moses* (1971) one of Isaac Hayes' most revered and best-known works. The multi-instrumental singer/songwriter and producer had been a central figure in the Memphis soul music revolution of the mid-1960s. Along with Booker T. and The MG's, Hayes' wrote and performed on more Stax sides than any other single artist. By the time of this release—his fifth overall, and first two-record set—Hayes had firmly established himself as a progressive soul artist. His stretched out and well-developed R&B jams, as well as his husky-voiced sexy spoken "raps" became key components in his signature sound. *Black Moses* not only incorporates those leitmotifs, but also reaffirms Hayes abilities as an unmistakably original arranger. Although a majority of the album consists of cover material, all the scores have been reconfigured and adapted in such a fundamental way that, for some listeners, these renditions serve as definitive. This is certainly true of the extended reworkings of Jerry Butler's "Brand New Me," and Esther Phillips' "You're Love Is So Doggone Good"—both of which are prefaced by the spoken prelude to coitus found in each respective installment of "Ike's Rap." The pair of Curtis Mayfield tunes—"Man's Temptation" and "Need to Belong to Someone"—are also worth noting for the layers of tastefully scored orchestration—from both Hayes and his long-time associate Johnny Allen. The pair's efforts remain fresh and discerning, rather than the dated ersatz strings and horn sections that imitators were glutting the soul and pop charts and airwaves with in the mid-1970s. Hayes' own composition, "Good Love," recalls the upbeat and jive talkin' "Hyperbolicsyllabicsesquedalymistic" from *Hot Buttered Soul* (1969), adding some spicy and sexy double-entendre in the chorus. Wisely, the CD reissue also reproduced Chester

Higgins' original tongue-in-cheek liner note essay giving the history and mythology of the *Black Moses* persona.

Lindsay Planer

Shaft
1971, Stax

Of the many wonderful blaxpoitation soundtracks to emerge during the early '70s, *Shaft* certainly deserves mention as not only one of the most lasting but also one of the most successful. Isaac Hayes was undoubtedly one of the era's most accomplished soul artists, having helped elevate Stax to its esteemed status; therefore, his being chosen to score such a high-profile major-studio film shouldn't seem like a surprise. And with "Theme From Shaft," he delivered an anthem just as ambitious and revered as the film itself, a song that has only grown more treasured over the years, after having been an enormously popular hit at the time of its release. Besides this song, though, there aren't too many more radio-targeted moments here. "Soulsville" operates effectively as the sort of down-tempo ballad Hayes was most known for, just as the almost 20-minute "Do Your Thing" showcased just how impressive the Bar-Kays had become, stretching the song to unseen limits with their inventive, funky jamming. For the most part, though, this double-LP features nothing but cinematic moments of instrumentation, composed and produced by Hayes while being performed by the Bar-Kays—some downtempo, others quite jazzy, nothing too funky, though. Even if it's not quite as enjoyable as Curtis Mayfield's *Superfly* due to its emphasis on instrumentals, *Shaft* still remains a powerful record; one of Hayes' pinnacle moments for sure.

Jason Birchmeier

Heatwave

Too Hot to Handle
1976, Epic

Too Hot to Handle was the debut album from the soul/funk ensemble Heatwave, and it was well received by R&B and pop fans. Their initial release was the disco anthem "Boogie Nights." From the suspenseful, interlude-like intro to the adamant vocal delivery, the single had a lasting effect on the charts. It peaked at numbers five and two on the *Billboard* R&B and pop charts, respectively. The ballad "Always and Forever" was and continues to be an ageless piece. Johnnie Wilder's vocal exhibition throughout the vamp is breathtaking. It peaked at number two on the *Billboard* R&B charts. These two releases were respectively certified platinum and gold singles. Heatwave did not waste any recording time. This album employs nothing but quality tracks. The moderately paced "Ain't No Half Steppin'" was received warmly by radio, and it remains a staple. While Rod Temperton was writing excellent songs, Johnnie Wilder's supreme vocals gave the songs their identity.

Craig Lytle

Jimi Hendrix

Are You Experienced?
1967, MCA

One of the most stunning debuts in rock history, and one of the definitive albums of the psychedelic era. On *Are You Experienced?*, Jimi Hendrix synthesized various elements of the cutting edge of 1967 rock into music that sounded both futuristic and rooted in the best traditions of rock, blues, pop, and soul. It was his mind-boggling guitar work, of course, that got most of the ink, building upon the experiments of  British innovators like Jeff Beck and Pete Townshend to chart new sonic territories in feedback, distortion, and sheer volume. It wouldn't have meant much, however, without his excellent material, whether psychedelic frenzy ("Foxey Lady," "Manic Depression," "Purple Haze"), instrumental freak-out jams ("Third Stone From the Sun"), blues ("Red House," "Hey Joe"), or tender, poetic compositions ("The Wind Cries Mary") that demonstrated the breadth of his songwriting talents. Not to be underestimated were the contributions of drummer Mitch Mitchell and bassist Noel Redding, who gave the music a rhythmic pulse that fused parts of rock and improvised jazz. Many of these songs are among Hendrix's very finest; it may be true that he would continue to develop at a rapid pace throughout the rest of his brief career, but he would never surpass his first LP in terms of consistently high quality. The British and American versions of the album differed substantially when they were initially released in 1967; MCA's 17-song CD reissue does everyone a favor by gathering all of the material from the two records in one place, adding a few B-sides from early singles as well.

Richie Unterberger

Freddie Hubbard

Red Clay
January 1970, CBS

This may be Freddie Hubbard's finest moment as a leader, in that it embodies and utilizes all of his strengths as a composer, soloist, and frontman. On *Red Clay*, Hubbard combines hard bop's glorious blues-out past with the soulful innovations of mainstream jazz in the 1960s, and reads them through the chunky groove innovations of 1970s jazz fusion. This session places the trumpeter in the company of giants such as tenor saxophonist Joe Henderson, pianist Herbie Hancock, bassist Ron Carter, and drummer Lenny White. Hubbard's five compositions all come from deep inside blues territory; these shaded notions are grafted onto funky hard bop melodies worthy of Horace Silver's finest tunes, and are layered inside the smoothed-over cadences of shimmering, steaming soul. The 12-minute-plus title track features a 4/4 modal opening and a spare electric piano solo woven through the twin horns of Hubbard and Henderson. It is a fine example of snaky groove music. Henderson even takes his solo outside a bit without ever moving out of the rhythmnatist's pocket. "Delightful" begins as a ballad with slow, clipped trumpet lines against a major key background, and opens onto a mid-tempo groover, then winds back into the dark, steamy heart of bluesy melodicism. The hands-down favorite here, though, is "The Intrepid Fox," with its

Miles-like opening of knotty changes and shifting modes, that are all rooted in bop's muscular architecture. It's White and Hancock who shift the track from underneath with large sevenths and triple-timed drums that land deeply inside the clamoring, ever-present riff. Where Hubbard and Henderson are playing against, as well as with one another, the rhythm section, lifted buoyantly by Carter's bridge-building bassline, carries the melody over until Hancock plays an uncharacteristically angular solo before splitting the groove in two and doubling back with a series of striking arpeggiatics. This is a classic, hands down.

Thom Jurek

Willie Hutch

The Mack
1973, Motown

When an act called Sisters Love were offered a cameo in the blaxploitation film *The Mack*, their manager suggested that Willie Hutch do the soundtrack. It becameto be one of the great '70s film scores, including a pair of classic funk tunes, "Brothers Gonna Work It Out" and the title cut. The results proved to be another soundtrack that far surpassed the quality of its film.

Ron Wynn

Incredible Bongo Band

Bongo Rock
1973, Mr. Bongo

A series of tracks laid down by relatively anonymous '70s studio musicians, this record would gain righteous fame as a hip-hop artifact, one of the first records to be extensively mined for beats. Heads will have no trouble recognizing the opening thumps of "Apache" or "Bongo Rock." Those less interested in the history of another form of music will find this less fascinating, more akin to *Persuasive Percussion* records than anything else.

Rob Ferrier

Instant Funk

Instant Funk
January 1979, Salsoul

Instant Funk, the nine-piece funk unit discovered by Bunny Sigler, created a stir in 1979 when Salsoul released the single "I Got My Mind Made Up (You Can Get It Girl)." Swirling, screaming horns announce the chorus; hand claps, tambourines and a maniacal rhythm guitar battle the heavy bottom; and a woman delivers erotic lines for added impact. Salsoul followed the number 20 pop and number one R&B (for three weeks) hit with "Crying," a race horse whose relentless beat only subsides near the fade; Carmichael's vocal is passionate, almost deranged. "Never Let Me Go Away," a rare Instant Funk ballad, was so overblown the melody got buried. Spooky voices and haunted-house sounds wallpaper "Dark Vader"'s comic-book lyrics and funky hooks. Rolling horns pump "I'll Be Doggone" (not the Marvin Gaye hit), a cooker that rolls for seven minutes. Four of the

eight tracks are killers; a pretty good average for a disco/funk group.

Andrew Hamilton

Weldon Irvine

Spirit Man
1975, RCA

Spirit Man channels the sonic sprawl of the preceding *Cosmic Vortex (Justice Divine)* to forge a tighter, more focused approach. Eschewing vocals altogether, it's Weldon Irvine's most balanced and complete recording, deftly combining massive funk grooves with ingenious electronic elements. Featuring a supporting cast including bassist Cleveland Freeman, trumpeters Charles Sullivan and Everett "Blood" Hollins, and saxophonist Sonny Fortune, *Spirit Man* parallels Herbie Hancock's groundbreaking fusion dates in both the imagination and ferocity of Irvine's keyboards as well as the extraterrestrial reach of its electronic effects. This music is deep, funky, and deeply funky.

Jason Ankeny

The Isley Brothers

3 + 3
1973, T Neck

Recorded in 1973, *3 + 3* was a major turning point for the Isley Brothers. With this album, the Isleys moved their T-Neck label from Buddah to Epic/CBS (which became Epic/Sony in the early '90s), and it was at Epic that they unveiled their new lineup. Lead singer Ronald Isley and his siblings O'Kelly and Rudolph remained, but the Isleys became a sextet instead of a trio when cousin Chris Jasper and younger brothers Ernie and Marvin were added. This new lineup was called 3 + 3, and the addition of Jasper on keyboards, Ernie on guitar, and Marvin on bass added exciting new elements to the Isleys' sound. One of finest R&B bassists of the 1970s, the ever-so-funky Marvin is in a class with heavyweights like Larry Graham and Louis Johnson—and Ernie is a stunning guitarist who is heavily influenced by Jimi Hendrix but has a distinctive style of his own. The Isleys had always been lovers of rock, but with the addition of Ernie, their sound became even more overtly rock-influenced. Nonetheless, the rock and pop elements didn't alienate R&B audiences, which ate this album up. The single "That Lady" (which is based on an Impressions-like gem they had recorded in 1964) was a major hit, and the Isleys are equally captivating on soul interpretations of Seals & Crofts' "Summer Breeze," James Taylor's "Don't Let Me Be Lonely Tonight," and the Doobie Brothers' "Listen to the Music." With this superb album, the Isley Brothers sounded better than ever—and they gained a lot of new fans without sacrificing the old ones.

Alex Henderson

The Heat Is On
1975, T Neck

1975's *The Heat Is On* was the third album that the Isley Brothers recorded with their 3 + 3 lineup, and by that time, the lineup had really perfected its attractive soul/rock sound. The Isleys were providing great R&B long before keyboardist Chris Jasper, bassist Marvin Isley, and the distinctive guitarist Ernie Isley came on board in 1973; nonetheless, the newcomers added a lot to the group and helped it provide some of its best recordings. Marvin's basslines are as funky as it gets, and the Jimi Hendrix-influenced Ernie is a killer guitarist; he would have been perfect for Deep Purple, Blue Öyster Cult, or Judas Priest if the Isley Brothers hadn't kept him busy in the 1970s. One of the 3 + 3 gems that no Isleys fans should be without is *The Heat Is On*, which is best known for the sweaty funk classic "Fight the Power" and the sexy quiet storm slow jam "For the Love of You." Lead vocalist Ronald Isley is as convincing on the funk scorchers as he is on caressing ballads like "Make Me Say It Again Girl" and "Sensuality." Meanwhile, "Hope You Feel Better Love" is brilliant because it contrasts those two sides of the 3 + 3 lineup—the verses are sweetly melodic, but the chorus is forceful and explosive. Superb from start to finish, *The Heat Is On* is among the Isleys' most essential albums.

Alex Henderson

Harvest for the World
1976, T Neck

The Isley Brothers came with love, funk, and the too seldom mentioned socially consicous songs; this album is titled after one of those social gems. However, "Who Loves You Better," with its disco flair, was the album's first release. Ronald Isley's aggressive delivery blends nicely with Ernie Isley's tantalizing guitar solos. It was a top three single on the *Billboard* R&B charts. The title track is a tour de force. Preceded by a mellow intro in which Ronald Isley's earnest plea rings with urgency, the timeless lyric and festive rhythm make "Harvest for the World" a welcomed anthem for all the people of the world. It cracked the *Billboard* R&B top ten at number nine. Ronald Isley changes his tone on some of these compositions by adding a roughness to his still smooth tenor, like on the relentless jams "People of Today" and "You Wanna Stay Down." Then there are those priceless ballads like "Let Me Know" and "Let Me Down Easy"; Ronald Isley sweetly caresses the lyric with compassion and agility. Neither of these two selections were releases but remain staples on R&B radio.

Craig Lytle

The Jackson 5

Diana Ross Presents the Jackson 5
1969, Motown

Less than two weeks before the 1960s were left to be deciphered in the history books, Motown unleashed *Diana Ross Presents the Jackson 5* (1969) and in doing so fittingly marked the beginning of a new era in crossover pop and soul. For all intents and purposes, this dozen-song disc introduced the world to the sibling talents of Jackie, Tito, Jermaine, Marlon, and most significantly of all, a prepubescent powerhouse named Michael Jackson. The brothers' inextricably tight vocal harmonies were fueled by the ebullience of youth and inexperience while the flames of their collective success were stoked with the funkified vibe of urban America. Immediately evident is the influence that Sly & the Family Stone (whose "Stand!" is an unmitigated zenith in the Jackson 5's care), James Brown, and even Funkadelic had on the J5. In fact, the quintet would actually cover George Clinton's "I Bet You" on their sophomore effort, *ABC* (1970). The burgeoning sounds coming out of Philly were having a similarly sizable impact, as evidenced by the addition of the Thom Bell/William Hart track "Can You Remember," which is one of the album's highlights. Another discernibly affective force was found closer to home, as they also drew on the considerable Motown back catalog with "My Cherie Amour," "Standing in the Shadows of Love," and a powerful reading of "(I Know) I'm Losing You." Under the moniker of "the Corporation," Motown staffers and artists including Bobby Taylor, instrumentalists Deke Richards (guitar), Freddie Perren (keyboard), and Fonce Mizell (keyboards), and the label's co-founder, Berry Gordy, came up with a handful of dominant originals. Prominent among them are the midtempo "Nobody" and their double-sided chart-topping single "I Want You Back" b/w the Smokey Robinson-penned "Who's Lovin' You." [The 2001 CD reissue of *Diana Ross Presents the Jackson 5* is coupled with their subsequent collection, *ABC*, and includes the supplementary "Oh, I've Been Blessed" from the very first J5 session at Motown.]

Lindsay Planer

Michael Jackson

Off the Wall
1979, Epic

Michael Jackson had recorded solo prior to the release of *Off the Wall* in 1979, but this was his breakthrough, the album that established him as an artist of astonishing talent and a bright star in his own right. This was a visionary album, a record that found a way to break disco wide open into a new world where the beat was undeniable, but not the primary focus—it was part of a colorful tapestry of lush ballads and strings, smooth soul and pop, soft rock, and alluring funk. Its roots hearken back to the Jacksons' huge mid-'70s hit "Dancing Machine," but this is an enormously fresh record, one that remains vibrant and giddily exciting years after its release. This is certainly due to Jackson's emergence as a blindingly gifted vocalist, equally skilled with overwrought ballads as "She's Out of My Life" as driving dancefloor shakers as "Working Day and Night" and "Get on the Floor," where his asides are as gripping as his delivery on the verses. It's also due to the brilliant songwriting, an intoxicating blend of strong melodies, rhythmic hooks, and indelible construction. Most of all, its success is due to the sound constructed by Jackson and producer Quincy Jones, a dazzling array of disco beats, funk guitars, clean mainstream pop, and unashamed (and therefore affecting) schmaltz that is utterly thrilling in its utter joy. This is highly professional, highly crafted music, and its details are evident, but the overall effect is nothing but pure pleasure. Jackson and Jones expanded this approach on the blockbuster *Thriller*, often with equally stunning results, but they never bettered it.

Stephen Thomas Erlewine

Thriller
1982, Epic

Off the Wall was a massive success, spawning four Top Ten hits (two of them number ones), but nothing could have prepared Michael Jackson for *Thriller*. Nobody could have prepared anybody for the success of *Thriller*, since the magnitude of its success was simply unimaginable—an album that sold 40 million copies in its initial chart run, with *seven* of its nine tracks reaching the Top Ten (for the record, the terrific "Baby Be Mine" and the pretty good ballad "The Lady in My Life" are not like the others). This was a record that had something for everybody, building on the basic blueprint of *Off the Wall* by adding harder funk, hard rock, softer ballads, and smoother soul—expanding the approach to have something for every audience. That alone would have given the album a good shot at a huge audience, but it also arrived precisely when MTV was reaching its ascendancy, and Jackson helped the network by being not just its first superstar, but first black star as much as the network helped him. This all would have made it a success (and its success, in turn, served as a new standard for success), but it stayed on the charts, turning out singles, for nearly two years because it was really, really good. True, it wasn't as tight as *Off the Wall*—and the ridiculous, late-night house-of-horrors title track is the prime culprit, arriving in the middle of the record and sucking out its momentum—but those one or two cuts don't detract from a phenomenal set of music. It's calculated, to be sure, but the chutzpah of those calculations (before this, nobody would even have thought to bring in metal virtuoso Eddie Van Halen to play on a disco cut) is outdone by their success. This is where a song as gentle and lovely as "Human Nature" coexists comfortably with the tough, scared "Beat It," the sweet schmaltz of the Paul McCartney duet "The Girl Is Mine," and the frizzy funk of "P.Y.T. (Pretty Young Thing)." And, although this is an undeniably fun record, the paranoia is already creeping in, manifesting itself in the record's two best songs: "Billie Jean," where a woman claims Michael is the father of her child, and the delirious "Wanna Be Startin' Something," the freshest funk on the album, but the most claustrophobic, scariest track Jackson ever recorded. These give the record its anchor and are part of the reason why the record is more than just a phenomenon. The other reason, of course, is that much of this is just simply great music.

Stephen Thomas Erlewine

Millie Jackson

Caught Up
1974, Southbound

Taking the drama of a love triangle to logical extremes, Millie Jackson's *Caught Up* turns the pitfalls of tainted love into the basis for a concept album (the seeds for soul music's explicit treatment of the topic having been planted by James Carr's "Dark End of the Street"). While the "other woman's" view is taken up initially on cuts like the R&B hit "If Loving You Is Wrong I Don't Want to Be Right," the wife's plight is

covered on the second half of the disc with revealing titles like "It's All Over but the Shouting." Jackson also delivers some of her patented racy commentary on the appropriately named "The Rap," while showing equal vigor in the album's wealth of fine vocal performances, including an impressive cover of Bobby Womack's "I'm Through Trying to Prove My Love to You." *Caught Up*'s standout track, though, is the version of Bobby Goldsboro's "Summer" that closes the record. Seemingly out of sync with the overriding concept, the song touches upon a girl's loss of innocence to an older man. One soon realizes, though, that beyond sexual awakening, Jackson is really emphasizing the point of no return: After the epiphany, one is sent hurdling toward the power struggles and politics of adult relations, including, potentially, the moral crossroads of infidelity. Luckily, as soon as your mind overloads from pop semiotics, the in-the-pocket grooves supplied by the Muscle Shoals Swampers provides the needed salve. Jackson shows both brains and soul on this fine release, creating what might be the only concept album one can dance and drink to.

Stephen Cook

Ahmad Jamal

The Awakening
February 1970, Impulse!

The music on this CD has been reissued many times, most recently in 1997. By 1970, pianist Ahmad Jamal's style had changed a bit since the 1950s, becoming denser and more adventurous while still retaining his musical identity. With bassist Jamil Nasser (whose doubletiming lines are sometimes furious) and drummer Frank Gant, Jamal performs two originals (playing over a vamp on "Patterns"), the obscure "I Love Music" and four jazz standards. Intriguing performances showing that Ahmad Jamal was continuing to evolve.

Scott Yanow

Bob James

One
April 1974, Tappan Zee

Bob James's first recording for his Tappan Zee label, which has been reissued on CD along with virtually James' entire output by Warner Bros., is typically lightweight. Although Grover Washington, Jr. has two spots on soprano and trumpeter Jon Faddis is in the brass section, James' dated Fender Rhodes keyboard is the lead voice throughout the six pieces, which include two adaptations of classical works. Only a lightly funky version of "Feel Like Making Love" rises above the level of pleasant background music.

Scott Yanow

Two
1975, Tappan Zee

Bob James largely defined pop/jazz crossover in the '70s. *Two*, reissued by Koch, is typical of his output. Mixing together aspects of pop, R&B and classical with just a touch of jazz, James (heard throughout on electric keyboards) put the emphasis on catchy melodies and lightly funky rhythms. The results range from insipid to pleasant, with a brass section, a string section, and vocalists (including Patti Austin) utilized to create what is essentially background music.

Scott Yanow

The Essential Collection: 24 Smooth Jazz Classics
2002, Metro Doubles

Issued by the U.K.-based Metro Doubles label in 2002, *Essential Collection: 24 Smooth Jazz Classics* only overlaps 2001's *Restoration* anthology with eight of the same tracks, and concentrates on material originally released from 1974 to 1984 (apart from 1995's "Ensenada Madness," everything fits into that time frame). A fine chronological overview of James' most productive period, this is a very attractive package that includes informative and insightful liner notes. "Nautilus," "Westchester Lady," "Take Me to the Mardi Gras," "Angela (Theme From Taxi)," "Touchdown," and "Sign of the Times" are among the inclusions. Naturally, this double-disc set can serve any number of purposes: as pleasant, occasionally funky background music, as proof of your extensive knowledge of hip-hop samples, or as cruel torture for your jazz purist peers.

Andy Kellman

Rick James

Come Get It!
1978, Motown

After returning to the U.S. from London, where he fronted the blues band Mainline, Rick James cut one album with White Cane before he turned to his own solo venture. By 1977, he'd begun working with the Stone City Band, emerging at the end of the year with an album's worth of delicious funk-rock fusion. Released in spring 1978, *Come Get It!* was a triumphant debut, truly the sum of all that had gone before, at the same time as unleashing the rudiments of what would become not only his trademark sound, but also his mantra, his manifesto—his self proclaimed punk-funk. Packed with intricate songs that are full of effusive energy, *Come Get It!* is marvelously hybridized funk, so tightly structured that, although they have the outward feel of funk's freewheeling jam, they never once cross the line into an uncontrolled frenzy. This is best

demonstrated across the monumental, eight-plus-minute "You and I." With enough funk bubbling under the surface to supplant the outward disco sonics of the groove, but brought back to earth via James' vocal interpolations, "You and I" became James' first R&B chart hit, effortlessly slamming into the top spot. "Mary Jane," meanwhile, was James' homage to marijuana—honoring the love affair through slang, it dipped into the Top Five in fall 1978. More importantly, though, it also offered up a remarkable preview of his subsequent vocal development. With nods to Earth, Wind & Fire on "Sexy Lady," *Motown* sonics on "Dream Maker," the passionate "Hollywood," and the classic club leanings of "Be My Lady," it's obvious that James was still very much in the throes of transition, still anticipating his future onslaught of hits and superstardom. Many of the songs here have a tendency toward the disco ethics that were inescapable in 1978, and have been faulted as such; nevertheless, what James achieved on this LP was remarkably fresh, and would prove vitally important to funk as it grew older during the next decade.

Amy Hanson

Bustin' Out of L Seven
1979, Motown

Rick James' second album, *Bustin' Out of L Seven*, maintained his status among R&B fans, almost topping the LP chart and spawning hits in the title track, "High on Your Love Suite," and "Fool on the Street," though none of them matched the popularity of the debut album's "You and I" or "Mary Jane." James managed an effective amalgam of recent R&B big-band styles, from Sly & the Family Stone to Earth, Wind & Fire and Funkadelic, overlaying the result with his jeeringly rendered sex-and-drugs philosophy. What was missing this time was a real pop crossover—if *Come Get It!* had suggested he could have the pop success of Earth, Wind & Fire, *Bustin' Out of L Seven* threatened that his work would find as restricted an audience as Funkadelic, and without the critical cachet.

William Ruhlmann

Street Songs
1981, Motown

Disappointed because *Garden of Love* wasn't as well received as it should have been, Rick James made a triumphant return to defiant, in-your-face funk with the triple-platinum *Street Songs*. This was not only his best-selling album ever, it was also his best period, and certainly the most exciting album released in 1981. The gloves came all the way off this time, and James is as loud and proud as ever on such arresting hits as "Super Freak," "Give It to Me Baby," and "Ghetto Life." Ballads aren't a high priority, but those he does offer (including his stunning duet with Teena Marie, "Fire and Desire") are first-rate. One song that's questionable (to say the least) is the inflammatory "Mr. Policeman," a commentary on police misconduct that condemns law enforcement in general instead of simply indicting those who abuse their authority. But then, the thing that makes this hot-headed diatribe extreme is what makes the album on the whole so arresting—honest, gut-level emotion. James simply follows what's in his gut and lets it rip. Even the world's most casual funksters shouldn't be without this pearl of an album.

Alex Henderson

The J.B.'s

Damn Right I Am Somebody
1974, People

Damn Right I Am Somebody captures the J.B.'s at the apex of their extraordinary powers. This James Brown-produced set is both their most fiercely polemical and their most musically daring, incorporating otherworldly electronic elements, eccentric time and rhythm shifts, and idiosyncratic studio effects to brilliantly articulate the increasing turmoil and insanity of the times. It's quite possibly the most challenging record ever released under the Brown aegis, favoring open-ended grooves and epic solos rooted in avant-jazz. The rhythms remain surgically precise and hypnotically intense, however, and every cut here, from the funk juggernaut "I'm Payin' Taxes, What Am I Buyin'?" to the righteously mellow "Same Beat," is a marvel. This is funk at its heaviest—musically, yes, but intellectually as well.

Jason Ankeny

Funky Good Time: The Anthology
February 1995, Polydor

The J.B.'s recorded under various billings in the early '70s, including the J.B.'s, Fred Wesley & the J.B.'s, Maceo & the Macks, the First Family, the Last Word, and others. This double CD gathers 30 of the prime tracks by all of the above configurations from the first half of the '70s, including all nine of their chart hits and quite a few rare singles and long versions. Often, James Brown himself chips in with incidental vocals (though this is mostly instrumental) and keyboards. The two-and-a-half-hour program can start to sound monotonous if taken all at once, but it's prime, often riveting funk, jammed with lockstep grooves that vary between basic R&B vamps and imaginative, almost jazzy improvisation.

Richie Unterberger

Syl Johnson

Twilight & Twinight (Masters Collection)
August 1996, Collectables

Syl Johnson has enjoyed a long recording career, first on King Records then for Peter Wright's Chi-town setups and stints with Hi, Delmark, and other labels. The Wright sessions, featured here, represent Johnson's finest and best-known tracks, many of which became substantial R&B hits. The Hi tracks are smoother and more majestic, but for raw soul, grits, guts, and conviction, these are the tracks that collectors and aficionados covet. Johnson combined uptown soul with urban blues and stayed on the R&B charts with aggressive numbers like "Come on Sock It to Me," "Different Strokes" (the era's buzz phrase), and "Dresses Too Short." "Concrete Reservation" is a sociopolitical song about the large, brick public housing projects in inner cities that many viewed as confining, without barriers, as the original Indian reservations. He plays the race card as adroitly as a bull walking through a china shop on "Is It Because I'm Black"; the message doesn't have to be explained on this one, Johnson slaps you in the face with it, heavy stuff for the '60s. "I'll Take Those Skinny Legs" is a takeoff of Joe Tex's "Skinny Legs and All," and you must check his gritty version of "Get Ready," which Johnson gives new implications. There are some good love songs too: "Together, Forever" by bass player Bernard Reed, Joshie Armstead's "I Feel an Urge," and the braggadocio "I Can Take Care of Business."

Andrew Hamilton

Grace Jones

Nightclubbing
1981, Island

By all means a phenomenal pop album that hit number nine on the black albums chart and crossed over to penetrate the pop charts at number 32, *Nightclubbing* saw Grace Jones working once again with reggae kings Sly Dunbar and Robbie Shakespeare twisting the knobs. *Nightclubbing* also continues Jones' tradition of picking excellent songs to reinterpret. This time out, the Police's "Demolition Man," Bill Withers' "Use Me," and Iggy Pop's "Nightclubbing" receive radical reinterpretations; "Nightclubbing" is glacial in both tempo and lack of warmth, while both "Use Me" and "Demolition Man" fit perfectly into Jones' lyrical scheme. Speaking of a lyrical scheme, "Pull Up to the Bumper" (number five black singles, number two club play) is so riddled with naughty double entendres—or is it just about parallel parking?—that it renders Musique's "In the Bush" as daring as Paul Anka's "Puppy Love." Drive it in between *what*, Grace? It's not just lyrics that make the song stick out; jingling spirals of rhythm guitar and a simplistic, squelching, mid-tempo rhythm make the song effective, even without considering Jones' presence. Sly & Robbie provide ideal backdrops for Jones yet again, casting a brisk but not bristly sheen over buoyant structures. Never before and never since has a precisely chipped block of ore been so seductive.

Andy Kellman

Eddie Kendricks

People...Hold On
May 1972, Tamla

Albums like this are why best-of and greatest-hits compilations aren't end-alls. One can find lots of good material that for a multitude of reasons never got released as singles, or if it did, went unnoticed as the flips of A-sides. The title track "My People Hold On" is one of Motown's most adventurous recordings with Eddie Kendricks; everything from African drums, a strong social message, and unorthodox backing chants makes the track a winner. Kendricks switches from his natural tenor to falsetto as easily as shifting gears in a Corvette, and no, you won't find it on *The Ultimate Collection*. Club favorite "Girl You Need a Change of Mind" features some wicked rhythms and urgent singing by Kendricks, while "If You Let Me" remains one of Eddie's best vocals; originally recorded by Jimmy Ruffin, Kendricks makes it his and his alone. The seductive slowies "Date With the Rain," "Day by Day," and "Just Memories" are aided by Eddie's sweet, innocent falsetto.

Andrew Hamilton

Kool & the Gang

Wild and Peaceful
September 1973, De Lite

Prior to James "JT" Taylor adding pop flavor vocals, which help garner a handful of top selling albums, this was Kool & the Gang's most successful album, spawning three bonafide R&B hits. Produced by Robert Bell, and featuring Donal Boyce's incredulous vocals, these songs have held up well. The fast, chugging "Jungle Boogie" was a club favorite, while "Funky Stuff," with its "whoa whoa whoa" hook, was slower and spacier than "Jungle Boogie." The band formerly known as the Jazziacs got their first R&B number one with "Hollywood Swinging," a slightly faster than mid-tempo song with whistles, festive ambiance and lead vocals by keyboardist Ricky West. All three hits were inspired by Manu Dibango's "Soul Makossa," and were recorded in one night at a studio in midtown Manhattan. The title cut flash backs to their prerecording jazz days, when they dazzled New Jerseyites with their playing skills.

Andrew Hamilton

Kraftwerk

Trans-Europe Express
1977, Capitol

Although *Autobahn* was a left-field masterpiece, *Trans-Europe Express* is often cited as perhaps the archetypal (and most accessible) Kraftwerk album. Melodic themes are repeated often and occasionally interwoven over deliberate, chugging beats, sometimes with manipulated vocals; the effect is mechanical yet hypnotic. Thematically, the record feels like parts of two different concept albums: one a meditation on the disparities between reality and image ("Hall of Mirrors" and "Showroom Dummies" share recurring images of glass, reflection, illusion, and confused identities, as well as whimsical melodies), and the other the glorification of Europe. There is an impressive composition paying homage to "Franz Schubert," but the real meat of this approach is

contained in the opening love letter, "Europe Endless," and the epic title track, which shares themes and lyrics with the following track, "Metal on Metal." The song "Trans-Europe Express" is similar in concept to "Autobahn," as it mimics the swaying motion and insistent drive of a cross-continent train trip. What ultimately holds the album together, though, is the music, which is more consistently memorable even than that on *Autobahn*. Overall, *Trans-Europe Express* offers the best blend of minimalism, mechanized rhythms, and crafted, catchy melodies in the group's catalog; henceforth, their music would take on more danceable qualities only hinted at here (although the title cut provided the basis for Afrika Bambaataa's enormously important dancefloor smash "Planet Rock").

Steve Huey

Computer World
1981, Warner Bros.

The last great Kraftwerk album, *Computer World* captured the band right at the moment when its pioneering approach fully broke through in popular music, thanks to the rise of synth pop, hip-hop, and electro. As Arthur Baker sampled "Trans-Europe Express" for "Planet Rock" and disciples like Depeche Mode, OMD, and Gary Numan scored major hits, *Computer World* demonstrated that the old masters still had some last tricks up their collective sleeves. Compared to earlier albums, it fell readily in line with *The Man-Machine*, eschewing side-long efforts but with even more of an emphasis on shorter tracks mixed with longer but not epic compositions. While the well-established tropes of the band were used again—electronically treated vocals, some provided by Speak and Spell toys; crisp rhythm blips; basslines and beats; haunting, quirky melodies—there's a ready liveliness to the songs, including the addictive "Pocket Calculator," with its perfectly deadpan portrait of "the operator" and his favorite tool, and the almost winsome "Computer Love." Cannily, the lyrical focus on newly accessible technology instead of cryptic futurism and vanished pasts matched this new of-the-now stance, and the result was a perfect balance between the new world of the album title and a withdrawn, bemused consideration of that world. The title track itself, with its lists detailing major organizations presumably all wired up, echoes the flow of *Trans-Europe Express*, serene and pondering. "Pocket Calculator" itself is more outrageously fun, thanks to the technical observation that "by pressing down a special key it plays a little melody." Others would take the band's advances and run with them, but with *Computer World* Kraftwerk—over a decade on from their start—demonstrated how they had stayed not merely relevant, but prescient, when nearly all their contemporaries had long since burned out.

Ned Raggett

Lafayette Afro Rock Band

Darkest Light: The Best of the Lafayette Afro Rock Band
October 1999, Strut

The name may not be familiar, but the Lafayette Afro Rock Band's grooves certainly are. A veritable sampler's paradise, snippets of their hip-hugger-tight funk have served as the bedrock of innumerable rap records, most notably Public Enemy's "Show 'Em Whatcha Got." *Darkest Light* assembles

15 tracks from the group's mid-'70s heyday, revealing a deep, versatile unit truly justified in adopting such an international name—their music indeed embraces both Afrobeat and Western psychedelia in equal measure, complete with hard-edged guitar riffs, incendiary sax breaks, and blistering rhythms. Although the title track inspired Public Enemy, "Hihache" also features a much-sampled drum intro and the relentless "Conga" later resurfaced on a volume of the *Ultimate Breaks and Beats* series. But to break this music down to its base elements is to do the greater whole a grave disservice—*Darkest Light* merits discussion alongside any of the great documents of classic funk.

Jason Ankeny

The Last Poets

The Last Poets
1970, Douglas

If rap could be traced to one logical source point, this exceptional piece of vinyl would be it, without question. Though the strict adherence to syncopated rhythms and standard song structures are absent, all the elements that would later become the hallmarks of hip-hop by the early 1980s (and predictable fare by the 1990s) are here: vivid depictions of street level violence, vivid apocalyptic predictions of racial genocide. All that is missing are pointless party anthems. But running through all the songs on the Last Poets' debut is an urgent sense of the need for radical action in the nation as well as the black community. In addition to railing against the injustices perpetrated by white America, the Poets' comment on the economic and social devastation of drugs ("Jones Comin' Down," "Two Little Boys"), complacency in urban families ("Wake Up Niggers," "When the Revolution Comes"), the emotional release of sex ("Black Thighs"), and the weight of oppression that leads to hopelessness ("Surprises"). At the same time, they warn of the dangers of half-hearted commitment to revolutionary change: "don't talk about revolution until you are ready to eat rats." In the same manner that Marvin Gaye's landmark album *What's Goin' On* depicted the problems that doomed black culture, the Last Poets are now seen by many as prophets. But also like Gaye, the realization that the problems depicted on *The Last Poets* are now much worse marks the record as an unheeded warning, far more than just a piece of Black Power kitsch.

John Duffy

This Is Madness
1971, Celluloid

A legendary set featuring a group of extremely controversial street poets. The Last Poets used offensive language brilliantly, talked in graphic detail about America's social and racial failures, and helped expose a wider audience to the sentiments of the '70s black nationalists. They were the forerunners of today's Afrocentric rappers, and also showed the way to a jazz/

rap union now being explored on both sides of the Atlantic. This has been reissued on CD.

Ron Wynn

Ronnie Laws

Pressure Sensitive
March–April 1975, Blue Note

Ronnie Laws has always been an R&B-oriented saxophonist miscast in the jazz world, starting with his early association with the rapidly declining Blue Note label. His debut album (reissued on CD) has a couple of decent melodies (the opening "Always There" is the most memorable), some soulful tenor and soprano playing by the leader in a style heavily influenced by Grover Washington, Jr., and vocals on only one of the eight selections; Laws's attempts to make it as a singer were still in the future. However, this obviously commercial effort (every song fades out before it hits the five-minute mark) can only be recommended in comparison to Ronnie Laws's later more inferior recordings.

Scott Yanow

Ramsey Lewis

Upendo Ni Pamoja
January 1972, Collectables

This marked Ramsey Lewis' third album for Columbia and the first to feature the Ramsey Lewis Trio. The most famous members had gone on to other successes. Red Holt and Eldee Young were signed to Atlantic as Young-Holt Unlimited, and of course later member Maurice White founded Earth, Wind and Fire. *Upendo Ni Pamoja* has the rhythm section of bassist Cleveland Eaton and drummer Morris Jennings. Unlike many early '70s sets, *Upendo Ni Pamoja* is a pretty straight-ahead date without Lewis indulging in tracks with funky overtones. Covers predominate here. The trio does a fairly true though subdued take on War's "Slippin' into Darkness" with Lewis on Fender Rhodes. Lewis' gentle playing is found throughout "People Make the World Go Round," although this version of the trio did an even better live take on the *Save the Children* soundtrack. The best cover, Michael Jackson's "Got to Be There," has Lewis playing a Steinway Concert Grand with an arrangement that spotlights the trio sound. The smooth title is one of Lewis' finest songs of the period. The problem with this is that few tracks stay with the listener. This is a cut or two away from being truly essential.

Jason Elias

Liquid Liquid

Liquid Liquid
August 1997, Mo' Wax

The angular, bass-propelled funk grooves of Liquid Liquid laid the groundwork for post-rock bands like Tortoise and Ui more than a decade before the fact—stripped of all excess and artifice, their hypnotically dub-like sound offered a starkly minimalist counterpoint to the prevailingly lush production of the concurrent disco movement, in the process impacting the development of everything from hip-hop to drum'n'bass. This superbly packaged, 18-track retrospective collects the sum of Liquid Liquid's official output, recorded between 1981 and 1983, and all things considered, it's remarkable just how prescient and modern the group's music really was. Although only the standout, "Cavern" (the basis for the Grandmaster Flash rap classic "White Lines"), is even remotely familiar in any strict sense, the remaining material, with its thickly fluid basslines and circular rhythms, will undoubtedly strike a chord of recognition in anyone versed in the sonic motifs of post-rock and electronica. Ui's Sasha Frere-Jones is thanked on the sleeve, but in truth he's the one owing the debt—for all intents and purposes, post-rock (and a whole lot more) starts here.

Jason Ankeny

Love Unlimited Orchestra

The Best of the Love Unlimited Orchestra
1995, Mercury

The Best of the Love Unlimited Orchestra collects 15 tracks by Barry White's groundbreaking instrumental support outfit. Their sound as assembled by White—thick layers of sweet strings, pulsing beats, chunky wah-wah guitars, plus tinkling piano and gently swelling horns—played a huge role in creating the blueprint for disco, not to mention countless porn soundtracks. In addition to backing White and his female protégées Love Unlimited, the Love Unlimited Orchestra also made their own recordings, naturally with White at the helm. Although they recorded up to 1983, their commercial heyday lasted from 1974–1977, when they charted regularly on the pop, R&B, and disco/club listings. They even scored a number one pop hit right out of the box with 1974's "Love's Theme," a watershed record in the history of disco. That's here, of course, plus the Orchestra's other chart hits: "Satin Soul," "Rhapsody in White," "Forever in Love," "My Sweet Summer Suite," "Bring It on Up," and their theme from the 1977 remake of *King Kong*. It's superbly evocative mood music, pretty much the instrumental equivalent of Barry White's trademark love-man come-ons. Anyone enamored of White's sound, or curious about the evolution of disco, would do well to pick this up.

Steve Huey

Cheryl Lynn

Cheryl Lynn
1978, Columbia

Ex-*Gong Show* contestant Cheryl Lynn hit paydirt with her self-titled debut album for Columbia. "Got to Be Real," one of those unavoidable disco-era hits—thanks to its instantly memorable bassline and Lynn's alternately soaring and barely contained giddiness—is one of the few singles of its level of success (number one black singles, number 11 club play, number 12 pop) to decrease in value with over-saturation. Thanks to that song and the multi-tiered "Star Love," *Cheryl Lynn* reached number five on the black albums chart and provided the artist with her time in the spotlight. It's easily her best full-length, full of solid album cuts that act as support for the key singles rather than attempting to match them or even duplicate them with forced hooks and bungled attempts at making a diverse listen. In fact, "You Saved My Day" is just as great as the hits and could've been bigger with the right support—nevertheless, it was a favorite of DJ Frankie Knuckles while he was at Chicago's infamous *Warehouse*. A strong debut that benefits from assured ease.

Andy Kellman

Galt MacDermot

Woman Is Sweeter/Shapes of Rhythm
June 2001, Kilmarnock

Remember the musical *Hair*? Remember the groovy rhythm tracks on "Let the Sunshine In" and "Where Do I Go?" Yeah, well, this guy here, Galt MacDermot, expatriate Canadian funk meister, is the cat who composed those jams—and in fact the music to the entire play. This CD brings together two of MacDermot's original LPs, both of them released in the '60s—one pre- and one post-*Hair*, one a session album and one a soundtrack, and both greasy in the future funk with cats like Idris Muhammad and Bernard Purdie laying down the beats behind the band. MacDermot is a driven pianist and organ grinder who sought one thing on these records: funky grooves. And he got them. Here's what's scary though: "Coffee Cold" (from *Shapes of Rhythm*) was recorded in 1966—prefiguring the rhythmic changes of James Brown's "Cold Sweat" in sequence and in key a full two years before Brown laid down his track. The feel of "Coffee Cold" is a bit whiter and smoother, but the jam is still an anthem, even with its cheese factor. MacDermot was a prophet of the groove that would overtake the late '60s and early '70s, and, were he a proud man, could have argued that more young musicians heard and took to heart the grooves he laid down in *Hair* than heard Allen Toussaint and Red Allen or Eddie Bo. The true feel of *Shapes of Rhythm* is like *Vince Guaraldi*'s Schroeder laying out the piano funk, seeking the groove inside the rhythm section and laying it out there. It's tough if ornate and it shimmers with real heat. The other disc, a soundtrack for Martine Barrat's movie *Woman Is Sweeter*, is a much dirtier, rawer affair altogether, and would have been worth the price of the CD alone. Here guitars chunk up in the cut with the bass, and the piano floats in the accents as drums and bass reign supreme. This was recorded immediately after *Hair*, and MacDermot wasn't in the mood to simply lay out some incidental music to a hippie flick. He took it down to its essence: rhythm, polyrhythm, drums, bass, and filthy nasty funk at insanely fast—for the time—tempos that were in fact symbolic of the orgiastic nature of his compositions. This wasn't just sex music, this was group sex symphonic music made with only a handful of instruments. These two albums comprise 26 tracks of pure groove-driven genius, with a bonus vocal version of "Coffee Cold" that the producers go hog-wild over in their notes, but it pretty much sucks compared to the rest of this—thank the gods they left it until the end. Yeah, you need this if you care about the influence of '60s groove at all. After all, Busta Rhymes did—check out the sample of MacDermot's "Space" on the rapper's "Woo-Hah!! Got You All in Check."

Thom Jurek

The Main Ingredient

Euphrates River
1974, RCA

While nothing soared as high as "Everybody Plays a Fool" from the *Bitter Sweet* LP, *Euphrates River* is tighter and has more zap than the previous year's beautiful but hitless *Afrodisiac*. They nailed Seals & Croft's "Summer Breeze"—the New Yorkers almost surpassed the Isley Brothers' soulful version. Cuba Gooding sings the upbeat and funky "California My Way" from the heart (the soul singer moved his family to L.A.—the only Main Ingredient to do so). The trio gives Stevie Wonder's "Don't You Worry About a Thing" all they can muster; this is an excellent rendition that should have done better on the charts. Their version of "Just Don't Want to Be Lonely" helped sell this LP; it was previously done by Blue Magic and Ronnie Dyson, but the Main Ingredient's version reigns supreme. Rolling, mid-tempo beaters make up the bulk of the tunes with "Euphrates" and "Happiness Is Just Around the Bend" as prime examples.

Andrew Hamilton

Mandrill

Just Outside of Town
1973, Collectables

It lacked the delicious hooks and tight funk of *Composite Truth*, but *Just Outside of Town* was as solid and confident a piece of music-making as the band ever accomplished. The single "Mango Meat" is a tough Latin funk number with some inspired group harmonizing, and Mandrill stretched out with a pair of love songs, "Never Die" and the aptly titled "Love Song," the latter beginning with a few minutes of atmospheric bliss that boasted unrealized cinematic/soundtrack possibilities. "Fat City Strut" moves back and forth between blasts of brass-powered funk and the sweet seduction of Latin percussion and a vibes solo. The distorted funk monster "Two Sisters of Mystery" is another classic, one that later enticed producer Gary G-Wiz to sample it for Public Enemy's "By the Time I Get to Arizona." The last two songs were very uncharacteristic for Mandrill, one a bluesy/country song with a pop gloss, the other an ambling instrumental led by an acoustic guitar and including a few out-of-place synthesizer shadings. It certainly wasn't Mandrill going out on top (for an album, or for its period at Polydor), but it certainly summed up the promise of one of funk's most courageous bands.

John Bush

Curtis Mayfield

Curtis
September 1970, Rhino

The first solo album by the former leader of the Impressions, *Curtis* represented a musical apotheosis for Curtis Mayfield—indeed, it was practically the "*Sgt. Pepper's*" album of '70s soul, helping with its content and its success to open the whole genre to much bigger, richer musical canvases than artists had previously worked with. All of Mayfield's years of experience of life, music, and people were pulled together into a rich, powerful, topical musical statement that reflected not only the most up-to-date soul sounds of its period, finely produced by Mayfield himself, and the immediacy of the times and their political and social concerns, but also embraced the most elegant R&B sounds out of the past. As a producer, Mayfield embraced the most progressive soul sounds of the era, stretching them out compellingly on numbers like "Move on Up," but also drew on orchestral sounds (especially harps), to achieve some striking musical timbres (check out "Wild and Free"), and wove all of these influences, plus the topical nature of the songs, into a neat, amazingly lean whole. There was only one hit single off of this record, "(Don't Worry) If There's a Hell Down Below We're All Going to Go," which made number three, but the album as a whole was a single entity and really had to be heard that way. In the fall of 2000, Rhino Records reissued *Curtis* with upgraded sound and nine bonus tracks that extended its running time to over 70 minutes. All but one are demos, including "Miss Black America" and "The Making of You," but mostly consist of tracks that he completed for subsequent albums; they're fascinating to hear, representing very different, much more jagged and stripped-down sounds. The upgraded CD concludes with the single version of "(Don't Worry) If There's a Hell Below We're All Going to Go."

Bruce Eder

Roots
1971, Rhino

Curtis Mayfield's visionary album, a landmark creation every bit as compelling and as far-reaching in its musical and extra-musical goals as Marvin Gaye's contemporary *What's Goin' On*. Opening on the hit "Get Down," the album soars on some of the sweetest and most eloquent—yet driving—soul sounds heard up to that time. Mayfield's growing musical ambitions, first manifested on the *Curtis* album, and his more sophisticated political sensibilities, presented with a lot of raw power on *Curtis Live!*, are pulled together here in a new, richer studio language, embodied in extended song structures ("Underground"), idealistic yet lyrically dazzling anthems ("We Got to Have Peace," "Keep On Keeping On," and, best of all, the soaring "Beautiful Brother of Mine"), and impassioned blues ("Now You're Gone"). The music is even bolder than the material on the *Curtis* album, with Mayfield expanding his instrumental range to the level of a veritable soul orchestra; and the recording is better realized, as Mayfield, with that album and a tour behind him, shows a degree of confidence that only a handful of soul artists of this era could have mustered. Charly Records had this album out on CD in the 1980s, but Rhino's acquisition of the Curtom catalog in 1996 led to a remastered and expanded reissue in 1999 with superior sound, detailed annotation, and the addition of four bonus tracks. Apart from a slow, funky, stripped-down but eminently listenable demo of "Underground" (which reveals just how sophisticated Mayfield's conceptions—forget the finished versions—of his songs were), the latter consist of the single edits of "Get Down," "We Got to Have Peace," and "Beautiful Brother of Mine." They seem redundant after the album versions, though they don't detract at all from the extraordinary value of this mid-priced CD.

Bruce Eder

Superfly
July 1972, Curtom

The choice of Curtis Mayfield to score the blaxploitation film *Superfly* was an inspired one. No other artist in popular music knew so well, and expressed through his music so naturally, the shades of gray inherent in contemporary inner-city life. His  debut solo album, 1970's *Curtis*, had shown in vivid colors that the '60s optimist (author of the civil-rights anthems "Keep On Pushing" and "People Get Ready") had added a layer of subtlety to his material; appearing on the same LP as the positive and issue-oriented "Move On Up" was an apocalyptic piece of brimstone funk titled "(Don't Worry) If There's a Hell Below, We're All Going to Go." For *Superfly*, Mayfield wisely avoids celebrating the wheeling-and-dealing themes present in the movie, or exploiting them, instead using each song to focus on a different aspect of what he saw as a plague on America's streets. He also steers away from explicit moralizing; through his songs, Mayfield simply tells it like it is (for the characters in the film as in real life), with any lessons learned the result of his vibrant storytelling and knack of getting inside the heads of the characters. "Freddie's Dead," one of the album's signature pieces, tells the story of one of the film's main casualties, a good-hearted yet weak-willed man caught up in the life of a pusher, and devastatingly portrays the indifference of those who witness or hear about it. "Pusherman" masterfully uses the metaphor of drug dealer as businessman, with the drug game, by extension, just another way to make a living in a tough situation, while the title track equates hustling with gambling ("The game he plays he plays for keeps/hustlin' times and ghetto streets/tryin' ta get over"). Ironically, the sound of *Superfly* positively overwhelmed its lyrical finesse. A melange of deep, dark grooves, trademarked wah-wah guitar, and stinging brass, *Superfly* ignited an entire genre of music, the blaxploitation soundtrack, and influenced everyone from soul singers to television-music composers for decades to come. It stands alongside *Saturday Night Fever* and *Never Mind the Bollocks Here's the Sex Pistols* as one of the most vivid touchstones of '70s pop music.

John Bush

Maze

Anthology
January 1996, Capitol

Maze have been a fan favorite since the mid-'70s; while they've received little critical notice or adulation except among soul and R&B scribes, Maze have seldom been out of the charts since making their debut on Capitol. Lead singer Frankie Beverly's roots extend back to classic doo wop and

East Coast soul; although he made the transition to funk, then urban material, Beverly always had plenty of soul and passion in his vocals. Maze also blazed their own musical trail; when such competitors as Earth, Wind & Fire, the Bar-Kays, Con Funk Shun, and Slave were featuring surging horn sections and jazz-tinged arrangements with heavy basslines, Beverly and company favored rock-influenced guitar parts juxtaposed against soulful organ riffs or synthesizer riffs and just a trace of reggae and/or Latin rhythm. Beverly enjoyed several hits on Capitol, but became unsatisfied with the label's inability to break the group beyond the R&B/funk market. They departed Capitol in the late '80s, and resurfaced on Warner Bros., where they continued making strong, distinctive releases. *Anthology* gathers the best (at least most of the best) singles the band did for Capitol, among them classics like "Southern Girl," "Before I Let Go," the complete "Joy and Pain," and "Happy Feelin's." British journalist David Nathan's notes are comprehensive, and nicely combine anecdotal and discographical references.

Ron Wynn

Les McCann

Talk to the People
May 1972, Atlantic

While *Invitation to Openness* was Les McCann's progressive statement of 1972, this was his populist sermon, with a title to match. With four vocals among the seven tracks, *Talk to the People* preaches earthily in the funky soul/jazz and R&B languages of the time, with some social comment besides. Having gone completely over to the Rhodes electric piano and Hohner clavinet, McCann became a fervent convert—indeed, he and Stevie Wonder were the funky-butt champs of the clavinet in the 1970s—and he could beat on them with the rhythmic snap of a conga drummer. "Shamading" may be the funkiest, hip-shaking thing Les has ever recorded; the cool, swaggering funkathon "North Carolina" runs a close second; and the best of the vocals is a very gritty and convincing treatment of Marvin Gaye's "What's Going On." Although there are some weak links in this chain of tunes, the highs are sky-high, and they represent some of Les' peak studio performances.

Richard S. Ginell

Gwen McCrae

Rockin' Chair
1975, Collectables

This album marked the long-playing debut of Gwen McCrae, a sultry voiced singer who remains popular with soul music cultists today. *Rockin' Chair* collects the material that she had been recording for the Cat label, a subsidiary of disco giant TK Records. Despite the fact that it was not technically conceived as an album, all the material on *Rockin' Chair* hangs together nicely: everything here was produced by Miami soul stalwart Steve Alaimo, who strikes an effective balance between silky soul and gospel-tinged funk on all the tracks. The obvious standout is the title tune, a mid-paced invitation to romance that frames McCrae's seductive vocal with stately horns and churning, infectious percussion. The end result is downright hypnotic and it deservedly became a massive hit on both the R&B and pop charts during 1975.

None of the remaining tracks are as instantly infectious as the title hit, but they all make for fine listening: "Move Me Baby" is a gently-loping funk jam built on some silky keyboard riffs, and "Your Love Is Worse Than a Cold Love" is a convincing declaration of frustrated passion that gets a gutsy, gospel-tinged treatment from McCrae. Trivia fans will also want to take note that Harry Casey of KC and the Sunshine Band lent a hand on the production of "Move Me Baby." However, the album's unsung gem is "90% Of Me Is You": this hypnotic tune is a grand showcase for McCrae's emotive skills, allowing her to unfold a tale of emotional enslavement over a sleek backing track that balances yearning strings with a moody funk groove. All in all, *Rockin' Chair* is an exciting collection that will appeal to any fans of 1970s soul.

Donald A. Guarisco

Gene McDaniels

Headless Heroes of the Apocalypse
1971, Label M

When *Headless Heroes of the Apocalypse* was first released in 1971, so the legend goes, Spiro Agnew himself called Atlantic Records to complain about the album's incendiary lyrics. Promotional efforts dried up, and since then, the album has become one of the great rare gems of the funk era. With this first-ever CD release from Label M, it is available again in all its strange, eclectic glory. McDaniels had earned his living as a producer and songwriter for artists like Roberta Flack and Gladys Knight, and was in all honesty not much of a singer, but somehow his clumsy lyrics and dry delivery combined to carry his message across. In an unthreatening manner that hardly warranted a call from the White House, McDaniels warns that man's struggles against each other are pointless, as some dark sinister force controls us all ("Headless Heroes"), and that protest without action is futile ("no amount of dancing is going to make us free," he sings in "Freedom Death Dance"). With a dry wit he recounts an episode of everyday racist brutality in "Supermarket Blues," and finds simple carnal pleasures in the acoustic folk-flavored "Susan Jane." It all gets wrapped up in an appealing stew that draws from rock, funk, folk, soul, and even free jazz. Considering the number of times McDaniels' sinewy beats and chunky guitar riffs have been sampled over the years, it's about time a proper re-release allowed listeners to hear the whole picture.

John Duffy

Jack McDuff

Moon Rappin'
December 1969, Blue Note

Moon Rappin' is one of Brother Jack McDuff's most ambitious efforts, a loose concept album that finds the organist exploring funky and spacy soundscapes. Unlike most McDuff records, there isn't a steady groove that flows throughout the record—the album flies into atmospheric territory that isn't strictly soul-jazz, but it's far from free. In many ways, *Moon Rappin'* is a fairly typical album of its time, boasting wah-wah guitars, flutes, spacious reverb, long bluesy vamps, orchestras, and disembodied backing vocals, but it also stands out from the pack in how it offers some excellent improvisation (including a rare piano spotlight on the title track) and unpredictable moments, like the stuttering organ and nearly

free interludes on "Made in Sweden." It's not strictly funky—it doesn't have the grit of early Brother Jack records, nor does it swing hard—but it proves that McDuff was as adept in adventurous territory as he was with the groove.

Stephen Thomas Erlewine

Jimmy McGriff

Soul Sugar
1971, Capitol

The Sonny Lester-produced *Soul Sugar* looms large in Jimmy McGriff's vast catalog—while it's a fool's errand to pick the organist's absolute funkiest recording, this one demands serious consideration. Without personnel credits, it's impossible to know who's backing McGriff here, but the rhythm section is nonetheless superb—cuts like "Dig on It" (later sampled by A Tribe Called Quest), "Fat Cakes," and "The Now Thing" rival the Meters for sheer soulfulness. The covers are no less impressive—while renditions of James Brown's "Ain't It Funky Now," Stevie Wonder's "Signed, Sealed, Delivered," and Aretha Franklin's "Spirit in the Dark" remain true to the spirit of the original recordings, the ingenious arrangements also allow McGriff and his band panoramic stretches of space to explore.

Jason Ankeny

Groove Grease
November 1971, Groove Merchant

This 1971 session finds McGriff continuing to do like so many other jazz musicians of the time: embrace and adapt to the emergence of funk and soul into mainstream music, and recontextualize it in a jazz arena. The results are an unsurprisingly delicious slice of jazz-funk made from the finest ingredients. The superb playing of Richard Davis on electric bass is unquestionably the anchor throughout the album's nine slices, leaving McGriff and company to follow suit with loose (but not too far out) improvisation that's as equally relaxing as it is invigorating. While McGriff's adventurous side is slightly tamed, it's that willingness to improv and blend together as a cohesive unit that makes *Groove Grease* such a tasty statement that is consistently fresh with repeated listenings.

Rob Theakston

Harold Melvin

Wake Up Everybody
1975, Philadelphia International

Even though Harold Melvin & the Blue Notes were an R&B group with much soul, the message in their music was truly profound, uplifting, thought provoking, and full of love. This album featured only two singles. The title track is a plea to the world to come together and rid the society of all its ills. Written by the prolific writing team of McFadden/Whitehead/Carstarphen, it conveys a message in line with the ideology of the album's producers. The connection felt when listening to the song permeates the soul, and will momentarily produce thoughts in one to make a change. This is a very moving song. It held on to the number one spot on the *Billboard* R&B charts for two consecutive weeks. The aggressive arrangement of "Tell the World How I Feel About 'Cha Baby" carried it to number seven on the charts. Other notables are "Keep on Lovin' You," "To Be Free to Be Who We Are," and "I'm Searching for a Love." Sharon Paige is featured on the balladic flow of the latter. "Don't Leave Me This Way" became a disco theme for Thelma Houston. This album was the final chapter of Harold Melvin & the Blue Notes featuring Theodore Pendergrass, who released a solo album the following year.

Craig Lytle

The Meters

The Meters
1969, Sundazed

This seminal New Orleans funk group's debut album features the semi-hit "Cissy Strut" and its follow-up, "Sophisticated Sissy." This 1999 reissue also offers two previously unreleased bonus tracks, "The Look of Love" and "Soul Machine." Other highlights include "Here Comes the Meter Man," "Live Wire," and "Sehorn's Farm."

Cub Koda

Look-Ka Py Py
January 1970, Josie

The second album by Art Neville's band continues the sound that made them New Orleans legends. In addition to the title track, there's plenty of funk aboard in songs like "Pungee," "9 'Til 5," "Rigor Mortis," "Funky Miracle," and "Yeah, You're Right." This 1999 reissue also features two previously unreleased bonus tracks, "Grass" and "Borro."

Cub Koda

Struttin'
1970, Sundazed

As the third full-length album released by the Meters, *Struttin'* may not appear to be drastically different than its predecessors, at least not on the surface. After all, the title of the lead single "Chicken Strut" intentionally recalls their previous biggest "Cissy Strut," and it has the same basic Meters groove. And if the essential sound remains unchanged, that's because that organic, earthy funk is the Meters' signature. Other groups have tried to replicate it, but nobody ever played it better. Because of that, *Struttin'* is an enjoyable record, even if it never quite feels like anything more focused than a series of jam sessions; after all, that's what it was. This time around, however, the Meters did make a conscious decision to emphasize vocals, and not just with shout-alongs on the chorus ("Chicken Strut," "Same Old Thing"), but with Art Neville's leads on covers of Ty Hunter's soulful uptown shuffle "Darling, Darling, Darling," Jimmy Webb's groovy ballad "Wichita Lineman," and Lee Dorsey's "Ride Your Pony" (the Meters provided support on the original recording). This gives the album a bit more diversity than its predecessors, which is welcome, even for devotees of the group's admittedly addictive sound. But the real difference is how the band seems willing to expand their signature sound. "Hand

Clapping Song" is a spare, syncopated breakdown without an obvious through-line, while "Joog" turns the group's groove inside out. These variations are entertaining—as entertaining as the vocals—and the songs that are solidly in the Meters tradition are also fun. The results are pretty terrific, though given the fact that *Struttin'* never really pulls itself into a coherent album, it may be the kind of first-rate record only aficionados of the band will need to seek out.

Stephen Thomas Erlewine

Funkify Your Life: The Meters Anthology
February 1995, Rhino

Rhino's *Funkify Your Life: The Meters Anthology* was the first truly comprehensive and widely available CD retrospective of the groundbreaking New Orleans funk band's work. These two chronologically arranged discs run down virtually every important track the band recorded under its own name, finally allowing a more general audience to hear why the Meters had earned such a stellar reputation among die-hard funk collectors and sample-minded hip-hoppers. Disc one, subtitled "The Josie Years," traces the group's 1969–1971 beginnings as a Booker T. & the MG's-like outfit, cutting brief instrumentals with a similar guitar/organ/bass/drums lineup. There were important differences, though; the Meters' arrangements usually carried the melody in single-note guitar lines, which gave them a distinctive calling card, and their rhythms were notably funkier. In fact, drummer Joseph "Ziggy" Modeliste pretty much establishes himself as a monster groove machine right from the beginning; his is a dominating rhythmic presence. This is the lean, earthy Meters sound most often imitated by latter-day funk revivalists like the Soul Fire label. Group vocals and wah-wah guitars start to pop up over the second half of the disc, setting the stage for their more ambitious major-label sound, which is documented on the second disc ("The Reprise/Warner Bros. Years"). Nearly all of these tracks are vocal numbers, "songs" in the more traditional sense, but the group also opens its sound up, allowing the members to show off their individual chops as soloists. There's more flash in this music, including plenty of nimble-fingered unison passages demonstrating that the band can be as tight as they are loose. It's more proof that the Meters were the most telepathic funk ensemble this side of the J.B.'s. Those with a casual interest can safely content themselves with the fine single-disc *Very Best of the Meters*, but for devoted funk fans, *Funkify Your Life* should be considered essential listening.

Steve Huey

The Mizell Brothers

Mizell
September 2005, Blue Note

Any jazz purist who hovered over record bins during the '70s knows to stay away from this, as one quick glance is likely to trigger flashbacks of feeling like a vampire shoved into daylight. Some background info: Fonce Mizell established his do-it-all studio career as part of the Corporation, a Motown team that worked for the Jackson 5, Martha Reeves & the Vandellas, and Edwin Starr. His brother Larry, who had recorded with him prior to the Motown gig, began working with him again—as Sky High Productions—on Donald Byrd's sharp left turn into funk, *Black Byrd*. In addition to inciting howls from purists, the session ignited Fonce and Larry's professional partnership and established their specific sound. Intricately arranged and often incorporating strings and state-of-the-art keyboards and synthesizers, their productions were supremely vibrant, funky, *and* slick, fusing dancefloor-friendly R&B and jazz to the point where there were no visible seams. Bobbi Humphrey, Gary Bartz, Rance Allen, and especially Byrd (a remarkable five-album run) all benefited from their genre-bending Blue Note sessions with the Mizells, showcased on this 11-track anthology. There's no point in singling anything out. Each track is filled with rich melodies, complex-elegant rhythms, and lush textures. Whether on a crowded dancefloor or driving with your partner on a summer evening just before sunset, everything translates. The two previously unreleased tracks—Bartz's blistering "Funked Up," featuring vocals from Syreeta, and the dynamite "N R Time," recorded during Humphrey's *Satin Doll* sessions (albeit without the flutist)—should seal the deal for collectors. As thoroughly enjoyable and representative as this disc is, it's somewhat arbitrary. Blame the Mizells for their quality control, not the people who put the set together. *Sky High*, a just-as-valuable 1998 set released in Europe, is concrete evidence of this fact, containing only two of the same selections. It reaches beyond the brothers' Blue Note work (a couple Johnny Hammond cuts, A Taste of Honey's "Boogie Oogie Oogie") and puts a different spin on their sessions with Allen, Bartz, Byrd, and Humphrey. Both sets still leave much to explore, including but in no way limited to Johnny Hammond's *Gears* and *Gambler's Life* (which are just as compulsory as the Byrd albums), Roger Glenn's *Reachin'*, and L.T.D.'s *Love to the World*.

Andy Kellman

The Moments

Those Sexy Moments
1974, Stang

Throughout the late '60s to the late '70s, the Moments were one of the premier and loved groups in R&B. Tracks like "Love on a Two Way Street" and "What's Your Name" may be preferred to other songs from more successful acts of the time. This 1974 album finds the group successfully changing with the times and exuding more confidence with their production and singing. That's the good news. The bad news is that the Moments were signed to a small label with one of the worst studios in the business. That fact makes most of this skilled but not sonically sound. That being said, *Those Sexy Moments* is a good mix of dance tracks and the ballads they were famous for. The breezy, "You've Come a Long Way" tells the tale of childhood through adulthood romance as Harry Ray sings the potentially unsettling "I wanted you then/but you were only five." The slow songs, "How Can I Love You" and "Look at Me" (not to be confused with their hit, "Look at Me (I'm in Love)"), both employ the guitar as sitar trick and have the groups' trademark harmonies. The best songs here are basically solo spots for Ray. The big hit here, the steamy "Sexy Mama," has him singing great lines

like, "This afternoon I know you like me/By tonight you're gonna love me." The innovative and melodic "Next Time That I See You" puts the spotlight on his underrated falsetto/tenor. For a group that never seemed to make undeniable albums, this effort has enough individual songs to make this worth looking for.

Jason Elias

Mtume

Juicy Fruit
1983, Epic

James Mtume's band Mtume hit its commercial and creative peak in 1983, when *Juicy Fruit* was released. The infectious, mildly risqué title song—which contains the controversial lyrics "I'll be your lollipop/ You can lick me everywhere"—

soared to number one on *Billboard*'s R&B singles chart and ended up being sampled by quite a few hip-hoppers, including the late Notorious B.I.G., aka Biggie Smalls (who used the infectious gem on his 1994 hit "Juicy"). Some of the people who heard the "Juicy Fruit" single on the radio back in 1983 bought the single but not the album, which was a mistake because the other tracks are also excellent. In fact, many of Mtume's hardcore fans agree that *Juicy Fruit* is the band's most essential album. This LP came at a time when funk was becoming increasingly technology-minded. Horn-driven funk bands were going out of style, and funksters were using a lot more keyboards and synthesizers. *Juicy Fruit* reflects that evolution; although not totally electronic, funk/ urban pearls like "Hips" and "Ready for Your Love" are very keyboard-minded. Only one horn player is employed on this release: jazz saxophonist Gary Bartz, who did his share of R&B sessions in the late '70s and early '80s but eventually returned to being a full-time jazz improviser. Throughout *Juicy Fruit*, James Mtume takes a very hands-on approach—in addition to producing the album and co-writing much of the material, he plays keyboards and provides some of the lead vocals (along with the expressive, big-voiced Tawatha Agee). *Juicy Fruit* isn't the only worthwhile album that James Mtume's band came out with in the 1980s; as a rule, his 1980s output was solid. But if you must limit yourself to one Mtume release, *Juicy Fruit* would be the best choice.

Alex Henderson

New Birth

Birth Day
1973, RCA

Under the banner The New Birth, from which they would later drop "the", this was the first album from the self-contained band; they came charging out of the starting gate with the gritty track "I Can Understand It." With vocals comparable to Bobby Womack, who also penned the number for himself, Leslie Wilson stepped into the lyric with total conviction. His vibrancy is augmented by a funky backing track, primarily a rumbling bass and soulful backing vocals. The single peaked at number four on the *Billboard* R&B charts after 12 weeks. The follow-up release was "Until It's Time for You to Go." Far from its predecessor, its arrangement is geared more toward a crossover audience, as it was previously a #40 hit for Elvis Presley in 1972. It peaked at #21 inside of ten weeks on the R&B charts for the New Birth. Nothing else made any chart noise from this album, but that does not represent the quality of this project. "Got to Get a Knutt" has a rather racy title, and rightly so. But the song takes on different themes within its mostly musical journey, including animated remarks taken from commercial jingles, riddles and the like. In addition to the urban-flavored "Theme from Buck & the Preacher" included on this album, the group gives its own rendition of the classic "Stop, Look, Listen (To Your Heart)," which does not live up to the original by the Stylistics and is the only marginal track.

Craig Lytle

The Ohio Players

Pain
1971, Westbound

Creatively, commercially, and conceptually, *Pain* was a major step forward for the Ohio Players. This 1971 album was quite a departure from their previous work—in the late '60s, the Midwesterners' forte had been raw, hard-edged Southern-style soul along the lines of Sam & Dave, Rufus Thomas, and Wilson Picket. But with *Pain*, they became a lot more experimental and unveiled an interesting, distinctive brand of funk that incorporated elements of jazz and blues as well as rock. The jazz influence is especially strong on "Never Had a Dream," "Singing in the Morning," and the hit title song, while "The Reds" is a progressive blues number that draws on jazz as well as psychedelic rock. It was with *Pain*, the Players' first album for Westbound, that they unveiled their goofy Granny character, which the funksters continued to have fun with on their subsequent Westbound releases but discontinued when they moved to Mercury with 1974's *Skin Tight*. And it was with *Pain* that they became famous (some would say infamous) for their erotic LP covers. Employing S&M/bondage imagery, *Pain*'s front cover was considered shocking in 1971. Although the Velvet Underground had written songs about S&M, and the British spy thriller *The Avengers* frequently hinted at kinky sex—Diana Rigg's Emma Peel character often dressed like a dominatrix—S&M and fetishism were very taboo subjects for Middle America in 1971. And not surprisingly, some retailers refused to carry *Pain*. But the album, although not huge, was a decent seller. With *Pain*,

the Ohio Players' Westbound period was off to an impressive and creative start.

Alex Henderson

Pleasure
1972, Westbound

When the Ohio Players recorded their second Westbound album, *Pleasure*, in 1972, they weren't as big as they would be from 1974–1976. But their popularity was growing—slowly but surely—and those who were hip to the band recognized it as one of the most cutting-edge acts in the funk field. A lot of bands were providing funk in 1972, but not many of them used jazz progressions as creatively as the Players use them on "Laid It," "Walked Away From You," and *Pleasure*'s title song. Those tracks are gems, and the Players are equally captivating on the sweet soul ballad "Varee Is Love." But the best known tune on the album is the goofy "Funky Worm," which employed the Players' amusing Granny character and was, in 1972, their biggest hit to date. Long after the band's popularity faded, "Funky Worm" would live on in the 1980s and 1990s thanks to the various hip-hoppers who sampled its irresistible bassline. Like *Pain* in 1971, *Pleasure* had a kinky cover that generated some controversy—the same bald woman who brandished a bullwhip and wore dominatrix attire on the front cover of *Pain* was chained up on the cover of *Pleasure*. Some folks found the Players' kinky LP covers intriguing, while others were shocked and offended. And the Players, having struggled in the 1960s, were happy to be noticed. But ultimately, it is the quality of the music—not the bondage-minded cover—that makes *Pleasure* a funk classic.

Alex Henderson

Funk on Fire: The Mercury Anthology
June 1995, Mercury

One hour, 54 minutes, and 12 seconds of innovative funk on two discs is nothing to sneeze at, particularly when the tracks are prime Ohio Players cuts. Mercury adroitly chronicles their chart-blazing career with full-length, unedited versions of winners and album treats. From the bluesy, strutting "Jive Turkey" to "More Than Love," the group displays its superb musicianship and ingenuity on 28 slabs of funk and soul. The guys proved they can slow jam with anyone on "Together" and the super-lush "Honey." The Ohio Players were affectionately known as Sugarfoot, Billy, Pee Wee, Merv, Diamond, Rock, and Satch, all of whom contributed collectively in the writing and production of all the songs. Everyone is familiar with the hits, and most of their fans already have them; it's the unsung pearl like "Good Luck Charm" that makes *Funk on Fire* a must—along with the convenience of having all these smokin' grooves in one sweet package.

Andrew Hamilton

Orgasm: The Very Best of the Westbound Years
June 1998, Westbound

The majority of music fans are familiar with the legendary Ohio Players through such mid-to-late '70s pop-funk hits as "Love Rollercoaster," "Fire," and "Fopp." What many don't realize is that the band had been around since the '60s, and released a trilogy of hard funk records from 1972–1973 on the Westbound label—*Pain*, *Pleasure*, and *Ecstasy*—that were easily comparable to the early '70s classics by their rival Westbound labelmates, Funkadelic. And since the albums have been out-of-print for some time, the European import *Orgasm: The Very Best of the Westbound Years* is a solid collection of tracks from this era. Included is the 1972 novelty hit "Funky Worm," as well as all the sizzling title tracks from the three albums. A pair of songs from outside the trilogy is added, "Climax" (one of the collection's best tracks) and a cover of Marvin Gaye's "What's Going On," both from 1974. A previously unissued track, "Ain't That Lovin' You (For More Reasons Than One)," is tacked on the end, making *Orgasm* an excellent anthology of the Ohio Players' early years, before they achieved mass mainstream success.

Greg Prato

The O'Jays

Back Stabbers
1972, Epic/Legacy

A major turning point for the O'Jays, *Back Stabbers* took the group to the top of the charts and made them household names in the R&B world. The O'Jays had been paying serious dues since the late '50s, and their perseverance payed off in a major way when the unsettling title song, the infectious "Time to Get Down," and the uplifting "Love Train" became their biggest hits up to that point. Indeed, this album did more than its part to help establish Kenneth Gamble and Leon Huff's Philadelphia International Records as the most successful soul label since Stax and Motown.

Alex Henderson

Ship Ahoy
1973, Epic/Legacy/Philadelphia Internat

The "other" O'Jays album masterpiece, *Ship Ahoy* combined shattering message tracks and stunning love songs in a fashion matched only by Curtis Mayfield's finest material. From the album cover showing a slave ship to the memorable title song and incredible "For the Love of Money," Gamble and Huff addressed every social ill from envy to racism and greed. Eddie Levert's leads were consistently magnificent, as were the harmonies, production and arrangements. "Put Your Hands Together" and "You Got Your Hooks In Me" would be good album cuts, but on *Ship Ahoy* they were merely icing on the cake.

Ron Wynn

Parliament

Osmium
1970, Invictus

The first Parliament album as such was a mixed-up mess of an affair—but would anyone expect anything less? The overall sound is much more Funkadelic than later Parliament, if with a somewhat more accessible feel. Things get going with an appropriately leering start, thanks to "I Call My Baby Pussycat," which makes something like "What's New, Pussycat?" seem like innocent, chaste conversation. After a stripped-down start, things explode into a full-on funk strut with heavy-duty guitar and slamming drums setting the way, while the singers sound like they're tripping without losing the soul—sudden music dropouts, vocal cut-ins, volume level tweaks, and more add to the off-kilter feeling. *Osmium*'s sound progresses from there—it's funk's fire combined with a studio freedom that feels like a blueprint for the future. Bernie Worrell's keyboard abilities are already clear, whether he's trying for hotel lounge jams or full freakiness; similarly, Eddie Hazel is clearly finding his own epic stoned zone to peel out some amazing solos at the drop of a hat. As for the subject matter and end results—who else but this crew could have come up with the trash-talking, yodeling twang of "Little Ol' Country Boy" in 1970 and still made it funky with all the steel guitar? Other fun times include the piano and vocal-into-full-band goofy romantic romp of "My Automobile" and "Funky Woman," where over a heavy groove (and goofy Worrell break) the titular character lives with the consequence of her stank: "She hung them in the air/ The air said this ain't fair!" Amidst all the nuttiness, there are some perhaps surprising depths—consider "Oh Lord, Why Lord/Prayer," which might almost be too pretty for its own good (Worrell's harpsichord almost verges on the sickly sweet) but still has some lovely gospel choir singing and heartfelt lyrics.

Ned Raggett

Up for the Down Stroke
1974, Casablanca

Kicking off with one of prime funk's purest distillations—the outrageously great title track, with a perfect party chorus line and uncredited horns (presumably the Horny Horns were involved somehow) adding to the monster beat and bass—*Up for the Down Stroke* finds Parliament in rude good health. As was more or less the case through the '70s, Parliament took a slightly more listener-friendly turn here than they did as Funkadelic, but often it's a difference by degrees. Just listening to some of Bernie Worrell's insane keyboard parts or Bootsy Collins' bass work here is enough to wake the dead. As always, Worrell in particular can suddenly surprise with his delicacy—the soft, understated flow of "I Just Got Back" may have lyrics that could be sung by Jon Anderson, at least at points, but the piano lines have subtle, dreamy grace, the antithesis of Rick Wakeman's masturbations. For that matter, Peter Chase's whistles are downright delightful, goofy, and sweet all at once. Slightly more oddball is "All Your Goodies Are Gone," which has a bit more upfront bite and some downright strange lyrics, delivered with a stoned, breathless tone and backed by unearthly choir arrangements. Eddie Hazel is still listed as present and contributing, though unfortunately not for long after, with Ron Bykowski, Gary Shider, and William Nelson also chipping in as needed. Hazel co-writes two of the songs; it's a pity "The Goose" runs out of steam toward the midpoint of its nine minutes, but it makes for pleasant background music if not Parliament at its unfettered best. In the meantime, Clinton and various familiar voices like Fuzzy Haskins and Grady Thomas keep the weird wigginess of the lyrics flowing. In a nod to the group's past, "(I Wanna) Testify," here simply called "Testify," gets a 1974-era work over.

Ned Raggett

Chocolate City
1975, Casablanca

"Chocolate City" stands out as a trademark P-Funk moment, with it's languid meandering, rich synth washes, and spoken-word vocals—a perfect way to jump start the album. From there, the album kicks into high gear, moving from one up-tempo R&B song to the next, every song driven by Bootsy's slippery bass riffs and most showered with harmonious vocal choruses. Every song has its quirks, with "Let Me Be" being the only song that gets too unconventional for its own good, featuring only synth, piano, and vocals. Most of the other songs are fairly equal, none being lackluster and none being too noteworthy, with the exception of "Together"; this song's soulful chorus drifts momentarily away from the funk for a moment, offering one of the album's most beautiful moments. For the most part, though, this isn't a beautiful album—it's fairly grimy with its funk-infused R&B thumping and worming relentlessly, never taking too much time to worry about catchy hooks. Yet for as understated as this stubborn focus is, never venturing too far into rock, disco, or jamming territory, it's an effective focus, making *Chocolate City* a slight improvement from *Up for the Down Stroke*. There's something rewarding about how consistent and focused this album is, probably because of its amazing lineup featuring Bootsy Collins, Bernie Worrel, and Eddie Hazel. As such, *Chocolate City* won't disappoint those looking for the R&B side of the P-Funk library.

Jason Birchmeier

Mothership Connection
February 1976, Casablanca

The addition of ex-JB's Fred Wesley and Maceo Parker to the Parliament roster on *Mothership Connection* elevated an already mind-blowing band into the best funk band of the '70s, arguably the best funk band ever. With these two funk veterans supplying the horns, Clinton had everything he could ask for in his already stellar group. The opening song, "P-Funk (Wants to Get Funked Up)," harkened back to the opening title track from Parliament's previous album, *Chocolate City*, laying down a languid synth aura for a spoken-word intro. When "P-Funk (Wants to Get Funked Up)" steps into second gear though, bringing in Bootsy's bass, Wesley's horn, Worrell's piano, and a chorus of vocalists, it's fairly evident just how large a step forward *Mothership Connection* is from the conventional R&B roots of *Chocolate City* and *Up for the Down Stroke*. The second song, "Mothership Connection (Star Child)," makes the differentiation glaringly evident, most noticeably when the song enters the cosmic, proto-hip-hop "swing down sweet chariot" bridge with its accompanying melody from beyond. The funk doesn't stop there though, with the remaining five songs keeping the tempo laden with dense interweaving rhythms, peaking on "Give Up the Funk (Tear the Roof Off the Sucker)." In the end, there's no questioning this album's impact, one that is still being felt via rap-induced aftershocks. In addition to its contemporary impact

and continued longevity, the album was a massive success for Clinton and company upon its release in 1975, elevating the P-Funk collective to unparalleled heights in terms of audience. Some Parliament albums may be flawless, and others may be innovative, but this is the P-Funk zenith in more ways than one, perfect as well as perennial.

Jason Birchmeier

The Clones of Dr. Funkenstein
September 1976, Casablanca

Come 1976, and Parliament got up to its usual tricks in that particular incarnation—right down to opening backwards-masked vocal weirdness plus sci-fi scenarios in the "Prelude," where "funk is its own reward." With Bernie Worrell and Fred Wesley splitting the horn arrangements and Clinton and Bootsy Collins taking care of the rest, the result is a concept album of sorts you can dance to. The clones get up and do their thing throughout, and if it's not *The Wall*, then that's all to its benefit. The immediate downside of *Clones* is that it's a fairly one-note record—every groove can just about be exchanged for any other one, unlike the wider variety apparent on other releases. Given Clinton and company's sheer work rate, something likely had to give and this is one of the stress points. There are a couple of stronger songs— "I've Been Watching You (Move Your Sexy Body)" is classic slow jam territory. Not exactly Barry White, but hearing Parliament tone it down just enough pays off, especially with Worrell's drowsy, sensuous horn charts. "Funkin' for Fun," meanwhile, brings the album to a strong, lively end, with just enough in the call-and-response vocals and horns to spark some extra energy into the proceedings. As is the case with most mid-to-late '70s Parliament, things may not be as deep as what was done as Funkadelic, but only those who always explicitly value lyrical worth have any cause to complain. Listening to the silly squeals and burbles on "Dr. Funkenstein" itself is pure fun with sound, while the good doctor's speech is scientific craziness. As one voice says out of nowhere, "Kiss me on my ego!" Special bonus—the utterly goofball cover photo, one of P-Funk's best.

Ned Raggett

Funkentelechy Vs. the Placebo Syndrome
1977, Casablanca

Parliament simply poured it on for this amazing album, clearly one of its all-time best. At least one band named itself after a lyric—Urge Overkill, taken from the song "Funkentelechy" itself—while the amount of times this album has been sampled for the music is uncountable. Besides having an absolutely wonderful name, it contained at least three of the finest Parliament tunes ever, including arguably its signature song. "Flash Light," which closes *Funkentelechy* on a riotous high, has it all—a brilliant fake ending, instant singalong value, a synth-bassline to kill for from Bernie Worrell, and so much more. As the album ends, so too does it begin, with a stone-cold classic—"Bop Gun (Endangered Species)." Starting with a brisk little guitar figure and beat, it turns into an instant party on all fronts, with great lead vocals and an addictive chorus, the Horny Horns and company hitting the grooves and blasting hard. Worrell's laser noises and shimmering keyboard leads and Cordell Mosson's monster bass squelches send everything all that much more over the top. Another song title says it all—"Sir Nose D'Voidoffunk (Pay Attention—B3M)." Treated with vocoders to an absurd degree, Sir Nose became the legendary enemy of funk, specifically the Starchild, on many a P-Funk recording (that's the two of them on the hilarious cover, the Starchild himself operating the Bop Gun). The throwaway lines in this song are almost legendary in and of themselves, while the music itself is a great slow build and burn rhythm that piles more on as it goes, with singers, horns, and more taking it to a climax. "Funkentelechy" and "The Placebo Syndrome" both have plenty of goodness as well, while "Wizards of Finance" is an amusing retro diversion, helping make *Funkentelechy* the highlight it is.

Ned Raggett

Motor Booty Affair
1978, Casablanca

By this point Parliament was one of the most accomplished and intelligent bands in music. With albums like *Mothership Connection* and *The Clones of Dr. Funkenstein*, George Clinton's druggy and patently eccentric humor often obscured the enviable musicianship throughout. *Motor Booty Affair* is no doubt another classic album and the perfect follow-up to 1977's *Funkentelechy Vs. the Placebo Syndrome*. On *Motor Booty Affair*, Clinton decides to yuck it up more with a great underwater concept and a few of his stronger alter egos, including the rhythmically challenged Sir Nose D' Void of Funk and his friend Rumpofsteelskin. The deft and airy "Mr. Wiggles" has Clinton taking on the persona of Wiggles, the "DJ of the affair" as he says: "Mr. Wiggles here on roller skates and a yo-yo/Acting a fool." The hypnotic "Rumpofsteelskin" has a great bassline and inventive and infectious background vocals. The closest thing to a ballad here is the astrologically savvy "(You're a Fish and I'm A) Water Sign." The well-produced "Aqua Boogie (A Psychoalphadiscobetabioaquadoloop)" with its handclaps and high-pitched basslines basically set the standards for the sound of R&B in the coming decade. The sleeper of the album, "One of Those Funky Things," is filled with timbales, congas, and Bernie Worrell's great synth signatures. The last track, "Deep," has great, understated riffs from the Horny Horns. Although many Parliament efforts can't be fully appreciated unless the whole catalogue is nearby, *Motor Booty Affair* stands on its own merits and sustains the laugh throughout.

Jason Elias

Ann Peebles

I Can't Stand the Rain
1974, Hi

The title song was an instant classic, and its lyrics are among the most moving and gripping in soul annals. This was Ann Peebles' finest album for Hi Records, and it should have been a massive success. Instead, while it's celebrated in Europe and now considered an anthem, it floundered and barely scraped the pop charts, although the single was her biggest R&B hit.

Ron Wynn

Esther Phillips

From a Whisper to a Scream
1990, Columbia

One of Esther Phillips finest '70s releases, *From a Whisper to a Scream* is the first of seven albums the singer recorded for CTI offshoot Kudu. Arranged and conducted by Pee Wee Ellis, the December 1971 session also involved principal players such as bassist Gordon Edwards, drummer Bernard Purdie, percussionist Airto, guitarists Cornel Dupree and Eric Gale, keyboardist Richard Tee, and saxophonists Hank Crawford and David Liebman. Setting the tone for Phillips' Kudu era, *Whisper* offers a series of spacious, yet fully arranged ballads of burning heartache, along with a handful of relatively funky numbers that do nothing to compromise her talent, dishing out loads of classy grit. It's a definite point of departure from the likes of *Esther Phillips Sings* and *And I Love Him*, her field of contemporaries closer to Al Green and Aretha Franklin than before. She grabs onto "Home Is Where the Hatred Is," Gil Scott-Heron's most harrowing rumination on drug dependency—which, at that point, wasn't even a year old—as if it were her very own, and it's all the more poignant given its parallels with her own life. (Its meaning was only compounded by her death in 1984.) Though there is absolutely nothing lacking in the album's more energetic moments, it's still the ballads that shine brightest, like the alternately fragile and explosive "From a Whisper to a Scream" (Allen Toussaint) and a staggering "Baby, I'm for Real" (Marvin and Anna Gordy, made popular by the Originals) so vulnerable yet commanding that it really should've closed the album. [Columbia's 1990 reissue adds several cuts from the session not present on the original LP.]

Andy Kellman

Home Is Where the Hatred Is: The Kudu Years 1971–1977
June 2004, Raven

The Rhino double-CD *The Best of Esther Phillips (1962–1970)* covered the period that most would agree was the singer's most artistically successful. As an 18-song disc that covers the period immediately following what was documented on the Rhino collection, *Home Is Where the Hatred Is: The Kudu Years 1971–1977* is a valuable supplement for those who want more artistically. However, as was the case with another idiosyncratic soul-pop singer who moved to CTI in the 1970s (Nina Simone), Phillips' '70s output was decidedly inferior to her '60s work, even if her vocal skills remained intact. It's respectable enough 1970s soul, with a slicker and funkier feel than her earlier sides, in keeping with the trends sweeping the world of R&B during the decade, getting into disco on her 1975 hit "What a Diff'rence a Day Makes." But while several major writers are covered on the songs selected for this anthology—Marvin Gaye, Allen Toussaint, Bill Withers, Joe Cocker, Jackie DeShannon, Gil Scott-Heron, and Gene McDaniels—not many of the selections are above average, leaving the most distinctive thing about them Phillips' odd if appealing pinched, slinky vocal tone. Songs really are necessary to raise singers who rely on cover material to a higher level, and the shortage of ace numbers is what separates Phillips' '70s records from those of someone like, say, Gladys Knight. The record's only disappointing, however, in that it doesn't show Phillips at the point where she was getting the most out of her abilities in the studio. It's mildly likable period '70s soul for the most part, if dull in places.

Richie Unterberger

Wilson Pickett

Wilson Pickett in Philadelphia
1970, Atlantic

After cutting most of his hits in the laid-back but gritty environs of the Deep South (most notably Mem-phis and Muscle Shoals), in 1970 Wilson Pickett decided to move with the times and headed to Phila-delphia, where his raw, bigger-than-life vocals were paired with the higher-gloss funk of song-writers and producers Kenny Gamble and Leon Huff. It may not have seemed like an ideal match on paper, but in the studio the results were inspired; on *Wilson Pickett in Phila-delphia*, Gamble and Huff kept the studio band on the good foot at all times, and Pickett's always passionate and forceful performance added whatever grease that might have been missing from the Philly session cats. (Not that they sound lacking in spirit, as Pickett inspires fiery performances from the band on cuts like "Engine, Engine Number 9" and "Run, Joey, Run.") While a few of the songs aren't quite up to snuff (especially the just-plain-silly "International Playboy"), and Pickett sound a lot better when he's tom-catting than when he's lovelorn (as on "Help The Needy"), the star still fires on all cylinders regardless of the material, and Gamble and Huff create first-class accommodations for his performances without losing touch with Pickett's gritty soul in the process. *Wilson Pickett in Philadelphia* was one of his last truly memorable sets for Atlantic Records; in 1973, he'd leave the label for RCA Victor, and his career as an R&B hit-maker would never truly recover.

Mark Deming

Pleasure

Accept No Substitutes
1976, Fantasy

Back in the '70s, AOR radio and soul radio were two very different formats—and not just because one played rock and the other played R&B. "AOR" stood for album-oriented rock, which was an accurate name because that format was, in fact, album-oriented; at AOR, album tracks that were never released as singles could be candidates for heavy rota-tion. Soul radio, however, was much more singles-oriented—an established soul radio DJ could play some album tracks here and there, but singles were the primary focus. And that wasn't good news for Pleasure, who were more of an album

act than a singles act. Pleasure recorded great albums, but for the most part, they didn't have the type of singles that drove program directors wild. *Accept No Substitutes*, Plea-sure's second album, is a perfect example of a record that is excellent but, as a rule, didn't blow program directors away. The funk gem "Let's Dance" had the makings of a radio hit, although radio didn't really take notice until the West Street Mob covered it in 1981. At any rate, Pleasure's relatively small group of hardcore fans loved this record. They loved the jazz-tinged funk of "Pleasure for Your Pleasure" and "I'm Mad"; they loved the mellow, laid-back quiet storm outlook of "The Love of My Life." *Accept No Substitutes* did contain one charting single: the hypnotic "Ghettoes of the Mind," which wasn't a huge smash but did become a minor hit and was a favorite at Pleasure's live gigs. Had '70s soul radio been as album-minded a medium as AOR radio, this Wayne Henderson-produced LP might have enjoyed heavy rotation. But in a medium that worshipped singles, *Accept No Substitutes* was fighting an uphill battle. Regardless, most Pleasure fans think of this LP as a highly respectable sophomore outing.

Alex Henderson

The Pointer Sisters

The Pointer Sisters
1973, MCA

With a big push from their Blue Thumb label, who introduced the band by way of a full-page ad in *Billboard* maga-zine, the Pointer Sisters took their eponymous debut straight to the top of the R&B charts in summer 1973 on the strengths of their penchant for mixing classic '60s R&B with fresh forward-thinking grooves. Add the sisters' harmonies and complex vocal moves, and there's no doubt the group was destined for a fast rise. Produced by David Rubinson, *The Pointer Sisters* contained effusive covers that cradled two of the Pointers' own compositions. That remarkable combo, then, allowed the Allen Toussaint classic "Yes We Can Can" to rub shoulders with the original "Jada," a boogie blues-shaded slab of jazz, and a perfect fingerprint of the eclectic style that would define the Pointers' core. That same bent also allowed them to give equal energy to the Willie Dixon gem "Wang Dang Doodle," a song which quickly became a live set favorite, and also to their own "Sugar." Other high points include "River Boulevard," a mid-tempo vocal that gives way to a light rock riot. It was easy to see exactly where the Pointer Sisters were headed. With talent to spare and an energy that was fresh and unending, this set emerges a cohesive and joyous cabaret, allowing the quartet to do what it does best. Listening to these earliest gems, it's no surprise, then, that the band would spend the better part of the next two decades in the charts.

Amy Hanson

Prince

Dirty Mind
October 1980, Warner Bros.

Neither *For You* nor *Prince* was adequate preparation for the full-blown masterpiece of Prince's third album, *Dirty Mind*. Recorded in his home studio, with Prince playing nearly every instrument, *Dirty Mind* is a stunning, audacious amalgam of funk, new wave, R&B, and pop, fueled by grinningly salacious sex and the desire to shock. Where other pop musicians suggested sex in lewd double-entendres, Prince left nothing to hide—before its release, no other rock or funk record was ever quite as explicit as *Dirty Mind*, with its gleeful tales of oral sex, threesomes, and even incest. Certainly, it opened the doors for countless sexually explicit albums, but to reduce its impact to mere profanity is too reductive—the music of *Dirty Mind* is as shocking as its graphic language, bending styles and breaking rules with little regard for fixed genres. Basing the album on a harder, rock-oriented beat more than before, Prince tries everything—there's pure new wave pop ("When You Were Mine"), soulful crooning ("Gotta Broken Heart Again"), robotic funk ("Dirty Mind"), rock & roll ("Sister"), sultry funk ("Head," "Do It All Night"), and relentless dance jams ("Uptown," "Partyup"), all in the space of half an hour. It's a breathtaking, visionary album, and its fusion of synthesizers, rock rhythms, and funk set the style for much of the urban soul and funk of the early '80s.

Stephen Thomas Erlewine

1999
February 1983, Warner Bros.

With *Dirty Mind*, Prince had established a wild fusion of funk, rock, new wave, and soul that signaled he was an original, maverick talent, but it failed to win him a large audience. After delivering the sound-alike album, *Controversy*, Prince revamped his sound and delivered the double album *1999*. Where his earlier albums had been a fusion of organic and electronic sounds, *1999* was constructed almost entirely on synthesizers by Prince himself. Naturally, the effect was slightly more mechanical and robotic than his previous work and strongly recalled the electro-funk experiments of several underground funk and hip-hop artists at the time. Prince had also constructed an album dominated by computer funk, but he didn't simply rely on the extended instrumental grooves to carry the album—he didn't have to when his songwriting was improving by leaps and bounds. The first side of the record contained all of the hit singles, and, unsurprisingly, they were the ones that contained the least amount of electronics. "1999" parties to the apocalypse with a P-Funk groove much tighter than anything George Clinton ever did, "Little Red Corvette" is pure pop, and "Delirious" takes rockabilly riffs into the computer age. After that opening salvo, all the rules go out the window—"Let's Pretend We're Married" is a salacious

extended lust letter, "Free" is an elegiac anthem, "All the Critics Love U in New York" is a vicious attack at hipsters, and "Lady Cab Driver," with its notorious bridge, is the culmination of all of his sexual fantasies. Sure, Prince stretches out a bit too much over the course of *1999*, but the result is a stunning display of raw talent, not wallowing indulgence.

Stephen Thomas Erlewine

Purple Rain
August 1984, Warner Bros.

Prince designed *Purple Rain* as the project that would make him a superstar, and, surprisingly, that is exactly what happened. Simultaneously more focused and ambitious than any of his previous records, *Purple Rain* finds Prince consolidating his funk and R&B roots while moving boldly into pop, rock, and heavy metal with nine superbly crafted songs. Even its best-known songs don't tread conventional territory: the bass-less "When Doves Cry" is an eerie, spare neo-psychedelic masterpiece; "Let's Go Crazy" is a furious blend of metallic guitars, Stonesy riffs, and a hard funk backbeat; the anthemic title track is a majestic ballad filled with brilliant guitar flourishes. Although Prince's songwriting is at a peak, the presence of the Revolution pulls the music into sharper focus, giving it a tougher, more aggressive edge. And, with the guidance of Wendy and Lisa, Prince pushed heavily into psychedelia, adding swirling strings to the dreamy "Take Me With U" and the hard rock of "Baby I'm a Star." Even with all of his new, but uncompromising, forays into pop, Prince hasn't abandoned funk, and the robotic jam of "Computer Blue" and the menacing grind of "Darling Nikki" are among his finest songs. Taken together, all of the stylistic experiments add up to a stunning statement of purpose that remains one of the most exciting rock & roll albums ever recorded.

Stephen Thomas Erlewine

Sign 'O' the Times
March 1987, Paisley Park

Fearless, eclectic, and defiantly messy, Prince's *Sign 'O' the Times* falls into the tradition of tremendous, chaotic double albums like *The Beatles*, *Exile on Main St.*, and *London Calling*— albums that are fantastic because of their overreach, their great sprawl.

Prince shows nearly all of his cards here, from bare-bones electro-funk and smooth soul to pseudo-psychedelic pop and crunching hard rock, touching on gospel, blues, and folk along the way. This was the first album Prince recorded without the Revolution since 1982's *1999* (the band does appear on the in-concert rave-up, "It's Gonna Be a Beautiful Night"), and he sounds liberated, diving into territory merely suggested on *Around the World in a Day* and *Parade*. While the music overflows with generous spirit, these are among the most cryptic, insular songs he's ever written. Many songs are left over from the aborted triple album *Crystal Ball* and the abandoned Camille project, a Prince alter ego personified by scarily sped-up tapes on "If I Was Your Girlfriend," the most disarming and bleak psycho-sexual song Prince ever wrote, as well as the equally chilling "Strange Relationship." These fraying relationships echo in the social chaos Prince writes about throughout the album. Apocalyptic imagery of drugs, bombs, empty sex, abandoned babies and mothers, and AIDS pop up again and again, yet he balances the despair with hope, whether it's God, love, or just having a good time. In its own roundabout way, *Sign 'O' the Times* is the sound of the late '80s—it's the sound of the good times collapsing and how all that doubt and fear can be ignored if you just dance those problems away.

Stephen Thomas Erlewine

The Black Album
1987, Paisley Park

Originally scheduled for release in November of 1987—following the double-album *Sign o' the Times* by a matter of months—Prince pulled *The Black Album* weeks before its release, guaranteeing it near-mythic status. Urban legends spread like wildfire: Prince believed it was too bleak to release; Warner Bros. balked at its explicit lyrics; no CDs were ever pressed, and all the LPs were destroyed. That final rumor was certainly untrue, since bootlegs immediately appeared, and when it finally received official release in the fall of 1994, nearly every die-hard fan already had the record. That limited-edition release of *The Black Album* turned out to be a bit anti-climatic, since the album itself isn't a lost masterwork—it's fun, but not much more. If anything, it's a little labored, as Prince works hard to win back the black audience he willfully abandoned after *Purple Rain*. So, he serves up "When 2 R in Love," an urban ballad every bit as nondescript as the genre, and offers "Dead on It," trying to one-up rappers with a mocking attack that winds up as one of the lamest things he ever waxed. The rest of the eight-song album is brilliant, pure funk, ranging from the unrelenting "Le Grind," a deliriously lustful plea to supermodel Cindy Crawford; the hyper-tense James Brown workout "2 Nigs United 4 West Compton"; to "Bob George," a perverse tale of a macho lunkhead (Prince, electronically affecting a deep, idiotic drawl) who discovers his lady just slept with Prince—or "that skinny motherf*cker with a high voice," as Bob calls him. All this may not add up to a lost classic, but it is a terrific little record that still delights, even after its mystique has faded.

Stephen Thomas Erlewine

Richard Pryor

...And It's Deep, Too! The Complete Warner Bros. Recordings (1968–1992)
October 2000, Rhino

Although some might give the nod to Andy Kaufman, Richard Pryor was arguably the most important, influential, and groundbreaking standup comic in America during the latter half of the '70s. Pryor's brilliantly perceptive, confrontational dissections of racial injustice paved the way for countless African-American comedians to tackle similar subject matter, and his brutal honesty about his personal life lent an extra depth to the edginess of his performances. Much of Pryor's best-known material appeared on the Warner Bros. label, and that body of work is reissued on CD for the first time as the mammoth nine-disc box set *...And It's Deep, Too!:*

The Complete Warner Bros. Recordings (1968–1992). The leap between the first and second discs (the albums *Richard Pryor* and *That Nigger's Crazy*, recorded in 1968 and 1974, respectively) is astonishing when heard back to back; Pryor moves from relatively traditional standup to inflammatory, foul-mouthed, deadly accurate send-ups of white America and its still poor treatment of African-Americans. Pryor only gets sharper over the rest of the box, which also contains the albums *...Is It Something I Said?*, *Bicentennial Nigger*, *Wanted: Live in Concert* (Parts 1 & 2), *Live on the Sunset Strip*, and *Here and Now*, which take you up to 1983. There's also a bonus disc titled "That "African-American" Is STILL Crazy: Good S**t from the Vaults," which compiles recorded outtakes from the '70s, '80s, and '90s, *plus* an 80-page booklet packed with tributes, informative essays, excerpts from interviews and Pryor's autobiography, and much more. The set may be huge and somewhat costly, but it's also a fitting tribute to one of the true giants of American comedy.

Steve Huey

RAMP

Come into Knowledge
1977, Blue Thumb

Centered around onetime Spinners utility players John Manuel (drums) and Landy Shores (guitar), Saturday Night Special—presumably named after Norman Connors' Reggie Lucas-written song of the same name—played in and around its hometown of Cincinnati during 1975 and 1976, basing live sets on reimagined versions of R&B hits that leaned toward sophisticated funk. Once Roy Ayers caught a gig and got involved, the band changed its name to RAMP ("Roy Ayers Music Productions") and recorded its one album, produced by Ayers with tight associates Edwin Birdsong and William Allen. The material swings between anti-gravity soul and hard-edged funk otherness, a unique mixture that could've only been encouraged or enhanced by Ayers and Birdsong. "Give It," one of Birdsong's contributions, tumbles and swings, repeatedly unfurling and recoiling, made all the more off-center by Sharon Matthews and Sibel Thrasher's frantic projections: "Earth can be lonely in the middle of the night/We must love now so our minds can take flight." "The American Promise," with all its nerved-up guitar scratches and alternately forthcoming and demanding assertions, could be mistaken for early Pointer Sisters or even Bohannon. The likes of "I Just Love You," "Daylight," "Come into Knowledge," and "Look into the Sky," along with a particularly radiant look at "Everybody Loves the Sunshine" (originally recorded less than a year prior for Ayers' album of the same title), drift along with sweet melodies and silken rhythmic layers that linger for days, rivaling similarly bliss-inducing, spiritually minded Ayers Ubiquity classics like "Searching" and "Red, Black and Green." Due to an untimely shake-up at the Blue Thumb label, the album was barely released, receiving nothing in the way of promotion beyond word of mouth. Few outside the band's local supporters and Ayers' keen following were in the know, and it languished in obscurity until A Tribe Called Quest sampled "Daylight" for "Bonita Applebum." Vinyl "reissues" surfaced. A couple tracks were licensed for compilations. Universal Japan put a stop to the nonsense in early 2007 by releasing the album for the first time on CD.

Andy Kellman

Otis Redding

The Dock of the Bay
February 1968, Atco

It was never sup-posed to be like this: "(Sittin' on) The Dock of the Bay" was supposed to mark a beginning of a new phase in Otis Redding's ca-reer, not an ending. Producer/guitarist Steve Cropper had a difficult task to perform in pull-ing together this album, the first of

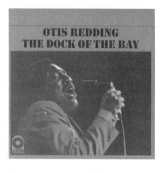

OTIS REDDING
THE DOCK OF THE BAY

several posthumous releases issued by Stax/Volt in the wake of Otis Redding's death. What could have been a cash-in effort or a grim memorial album instead became a vivid, exciting presentation of some key aspects of the talent that was lost when Redding died. *Dock of the Bay* is, indeed, a mixed bag of singles and B-sides going back to July of 1965, one hit duet with Carla Thomas, and a pair of previously unissued tracks from 1966 and 1967, respectively. There's little cohesion, stylistic or otherwise, in the songs, especially when the title track is taken into consideration—nothing else here resembles it, for the obvious reason that Redding never had a chance to follow it up. Despite the mix-and-match na-ture of the album, however, this is an impossible record not to love. Cropper chose his tracks well, selecting some of the strongest and most unusual among the late singer's orphaned songs: "I Love You More Than Words Can Say" is one of Redding's most passionate performances; "Let Me Come on Home" presents an ebullient Otis Redding accompanied by some sharp playing; and "Don't Mess With Cupid" begins with a gorgeous guitar flourish and blooms into an intense, pounding, soaring showcase for singer and band alike. No one could complain about the album then, and it still holds more than three decades later. Reissued on CD by the Atco label through Rhino Records in excellent sound.

Bruce Eder

Minnie Riperton

Adventures in Paradise
1975, Epic

Adventures in Paradise, the follow-up to *Perfect Angel*—an album featuring Minnie Riperton's biggest hit, much as-sistance from Stevie Wonder and several of his associates, as well as an iconic outer sleeve—tends to be viewed as a flop, at least by those who disregard Minnie as a novelty one-hit wonder. If the album is a flop on principle because none of its three singles were as big as "Lovin' You," or because Stevie was no longer around, so be it, but it's borderline classic by any other measure. The key collaborators here, outside of Minnie's songwriting husband Richard Rudolph, include keyboardist Joe Sample, guitarist Larry Carlton, saxophonist Tom Scott, and harpist Dorothy Ashby. Hardly poor substitutes. Most importantly, the album's three central

songs were co-written with Leon Ware, who had come up with the Jackson 5's "I Wanna Be Where You Are" and was on the brink of writing what would become the entirety of Marvin Gaye's *I Want You*, along with his own excellent *Musical Massage*. Each of the Riperton/Rudolph/Ware songs ooze playful sensuality, desire, and lust—especially "Inside My Love" (a Top 30 R&B single), a swooning slow jam filled with double entendres. If it weren't for the supremely seductive innocence in Minnie's voice, the words would likely fall flat in their directness ("You can see inside me/Will you come inside me?/Do you wanna ride inside my love?") The opener, "Baby, This Love I Have," is even more heated, with Minnie's frustrated yearning wrapped around a lithe arrange-ment. (It's gentle six-note guitar-and-bass intro would later resurface in A Tribe Called Quest's "Check the Rhime.") The songs written by Minnie and Rudolph alone match up well with the best of *Perfect Angel*, and they're deceptively eclectic, mixing and matching soul and rock with touches of country and adult pop. The album was tailor made for the kind of '70s radio format that would not balk at spinning Boz Scaggs, LTD, and Fleetwood Mac back-to-back-to-back. But, for whatever reason (poor promotion, closed minds), it did not do nearly as well as it deserved.

Andy Kellman

Rose Royce

Rose Royce II: In Full Bloom
1977, Whitfield

As strong as any of the songs featured on 1976's *Car Wash* soundtrack, Rose Royce's 1977 outing, *Rose Royce II: In Full Bloom*, allowed them to fully shine in their own right and on their own terms. Although their early incarnation as Total Concept

Unlimited had paired them with Motown label mates the Temptations and given them clout in the label stable, it was the addition of powerhouse vocalist Gwen Dickey and con-tinued pairing with über-producer Norman Whitfield that brought the band into their own. Packed with tight funk jams and horn-heavy construction, tempered only occasion-ally by Dickey's sweet ballads, *Rose Royce II: In Full Bloom* is a disco-funk masterpiece—a pure fusion of both genres that works better than it has a right to, courtesy of both the band's own confidence and Whitfield's artful magic. The wistful and absolutely sublime ballad "Wishing on a Star" opens the set and should have been a chart-heavy hitter. In fact, it reached only number 52 on the R&B charts, proving that the band's fans were truly in the mood to dance. Rose Royce wouldn't disappoint, as the nine-minute funk monster "Do Your Dance" was uncaged. Shaved to a four-minute highlights version, the song gave the band a Top Five R&B hit. The full album version, however, is a far superior work-out, while the equally funky "You Can't Please Everybody" and eight-minute epic "It Makes You Feel Like Dancin'" keep the groove moving smoothly. Rose Royce may have shot to stardom with the *Car Wash* craze, but they are far better without the celluloid glitter covering up their own pure gold.

Amy Hanson

Diana Ross

Diana Ross
February 1976, Motown

Diana Ross landed one of the decade's definitive singles with "Love Hangover," instantly making this a major hit album. While it surprisingly didn't sell as well as some 1980s LPs, the single was a double chart-topper and a huge club hit for much of the next two years. It vaulted the album into the pop Top 10 and even managed to break the follow-up single onto the charts.

Ron Wynn

Rotary Connection

Rotary Connection
1967, Chess

The most inexplicable aspect of Rotary Connection's debut is that its strange and experimental qualities are often referred to as charming but dated, while Love's *Forever Changes* (released the same year), a record that is just a shade less bizarre and no more psychedelic, is universally viewed as timeless. There's no mistaking that this is hardly a flawless record—this band, more an experiment than anything else, was only beginning to find its feet. For every cover that radically reshapes the original and either stuns ears or elicits screams of blasphemy ("Like a Rolling Stone"), there's one that falls completely flat in its blandness ("Soul Man"). And for every original that is rife with otherworldly melodies and luscious combinations of countless musical styles ("Memory Band"), there's something like the ghostly "what you've just heard" audio collage/megamix that closes out the album ("Rotary Connection"). The consensus seems to be that this is the only essential record this group released, and that they were such an oddball entity that this is all one can take of them. That's just plain silly, evident from any number of the sparkling moments found on the LPs that followed. Minnie Riperton had yet to take the spotlight she deserved in this group—so in a sense, this could be seen as the *least*-representative Rotary Connection record, as fascinating as it is. Some strange force carried it to the Top 40 of the album chart, not that it was undeserving.

Andy Kellman

Patrice Rushen

Straight from the Heart
1982, Elektra

An early '80s jazz-pop-R&B synthesis as durable and pleasing as any other, *Straight from the Heart* was Patrice Rushen's most successful album, at least from a sales standpoint: it peaked at number 14 on the pop chart, 25 slots higher than 1980's *Pizzazz*. Still working with a core group of

associates—including Freddie Washington, Charles Mims, Paul M. Jackson, and Marlo Henderson (along with a still young Gerald Albright)—that went back to her earlier Elektra albums, the material here is as slick as ever, but not at the expense of lighter rhythms or less memorable melodies. Much of the album's popularity can be attributed to the club hit "Forget Me Nots," Rushen's most-known single—a breezy, buoyant mixture of handclaps, fingersnaps, twisting bass, and Rushen's typically blissful (and not overplayed) electric piano, not to mention the incorporation of a *bad* bass-and-percussion breakdown. (If you were born after the mid-'70s or so, you'd be more likely to recognize the song as the basis of Will Smith's "Men in Black.") Beyond a forgettable ballad or two, the only disappointment is the Brenda Russell collaboration on "Breakout!," where rock affectations (gnarling electric guitar, grimacing vocal tactics that suit neither Rushen nor Russell) damage what could've been a bigger hit. "Remind Me," despite not being released as a single, is a sweet and low-slung groove that has been sampled and interpolated by no less than a dozen significant rap and R&B songs—including Faith Evans' "Fallin' in Love," Notorious B.I.G.'s "Unbelievable," MoKenStef's "He's Mine," and Junior M.A.F.I.A.'s "I Need You Tonight." But it's not like anything about this album requires that kind of validation. [Rhino's 1996 reissue adds the 12" versions of all three singles, including seven very replayable minutes of "Forget Me Nots," as well as two single edits.]

Andy Kellman

Tom Scott

Tom Scott & the L.A. Express
August–September 1973, Ode

Most of Tom Scott's GRP albums of the '80s and '90s have been shallow, formulaic releases offering little evidence of the saxman's improvisatory skills. But most of his earlier recordings of the 1970s were appealing jazz/funk/R&B efforts that, although commercial and highly accessible, demonstrated his capabilities as a soloist. If the version of Scott's L.A. Express band heard on this album (reissued on CD in 1996) brings to mind the Crusaders, it's because two of its members, keyboardist Joe Sample and guitarist Larry Carlton, were also Crusaders members. Although the Express was never in a class with that band, it was a likable unit defined by its cohesiveness, warmth and spontaneity. As slick as the Express was, it took risks. It's hard to imagine Scott providing a funk-drenched version of John Coltrane's "Dahomey's Dance" as he does here—or incorporating Middle Eastern influences as he does on "King Cobra"—on his calculated GRP recordings of the '90s. Solid jazz-funk like "L.A. Expression" and "Nunya" is well worth hearing. And "Spindrift," though congenial and mellow, is far more substantial than the "muzak" with which he would later inundate us.

Alex Henderson

Gil Scott-Heron

Small Talk at 125th and Lenox
1970, RCA

Disregard the understated title; *Small Talk at 125th and Lenox* was a volcanic upheaval of intellectualism and social critique, recorded live in a New York nightclub with only bongos and conga to back the street poet. Here Scott-Heron introduced some of his most biting material, including the landmark "The Revolution Will Not Be Televised" as well as his single most polemical moment: the angry race warning "Enough." Still, he balances the tone and mood well, ranging from direct broadsides to clever satire. He introduces "Whitey on the Moon" with a bemused air ("wanting to give credit where credit is due"), then launches into a diatribe concerning living conditions for the neglected on earth while those racing to the moon receive millions of taxpayer dollars. On "Evolution (And Flashback)," Scott-Heron laments the setbacks of the civil rights movement and provides a capsule history of his race, ending sharply with these words: "In 1960, I was a negro, and then Malcolm came along/Yes, but some nigger shot Malcolm down, though the bitter truth lives on/Well, now I am a black man, and though I still go second class/Whereas once I wanted the white man's love, now he can kiss my ass." The only sour note comes on a brush with homophobia, "The Subject Was Faggots."

John Bush

Pieces of a Man
1971, RCA

After decades of influencing everyone from jazz musicians to hip-hop stars, *Pieces of a Man* set a standard for vocal artistry and political awareness that few musicians will ever match. Scott-Heron's unique proto-rap style influenced a generation of hip-hop artists, and nowhere is his style more powerful than on the classic "The Revolution Will Not Be Televised." Even though the media—the very entity attacked in this song—has used, reused, and recontextualized the song and its title so many times, its message is so strong that it has become impossible to co-opt. Musically, the track created a formula that modern hip-hop would follow for years to come: bare-bones arrangements featuring pounding basslines and stripped-down drumbeats. Although the song features plenty of outdated references to everything from Spiro Agnew and Jim Webb to *The Beverly Hillbillies*, the force of Scott-Heron's well-directed anger makes the song timeless. More than just a spoken word poet, Scott-Heron was also a uniquely gifted vocalist. On tracks like the reflective "I Think I'll Call It Morning" and the title track, Scott-Heron's voice is complemented perfectly by the soulful keyboards of Brian Jackson. On "Lady Day and John Coltrane," he not only celebrates jazz legends of the past in his words but in his vocal performance, one that is filled with enough soul and innovation to make Coltrane and Billie Holiday nod their heads in approval. More than three decades

after its release, *Pieces of a Man* is just as—if not more—powerful and influential today as it was the day it was released.

Jon Azpiri

Winter in America
September–October 1973, Strata East

Gil Scott-Heron was at his most righteous and provocative on this album. The title cut was a moving, angry summation of the social injustices Scott-Heron felt had led the nation to a particularly dangerous period, while "The Bottle" was a great treatise on the dangers of alcohol abuse. He also offered his thoughts on Nixon's legacy with "The H2O Gate Blues," a classic oral narrative. Brian Jackson's capable keyboard, acoustic piano and arranging talents helped make this a first-rate release, one of several the duo issued during the 1970s.

Ron Wynn

Marlena Shaw

Spice of Life
1969, Cadet

Marlena Shaw's penchant for stylistic variety is certainly evident on this, her sophomore release. Cut for the Cadet label in 1969, *Spice of Life* ranges from soul and proto-funk to jazz and MOR-hued material. Shaw shines throughout, showing her power on politically charged, Aretha-styled cuts like "Woman of the Ghetto" and "Liberation Conversation," while also delivering supple interpretations of such traditional jazz fare as "Go Away Little Boy" (shades of Nancy Wilson). And with a gutsy take on "Stormy Monday," it's clear Shaw doesn't shrink from the blues either. Across this sound spectrum, arrangers Richard Evans and Charles Stepney envelope Shaw in unobtrusive yet exciting pop-soul environs, throwing kalimba runs (a few years before Earth, Wind & Fire picked up on the instrument), psych guitar accents, and bongo-fueled organ riffs into the mix. Their widescreen touch is particularly well essayed on strings-and-brass standouts like the Bacharach-inspired Barry Mann & Cynthia Weil composition "Looking Through the Eyes of Love" and Ashford & Simpson's "California Soul" (a classic reading heavily favored by the crate-digging set). A perfect way to get familiar with Shaw's impressive early work.

Stephen Cook

Skull Snaps

Skull Snaps
1974, Charly

Original vinyl copies of Skull Snaps' one and only LP continue to exchange hands on the rare groove market for three figures. There are two reasons for this: one, it's rare, and two, the drum breaks from the album have been feasted upon for samples so frequently that samples of the samples have likely been sampled. It's not that the album is spectacular—it's merely a decent early '70s funk record from some accomplished musicians who don't exactly leave a trademark of their own throughout its nine songs. This soul-drenched funk album is most notable for the drums of "It's a New Day." It's the album's strongest cut, and the opening drum pattern is as ubiquitous they come—you can hear it get put to re-use in well over two dozen popular rap songs. Anyone who likes hard funk will find much to like—the vocals are gruff, the rhythms are tough yet nimble (the drums are crisp and smacking throughout), and the subject matter takes on everything from pimps to romance to everyday relationships. Charly reissued the album on CD in 1995.

Andy Kellman

Slave

Slave
1977, Cotillion

The debut album from the Ohio-based funk aggregate Slave was a grand success, but resulted in the release of only one single, "Slide." Being the only single released from the album, "Slide" had no problem gaining airplay with its gothic introduction, animated vocals, and rumbling bassline. The funk anthem claimed the number one spot on the *Billboard* R&B charts inside of 20 weeks. The other cuts on the album continue the aggressive funk assault, but with subtle passion and their own distinctive arrangements. The exception is "Son of Slide," which is identical to the album's big hit, except that it's an instrumental save a brief chorus chant. The only ballad is "The Happiest Days," a sweet soul song arranged in the vein of the Ohio Players with its horns, lead and backing vocals.

Craig Lytle

Sly & the Family Stone

Life
1968, Epic/Legacy

Just a matter of months after *Dance to the Music*, Sly & the Family Stone turned around and delivered *Life*, a record that leapfrogged over its predecessor in terms of accomplishment and achievement. The most noteworthy difference is the heavier reliance on psychedelics and fuzz guitars, plus a sharpening of songcraft that extends to even throwaways like "Chicken." As it turned out, *Life* didn't have any hits—the double A-sided single "Life"/ "M'Lady" barely cracked the Top 100—yet this feels considerably more song-oriented than its predecessor, as each track is a concise slice of tightly wound dance-funk. All the more impressive is that the group is able to strut their stuff within this context, trading off vocals and blending into an unstoppable force where it's impossible to separate the instruments, even as they solo. The songwriting might still be perfunctory or derivative in spots—listen to how they appropriate "Eleanor Rigby" on "Plastic Jim"—but what's impressive is how even the borrowed or recycled moments sound fresh in context. And then there are the cuts that work on their own, whether it's the

aforementioned double-sided single, "Fun," "Dynamite!," or several other cuts here—these are brilliant, intoxicating slices of funk-pop that get by as much on sound as song, and they're hard to resist.

Stephen Thomas Erlewine

Stand!
May 1969, Sony

Stand! is the pinnacle of Sly & the Family Stone's early work, a record that represents a culmination of the group's musical vision and accomplishment. *Life* hinted at this record's boundless enthusiasm and blurred stylistic boundaries, yet everything simply gels here, resulting in no separation between the astounding funk, effervescent irresistible melodies, psychedelicized guitars, and deep rhythms. Add to this a sharpened sense of pop songcraft, elastic band interplay, and a flowering of Sly's social consciousness, and the result is utterly stunning. Yes, the jams ("Don't Call Me Nigger, Whitey," "Sex Machine") wind up meandering ever so slightly, but they're surrounded by utter brilliance, from the rousing call to arms of "Stand!" to the unification anthem "Everyday People" to the unstoppable "I Want to Take You Higher." All of it sounds like the Family Stone, thanks not just to the communal lead vocals but to the brilliant interplay, but each track is distinct, emphasizing a different side of their musical personality. As a result, *Stand!* winds up infectious and informative, invigorating and thought-provoking—stimulating in every sense of the word. Few records of its time touched it, and Sly topped it only by offering its opposite the next time out.

Stephen Thomas Erlewine

Greatest Hits
November 1970, Epic

Released in 1970 during the stopgap between *Stand!* and *There's a Riot Goin' On, Greatest Hits* inadvertently arrived at precisely the right moment, summarizing Sly & the Family Stone's joyous hit-making run on the pop and R&B charts. Technically, only four songs here reached the Top Ten, with only two others hitting the Top 40, but judging this solely on charts is misleading, since this is simply a peerless singles collection. This summarizes their first four albums perfectly (almost all of *Stand!* outside of the two jams and "Somebody's Watching You" is here), adding the non-LP singles "Hot Fun in the Summertime," "Thank You (Falettinme Be Mice Elf Agin)," and "Everybody Is a Star," possibly the loveliest thing they ever recorded. But, this isn't merely a summary (and, if it was just that, *Anthology*, the early '80s comp that covers *Riot* and *Fresh* would be stronger than this), it's one of the greatest party records of all time. Music is rarely as vivacious, vigorous, and vibrant as this, and captured on one album, the spirit, sound, and songs of Sly & the Family Stone are all the more stunning. Greatest hits don't come better than this—in fact, music rarely does.

Stephen Thomas Erlewine

There's a Riot Goin' On
November 1971, Epic

It's easy to write off *There's a Riot Goin' On* as one of two things—Sly Stone's disgusted social commentary or the beginning of his slow descent into addiction. It's both of these things, of course, but pigeonholing it as either winds up dismissing the album as a whole, since it is so bloody hard to categorize. What's certain is that *Riot* is unlike any of Sly & the Family Stone's other albums, stripped of the effervescence that flowed through even such politically aware records as *Stand!* This is idealism soured, as hope is slowly replaced by cynicism, joy by skepticism, enthusiasm by weariness, sex by pornography, thrills by narcotics. Joy isn't entirely gone—it creeps through the cracks every once and awhile and, more disturbing, Sly revels in his stoned decadence. What makes *Riot* so remarkable is that it's hard not to get drawn in with him, as you're seduced by the narcotic grooves, seductive vocals slurs, leering electric pianos, and crawling guitars. As the themes surface, it's hard not to nod in agreement, but it's a junkie nod, induced by the comforting coma of the music. And damn if this music isn't funk at its deepest and most impenetrable—this is dense music, nearly impenetrable, but not from its deep grooves, but its utter weariness. Sly's songwriting remains remarkably sharp, but only when he wants to write—the foreboding opener "Luv N' Haight," the scarily resigned "Family Affair," the cracked cynical blues "Time," and "(You Caught Me) Smilin'." Ultimately, the music is the message, and while it's dark music, it's not alienating—it's seductive despair, and that's the scariest thing about it.
Stephen Thomas Erlewine

Fresh
June 1973, Epic

Fresh expands and brightens the slow grooves of *There's a Riot Goin' On*, turning them, for the most part, into friendly, welcoming rhythms. There are still traces of the narcotic haze of *Riot*, particularly on the brilliant, crawling inversion of "Que Sera, Sera," yet this never feels like an invitation into a junkie's lair. Still, this isn't necessarily lighter than *Riot*—in fact, his social commentary is more explicit, and while the music doesn't telegraph his resignation the way *Riot* did, it comes from the same source. So, *Fresh* winds up more varied, musically and lyrically, which may not make it as unified, but it does result in more traditional funk that certainly is appealing in its own right. Besides, this isn't conventional funk—it's eccentric, where even concise catchy tunes like "If You Want Me to Stay" seem as elastic as the opener, "In Time." That's the album's ultimate charm—it finds Sly precisely at the point where he's balancing funk and pop, about to fall into the brink, but creating an utterly individual album that wound up being his last masterwork and one of the great funk albums of its era.
Stephen Thomas Erlewine

Jimmy Smith

Root Down
February 1972, Verve

Toward the end of his stint with Blue Note, Jimmy Smith's albums became predictable. Moving to Verve in the mid-'60s helped matters considerably, since he started playing with new musicians (most notably nice duets with Wes Montgomery)

and new settings, but he never really got loose, as he did on select early Blue Note sessions. Part of the problem was that Smith's soul-jazz was organic and laid-back, *relaxed* and funky instead of down and dirty. For latter-day listeners, aware of his reputation as the godfather of modern soul-jazz organ (and certainly aware of the Beastie Boys' name drop), that may mean that Smith's actual albums all seem a bit tame and restrained, classy, not funky. That's true of the bulk of Smith's catalog, with the notable exception of *Root Down*. Not coincidentally, the title track is the song the Beasties sampled on their 1994 song of the same name, since this is one of the only sessions that Smith cut where his playing his raw, vital, and earthy. Recorded live in Los Angeles in February 1972, the album captures a performance Smith gave with a relatively young supporting band who were clearly influenced by modern funk and rock. They push Smith to playing low-down grooves that truly cook: "Sagg Shootin' His Arrow" and "Root Down (And Get It)" are among the hottest tracks he ever cut, especially in the restored full-length versions showcased on the 2000 Verve By Request reissue. There are times where the pace slows, but the tension never sags, and the result is one of the finest, most exciting records in Smith's catalog. If you think you know everything about Jimmy Smith, this is the album for you.
Stephen Thomas Erlewine

Johnny "Hammond" Smith

Gears
1975, Milestone/OJC

By the mid-'70s, the embracing and assimilation of soul and funk elements into the jazz vernacular had come full steam. Artists and producers from both communities were exchanging ideas and sounds that once again challenged jazz purists' definitions of what jazz "should" be. These collaborations were often scoffed at by academics and critics attempting to pigeonhole and quantify jazz into an academic exercise ripe with songbook predictability and sonic parameters. Thankfully, the record-buying public at large had the good sense to politely ignore these people and continue purchasing records with these new sounds, largely concocted by the production team of Larry and Fonce Mizell. This time around, their subject was Johnny "Hammond" Smith who proves to be more than up to the task of playing around and inside the Mizell's string arrangements which foreshadowed the early days of disco. In fact, two of the cuts found on *Gears*—"Fantasy" and "Los Conquistadores Chocolates"—were played extensively at the early Loft parties hosted by legendary DJ David Mancuso, as well as at the club many consider to be the true home of disco, the Paradise Garage in NYC. *Gears* starts off innocently enough with "Tell Me What To Do," which could have easily found its way on to a Donald Byrd album from this period, but then kicks into full steam with "Los Conquistadores Chocolates," a six-and-a-half-minute *tour de force* of funk, soul, jazz and disco all rolled into one. Hammond is in fine form throughout with crisp playing; never over improvising, but playing only what's necessary to help the music move along at a brisk pace. This is unquestionably another jewel in a treasure chest already filled with so many for the Mizell production team, and a great performance by Hammond to keep up with his contemporaries who refuse to be held back by conventional wisdom.

Rob Theakston

Lonnie Liston Smith

Expansions
1974, Flying Dutchman

When Lonnie Liston Smith left the Miles Davis band in 1974 for a solo career, he was, like so many of his fellow alumni, embarking on a musical odyssey. For a committed fusioneer, he had no idea at the time that he was about to enter an abyss that it would take him the better part of two decades to return from. Looking back upon his catalog from the period, this is the only record that stands out—not only from his own work, but also from every sense of the word: It is fully a jazz album, and a completely funky soul-jazz disc as well. Of the seven compositions here, six are by Smith, and the lone cover is of the Horace Silver classic, "Peace." The lineup includes bassist Cecil McBee, soprano saxophonist David Hubbard, tenor saxophonist Donald Smith (who doubles on flute), drummer Art Gore, and percussionists Lawrence Killian, Michael Carvin, and Leopoldo. Smith plays both piano and electric keyboards and keeps his compositions on the jazzy side—breezy, open, and full of groove playing that occasionally falls over to the funk side of the fence. It's obvious, on this album at least, that Smith was not completely comfortable with Miles' reliance on hard rock in his own mix. Summery and loose in feel, airy and free with its in-the-cut beats and stellar piano fills, *Expansions* prefigures a number of the "smooth jazz" greats here, without the studio slickness and turgid lack of imagination. The disc opens with the title track, with one of two vocals on the LP by Donald Smith (the other is the Silver tune). It's typical "peace and love and we've got to work together" stuff from the mid-'70s, but it's rendered soulfully and deeply without artifice. "Desert Nights" takes a loose Detroit jazz piano groove and layers flute and percussion over the top, making it irresistibly sensual and silky. It's fleshed out to the bursting point with Smith's piano; he plays a lush solo for the bridge and fills it to the brim with luxuriant tones from the middle register. "Summer Days" and "Voodoo Woman" are where the electric keyboards make their first appearance, but only as instruments capable of carrying the groove to the melody quickly, unobtrusively, and with a slinky grace that is infectious. The mixed bag/light-handed approach suits Smith so well here that it's a wonder he tried to hammer home the funk and disco on later releases so relentlessly. The music on *Expansions* is timeless soul-jazz, perfect in every era. Of all the fusion records of this type released in the mid-'70s, *Expansions* provided smoother jazzers and electronica's sampling wizards with more material that Smith could ever have anticipated. The French CD reissue is a 24-bit remaster with pristine sound and balance.

Thom Jurek

Dr. Lonnie Smith

Move Your Hand
August 1969, Blue Note

Move Your Hand was recorded live at *Club Harlem* in Atlantic City on August 9, 1969. Organist Lonnie Smith led a small combo—featuring guitarist Larry McGee, tenor saxist Rudy Jones, bari saxist Ronnie Cuber, and drummer Sylvester Goshay—through a set that alternated originals with two pop covers, the Coasters' "Charlie Brown" and Donovan's "Sunshine Superman." Throughout, the band works a relaxed, bluesy, and, above all, funky rhythm; they abandon improvisation and melody for a steady groove, so much that the hooks of the two pop hits aren't recognizable until a few minutes into the track. No one player stands out, but *Move Your Hand* is thoroughly enjoyable, primarily because the group never lets their momentum sag throughout the session. Though the sound of the record might be somewhat dated, the essential funk of the album remains vital.

Stephen Thomas Erlewine

Drives
January 1970, Blue Note

Lonnie Smith had the raw skills, imagination, and versatility to play burning originals, bluesy covers of R&B and pop, or skillful adaptations of conventional jazz pieces and show tunes. Why he never established himself as a consistent performer remains a mystery, but this 1970 reissue shows why he excited so many people during his rise. Smith's solos on "Spinning Wheel" and his own composition, "Psychedelic PI," are fleet and furious, boosting the songs from interesting to arresting. He's also impressive on "Seven Steps to Heaven," while the array of phrases, rhythms, and voicings on "Who's Afraid of Virginia Woolf?" demonstrate a mastery of the organ's pedals and keys rivaling that of the instrument's king, Jimmy Smith.

Ron Wynn

The Spinners

Spinners
1972, Rhino

A superb album, arguably their finest, though not their biggest, crossover work. The Spinners teamed with Thom Bell and made Motown look stupid with this album of glorious anthems. "I'll Be Around" and "Could It Be I'm Falling in Love" ended any discussions, mentions, or even thoughts of their former lead singer G.C. Cameron, as Phillippe Wynne was emerging as the king of immaculate, sophisticated soul. They had three R&B chart toppers from this album and were now dominating the Motown acts they once idolized.

Ron Wynn

The Staple Singers

The Ultimate Staple Singers: A Family Affair
September 2004, Kent/Ace

Considering what a long, popular, and respected career the Staple Singers had, it's surprising that there was no comprehensive compilation prior to this 2004 release that spanned their gospel and soul eras, from the 1950s to the 1980s. You can count on the Ace group of labels to do these things right, however, and this two-CD, 44-song set is a very good summary of their career highlights, even if it inevitably can't include all of their outstanding performances. All of their big soul hits are here, naturally, but what makes this especially available is the presence of much material predating their hookup with Stax in the late '60s. The earliest recording goes all the way back to 1953, and the first half or so of disc one is all pre-Stax, with gospel sides from the mid-'50s through the mid-'60s for various labels, including "This May Be the Last Time" (which famously helped inspire the Rolling Stones' "The Last Time"), "Uncloudy Day," and their cover of Bob Dylan's "A Hard Rain's a-Gonna Fall." Their transition from gospel to soul on Epic in the mid-'60s is also represented by a handful of sides, including Pop Staples' "Why (Am I Treated So Bad)" and their low-charting cover of Buffalo Springfield's "For What It's Worth." And while their Stax era is understandably covered with far greater depth than any other, some relatively little-known worthy efforts from that period are here alongside the hits. There are, for instance, socially conscious "message songs" such as "The Ghetto," "Long Walk to DC," "When Will We Be Paid for the Work We Did," and "Who Took the Merry Out of Christmas"; unreleased solo sides by Pop Staples and Mavis Staples; and a remix of their "Oh La De Da" single that removes the fake audience noise. A few post-Stax tracks with slicker production are here too (among them their huge 1975 hit "Let's Do It Again"), and while it could be argued that a few more pre-Stax numbers would have been more artistically satisfying, it does round off the documentation of this major group's work, augmented by a detailed history in the 28-page booklet.

Richie Unterberger

Edwin Starr

Hell up in Harlem
1974, Motown

With productions and songs from Freddie Perren and Fonce Mizell, *Hell Up in Harlem* is the scathing and soulful soundtrack of the motion picture starring Fred Williamson. This was Edwin Starr's last album for Motown which probably accounts for the woeful lack of promotion. Two singles were

released, *Hell Up in Harlem*, the first, should have remained an album cut, as its appeal was limited, despite a dogmatic vocal by Edwin. However, the follow up, "Big Papa," should have been a monster. Written by Freddie Perren, it has the same power, forcefulness and drive of numbers that Norman Whitfield had produced on Rare Earth and the Temptations. The flips of both singles, "Don't It Feel Good to Be Free" and "Like We Used to Do," are mellower than the push sides. The bone picker, however, is "Easin' In," a great mid-tempo number with cool backing vocals, and a great reading from Starr, it has chart buster written all over it, yet Motown never released it as a single. Mind boggling, since Starr's final single for Berry's empire, "Who's Right Or Wrong," backed with "Lonely Rainy Days in San Diego," dropped six months after "Papa," but doesn't rate with "Easin'." Even more puzzling is why Phillips, which owns the Motown masters, hasn't reissued this winner on CD.

Andrew Hamilton

Steely Dan

Aja
1977, MCA

Steely Dan hadn't been a real working band since *Pretzel Logic*, but with *Aja*, Walter Becker and Donald Fagen's obsession with sonic detail and fascination with composition reached new heights. A coolly textured and immaculately produced collection of sophisticated jazz-rock, *Aja* has none of the overt cynicism or self-consciously challenging music that distinguished previous Steely Dan records. Instead, it's a measured and textured album, filled with subtle melodies and accomplished, jazzy solos that blend easily into the lush instrumental backdrops. But *Aja* isn't just about texture, since Becker and Fagen's songs are their most complex and musically rich set of songs—even the simplest song, the sunny pop of "Peg," has layers of jazzy vocal harmonies. In fact, Steely Dan ignores rock on *Aja*, preferring to fuse cool jazz, blues, and pop together in a seamless, seductive fashion. It's complex music delivered with ease, and although the duo's preoccupation with clean sound and self-consciously sophisticated arrangements would eventually lead to a dead end, *Aja* is a shining example of jazz-rock at its finest.

Stephen Thomas Erlewine

The Stylistics

The Stylistics
1971, Amherst

The brilliant album that got everything started. Heads turned, people snapped to attention (women especially), and the "sweet" soul fraternity was turned on its head when this five-member group featuring the sugary, sweeping falsetto of Russell Tompkins, Jr. hit the scene with such singles as "Betcha by Golly Wow," "People Make the World Go Round," and "Stop, Look and Listen to Your Heart." His delivery, shimmering style, and brilliant pacing and control temporarily rendered almost every other "sweet" soul vocalist and group speechless; pretty soon, the Delfonics, Blue Magic, Moments, and others would fight back, but in 1972, everyone was playing catch-up to The Stylistics.

Ron Wynn

The Sylvers

Boogie Fever: The Best of the Sylvers
1995, Razor & Tie

Boogie Fever: The Best of the Sylvers is a definitive 16-track collection that contains all of the group's hits, from "Fool's Paradise" to "Falling for Your Love." In between, the Top Ten R&B hits "Wish That I Could Talk to You," "Boogie Fever," "Hot Line" and "High School Dance" are heard, as are a number of smaller hits. Not all of the songs are as infectious or memorable as the big hits, but they're solid disco and soul cuts. And there's never been a collection of Sylvers material as strong as this excellent disc.

Stephen Thomas Erlewine

Foster Sylvers

Foster Sylvers
1973, Pride

Dismiss Foster Sylvers as little more than a poor man's Michael Jackson if you must, but damn, the smash "Misdemeanor" lays to waste everything MJ recorded solo until "Don't Stop Til You Get Enough"—a sinuous, loping evocation of street-smart puppy love, it's one of the most underrated funk jams ever. Sylvers was just eleven years old when he cut this preternaturally accomplished solo effort, aided and abetted by arrangers Jerry Peters, David Crawford and King Errison—comprised largely of covers including "I'm Your Puppet," "Mockingbird" and "Lullabye/Uncle Albert," the material is often too slight or too obvious for its own good, but Sylvers is such an ebullient and charming singer that the positives far outweigh the negatives.

Jason Ankeny

The Temptations

All Directions
July 1972, Motown

A monster album, the one that put them back in the spotlight and signaled that Norman Whitfield had saved the day. Damon Harris had replaced Eddie Kendricks, and there were many doubters convinced the band was finished. Instead, Whitfield revitalized them via the majestic single, "Papa Was a Rollin' Stone." Despite its length, Whitfield's decision to open with an extensive, multi-layered musical suite and tease listeners was a master stroke. By the time Dennis Edwards' voice came rushing in, no one would dare turn it off. The single, as well as "Law Of The Land" and others, ended the funeral arrangements that had been prepared for The Temptations.

Ron Wynn

Joe Tex

Live and Lively
February 1968, Atlantic

Fantastic reproduction of a 1968 show—who knows how much overdubbing was done, and when the feel is this spontaneous and funky, who cares? He tears up stuff like "Get Out of My Life, Woman," "Love is a Hurtin' Thing," and even "That's Life." But the real meat is in his hits: "Skinny Legs and All" is a true climax, but only because part of what it follows is "A Woman's Hands," "Papa Was, Too," and other originals, all of them topping the standards. Arguably the definitive Joe Tex document. (The liner notes, by a St. Louis DJ, are among the worst in even the shabby history of '60s R&B notes, but that just makes them funnier.)

Dave Marsh

The Very Best of Joe Tex
November 1996, Rhino

An old friend of mine once said he considered listening to Joe Tex a viable alternative to seeing a marriage counselor; it was his opinion if you sat down with Joe's records and heeded his advice on keeping a happy home, chances were good you'd end up doing the right thing. And while Joe Tex had a great voice (a rich tenor whose openness and warmth tended to belie its strength and agility) and cut some of the most engaging Southern soul sides of the 1960's (as well as some potent 70's funk), what really set him apart were his songs, which with humor, charm and down-home horse sense offered plenty of hard-won advice on dealing with the ups and downs of life and love. While the albums Tex cut for Atlantic in the 1960's are consistently strong and worth hearing, many are not widely available in the United States; fortunately, this sixteen-cut sampler brings together many of biggest and most memorable hits, including "Skinny Legs And All," "You Got What It Takes," "The Love You Save (May Be Your Own)," and "S.Y.S.L.J.F.M. (The Letter Song)," as well as a few of his best latter-day dance tracks, such as "I Gotcha" and the memorably titled "Ain't Gonna Bump No More With No Big Fat Woman." *The Very Best Of Joe Tex* is a fine introduction to an artist well worth your attention; it's better than watching *Dr. Phil*, and you can dance to it, too!

Mark Deming

Rufus Thomas

The Best of Rufus Thomas: Do the Funky Somethin'
April 1996, Rhino

The Best of Rufus Thomas: Do the Funky Somethin' is an overdue, career-spanning collection of Thomas' best material, centering around his Stax hits from the '60s and early '70s. The whole "dog" series of novelty dance songs from 1963–1964 is here, as well as the hit "Jump Back" and a clutch of Stax singles that weren't hits but became pretty well-known anyway, like "Sister's Got a Boyfriend" and "Sophisticated Sissy." There are also the early '70s funk-dance hits "Do the Funky Chicken," "(Do The) Push and Pull," "The Breakdown," and "Do the Funky Penguin," a couple of '60s duets with his daughter Carla, and his 1953 blues single "Bear Cat (The Answer to Hound Dog)," the first hit on Sun Records. A few other compilations have gone into specific phases of his career in greater depth, but this is certainly the best overview of a man who offered some of the funkiest and funniest Memphis soul around.

Richie Unterberger

Trouble Funk

Drop the Bomb
1982, Sequel

Masters of Washington, D.C.'s '80s go-go craze, Trouble Funk brought early hip-hop (the group was part of Sugarhill Records) to the dancefloor with deep bass, propulsive rhythms, and party lyrics. Being even more inspired by '70s funk bands like Chic, Cameo, and the Gap Band than either the Sugar Hill Gang or Grandmaster Flash, Trouble Funk and other go-go acts like EU and Chuck Brown used the MC to conduct party-time call-and-response sessions and not generally for street poetry raps à la Melle Mel and Kurtis Blow. A celebratory atmosphere certainly prevails on Sequel Records' fine Trouble Funk collection *Drop the Bomb*, with many of the band's prime dance hits like the title track, "Get on Up," and "Let's Get Hot" being featured in their extended versions. The band's nasty synth licks, up-front percussion, and sinewy funk guitar lines keep the music pumping throughout, while both the go-go/rap hybrid "Pump Me Up" and Barry White-inspired soul ballad "Don't Try to Use Me" show off the group's musical flexibility. The set is rounded out with the ten-minute, bring-the-house-down jam "Supergrit," which nicely incorporates the funk of Kool & the Gang and Earth, Wind & Fire into the go-go mix. This is a great introduction to both Trouble Funk's music and the go-go sound.

Stephen Cook

The Undisputed Truth

Smiling Faces: The Best of Undisputed Truth
June 2003, Motown

While "Smiling Faces Sometimes" was unquestionably their biggest commercial success, the Undisputed Truth had many an underground soul circuit success with other hits over their decade-long career. This compiles a dozen of their greatest hits, starting with the aforementioned big hit and tearing through to Whitfield compositions that would become hits for other bands, "Ball of Confusion" and "Papa Was a Rolling Stone." The group members leave no room to question

whether they were talented or not, as song after song they exemplify how in sync they were with one another and feature extended song workouts similar in vein to early Parliament jam sessions. This is nowhere near as thorough as 2002's *Essential Collection*, but that's not necessarily a bad thing, as only die-hard fans would be interested in that much comprehensive material. This would be an ideal place for curious listeners to familiarize themselves with the Undisputed Truth's career.

Rob Theakston

Michal Urbaniak

The Beginning
1973, Catalyst

The title of this double LP is not quite accurate, for rather than being *The Beginning* of violinist Michal Urbaniak's career (he had recorded as early as 1969), it was close to the end of his stay in his native Poland; he would defect to the U.S. within a year. The music (all but one song is an Urbaniak original) falls into the fusion area and gives listeners a strong early dosage of Urbaniak (who also plays soprano, tenor and flute), his wife Urszula Dudziak (an innovative avant-garde singer), and Adam Makowicz. While Makowicz would become famous in the U.S. for his Art Tatum-inspired acoustic piano work, here he is heard on the Fender Rhodes and clavinet. The passionate playing is somewhat dated, yet due to its exploratory nature and spirit, also somewhat timeless. This twofer from the long-defunct Catalyst label will be quite difficult to find.

Scott Yanow

Melvin Van Peebles

Sweet Sweetback's Baadasssss Song
March 1997, Stax

Melvin Van Peebles' *Sweet Sweetback's Baadasssss Song* was an important film that paved the way for black filmmakers in American cinema in general, and in the 1970s blaxploitation genre in particular. Van Peebles hasn't been nearly as well known as a musician as he has a filmmaker, but he did compose the soundtrack, which was performed by Earth, Wind & Fire, who had then just released their first album. Heard on its own, the soundtrack, unlike *Superfly* or *Shaft*, is not a significant musical achievement. It's serviceable period funk-soul, both instrumental and vocal, sprinkled with some dialog from the film, although it did make number 13 on the soul album charts. "Hoppin' John" is an obvious James Brown-inspired tune, though sung with considerably less than Brown himself would have mustered. "Come On Feet Do Your Thing" is the cut most like Van Peebles' pre-rap excursions on A&M Records, which is unsurprising, as he had already recorded it on his A&M album *Ain't Supposed to Die a Natural Death*. *Sweet Sweetback's* has been reissued as one disc of the two-CD release *The Melvin Van Peebles Collection*, which also includes the 1972 original cast recording of *Don't Play Us Cheap*, the Broadway production (originally a film) that Van Peebles staged, and for which he also composed the music.

Richie Unterberger

War

All Day Music
February 1971, Rhino

As controlled as their self-titled debut was loose, War's sophomore effort, *All Day Music*, appearing a little over six months later in November 1971, was packed with subtly understated grooves. A hit with the fans, the LP peaked in the Top Ten, ultimately spending a massive 39 weeks on the charts. Side one is a gorgeous slab of mellow grooves and jazzed funk highlighted by both the title track and "Get Down," while "That's What Love Can Do" is an outstanding, textured, sleepy love affair revolving around the band's superior vocal harmonies and a tenor sax solo. The light, spare rhythm is like a warm treacle binding. With just three songs picking up the second half, War steps up the pace across the Latin-influenced jam "Nappy Head," the funky, bass-laden "Slipping Into the Darkness," and the all-out electric blues jam that rips through the prototype "Baby Brother." The latter was recorded live on June 30, 1971, at California's *Hollywood Bowl* and would, in revised and seriously edited form, be reborn as the monster "Me and Baby Brother" on War's *Deliver the Word* opus. Not nearly as fiery (with the exception of "Baby Brother," of course) as either their live performances or later albums, *All Day Music* is still one of this band's best-ever efforts. At times mellow enough to border on horizontal, the songs are filled with such texture and such rich intent that even in the band's quietest breath there is a funky resonance that fulfills Lee Oskar's vision fully.

Amy Hanson

Grover Washington, Jr.

Feels So Good
May & July 1975, Motown

The aptly titled and much-sampled *Feels So Good* represents the creative apex of Grover Washington, Jr.'s sublime electric funk sound. Its shimmering, soulful grooves refute the argument that smooth jazz is little more than mere ambience, combining expert playing and intricate songwriting to create music that is both compelling and comforting. Arranger Bob James is in top form here, creating the spacious, rich milieus that are his trademark, but regardless of the name above the title, bassist Louis Johnson is the real star of the show. His supple rhythms percolate like coffee, adding oomph to the bottom of highlights "Hydra" and "Knucklehead" while Washington's cream-and-sugar soprano sax solos soar over the top.

Jason Ankeny

Johnny "Guitar" Watson

Ain't That a Bitch
1976, Collectables

Coming out of Houston's fertile blues scene with Albert Collins and Johnny Copeland, Johnny "Guitar" Watson trod the same route to fame that his peers did in the latter half of the '50s and for most of the '60s. Unlike Collins and Copeland, though, Watson found his biggest success as a funkster in the '70s. And lest one thinks of an aging blues legend embarrassing himself aping the innovations of George Clinton and Sly Stone, Watson found a singular groove by slicking up his already urbane blues style with lots of tasty horn arrangements, plenty of fat basslines, and wah-wah-issue guitar licks. The latter element, of course, was to be expected from a virtuoso such as Watson. And whether reeling off one of his subtle solos or blending in with the band, the reborn blues star was never less than compelling. *Ain't That a Bitch*, from 1976, heralded Watson's new funk era with plenty of guitar treats and one of the best batch of songs he ever cooked up. The variety here is stunning, ranging from the calypso-based blues swinger "I Need It" to the quiet storm soul ballad "Since I Met You Baby." In between, Watson goes widescreen with the comic book funk of "Superman Lover" and eases into an after-hours mood on the organ-driven jazz and blues gem "I Want to Ta-Ta You Baby." Besides the fine Watson roundups on the Rhino and Charly labels, *Ain't That a Bitch* works beautifully as a first-disc choice for newcomers, especially those who want to hear the '70s funk material.

Stephen Cook

Watts Prophets

Things Gonna Get Greater: The Watts Prophets 1969–1971
September 2005, Water

Water Records—the incomparable, mysterious reissue label—has outdone themselves this time by reissuing the first two albums by the Watts Prophets, a spoken-word poetry group that grew out of the Watts Writers' Workshop. The Prophets—Anthony "Amde" Hamilton, Richard Dedeaux, Otis O'Solomon and later Dee Dee McNeil—were not as well-known nationally as their East Coast contemporaries the Last Poets, but they have influenced and have been sampled by countless hip-hop artists. The two recordings featured here, 1969's *Black Voices: On the Streets in Watts* and 1971's *Rappin' Black in a White World*, are seminal documents of the Black Power struggle that was wiped out by the FBI's Cointelpro operation, incarceration, death, poverty and other persecutions from the power culture. The albums are presented here in reverse order—as Water is wont to do—and, aesthetically, it makes sense. *Rappin' Black in a White World* features McNeil's bluesed-out piano, her deeply influential proto-feminist poem "There's a Difference Between a Black Man and a Nigger," and the wonderfully haunting yet poignant "Sell Your Soul." Her voice and piano textures the suit on the first side of the disc. Dedeaux's "Amerikkka" is the highlight of the set with its righteous anger and deep rhythmic heartbeat. On *Black Voices: On the Streets in Watts* it is Hamilton's voice that startles, exhorts and occasionally frightens the listener. It's immediate, direct from the street and in your face. The album is rawer, less connected track for track, more slice of life, from the gut. Ragged, wailing saxophones and hand drums color the poetic proceedings that insist on revolution and a holistic approach to living while being suffocated and eaten alive in the white America. These records are not for everybody, but then, they never were. They are for those who can handle the truth that is still the truth. The game and its rules haven't changed; only the adornments and surfaces have changed. This is rap, hard, immediate and angry; it's a heart full of soul and a belly full of hard beauty that rings like a cry from the wilderness. Welcome to the real hardcore.

Thom Jurek

Weather Report

Sweetnighter
February 1973, Columbia

Right from the start, a vastly different Weather Report emerges here, one that reflects co-leader Joe Zawinul's developing obsession with the groove. It is the groove that rules this mesmerizing album, leading off with the irresistible 3/4 marathon deceptively tagged as the "Boogie Woogie Waltz" and proceeding through a variety of Latin-grounded hip-shakers. It is a record of discovery for Zawinul, who augments his Rhodes electric piano with a funky wah-wah pedal, unveils the ARP synthesizer as a melodic instrument and sound-effects device, and often coasts along on one chord. The once fiery Wayne Shorter has been tamed, for he now contributes mostly sustained ethereal tunes on soprano sax, his tone sometimes doubled for a pleasing octave effect. The wane of freewheeling ensemble interplay is more than offset by the big increase in rhythmic push; bassist Miroslav Vitous, drummer Eric Gravatt, and percussionist Dom Um Romao are now cogs in one of jazz's great swinging machines.

Richard S. Ginell

Barry White

I've Got So Much Love to Give
1973, 20th Century

It was no real surprise when Barry White's 1973 debut LP, *I've Got So Much to Give*, rocketed to the top of the R&B charts in April. The sound of whispered voices, half-empty champagne bottles, and rumpled satin sheets, its seamless blend of lush instrumentals and rich, deep vocal numbers was delivered with a suave coolness that shook up the mores of traditional '60s-style soul and turned it into something so sexy that blush and groove vied for the same space. The album is built around the massive "I'm Gonna Love You Just a Little More Baby," which scored White both his first charting

single and his first ever number one—and remains, for many, the song to which White's style is indelibly inked. With just a little funk behind the strings and keys, it's White's quietly-spoken declaration of love-without-innuendo that completes the mood, long before he turns to verse and chorus. Silly, perhaps; thrilling, definitely; and titillating—it depended on who you spoke to. "I've Got So Much to Give," the follow-up hit, follows that format—of course it does. But the novelty of White's approach, coupled with the universality of his subject matter, ensured that there was no sense of having heard it all before. Indeed, even with two such groundbreaking songs to lead the way, the three remaining tracks only maintain the mood and prolong the pleasure, completing a concerto that spans the full gamut of romantic emotion—an astonishing "Standing in the Shadows of Love," the yearning "Bring Back My Yesterday," and the absolutely joyful "I Found Someone." Together, too, they amount to some of the purest, easiest material White ever recorded.

Amy Hanson

Barry White Sings for Someone You Love
1977, 20th Century

This was Barry White's first bona fide success in close to two years. It is due in part to the slight change of his music formula. After albums such as the Love Unlimited Orchestra's *Music Maestro, Please* and 1976's *Is This Whatcha Wont?* disappeared without a trace, White ended his over the top musical extravagance and returned with a sleeker more relaxed style. *Barry White Sings for Someone You Love* is often so laid back, it's almost reclining. This album biggest hit was "It's Ecstasy When You Lay Down Next to Me." That song more than anything else here typified White's new and improved production style and offered one of his drollest vocals. The amazing "Oh What a Night" has him effortlessly capturing the drama of R&B from a decade or two earlier and it is both sensual and romantic. The sleeper of the album, "I Never Thought I'd Fall In Love With You," is lush, confident, and assured. If it appeared on an album before this, it's doubtful White could have gotten the subtle musical nuances or the plaintive vocal. As for pure ballads, "You Turned My Whole World Around" and "Of All the Guys in the World" are good, but with their interchangeable dirge-like paces, they practically cancel one another out. *Barry White Sings for Someone You Love* in essence restarted White's career and contains some of his best work.

Jason Elias

Marva Whitney

It's My Thing
1969, King

Like any disc produced by James Brown and featuring the mighty JB's as a backing group, *It's My Thing* is a stone-cold funky record. Marva Whitney sang in the James Brown Revue from 1967 to 1969, and in 1969 she released this record.

Not only did Brown produce but he wrote or co-wrote most of the tracks and it basically sounds like a James Brown record with a female singer. A tough, aggressive female singer. Marva sounds like she could take any comers and leave them shaking in their go-go boots. From the opening blast of "It's My Thing, Pt. 1 and Pt. 2," a rewrite of the Isley Brothers' "It's Your Thing," she shouts, exhorts, wails, and basically lets it all hang out as the band lays down groove after groove. Thankfully after four exhausting tracks, Marva slows it down with "If You Love Me," an Otis Redding-style broken-hearted ballad. After an instrumental break she jumps right back into the funky fray with "Unwind Yourself," which features a classic horn line and some gritty vocalizing from Marva. The rest of the record follows this pattern of a couple of stompers and a ballad. The highlight of the record is "I'm Tired I'm Tired I'm Tired (Things Better Change Before It's Too Late)," a funky (yes, every track on this disc is funky) lament that details just how tired Marva is of society putting her down. Check out Brown going wild in the background about halfway through the song. The disc has five bonus tracks added to the original album, including the slow-burning "I Made a Mistake Because It's Only You, Pts. 1 & 2" and a duet with Janies Brown on "Sunny." This is a great record and it is a pity that it is on such a tiny label and not one of the major reissue labels because Marva deserves wider recognition. By all means seek this one out.

Tim Sendra

Larry Willis

Inner Crisis
1973, Groove Merchant

Inner Crisis by Larry Willis is one of the very finest examples of electric jazz-funk from the mid-'70s. With sidemen who included guitarist Roland Prince, drummer Al Foster, tenor saxophonist Harold Vick, and trombonist Dave Bargeron, as well as bassists Eddie Gomez (acoustic) and Roderick Gaskin (electric), Willis assembled a session that was long on composition and tight on the big groove. Willis' long front lines accentuated deep soul and blues' cadences that were hallmarks of music that walked the line between tough lean groove and the pulsating rhythm of disco without losing its jazz roots to sterile fusion tropes, thanks in large part to his willingness as a pianist to play as part of an ensemble rather than as a soloist. Tracks such as "153rd Street Theme," with its loping saxophone lines juxtaposed against deep groove basslines, offer a deeper perspective on the funk; the shimmering modal intensity of the title cut nods to the expansiveness of Miles Davis' "In a Silent Way," and the blissed-out soul of "Journey's End," accentuates the wide-open engagement with lyricism that was frequently left out of the electric jazz equation during the period. Along with the other tracks here, they offer a moving, wonderfully conceived and articulated aspect of the music that has been sadly overlooked by all but the most devoted fans of the genre.

Thom Jurek

Reuben Wilson

Love Bug
March & October 1969, Blue Note

Love Bug was an attempt to establish Reuben Wilson as an organist with either the vision of Larry Young or the fiery style of John Patton, and while it comes up short on both accounts, it nevertheless remains quite enjoyable. Working with an impressive backing band of guitarist Grant Green, trumpeter Lee Morgan, tenor saxophonist George Coleman and drummer Idris Muhammad, Wilson leads his band through a number of soul-jazz workouts, none of which ever really catch fire. Instead of working tight, funky grooves, the quintet tends to spiral off into vaguely experimental territory, which loses sight of the spirit of the song. Still, Green has a number of shining moments, as does Morgan and Coleman—in fact, they tend to overshadow Wilson, who nevertheless turns in a fine performance. Nevertheless, there are flashes on *Love Bug*, particularly on "Hot Rod" and the bonus track "Hold On, I'm Comin'," that demonstrate the organist coming into his own.

Stephen Thomas Erlewine

Blue Mode
December 1969, Blue Note

If *Love Bug* skirted the edges of free jazz and black power, *Blue Mode* embraces soul-jazz and Memphis funk in no uncertain terms. Opening with the cinematic, stuttering "Bambu" and running through a set of relaxed, funky grooves—including covers of Eddie Floyd's "Knock on Wood" and Edwin Starr's "Twenty-Five Miles"—*Blue Mode* isn't strictly a jazz album, but its gritty, jazzy vamps and urban soul-blues make it highly enjoyable. Reuben Wilson has a laid-back, friendly style and his supporting band—tenor saxophonist John Manning, guitarist Melvin Sparks, and drummer Tommy Derrick—demonstrate a similarly warm sense of tone. While none of them break through with any improvisations that would satiate hardcore jazz purists, they know how to work a groove, and that's what makes *Blue Mode* a winner.

Stephen Thomas Erlewine

Bill Withers

Still Bill
1972, Sussex

Bill Withers came into his own on his third album, *Still Bill*. Released in 1972, the record is a remarkable summation of a number of contemporary styles: the smooth soul coming out of Philly, smoky, late-night funk via Bobby Womack, bluesy Southern soul, and '70s singer/songwriterism. It's rich, subtly layered music, but its best attribute is that it comes on easy, never sounding labored or overworked. In fact, it takes several spins of the album to realize just how versatile Withers is on *Still Bill*, to hear how he makes intricate, funky rhythms sound as effortless and simple as the album's best-known song, the gospel-tinged inspirational anthem "Lean on Me." That's the genius behind Withers' music: it's warm and easily accessible, but it has a depth and complexity that reveals itself over numerous plays—and, given the sound and feel of the music, from the lush arrangements to his comforting voice, it's easy to want to play this again and again. Then there's the quality of the songwriting, which is as assured on the grooving "Lonely Town, Lonely Street" as it is on the suspicious, paranoid "Who Is He (And What Is He to You)?" or "Use Me," where he happily submits to being used by his object of affection. This high level of songwriting is sustained throughout the record, making this the greatest testament to his considerable gifts. [The 2003 reissue contains two bonus tracks from his *Live at Carnegie Hall* album.]

Stephen Thomas Erlewine

Bobby Womack

Across 110th Street
December 1972, Charly

The soundtrack to a relatively little-known 1972 blaxploitation film featured songs written and performed by Bobby Womack, as well as a musical score by J.J. Johnson. Although the inconsistency of the approach precluded a musical statement along the lines of *Superfly*, it's an interesting find for those looking for little-heeded early '70s soul with funk and rock influences. Womack's cuts count among his better material, and even if the title track cops much of its attitude from *Superfly*, it has a satisfyingly tough soul-rock groove of its own. "If You Want My Love" is a good grainy ballad, "Quicksand" a propulsive number well-suited for action scenes, and "Do It Right" in the mold of James Brown, but more rock-oriented. Johnson's instrumental contributions, while not as interesting, set a nice period soul-jazz mood, and there are nifty periodic washes of electronic effects in both composers' contributions.

Richie Unterberger

Stevie Wonder

Talking Book
October 1972, Motown

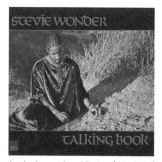

After releasing two "head" records during 1970–71, Stevie Wonder expanded his compositional palate with 1972's *Talking Book* to include societal ills as well as tender love songs, and so recorded the first smash album of his career. What had been hinted at on the intriguing project *Music of My Mind* was here focused into a laser beam of tight songwriting, warm electronic arrangements, and ebullient performances—altogether the most realistic vision of musical personality ever put to wax, beginning with a disarmingly simple love song, "You Are the Sunshine of My Life" (but of course, it's only the composition that's simple). Stevie's not always singing a tender ballad here—in fact, he flits from contentment to mistrust to promise to heartbreak within the course of the first four songs—but he never fails to render each song in the most

vivid colors. In stark contrast to his early songs, which were clever but often relied on the Motown template of romantic metaphor, with *Talking Book* it became clear Stevie Wonder was beginning to speak his mind and use personal history for material (just as Marvin Gaye had with the social protest of 1971's *What's Going On*). The lyrics became less convoluted, while the emotional power gained in intensity. "You and I" and the glorious closer "I Believe (When I Fall in Love It Will Be Forever)" subtly illustrate that the conception of love can be stronger than the reality, while "Tuesday Heartbreak" speaks simply but powerfully: "I wanna be with you when the nighttime comes / I wanna be with you till the daytime comes." Ironically, the biggest hit from *Talking Book* wasn't a love song at all; the funk landmark "Superstition" urges empowerment instead of hopelessness, set to a grooving beat that made it one of the biggest hits of his career. It's followed by "Big Brother," the first of his directly critical songs, excoriating politicians who posture to the underclass in order to gain the only thing they really need: votes. With *Talking Book*, Stevie also found a proper balance between making an album entirely by himself and benefiting from the talents of others. His wife Syreeta and her sister Yvonne Wright contributed three great lyrics, and Ray Parker, Jr. came by to record a guitar solo that brings together the lengthy jam "Maybe Your Baby." Two more guitar heroes, Jeff Beck and Buzzy Feton, appeared on "Lookin' for Another Pure Love," Beck's solo especially giving voice to the excruciating process of moving on from a broken relationship. Like no other Stevie Wonder LP before it, *Talking Book* is all of a piece, the first unified statement of his career. It's certainly an exercise in indulgence but, imitating life, it veers breathtakingly from love to heartbreak and back with barely a pause.

John Bush

Innervisions
August 1973, Motown

When Stevie Wonder applied his tremendous songwriting talents to the unsettled social morass that was the early '70s, he produced one of his greatest, most important works, a rich panoply of songs addressing drugs, spirituality, political ethics, the unnecessary perils of urban life, and what looked to be the failure of the '60s dream—all set within a collection of charts as funky and catchy as any he'd written before. Two of the highlights, "Living for the City" and "Too High," make an especially deep impression thanks to Stevie's narrative talents; on the first, an eight-minute mini-epic, he brings a hard-scrabble Mississippi black youth to the city and illustrates, via a brilliant dramatic interlude, what lies in wait for innocents. (He also uses his variety of voice impersonations to stunning effect.) "Too High" is just as stunning, a cautionary tale about drugs driven by a dizzying chorus of scat vocals and a springing bassline. "Higher Ground," a funky follow-up to the previous album's big hit ("Superstition"), and "Jesus Children of America" both introduced Wonder's interest in Eastern religion. It's a tribute to his genius that he could broach topics like reincarnation and transcendental meditation in a pop context with minimal interference to the rest of the album. Wonder also made no secret of the fact that "He's Misstra Know-It-All" was directed at Tricky Dick, aka Richard Milhouse Nixon, then making headlines (and destroying America's faith in the highest office) with the biggest political scandal of the century. Putting all these differing themes and topics into perspective was the front cover, a striking piece by Efram Wolff portraying Stevie Wonder as the blind visionary, an artist seeing far better than those around him what was going on in the early '70s, and using his astonishing musical gifts to make this commentary one of the most effective and entertaining ever heard.

John Bush

Songs in the Key of Life
September 1976, Motown

Songs in the Key of Life was Stevie Wonder's longest, most ambitious collection of songs, a two-LP (plus accompanying EP) set that—just as the title promised— touched on nearly every issue under the sun, and did it all with ambitious (even for him), wide-ranging arrangements and some of the best performances of Wonder's career. The opening "Love's in Need of Love Today" and "Have a Talk With God" are curiously subdued, but Stevie soon kicks into gear with "Village Ghetto Land," a fierce exposé of ghetto neglect set to a satirical baroque synthesizer. Hot on its heels comes the torrid fusion jam "Contusion," a big, brassy hit tribute to the recently departed Duke Ellington in "Sir Duke," and (another hit, this one a Grammy winner as well) the bumping poem to his childhood, "I Wish." Though they didn't necessarily appear in order, *Songs in the Key of Life* contains nearly a full album on love and relationships, along with another full album on issues social and spiritual. Fans of the love album *Talking Book* can marvel that he sets the bar even higher here, with brilliant material like the tenderly cathartic and gloriously redemptive "Joy Inside My Tears," the two-part, smooth-and-rough "Ordinary Pain," the bitterly ironic "All Day Sucker," or another classic heartbreaker, "Summer Soft." Those inclined toward Stevie Wonder the social-issues artist had quite a few songs to focus on as well: "Black Man" was a Bicentennial school lesson on remembering the vastly different people who helped build America; "Pastime Paradise" examined the plight of those who live in the past and have little hope for the future; "Village Ghetto Land" brought listeners to a nightmare of urban wasteland; and "Saturn" found Stevie questioning his kinship with the rest of humanity and amusingly imagining paradise as a residency on a distant planet. If all this sounds overwhelming, it is; Stevie Wonder had talent to spare during the mid-'70s, and instead of letting the reserve trickle out during the rest of the decade, he let it all go with one massive burst. (His only subsequent record of the '70s was the similarly gargantuan but largely instrumental soundtrack *Journey Through the Secret Life of Plants*.)

John Bush

Charles Wright

Express Yourself
1970, Warner Bros.

The quintessential Charles Wright & the Watts 103rd Street Rhythm Band record, *Express Yourself* displays the purposefully sloppy rhythms and shout vocals that would make this band a legend in soul circles. Every track on this album

is a classic, from the oft-sampled and high-charting pop single "Express Yourself" to the first of many readings of "I Got Love" that would appear on the band's records— and even Wright's solo works for years to come. The aching balladry of "Tell Me What You Want Me to Do" and the complex compositions "High as Apple Pie—Slice 1" and "High as Apple Pie—Slice 2" showcase a versatility found in other West Coast collectives such as War. Perhaps the treasure of this album is the opener, "Road Without an End," a charming, stepping groover punctuated by choppy horns and snapping drums that blend beautifully with one of Wright's best vocals of his career, all accented by sweeping strings. *Express Yourself* is '70s soul at its most creative and satisfying.

Douglas Siwek

Young-Holt Unlimited

Soulful Strut
December 1968, Brunswick

It's unclear how much actual playing the Young-Holt Trio does on their debut LP. "*Soulful Strut*." The title track happens to be the instrumental track of "Am I The Same Girl," by Barbara Acklin, with Acklin's vocal removed and the piano raised in the mix. Likewise for "Please Sunrise," "Love Makes A Woman," and "Just Ain't No Love," all songs that Acklin recorded. The trio consisted of Ken Chaney (piano), and Eldee Young (bass, cello, vocals), and Issac Holt (drums), formerly of the Ramsey Lewis Trio. Whether a fast one got pulled or not, the 10 tracks make for enjoyable and delightful listening. Excellent old school, smooth jazz.

Andrew Hamilton

PLAYLISTS

Cold Chillin' Label Playlist

Kool G Rap & DJ Polo: "It's a Demo"
MC Shan: "Jane, Stop This Crazy Thing"
Roxanne Shante: "Have a Nice Day"
Kool G Rap & DJ Polo: "Riker's Island"
Big Daddy Kane: "Ain't No Half Steppin'"
Marley Marl: "The Symphony"
Biz Markie: "Vapors"
Grand Daddy I.U.: "Pick Up the Pace"
Chubb Rock: "Road to the Riches"
Diamond Shell: "Oh, What a Night"
MC Shan: "I Pioneered This"
Biz Markie: "Just a Friend"
Big Daddy Kane: "Smooth Operator"
Kool G Rap & DJ Polo: "Streets of New York"
Masta Ace: "Me and the Biz"
Kool G Rap & DJ Polo: "Ill Street Blues"

Def Jam Label Playlist

T La Rock & Jazzy Jay: "It's Yours"
LL Cool J: "I Need a Beat"
LL Cool J: "Rock the Bells"
Hollis Crew: "It's the Beat"
Beastie Boys: "The New Style"
Jazzy Jay: "Def Jam"
Original Concept: "Knowledge Me"
Nikki D: "Daddy's Little Girl"
Downtown Science: "Room to Breathe"
Public Enemy: "Welcome to the Terrordome"
Slick Rick: "Children's Story"
3rd Bass: "Steppin' to the AM"
LL Cool J: "Goin' Back to Cali"
Public Enemy: "Welcome to the Terrordome"
EPMD: "Gold Digger"
Terminator X: "Buck Whylin'"
Redman: "Time 4 Sum Aksion"
Onyx: "Throw Ya Gunz"

Enjoy Label Playlist

Grandmaster Flash & the Furious Five:
    "Superappin'"
Treacherous Three: "At the Party"
Spoonie Gee & Treacherous Three: "New Rap
    Language"
Funky 4 + 1: "Rappin' and Rocking the House"
Treacherous Three: "The Body Rock"
Kool Kyle the Starchild & the Disco Dolls: "Do You
    Like That Funky Beat"
Disco Four: "Move to the Groove"
Fearless Four: "Feel the Heartbeat"
Treacherous Three: "Put the Boogie in Your Body"
Disco Four: "Do It, Do It"

Spanish Fly & the Terrible Two: "Spanglish"
Fearless Four: "Rockin' It"
Masterdon Committee: "Funk Box Party"

Profile Label Playlist

Dr. Jeckyll & Mr. Hyde: "Genius Rap"
Disco Four: "We're at the Party"
Run-D.M.C.: "It's Like That"
Run-D.M.C.: "Hard Times"
Fresh 3 MCs: "Fresh"
Pumpkin: "King of the Beat"
The Rake: "Street Justice"
Run-D.M.C.: "Rock Box"
Rammelzee vs. K-Rob: "Beat Bop"
Pumpkin & the Profile: "Here Comes That Beat!"
Dr. Jeckyll & Mr. Hyde: "Fast Life"
Run-D.M.C.: "King of Rock"
Run-D.M.C.: "My Adidas"
Sweet Tee & DJ Jazzy Joyce: "It's My Beat"
Dana Dane: "Nightmares"
Twin Hype: "Do It to the Crowd"
Rob Base & DJ E-Z Rock: "It Takes Two"
Run-D.M.C.: "Run's House"
Special Ed: "I Got It Made"
Low Profile: "Pay Ya Dues"
Poor Righteous Teachers: "Rock Dis Funky Joint"
Special Ed: "The Mission"
DJ Quik: "Tonight"
2nd II None: "Be True to Yourself"
N2Deep: "Back to the Hotel"

Sugarhill Label Playlist

Sugarhill Gang: "Rapper's Delight"
Sequence: "Funk You Up"
Sequence & Spoonie Gee: "Monster Jam"
Grandmaster Flash & the Furious Five: "Freedom"
Sugarhill Gang: "Eighth Wonder"
Grandmaster Flash: "The Adventures of Grandmas-
    ter Flash on the Wheels of Steel"
Funky 4 + 1: "That's the Joint"
Spoonie Gee: "Spoonie Is Back"
Mean Machine: "Disco Dream"
Crash Crew: "We Want to Rock"
Grandmaster Flash & the Furious Five: "The
    Message"
Busy Bee: "Making Cash Money"
Fearless Four: "Yes We Can Can"
Grandmaster Melle Mel: "White Lines (Don't Do It)"
Treacherous Three: "Action"
Grandmaster Flash & the Furious Five: "New York,
    New York"
Crash Crew: "On the Radio"

Tommy Boy Label Playlist

Afrika Bambaataa & Soul Sonic Force: "Planet Rock"
Afrika Bambaataa & Soul Sonic Force: "Looking for the Perfect Beat"
Afrika Bambaataa & the Jazzy 5: "Jazzy Sensation"
GLOBE & Whiz Kid: "Play That Beat, Mr. DJ"
Planet Patrol: "Play at Your Own Risk"
The Jonzun Crew: "Pack Jam (Look Out for the OVC)"
Stetsasonic: "Talkin' All That Jazz"
De La Soul: "Me, Myself, and I"
De La Soul: "Buddy"
Queen Latifah: "Ladies First"
Digital Underground: "The Humpty Dance"
Digital Underground: "Doowutchyalike"
Paris: "Break the Grip of Shame"
Naughty by Nature: "O.P.P."
Naughty by Nature: "Everything's Gonna Be Alright"
House of Pain: "Jump Around"

Tuff City Label Playlist

Spoonie Gee: "The Big Beat"
Cold Crush Brothers: "Punk Rock Rap"
Davy DMX: "One for the Treble (Fresh)"
Cold Crush Brothers: "Fresh, Fly, Wild, and Bold"
Freddy B & the Mighty Mic Masters: "The Main Event"
Spoonie Gee: "The Godfather"
Spoonie Gee: "Take It Off"
The 45 King: "The 900 Number"
Lakim Shabazz: "Black Is Back"
YZ: "In Control of Things"

Wild Pitch Label Playlist

Latee: "This Cut's Got Flavor"
Chill Rob G: "Dope Rhymes"
Gang Starr: "Words I Manifest (Remix)"
Chill Rob G: "Court Is Now in Session"
Main Source: "Looking at the Front Door"
Lord Finesse & DJ Mike Smooth: "Strictly for the Ladies"
Main Source: "Just Hangin' Out"
UMCs: "One to Grow On"
Ultramagnetic MCs: "Two Brothers with Checks (San Francisco, Harvey)"
O.C.: "Time's Up"
The Coup: "Not Yet Free"
Brokin English Klick: "Who's da Gangsta?"

Diamond Production Playlist

Ultimate Force: "I'm Not Playing"
Brand Nubian: "Punks Jump Up to Get Beat Down"
Diamond & the Psychotic Neurotics: "Sally Got a One Track Mind"
Showbiz & AG: "Soul Clap"
Illegal: "Crumbsnatcher"
Fat Joe da Gangsta: "Watch the Sound"

Fu-Schnickens: "Sneaking Up on Ya"
House of Pain: "Word Is Bond"
Ed OG & da Bulldogs: "Streets of the Ghetto"
Nefertiti: "Family Tree"
Lord Finesse & DJ Mike Smooth: "Funky Technician"

DJ Mark the 45 King Production/Remix Playlist

DJ Mark the 45 King: "The 900 Number"
Queen Latifah: "Ladies First"
Def Jef: "Don't Sleep (Open Your Eyes)"
Apache: "Do Fa Self"
Lakim Shabazz: "Pure Righteousness"
Gang Starr: "Gusto"
X Clan: "Heed the Word of the Brother"
Salt-N-Pepa: "My Mic Sounds Nice (Remix)"
King Sun: "Fat Tape"
Chill Rob G: "Court Is Now in Session"
Dr. Dre & Ed Lover: "Who's the Man"
Latee: "No Tricks"
Eric B. & Rakim: "Microphone Fiend (Remix)"

Marley Marl Production Playlist

Roxanne Shante: "Roxanne's Revenge"
Marley Marl: "Marley Marl Scratch"
Kool G Rap & DJ Polo: "It's a Demo"
Biz Markie: "Nobody Beats the Biz"
Big Daddy Kane: "Raw"
Spoonie Gee: "The Godfather"
LL Cool J: "The Boomin' System"
Intelligent Hoodlum: "Black and Proud"
MC Lyte: "Cappucino"
MC Shan: "Kill That Noise"
Heavy D & the Boyz: "Gyrlz, They Love Me"
Dimples D: "Sucker DJs (I Will Survive)"
Monie Love: "Full Term Love"
Lords of the Underground: "Tic Toc"
Master Ace: "Music Man"

Rick Rubin Production Playlist

T la Rock & Jazzy Jay: "It's Yours"
LL Cool J: "I Need a Beat"
LL Cool J: "I Can't Live Without My Radio"
Jazzy Jay: "Def Jam"
Hollis Crew: "It's the Beat"
Beastie Boys: "She's on It"
Jimmy Spicer: "This Is It"
Run-D.M.C.: "My Adidas"
Run-D.M.C.: "It's Tricky"
Beastie Boys: "No Sleep till Brooklyn"
The Junkyard Band: "The Word"
LL Cool J: "Going Back to Cali"
Sir Mix-A-Lot: "Baby Got Back"

Sampled on A Tribe Called Quest's *The Low End Theory*

The Last Poets: "Time" ("Excursions")
The Last Poets: "Tribute to Obabi" ("Excursions")
Shades of Brown: "The Soil I Tilled for You"

("Excursions")

Art Blakey & the Jazz Messengers: "A Chant for Bu" ("Excursions")

Jack DeJohnette's Direction: "Minya's the Mooch" ("Buggin' Out")

Lonnie Smith: "Spinning Wheel" ("Buggin' Out")

Michal Urbaniak: "Ekim" ("Buggin' Out")

Eric Mercury: "Long Way Down" ("Rap Promoter")

The New Birth: "Keep on Doin' It" ("Rap Promoter")

Sly & the Family Stone: "Stand" ("Rap Promoter")

Eighties Ladies: "Turned on to You" ("Butter")

Chuck Jackson: "I Like Everything About You" ("Butter")

Gary Bartz: "Gentle Smiles" ("Butter")

Weather Report: "Young and Fine" ("Butter")

Heatwave: "The Star of a Story" ("Verses from the Abstract")

Joe Farrell: "Upon This Rock" ("Verses from the Abstract")

James Brown: "Funky President" ("Show Business")

The Fatback Band: "Wicky-Wacky" ("Show Business")

Grant Green: "Down Here on the Ground" ("Vibes and Stuff")

Jackie Jackson: "Is It Him or Me?" ("The Infamous Date Rape")

Cannonball Adderley: "The Steam Drill" ("The In-famous Date Rape")

Les McCann: "North Carolina" ("The Infamous Date Rape")

Average White Band: "Love Your Life" ("Check the Rhime")

Minnie Riperton: "Baby, This Love I Have" ("Check the Rhime")

Grover Washington, Jr.: "Hydra" ("Check the Rhime")

Bobby Byrd: "Hot Pants... I'm Coming, I'm Coming, I'm Coming" ("Everything Is Fair")

Funkadelic: "Let's Take It to the People" ("Every-thing Is Fair")

Harlem Underground Band: "Ain't no Sunshine" ("Everything is Fair")

The Five Stairsteps: "Don't Change Your Love" ("Jazz [We've Got]")

Sly & the Family Stone: "Sing a Simple Song" ("Jazz [We've Got]")

Freddie Hubbard: "Red Clay" ("Jazz [We've Got]")

Lucky Thompson: "Green Dolphin Street" ("Jazz [We've Got]")

Paul Humphrey & the Cool-Aid Chemists: "Uncle Willie's Dream" ("What?")

The Emotions: "Blind Alley" ("Scenario")

Kool & the Gang: "Give It Up" ("Scenario")

Kool & the Gang: "Soul Vibrations" ("Scenario")

Ohio Players: "Ecstasy" ("Scenario")

Brother Jack McDuff: "Oblighetto" ("Scenario")

Sampled on De La Soul's *3 Feet High and Rising*

Banbarra: "Shack Up" ("The Magic Number")

Don Covay: "The Overtime Man" ("The Magic Number")

Syl Johnson: "Different Strokes" ("The Magic Number")

Cymande: "Bra" ("Change in Speak")

Mad Lads: "No Strings Attached" ("Change in Speak")

Ashford & Simpson: "Solid" ("Cool Breeze on the Rocks")

Michael Jackson: "Rock with You" ("Cool Breeze on the Rocks")

Vaughn Mason & Crew: "Bounce, Rock, Skate, Roll" ("Cool Breeze on the Rocks")

Treacherous Three: "The Body Rock" ("Cool Breeze on the Rocks")

The New Birth: "Got to Get a Knutt" ("Can U Keep a Secret?")

Lyn Collins: "Think (About It)" ("Jenifa Taught Me [Derwin's Revenge]")

Curtis Mayfield: "Back to the World" ("Ghetto Thang")

The Blackbyrds: "Rock Creek Park" ("Ghetto Thang")

Kraftwerk: "Trans-Europe Express" ("Ghetto Thang")

Mad Lads: "Make This Young Lady Mine" ("Eye Know")

Steely Dan: "Peg" ("Eye Know")

Otis Redding: "Sittin' on the Dock of the Bay" ("Eye Know")

Patrice Rushen: "Remind Me" ("Eye Know")

Sly & the Family Stone: "Sing a Simple Song" ("Eye Know")

Percy Sledge: "Stand by Me" ("Take It Off")

The Headhunters: "God Made Me Funky" ("Take It Off")

Jarmels: "A Little Bit of Soap" ("A Little Bit of Soap")

Ben E. King: "Don't Play That Song" ("A Little Bit of Soap")

People's Choice: "I Likes to Do It" ("Tread Water")

Melvin Bliss: "Synthetic Substitution" ("Potholes in My Lawn")

Brother Soul: "Cookies" ("Potholes in My Lawn")

Parliament: "Little Old Country Boy" ("Potholes in My Lawn")

War: "Magic Mountain" ("Potholes in My Lawn")

The Detroit Emeralds: "Baby Let Me Take You (In My Arms)" ("Say No Go")

The Emotions: "You Got the Best of My Love" ("Say No Go")

MFSB: "Get Down with the Philly Sound" ("Say No Go")

Sly & the Family Stone: "Crossword Puzzle" ("Say No Go")

Hall & Oates: "I Can't Go for That (No Can Do)" ("Say No Go")

Average White Band: "Schoolboy Crush" ("Do as De La Does")
Bar-Kays: "Son of Shaft" ("Plug Tunin'")
Manzel: "Midnight Theme" ("Plug Tunin'")
The Invitations: "The Writing's on the Wall" ("Plug Tunin'")
Commodores: "Girl, I Think the World About You" ("Buddy")
The Five Stairsteps: "Don't Change Your Love" ("Buddy")
The Five Stairsteps: "Ooh Child" ("Buddy")
Eddie Harris: "Get on Up and Dance" ("Buddy")
Sly & the Family Stone: "Poet" ("Description")
Edwin Birdsong: "Rapper Dapper Snapper" ("Me, Myself, and I")
James Brown: "The Little Groove Maker" ("Me, Myself, and I")
Funkadelic: "Knot Just (Knee Deep)" ("Me, Myself, and I")
GQ: "Disco Nights (Rock, Freak)" ("Me, Myself, and I")
Ohio Players: "Funky Worm" ("Me, Myself, and I")
Sequence: "Funk You Up" ("This Is a Recording 4 Living in a Fulltime Era")
Treacherous Three: "Feel the Heartbeat" ("This Is a Recording 4 Living in a Fulltime Era")

Sampled on Beastie Boys' *Paul's Boutique*

Idris Muhammad: "Loran's Dance" ("To All the Girls")
Rose Royce: "Born to Love You" ("Shake Your Rump")
Harvey Scales: "Dancing Room Only" ("Shake Your Rump")
Ronnie Laws: "Tell Me Something Good" ("Shake Your Rump")
Alphonse Mouzon: "Funky Snakefoot" ("Shake Your Rump")
Donny Hathaway: "Magnificent Sanctuary Band" ("Johnny Ryall")
Jean Knight: "Mr. Big Stuff" ("Johnny Ryall")
DJ Grand Wizard Theodore: "Military Cut (Scratch Mix)" ("Johnny Ryall")
Commodores: "I'm Ready" ("Egg Man")
Lightnin' Rod: "Sport" ("Egg Man")
Curtis Mayfield: "Superfly" ("Egg Man")
Sly & the Family Stone: "Dance to the Music" ("Egg Man")
The Fatback Band: "Put Your Love in My Care" ("High Plains Drifter")
James Brown: "Get Up, Get Into It, Get Involved" ("The Sounds of Science")
Isaac Hayes: "Walk from Regio's" ("The Sounds of Science")
Sly & the Family Stone: "Poet" ("3-Minute Rule")
Sly & the Family Stone: "Brave and Strong" ("3-Minute Rule")
Bar-Kays: "Holy Ghost" ("Hey, Ladies")
James Brown: "Ain't It Funky" ("Hey, Ladies")
Cameo: "Shake Your Pants" ("Hey, Ladies")
Commodores: "Machine Gun" ("Hey, Ladies")
Kool & the Gang: "Jungle Boogie" ("Hey, Ladies")

Roger: "So Ruff, So Tuff" ("Hey, Ladies")
Edwin Starr: "War" ("Hey, Ladies")
The Incredible Bongo Band: "Last Bongo in Belgium" ("Looking Down the Barrel of a Gun")
Funkadelic: "I'll Bet You" ("Car Thief")
Jackson 5: "I'll Bet You" ("Car Thief")
Funk Factory: "Rien Ne Va Plus" ("Car Thief")
Trouble Funk: "Drop the Bomb" ("Car Thief")
Dennis Coffey & the Detroit Guitar Band: "Getting It On" ("What Comes Around")
Gene Harris & the Three Sounds: "Put on Train" ("What Comes Around")
Rose Royce: "Do Your Dance" ("Shadrach")
Sly & the Family Stone: "Loose Booty" ("Shadrach")
Trouble Funk: "Good to Go" ("Shadrach")
B-Side & Fab Five Freddy: "Change le Beat" ("B-Boy Bouillabaisse")

Sampled by Eric B. & Rakim

The Average White Band: "Schoolboy Crush" ("Microphone Fiend")
Baby Huey: "Listen to Me" ("Follow the Leader")
James Brown: "Funky Drummer" ("Lyrics of Fury")
Johnny Hammond: "Breakout" ("Casualties of War")
Bobbi Humphrey: "Blacks and Blues" ("Keep the Beat")
Bob James: "Night on Bald Mountain" ("Let the Rhythm Hit 'Em")
Little Richard: "Tutti Frutti" ("Move the Crowd")
Positive Force: "We Got the Funk" ("Let the Rhythm Hit 'Em")
Fonda Rae: "Over Like a Fat Rat" ("Eric B. Is President")
Rotary Connection: "Life Could" ("Rest Assured")
Skull Snaps: "It's a New Day" ("Step Back)
Rufus Thomas: "Do the Funky Penguin" ("Let the Rhythm Hit 'Em")
24 Carat Black: "Ghetto: Misfortune's Wealth" ("In the Ghetto")
Esther Williams: "Last Night Changed It All" ("I Know You Got Soul")

Sampled by N.W.A

James Brown: "Give It Up or Turnit a Loose" ("100 Miles and Runnin'")
Charles Wright & the Watts 103rd Street Rhythm Band: "Express Yourself" ("Express Yourself")
William DeVaughn: "Be Thankful for What You Got" ("Eight Ball")
The Honey Drippers: "Impeach the President" ("Gangsta Gangsta")
Syl Johnson: "Different Strokes" ("Real N*ggaz Don't Die")
Jimmy Castor Bunch: "It's Just Begun" ("Gangsta Gangsta")
The Dramatics: "Get Up and Get Down" ("Approach to Danger")
Herman Kelly & Life: "Dance to the Drummer's Beat" ("Dopeman")

Funkadelic: "Get Off Your Ass and Jam" ("100 Miles and Runnin'")
ESG: "UFO" ("Real N*ggaz Don't Die")
Steve Arrington's Hall of Fame: "Weak at the Knees" ("Gangsta Gangsta")
Lalo Schifrin: "Scorpio" ("Approach to Danger")

Sampled by Public Enemy

Banbarra: "Shack Up!" ("Yo! Bum Rush the Show")
Bar-Kays: "Holy Ghost" ("Fear of a Black Planet")
James Brown: "Cold Sweat" ("Prophets of Rage")
Bobby Byrd: "I Know You Got Soul" ("Fight the Power")
George Clinton: "Atomic Dog" ("Can't Truss It")
Dennis Coffey: "Scorpio" ("Night of the Living Baseheads")
Funkadelic: "Get Off Your Ass and Jam" ("Bring the Noise")
Isaac Hayes: "Hyperbolicsyllabicsesquedalymistic" ("Black Steel in the Hour of Chaos")
Instant Funk: "I Got My Mind Made Up" ("Welcome to the Terrordome")
The JB's: "Gimme Some More" ("Cold Lampin' with Flavor")
Kool & the Gang: "Who's Gonna Take the Weight" ("Louder Than a Bomb")
Lafayette Afro-Rock Band: "Darkest Light" ("Show 'Em What Cha Got")
Mandrill: "Two Sisters of Mystery" ("By the Time I Get to Arizona")
The New Birth: "Got to Get a Knutt" ("Lost at Birth")
Parliament: "Flashlight" ("Night Train")
Prince & the Revolution: "Let's Go Crazy" ("Brothers Gonna Work It Out")
Slave: "Slide" ("Can't Truss It")

Tracks That Sampled James Brown's "Funky Drummer"

Above the Law: "Untouchable"
Lakim Shabazz: "Black Is Back"
Eazy-E: "We Want Eazy"
Eric B. & Rakim: "Lyrics of Fury"
Geto Boys: "Mind of a Lunatic"
Ice Cube: "Endangered Species"
Kool G Rap & DJ Polo: "It's a Demo"
Kool Moe Dee: "Knowledge Is King"
Leaders of the New School: "Teachers, Don't Teach Us Nonsense!"
LL Cool J: "Mama Said Knock You Out"
Mantronix: "Fresh Is the Word"
N.W.A: "F*ck tha Police"
Public Enemy: "Bring the Noise"
Son of Bazerk: "One Time for the Rebel"
Stetsasonic: "Sally"

Tracks That Sampled Mountain's "Long Red"

Compton's Most Wanted: "Growin' up in the Hood"

EPMD: "It's My Thing"
Eric B. & Rakim: "Eric B. Is President"
Ice Cube: "The Birth"
MC Shan: "So Fresh"
Nas: "It Ain't Hard to Tell"
Pete Rock & CL Smooth: "Return of the Mecca"
Public Enemy: "Louder Than a Bomb"
A Tribe Called Quest: "Jazz (We've Got)"
Young Black Teenagers: "Roll with the Flavor"

Tracks That Sampled the Incredible Bongo Band's "Apache"

Chubb Rock: "Three Men at Chung King"
DJ Jazzy Jeff & the Fresh Prince: "Live at Union Square"
Double D & Steinski: "Lesson 1"
Geto Boys: "Do It like a G.O."
Leaders of the New School: "My Ding-A-Ling"
LL Cool J: "You Can't Dance"
MC Hammer: "Turn This Mutha Out"
Kool Moe Dee: "Way, Way Back"
Sugarhill Gang: "Apache Rap"
Young MC: "Know How"

Tracks That Sampled Bob James' "Nautilus"

EPMD: "Brothers on My Jock"
Eric B. & Rakim: "Follow the Leader"
The Jungle Brothers: "Book of Rhyme Pages"
Leaders of the New School: "Show Me a Hero"
Nice & Smooth: "No Delayin'"
Run-D.M.C.: "Beats to the Rhyme"
Main Source: "Live at the Barbecue"
Onyx: "Throw Ya Gunz"
Public Enemy: "Anti-N*gger Machine"
Slick Rick: "Children's Story"
A Tribe Called Quest: "Clap Your Hands"
Ultramagnetic MCs: "Ced Gee (Delta Force One)"

Tracks That Sampled Billy Squier's "Big Beat"

Run-D.M.C.: "Here We Go"
UTFO: "Roxanne, Roxanne"
Big Daddy Kane: "Ain't No Half Steppin'"
Special Ed: "The Mission"
Ice Cube: "Jackin' for Beats"
Rodney O & Joe Cooley: "Get Ready to Roll"
Naughty by Nature: "Wickedest Man Alive"
Kriss Kross: "Da Bomb"
MC Shan: "Born to Be Wild"
X Clan: "A Day of Outrage, Operation Snatchback"

Unlikely Sample Sources

Can: "Vitamin C" (The Pharcyde: "Hey You")
Tracy Chapman: "Fast Car" (Nice & Smooth: "Sometimes I Rhyme Slow")
Peter Gabriel: "Sledgehammer" (3rd Bass: "Pop Goes the Weasel")
Edie Brickell & New Bohemians: "What I Am" (Brand Nubian: "Slow Down")

Blood, Sweat & Tears: "Spinning Wheel" (Public Enemy: "Night Train")

Billy Joel: "Stiletto" (Kool G Rap & DJ Polo: "Road to the Riches")

Steve Miller Band: "The Joker" (Geto Boys: "Gangster of Love")

Lynyrd Skynyrd: "Sweet Home Alabama" (Geto Boys: "Gangster of Love")

Lou Reed: "Walk on the Wild Side" (A Tribe Called Quest: "Can I Kick It")

The Turtles: "You Showed Me" (De La Soul: "Transmitting Live from Mars")

The Turtles: "Buzzsaw" (D-Nice: "They Call Me D-Nice")

Ferrante & Teicher: "Midnight Cowboy" (A Tribe Called Quest: "Show Business")

The Knack: "My Sharona" (Run-D.M.C.: "It's Tricky")

Joe Cocker: "Woman to Woman" (EPMD: "Knick Knack Patty Wack")

Little Feat: "Fool Yourself" (A Tribe Called Quest: "Bonita Applebum")

Sweet: "Ballroom Blitz" (Beastie Boys: "Hey, Ladies")

Babe Ruth: "The Mexican" (Afrika Bambaataa & Soul Sonic Force: "Planet Rock")

Michael McDonald: "I Keep Forgettin'" (Warren G: "Regulate")

Rush: "Tom Sawyer" (Mellow Man Ace: "Welcome to My Groove")

Jack Bruce: "Statues" (Souls of Mischief: "That's When Ya Lost")

Boz Scaggs: "Lowdown" (Sparky D: "Throwdown")

Eric Clapton: "I Shot the Sheriff" (EPMD: "Strictly Business")

Hall & Oates: "I Can't Go for That (No Can Do)" (Above the Law: "VSOP")

Three Dog Night: "I Can Hear You Calling" (MC Lyte: "I Am the Lyte")

Toto: "Georgy Porgy" (MC Lyte: "Poor Georgie")

Van Halen: "Jamie's Crying" (Tone Loc: "Wild Thing")

Tom Waits: "Down in the Hole" (3rd Bass: "Flippin' off the Wall like Lucy Ball")

Frank Zappa: "Son of Mr. Green Genes" (Black Moon: "Ack Like U Want It")

TIMELINE: ALBUMS THAT CAPTURED A YEAR

The prime years of the golden age of old school ran from 1984–1994. Here are the albums that captured the sound of those years the best.

1984

Fat Boys: *Fat Boys*
Run-D.M.C.: *Run-D.M.C.*
Egyptian Lover: *On the Nile*
Whodini: *Escape*
Kurtis Blow: *Ego Trip*

1985

Run-D.M.C.: *King of Rock*
LL Cool J: *Radio*
Mantronix: *Mantronix: The Album*

1986

Run-D.M.C.: *Raising Hell*
Doug E Fresh: *Oh My God!*
Afrika Bambaataa: *Planet Rock: The Album*
Whodini: *Back in Black*
Salt-N-Pepa: *Hot Cool & Vicious*
Beastie Boys: *Licensed to Ill*
Stetsasonic: *On Fire*

1987

LL Cool J: *Bigger and Deffer*
Ice T: *Rhyme Pays*
Eric B & Rakim: *Paid in Full*
Two Live Crew: *Move Something*
Schoolly D: *Adventures of Schoolly D*
Public Enemy: *Yo! Bum Rush the Show*
Fat Boys: *Crushin'*
Boogie Down Productions: *Criminal Minded*

1988

Run-D.M.C.: *Tougher Than Leather*
Marley Marl: *In Control, Vol. 1*
Ice T: *Power*
DJ Jazzy Jeff & The Fresh Prince: *He's the DJ, I'm the Rapper*
Eric B & Rakim: *Follow the Leader*
Ultramagnetic MCs: *Critical Breakdown*
Slick Rick: *Great Adventures of Slick Rick*
MC Lyte: *Lyte as a Rock*
Kid N Play: *2 Hype*
Jungle Brothers: *Straight Out the Jungle*
EPMD: *Strictly Business*
Eazy E: *Eazy Duz It*
Boogie Down Productions: *By All Means Necessary*
Rob Base: *It Takes Two*
Stetsasonic: *In Full Gear*

Biz Markie: *Goin' Off*
Public Enemy: *It Takes a Nation of Millions*
Big Daddy Kane: *Long Live the Kane*

1989

Young MC: *Stone Cold Rhymin'*
LL Cool J: *Walking with a Panther*
De La Soul: *3 Feet High and Rising*
DOC: *No One Can Do It Better*
2 Live Crew: *As Nasty as They Wanna Be*
Tone Loc: *Loced After Dark*
N.W.A.: *Straight Outta Compton*
EPMD: *Unfinished Business*
Neneh Cherry: *Raw Like Sushi*
Beastie Boys: *Paul's Boutique*
Boogie Down Productions: *Ghetto Music: The Blueprint of Hip-Hop*
Big Daddy Kane: *It's a Big Daddy Thing*
Ice T: *Iceberg/Freedom of Speech*
DJ Jazzy Jeff: *And in This Corner*
Biz Markie: *Biz Never Sleeps*
3rd Bass: *Cactus Album*
Queen Latifah: *All Hail the Queen*
Jungle Brothers: *Done by the Forces of Nature*
Special Ed: *Youngest in Charge*

1990

Run-D.M.C.: *Back from Hell*
Vanilla Ice: *To the Extreme*
Poor Righteous Teachers: *Holy Intellect*
Kid N Play: *Kid N Play's Funhouse*
Ice Cube: *Kill at Will*
Geto Boys: *Geto Boys*
Afros: *Kickin' Afrolistics*
Brand Nubian: *One for All*
Digital Underground: *Sex Packets*
MC Hammer: *Please Hammer, Don't Hurt 'Em*
Public Enemy: *Fear of a Black Planet*
Salt-N-Pepa: *Blacks' Magic*
Tribe Called Quest: *People's Instinctive Travels*
Ice Cube: *AmeriKKKAs Most Wanted*
Boogie Down Productions: *Edutainment*
N.W.A.: *100 Miles and Runnin'*
LL Cool J: *Mama Said Knock You Out*
Paris: *Devil Made Me Do It*
Too Short: *Life Is…Too Short*
EPMD: *Business as Usual*

1991

Leaders of the New School: *Future Without a Past*
Del tha Funkee Homosapien: *I Wish My Brother George Was Here*
Gang Starr: *Step in the Arena*
Dream Warriors: *And Now, the Legacy Begins*
Digital Underground: *This Is an EP Release*
De La Soul: *De La Soul Is Dead*
Ice T: OG: *Original Gangster*
Son of Bazerk: *Bazerk Bazerk Bazerk*
N.W.A.: *Niggaz4life*
3rd Bass: *Derelicts of Dialect*
Geto Boys: *We Can't Be Stopped*
Stetsaonic: *Blood, Sweat, and No Tears*
Slick Rick: *Ruler's Back*
DJ Jazzy Jeff: *Homebase*
PM Dawn: *Of the Heart, Of the Soul*
Cypress Hill: *Cypress Hill*
Naughty By Nature: *Naughty by Nature*
Tribe Called Quest: *Low End Theory*
Public Enemy: *Apocalypse 91...The Enemy Strikes Black*
Scarface: *Mr. Scarface Is Back*
Digital Underground: *Sons of the P*
Ice Cube: *Death Certificate*
Main Source: *Breaking Atoms*
Scarface: *Mr. Scarface Is Back*

1992

Pete Rock & CL Smooth: *Mecca and the Soul Brother*
Disposable Heroes of Hiphoprisy: *Hypocrisy Is the Greatest*
Eric B & Rakim: *Don't Sweat the Technique*
Lench Mob: *Guerillas in tha Mist*
Pharcyde: *Bizarre Ride II the Pharcyde*
Paris: *Sleeping with the Enemy*
Heavy D: *Blue Funk*
Basehead: *Play with Toys*
Fu Schnickens: *FU Don't Take It Personal*
Boogie Down Productions: *Sex and Violence*
Arrested Development: *Three Years, Five Months, and Two Days*
Kriss Kross: *Totally Krossed Out*
Das EFX: *Dead Serious*
Beastie Boys: *Check Your Head*
Gang Starr: *Daily Operation*
House of Pain: *House of Pain*
EPMD: *Business Never Personal*
Brand New Heavies: *Heavy Rhyme Experience*

Redman: *Whut? Thee Album*
Neneh Cherry: *Homebrew*
Doctor Dre: *Chronic*
Brand Nubian: *In God We Trust*
Showbiz & AG: *Runaway Slave*
Diamond D & the Psychotic Neurotics: *Stunts, Blunts, and Hip-Hop*
Ice Cube: *Predator*

1993

Erick Sermon: *No Pressure*
Onyx: *Bacdafucup*
Guru: *Jazzmatazz, Vol. 1*
Lords of the Underground: *Here Come the Lords*
Brand Nubian: *In God We Trust*
Two Pac: *Strictly 4 My NIGGAZ*
Naughty By Nature: *19 Naughty III*
Tha Alkaholiks: *21 and Over*
Funkdoobiest: *Which Doobie U B?*
Cypress Hill: *Black Sunday*
Jungle Brothers: *J Beeez with the Remedies*
Souls of Mischief: *93 'Til Infinity*
De La Soul: *Buhloone Mindstate*
Digable Planets: *Reachin'*
Salt-N-Pepa: *Very Necessary*
Wu Tang Clan: *Enter the Wu-Tang (36 Chambers)*
Tribe Called Quest: *Midnight Marauders*
US3: *Hand on the Torch*
DAS EFX: *Straight Up Sewaside*
Snoop Dogg: *Doggystyle*
Domino: *Domino*
Black Moon: *Enta da Stage*
KRS-One: *Return of the Boom Bap*

1994

Pete Rock & CL Smooth: *Main Ingredient*
Nas: *Illmatic*
Outkast: *Southernplayalisticadillac*
Jeru the Damaja: *Sun Rises in the East*
Warren G: *Regulate...G Funk Era*
House of Pain: *Same as It Ever Was*
Coolio: *It Takes a Thief*
Gravediggaz: *6 Feet Deep*
Notorious BIG: *Ready to Die*
Spearhead: *Home*
Digable Planet: *Blowout Comb*
Fu Schnickens: *Nervous Breakdown*
Common: *Resurrection*
Organized Konfusion: *Stress: The Extinction Agenda*
Beastie Boys: *Ill Communication*